PAPER MARIO™
Sticker Star

TABLE OF CONTENTS

HOW TO USE THIS GUIDE

This guide contains all the information you'll need to complete every task, collect every item, and uncover every secret in the game. With our labeled maps, detailed walkthrough, and proven strategies, you'll always know where to go and what to do when you get there!

HOW TO PLAY

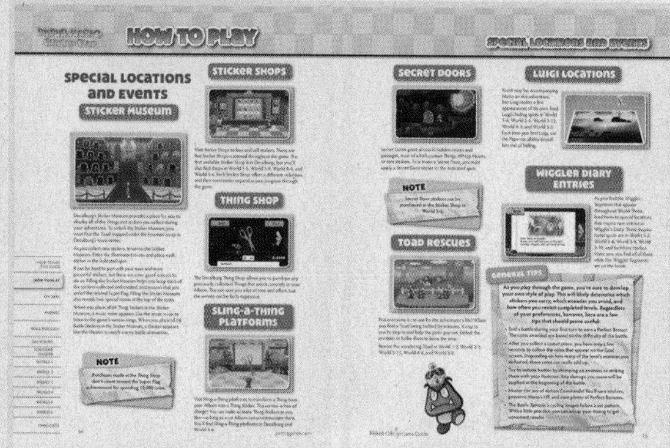
HOW TO PLAY
SPECIAL LOCATIONS AND EVENTS
STICKER MUSEUM
STICKER SHOPS
THING SHOP
SLING-A-THING PLATFORMS
SECRET DOORS
LUIGI LOCATIONS
WIGGLER DIARY ENTRIES
TOAD RESCUES
GENERAL TIPS
NOTE

This section covers the game's basic mechanics and features. If you're playing the game for the first time, use this chapter to learn how to control Mario, when to use his abilities, how to unlock new areas, and which collectible items you should expect to find as you play through the game.

STICKERS

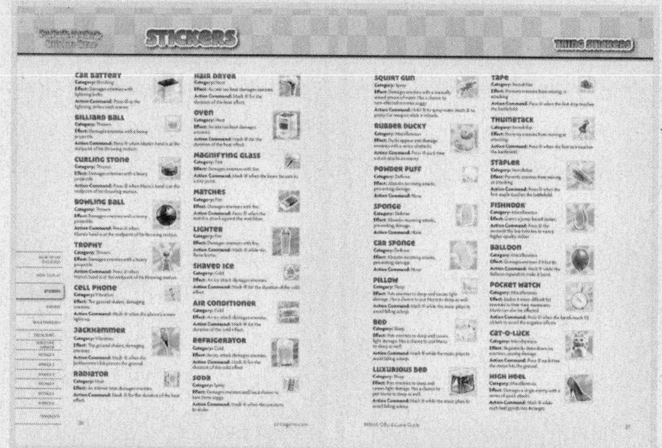
STICKERS
THING STICKERS

This chapter contains vital details about the game's stickers. Stickers are used in battle and during exploration, so it's essential to understand the properties of each one.

Enemies

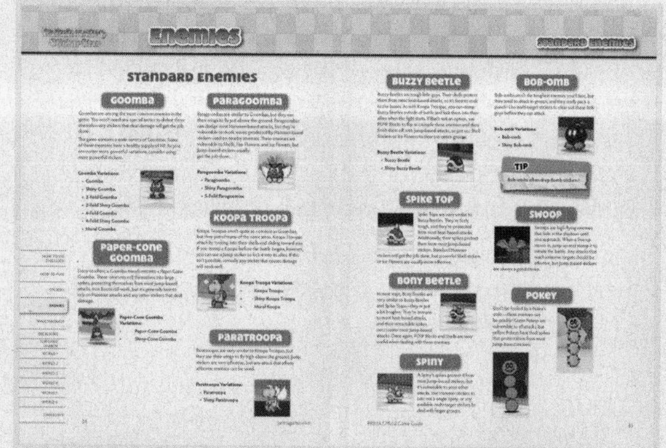
ENEMIES
STANDARD ENEMIES
GOOMBA
PARAGOOMBA
PAPER-CONE GOOMBA
KOOPA TROOPA
PARATROOPA
BUZZY BEETLE
SPIKE TOP
BONY BEETLE
SPINY
BOB-OMB
TIP
SWOOP
POKEY

This section offers some details about the enemies you'll face during your adventure.

WALKTHROUGH

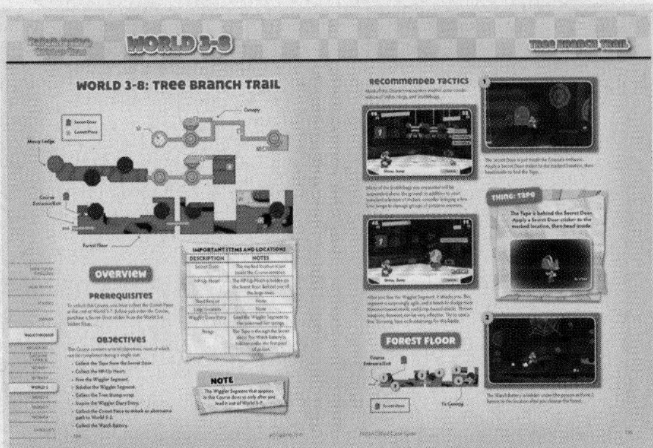

The walkthrough contains step-by-step instructions to help you complete every Course, collect every item, and uncover every secret. Each Course's walkthrough begins with a map of the area, followed by a brief overview of available objectives, collectible items, and basic tactics for expected encounters. The Course is then divided into several smaller areas, making it much easier to keep track of important locations and items.

On the area maps, we've labeled key locations with numbered icons. For more details about a location, look for the subsequent picture marked with the corresponding number. Lettered icons indicate a transition between two seemingly unrelated points. Warp pipes, secret passages, and vertical paths are often indicated by the corresponding icons in two different areas.

If an area requires additional visits—and most of them do—the details are provided at the end of each Course's walkthrough.

CHECKLISTS

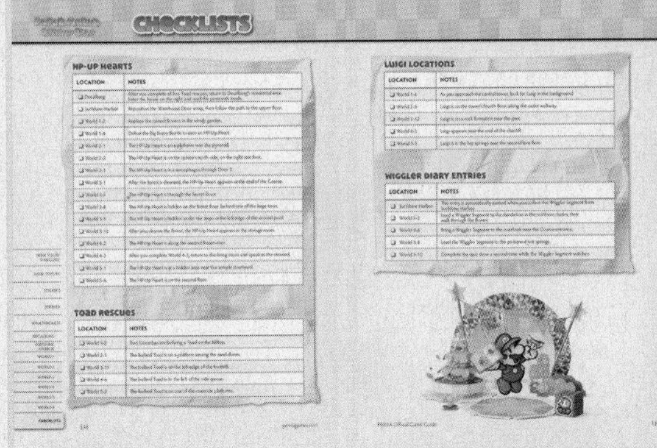

We've put together some handy checklists to help you keep track of the game's optional objectives.

NOTE

This game provides you with a great deal of freedom concerning which tasks you complete and when you might choose to do so. As such, each Course's walkthrough is simply a series of recommended visits. Most Courses are divided into one primary play-through, followed by faster, more efficient visits to take care of any unfinished business after you obtain the required items. It's important to note, however, that you can complete most objectives over any number of visits.

Don't be afraid to explore areas out of order, revisit completed Courses to collect extra Battle Stickers, or to leave a Course unfinished if it proves too difficult at that point in the game.

There are many ways to play this game; simply use the method that you find the most enjoyable!

The Basics

Using the World-Map

The World-Map is used to travel between available Courses. While you navigate the World-Map, the 3D Screen displays Mario's HP, the name of your selected Course, and your current coin count.

The marker at each Course's location changes color based on the status of the Course:

- **A red marker indicates that you haven't collected any of the Course's Comet Pieces.**
- **A blue marker indicates that you've collected all of the Course's Comet Pieces, or that the Course is a previously visited neutral area.**
- **A yellow marker indicates that at least one Comet Piece remains in a previously visited Course.**

Your most recent save location is indicated by a flag near the corresponding Course.

WORLD-MAP CONTROLS

Move	Circle Pad
Open/close Album	Ⓧ
View sticker details	Ⓨ (while the Album is open)
Select Album page	L or R (while the Album is open)
Auto-sort stickers	START (while the Album is open)
Return to title screen	START (while the Album is closed)

Exploring Courses

While you play through a Course, you'll spend the bulk of your time navigating obstacles, solving puzzles, and searching for collectible items.

FIELD CONTROLS

Move	Circle Pad
Jump	Ⓐ
Interact	Ⓐ (when standing near an interactive object)
Peel	Hold Ⓐ (when standing near a sticker)
Paperize	Ⓨ
Swing Hammer	Ⓑ
Talk to Kersti	L
Open/close Album	Ⓧ
View sticker details	Ⓨ (while the Album is open)
Select Album page	L or R (while the Album is open)
Auto-sort stickers	START (while the Album is open)
Exit a previously completed Course	START

Battling Enemies

Battles typically begin whenever you make contact with an enemy. During a battle, the 3D Screen displays Mario's HP and the combined HP of your opponents. To win a battle, you must use stickers to drain your enemies' HP before Mario's HP runs out.

BATTLE CONTROLS

Action Command	Ⓐ (when attacking or defending)
Battle Spinner	Ⓧ (at the start of your turn)
Select Album page	L or R
View sticker details	Ⓨ

Using the Touch Screen

The Touch Screen is used to manage your Album. Use the stylus to rearrange your stickers, switch tabs, and make selections.

NOTE

Some commands only become available as you progress through the game. Many commands are contextual and cannot be used in certain situations. Keep an eye out for notifications about available commands.

Abilities

NOTE

Not all abilities are available at all times. Some abilities are introduced as you progress through the game, and other abilities are temporarily disabled when you lose your companion or equipment.

Jump

Jumping is Mario's simplest ability, but it's also the most important! Jump to reach higher ground, avoid obstacles, and stomp vulnerable enemies before you enter battle.

Hammer

The Hammer is a surprisingly versatile tool! Use the Hammer to topple unstable objects, drive stakes into the ground, and smash vulnerable enemies before you enter battle. Once a battle begins, the Hammer allows you to use Hammer-based stickers.

HOW TO USE THIS GUIDE
HOW TO PLAY
STICKERS
ENEMIES
WALKTHROUGH
DECALBURG
SURFSHINE HARBOR
WORLD 1
WORLD 2
WORLD 3
WORLD 4
WORLD 5
WORLD 6
CHECKLISTS

Paperize

Early in the game, Kersti introduces the Paperize ability. When you activate the Paperize ability, the environment turns into a two-dimensional image. Paperize special locations to reveal secrets, apply stickers, and manipulate important objects.

Run

When you find yourself unprepared for an encounter, you can run from the battle. Instead of selecting stickers at the start of your turn, select the "run" option that appears at the top of your Album.

TIP

There's always a chance that an attempt to run from battle will fail. As you run, rapidly tap Ⓐ to dim the battlefield until you leave the battle or fall to the ground.

Battle Spinner

Early in the game, Kersti introduces the Battle Spinner. During combat, the Battle Spinner gives you a chance to use multiple stickers in a single turn. This ability can only be used at the beginning of your turn, and each use costs three coins. Match two images to earn an extra attack. Match all three images to win the jackpot. In addition to granting two extra attacks, the jackpot triggers a bonus effect.

JACKPOT BONUSES

IMAGES	EFFECT
Coin × 3	You receive coins.
Fire Flower × 3	Grounded and low-flying enemies take damage.
Lightning × 3	Enemies take damage; enemy attacks might miss.
POW Block × 3	Grounded enemies are crumpled.
Mushroom × 3	Restores some of your HP.
Poison Mushroom × 3	You are poisoned; contact poisons enemies.

TIP

In exchange for coins, the Battle Spinner will automatically match the first two images, guaranteeing you at least one extra attack-during your turn. The cost for this ability goes up each time you use it during a single battle.

Action Commands

During a battle, Action Commands can be used to increase the potency of your stickers and to reduce damage caused by enemy attacks. Most Action Commands require precision timing, so it's important to recognize each opportunity as it presents itself.

When Mario Jumps

Whenever a sticker causes Mario to jump, press Ⓐ to perform an Action Command at the moment he leaves the ground and each time he lands. This applies not only to Jump-based stickers, but also to Shells, POW Blocks, and many other stickers. This generally extends the attack and/or boosts its power, causing much more damage to your enemies.

When Mario Shines

When Mario winds up for an attack, a shine often appears on his hands or his weapon. Look for this shine when Mario swings a Hammer, or when he reels back to throw a projectile, The shine only lasts for a second, but it grows more intense until it disappears. Press Ⓐ to use an Action Command just before the shine vanishes.

When Mario Raises His Arms

When Mario uses Mushrooms, 1Ups, and certain Thing Stickers, he raises his hands in the air and spins around three times. Press Ⓐ just before Mario stops spinning to increase the effectiveness of the sticker.

To Block an Attack

During an enemy's turn, use the Action Command to block incoming attacks. Mario only blocks for a moment, so press Ⓐ just before the enemy or projectile makes contact.

NOTE

Depending on the specific attack, defensive stickers like the Spike Helmet or Frog Suit allow you to counter or dodge instead of blocking.

Button Mashing

Not all maneuvers call for precision timing—sometimes you just have to tap Ⓐ repeatedly. The more times you tap the button, the better your chances of a successful outcome. Use button mashing when you run from battle, defend against a sustained attack, or use certain Thing Stickers.

NOTE

When you perform an Action Command, look for notices about your timing. Earn "Excellent" ratings to make the most of each sticker, and to earn the related Super Flag achievement.

Game Progression

To complete the game, you must recover the six Royal Stickers and rescue Peach from Bowser. This, of course, is not as simple as it sounds!

Unlocking New Areas

The game begins in Decalburg, in the aftermath of the Sticker Festival. When you first reach the World-Map, you can visit any of the four adjacent areas. To unlock additional areas, you must recover the Comet Pieces scattered throughout the game and complete a variety of other tasks.

As you progress through the game, you'll encounter puzzles and obstacles that require items located in different Courses. This effectively limits the order in which you can complete certain Courses, but you're free to explore any available Course at any time. After you collect the required item, simply revisit the Course and take care of any unfinished business.

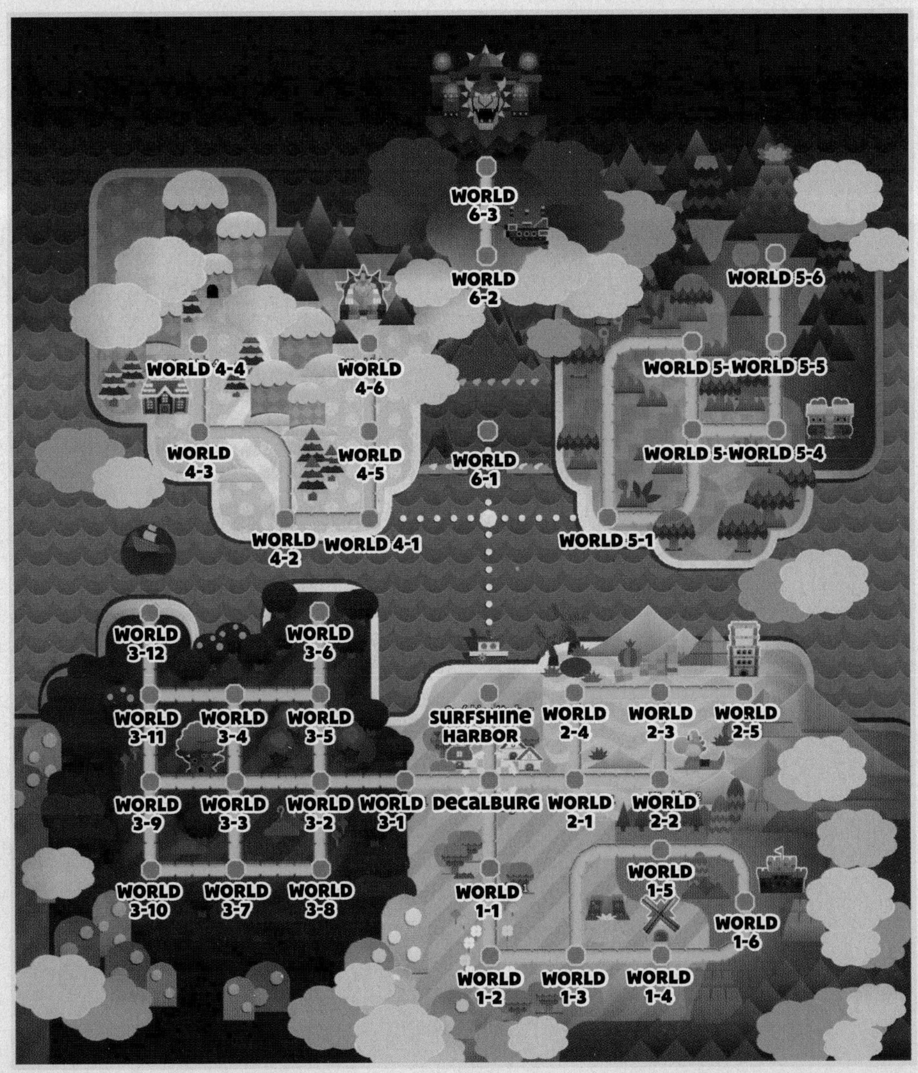

SUPER FLAGS

As Decalburg rebuilds the Sticker Festival, eight Super Flags appear on the festival grounds. When you meet the conditions written on each Super Flag, it unfurls in celebration of your achievement.

To unfurl all eight Super Flags, you must complete these tasks:

- **Collect all Comet Pieces.**
- **Make all Secret Doors appear.**
- **Fill the Sticker Museum with every possible sticker type.**
- **Find all HP-Up Hearts.**
- **Spend a total of 10,000 coins in the Sticker Shops.**
- **Get a Perfect Bonus in 500 battles.**
- **Perform 1,000 Excellent attacks.**
- **Hit the Battle Spinner jackpot 50 times.**

Return to the Super Flags at any time to check your progress in each task.

ITEMS AND OBJECTS

PICKUPS AND COLLECTIBLE ITEMS

BATTLE STICKERS

Battle Stickers are used to battle enemies and solve puzzles, making them the most important collectible items in the game. Luckily, they're also the most common. You'll find these stickers posted on walls, hidden in Blocks, and left behind by defeated enemies.

Collected stickers are stored in your Album. The Album can only accommodate a limited number of stickers, but you can earn additional Album pages by defeating the bosses lurking in the last Course of each world. Stickers come in a variety of sizes, so your choice of stickers determines how many your Album can hold at a given time.

TIP

The game contains 96 different Battle Stickers and 64 Thing Stickers. Like Battle Stickers, Thing Stickers are used to battle enemies and solve puzzles. Rather than appearing in the environment, however, Thing Stickers must be created at Sling-a-Thing platforms.

Scraps

Scraps are pieces of the environment that can be moved or adjusted to solve puzzles and open new paths. Collected scraps are stored in your Album. Once a scrap is applied to the appropriate spot, it can no longer be manipulated.

Things

There are 64 Things scattered in various locations throughout the game. After you collect a Thing, visit a Sling-a-Thing platform to convert it into a Thing Sticker. When you do, the Thing is returned to its original location.

Hearts

Collect Hearts to replenish Mario's HP. The amount of HP gained depends on the size of the Heart.

HP-Up Hearts

Each time you collect an HP-Up Heart, Mario's maximum HP is permanently increased by 5 points. There are 16 HP-Up Hearts hidden throughout the game—collect them all to increase Mario's HP by 80 points.

As an added bonus, HP-Up Hearts also combine to increase the damage done by any Hammer strikes and stomps you perform outside of battle. This allows you to finish weaker enemies without using any stickers.

Coins

If you want to purchase items or take advantage of the Battle Spinner, you'll need a steady supply of coins. Collect the coins floating in the environment, hidden in secret areas, and dropped by defeated enemies.

Comet Pieces

Most hostile Courses contain at least one Comet Piece. Collect Comet Pieces to unlock new paths on the World-Map.

ROYAL STICKERS

Each of the game's six worlds contains a Royal Sticker. To rescue Peach and complete the game, you must collect them all. When you defeat a world's boss, collect the Royal Sticker it leaves behind.

SUPER STARS

Collect Super Stars to gain temporary invincibility. While the effect lasts, enemies are defeated on contact. Super Stars are very rare—when you spot one, be sure you make the most of it.

SPECIAL OBJECTS

BLOCKS

? BLOCKS

You'll find ? Blocks throughout the game. To collect its contents, jump up to hit a ? Block from below, or strike it with your Hammer.

HIDDEN BLOCKS

Hidden Blocks appear only when you hit them from below or strike them with your Hammer. When you spot a blue flower, chances are that there's at least one Hidden Block in the area. They always contain useful items, and they often serve as secret platforms. When a sticker or ledge seems to be out of reach, search the area for conveniently located Hidden Blocks.

PAPERIZATION BLOCKS

To reveal a Paperization Block, you must activate the Paperize ability and apply a sticker to the indicated spot. The contents of a Paperization Block are determined by the sticker you use to reveal it. Each sticker has four possible results. (See the "Stickers" chapter for details.)

TIP

When you use a sticker to reveal a Paperization Block, one of four possible outcomes is randomly selected. There's no way to guarantee you'll get the result you're hoping for.

HP Blocks

When you find an HP Block, hit it to refill Mario's HP. There's no limit to how many times you can use an HP Block, so never pass one up.

Save Blocks

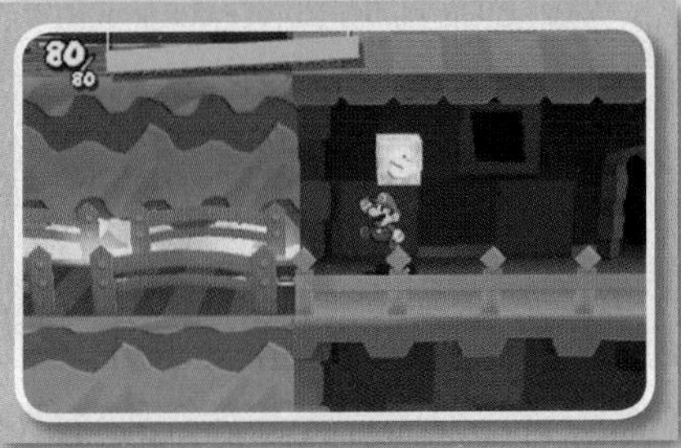

Save Blocks allow you to save your progress within a Course. If an unfortunate accident forces you to restart the Course, you can then jump directly to the Save Block's location.

Bowser Tape

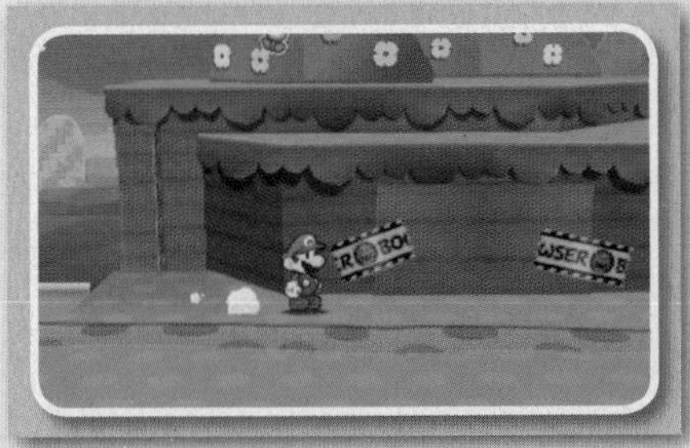

You'll find Bowser tape scattered throughout the game. Peel Bowser tape to free objects and reveal new paths.

Stakes

Stakes anchor chained objects and enemies to specific locations. When you find a stake, hit it with your Hammer to break the chain free.

Signs

Signs usually contain important or amusing information. Take the time to read every sign you find.

Warp Pipes

Warp pipes allow you to move between two areas within a Course. These pipes often serve as shortcuts, but sometimes they're the only way to reach certain areas.

Special Locations and Events

Sticker Museum

Decalburg's Sticker Museum provides a place for you to display all of the Things and stickers you collect during your adventures. To unlock the Sticker Museum, you must free the Toad trapped under the Fountain scrap in Decalburg's town center.

As you collect new stickers, return to the Sticker Museum. Enter the illuminated rooms and place each sticker in the indicated spot.

It can be hard to part with your rarer and more powerful stickers, but there are some good reasons to do so. Filling the Sticker Museum helps you keep track of the stickers collected and created, and ensures that you unfurl the related Super Flag. Filling the Sticker Museum also reveals two special rooms at the top of the stairs.

When you place all 64 Thing Stickers in the Sticker Museum, a music room appears. Use the music room to listen to the game's various songs. When you place all 96 Battle Stickers in the Sticker Museum, a theater appears. Use the theater to watch enemy battle animations.

NOTE

Purchases made at the Thing Shop don't count toward the Super Flag achievement for spending 10,000 coins.

Sticker Shops

Visit Sticker Shops to buy and sell stickers. There are five Sticker Shops scattered throughout the game The first available Sticker Shop is in Decalburg, but you'll also find shops in World 1-5, World 3-6, World 4-4, and World 5-6. Each Sticker Shop offers a different selection, and their inventories expand as you progress through the game.

Thing Shop

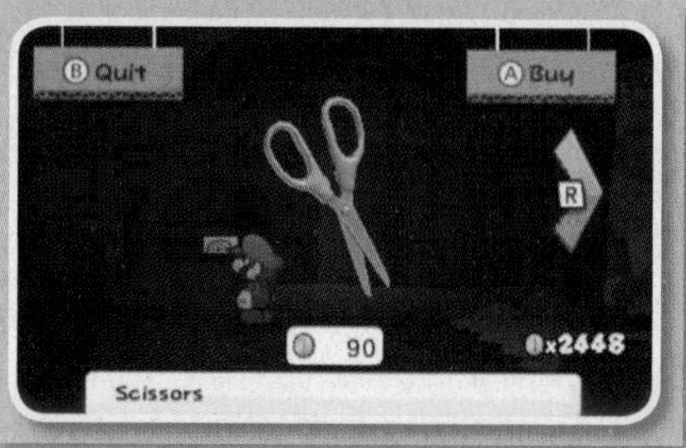

The Decalburg Thing Shop allows you to purchase any previously collected Things that aren't currently in your Album. This can save you a lot of time and effort, but the service can be fairly expensive.

Sling-a-Thing Platforms

Visit Sling-a-Thing platforms to transform a Thing from your Album into a Thing Sticker. This service is free of charge! You can make as many Thing Stickers as you like—as long as your Album can accommodate them. You'll find Sling-a-Thing platforms in Decalburg and World 3-6.

Secret Doors

Secret Doors grant access to hidden rooms and passages, most of which contain Things, HP-Up Hearts, or rare stickers. To activate a Secret Door, you must apply a Secret Door sticker to the indicated spot.

NOTE

Secret Door stickers can be purchased at the Sticker Shop in World 3-6.

Toad Rescues

Not everyone is cut out for the adventurer's life! When you find a Toad being bullied by enemies, it's up to you to step in and help the poor guy out. Defeat the enemies or bribe them to leave the area.

Rescue the wandering Toad in World 1-2, World 2-1, World 3-11, World 4-6, and World 5-2.

Luigi Locations

Kersti may be accompanying Mario on this adventure, but Luigi makes a few appearances of his own. Find Luigi's hiding spots in World 1-6, World 2-5, World 3-12, World 4-5, and World 5-5. Each time you find Luigi, use the Paperize ability to pull him out of hiding.

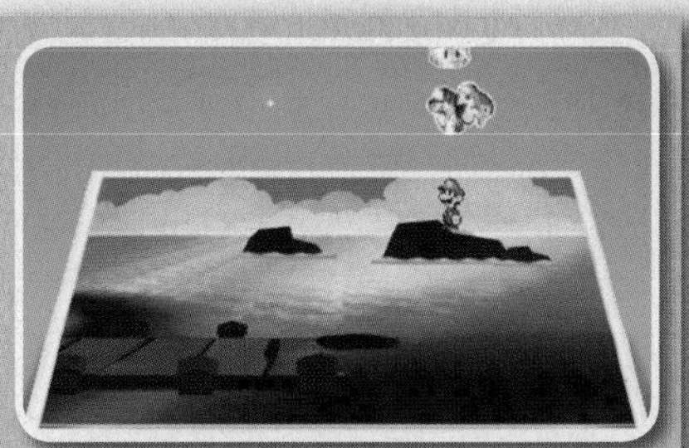

Wiggler Diary Entries

As you find the Wiggler Segments that appear throughout World Three, lead them to special locations that inspire new entries in Wiggler's Diary. These inspirational spots are in World 3-2, World 3-6, World 3-8, World 3-10, and Surfshine Harbor. Make sure you find all of them while the Wiggler Segments are on the loose.

General Tips

As you play through the game, you're sure to develop your own style of play. This will likely determine which stickers you carry, which enemies you avoid, and how often you revisit completed Courses. Regardless of your preferences, however, here are a few tips that should prove useful:

- End a battle during your first turn to earn a Perfect Bonus! The coins awarded are based on the difficulty of the battle.
- After you collect a Comet Piece, you have only a few seconds to collect the coins that appear on the Goal screen. Depending on how many of the Course's enemies you defeated, these coins can really add up.
- Try to initiate battles by stomping on enemies or striking them with your Hammer. Any damage you cause will be applied at the beginning of the battle.
- Master the use of Action Commands! You'll save stickers, preserve Mario's HP, and earn plenty of Perfect Bonuses.
- The Battle Spinner's cycling images follow a set pattern. With a little practice, you can adjust your timing to get consistent results.

As you progress through the game, you'll use stickers to battle enemies, solve puzzles, and reveal Paperization Blocks. Battle Stickers can be collected in the game's courses and purchased from Sticker Shops. Thing Stickers must be created at Sling-a-Thing platforms, but they're well worth the time and effort it takes to do so.

Although you're sure to develop preferences for certain stickers, every sticker is effective when it's used properly. Your success depends on learning the strengths and weaknesses of each sticker, and mastering the available Action Commands.

Battle Stickers

Worn-Out Jump

Attack Power: ✳

Attack Range: Ground/low altitude/air

Sticking Points: A jump-and-stomp attack so weak that reputable shops are too ashamed to stock this sticker.

Action Command: Hit Ⓐ each time Mario lands to perform up to five stomps.

Jump

Attack Power: ✳

Attack Range: Ground/low altitude/air

Sticking Points: A jump-and-stomp attack. A word to the wise: Do *not* use this attack on spiked enemies or you'll regret it.

Action Command: Hit Ⓐ each time Mario lands to perform up to five stomps.

Shiny Jump

Attack Power: ✳✳

Attack Range: Ground/low altitude/air

Sticking Points: A fairly strong and fairly fair jump-and-stomp attack. Shininess aside, it's still a bad choice for spiked foes.

Action Command: Hit Ⓐ each time Mario lands to perform up to five stomps.

Flashy Jump

Attack Power: ✳✳✳

Attack Range: Ground/low altitude/air

Sticking Points: A pretty strong and pretty pretty jump-and-stomp attack. No amount of flash will make it good against spiky baddies.

Action Command: Hit Ⓐ each time Mario lands to perform up to five stomps.

Big Shiny Jump

Attack Power: ✳✳✳✳

Attack Range: Ground/low altitude/air

Sticking Points: A bit bigger and shinier than the standard model, this jump attack also boasts some crumpling power.

Action Command: Hit Ⓐ each time Mario lands to perform up to five stomps.

Megaflash Jump

Attack Power: ✳✳✳✳✳

Attack Range: Ground/low altitude/air

Sticking Points: A big, strong, flashy attack blessed with great power and solid crumpling ability. Tell me this thing doesn't look cool.

Action Command: Hit Ⓐ each time Mario lands to perform up to five stomps.

Iron Jump

Attack Power: ✳

Attack Range: Ground/low altitude/air

Sticking Points: As the name implies, this is a Battle Sticker that laughs in the face of spiked foes. Feel free to laugh along with it.

Action Command: Hit Ⓐ each time Mario lands to perform up to five stomps.

Shiny Iron Jump

Attack Power: ✳✳

Attack Range: Ground/low altitude/air

Sticking Points: An attack that delivers a slightly stronger stomp on spiked enemies. Though made of iron, it's quite light!

Action Command: Hit Ⓐ each time Mario lands to perform up to five stomps.

Flashy Iron Jump

Attack Power: ✳✳✳

Attack Range: Ground/low altitude/air

Sticking Points: A compact and pretty powerful stomp that doesn't mind spiked landings. Who knew iron could be so pretty?

Action Command: Hit Ⓐ each time Mario lands to perform up to five stomps.

Big Shiny Iron Jump

Attack Power: ✳✳✳✳

Attack Range: Ground/low altitude/air

Sticking Points: A strong stomp attack designed for spiked enemies. You really would think such a big iron sticker would be heavy.

Action Command: Hit Ⓐ each time Mario lands to perform up to five stomps.

Megaflash Iron Jump

Attack Power: ✳✳✳✳✳

Attack Range: Ground/low altitude/air

Sticking Points: An extreme stomp attack that crushes all spiked enemies. This thing is almost not fair in battle.

Action Command: Hit Ⓐ each time Mario lands to perform up to five stomps.

Hopslipper

Attack Power: ✳

Attack Range: Ground/low altitude/air

Sticking Points: A slightly weak attack befitting a slipper, but capable of up to 10 jumps if your timing is on.

Action Command: Hit Ⓐ each time Mario lands to perform up to 10 attacks.

Shiny Hopslipper

Attack Power: ✳✳

Attack Range: Ground/low altitude/air

Sticking Points: A less-than-powerful attack that can stomp up to 10 times using wonderful spring technology.

Action Command: Hit Ⓐ each time Mario lands to perform up to 10 stomps.

Flashy Hopslipper

Attack Power: ✳✳✳

Attack Range: Ground/low altitude/air

Sticking Points: A flashy sticker that doesn't exactly look cool, seeing as it's a slipper with a spring on it. But it can stomp 10 times!

Action Command: Hit Ⓐ each time Mario lands to perform up to 10 stomps.

Big Shiny Hopslipper

Attack Power: ✳✳✳✳

Attack Range: Ground/low altitude/air

Sticking Points: An attack whose size hides weak power. But 10 jumps does mean 10 attacks, so it's got that going for it.

Action Command: Hit Ⓐ each time Mario lands to perform up to 10 stomps.

Megaflash Hopslipper

Attack Power: ✳✳✳✳✳

Attack Range: Ground/low altitude/air

Sticking Points: A big, shiny...slipper. Still, if you can land 10 jumps, it's a *mean* slipper. So just lay off with the slipper hate.

Action Command: Hit Ⓐ each time Mario lands to perform up to 10 stomps.

Line Jump

Attack Power: ✳

Attack Range: Ground/low altitude/air

Sticking Points: An attack that lets you stomp foe after foe with decreasing power, but only if you have good jump timing.

Action Command: Hit Ⓐ each time Mario lands to stomp each enemy up to three times.

Shiny Line Jump

Attack Power: ✳✳

Attack Range: Ground/low altitude/air

Sticking Points: A Line Jump with a bit more oomph. Try to stomp each enemy three times, since three is better than two or one.

Action Command: Hit Ⓐ each time Mario lands to stomp each enemy up to three times.

Flashy Line Jump

Attack Power: ✳✳✳

Attack Range: Ground/low altitude/air

Sticking Points: A flashy-looking Line Jump with flashy-feeling attack power. It's got the max power of the small Line Jump line.

Action Command: Hit Ⓐ each time Mario lands to stomp each enemy up to three times.

Big Shiny Line Jump

Attack Power: ✳✳✳✳

Attack Range: Ground/low altitude/air

Sticking Points: A sticker whose jump in size mirrors a jump in jumping-attack power. Foes will line up to take their whupping!

Action Command: Hit Ⓐ each time Mario lands to stomp each enemy up to three times.

Megaflash Line Jump

Attack Power: ✳✳✳✳✳

Attack Range: Ground/low altitude/air

Sticking Points: The strongest sticker in the Line Jump line. Enjoy the megapower as you stomp each enemy up to three times!

Action Command: Hit Ⓐ each time Mario lands to stomp each enemy up to three times.

Flashy Clone Jump

Attack Power: ✳✳✳

Attack Range: Ground/low altitude/air

Sticking Points: An attack that sends four clones leaping in succession. This attack can sometimes crumple foes, too.

Action Command: Hit Ⓐ each time Mario lands to deal increased damage.

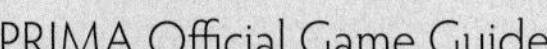

BIG SHINY CLONE JUMP

Attack Power: ✶✶✶✶

Attack Range: Ground/low altitude/air

Sticking Points: A sparkling clone attack with power befitting the sticker's size and raw, untamed sparklability.

Action Command: Hit Ⓐ each time Mario lands to deal increased damage.

MEGAFLASH CLONE JUMP

Attack Power: ✶✶✶✶✶

Attack Range: Ground/low altitude/air

Sticking Points: An attack that unleashes the four strongest clones and delivers a strong crumpling effect. Wow.

Action Command: Hit Ⓐ each time Mario lands to deal increased damage.

FLASHY INFINIJUMP

Attack Power: ✶✶✶

Attack Range: Ground/low altitude/air

Sticking Points: An attack with weak power but unreal stamina. Go for the maximum 100 jumps. Yes, you read that right.

Action Command: Hit Ⓐ each time Mario lands to perform up to 100 stomps.

BIG SHINY INFINIJUMP

Attack Power: ✶✶✶✶

Attack Range: Ground/low altitude/air

Sticking Points: A slightly bigger sticker that still has weak power. But c'mon, 100 stomps! 100 stomps is pretty solid.

Action Command: Hit Ⓐ each time Mario lands to perform up to 100 stomps.

MEGAFLASH INFINIJUMP

Attack Power: ✶✶✶✶✶

Attack Range: Ground/low altitude/air

Sticking Points: An attack said to bring enlightenment if you make your mind blank and become one with your jump.

Action Command: Hit Ⓐ each time Mario lands to perform up to 100 stomps.

WORN-OUT HAMMER

Attack Power: ✶

Attack Range: Ground/low altitude

Sticking Points: A Battle Sticker that doesn't look so hot. To be completely honest, it doesn't work so hot, either.

Action Command: Hit Ⓐ just before Mario's shine vanishes to deal increased damage.

HAMMER

Attack Power: ✶

Attack Range: Ground/low altitude

Sticking Points: A Hammer that can pound enemies flat but is useless against flying enemies. Use it wisely.

Action Command: Hit Ⓐ just before Mario's shine vanishes to deal increased damage.

SHINY HAMMER

Attack Power: ✶✶

Attack Range: Ground/low altitude

Sticking Points: A stronger Hammer attack. It will build power as you hold your windup, but don't overdo it or the head will pop off!

Action Command: Hit Ⓐ just before Mario's shine vanishes to deal increased damage.

FLASHY HAMMER

Attack Power: ✶✶✶

Attack Range: Ground/low altitude

Sticking Points: Like many others, a Hammer that can damage enemies near its main target. Plan for collateral damage!

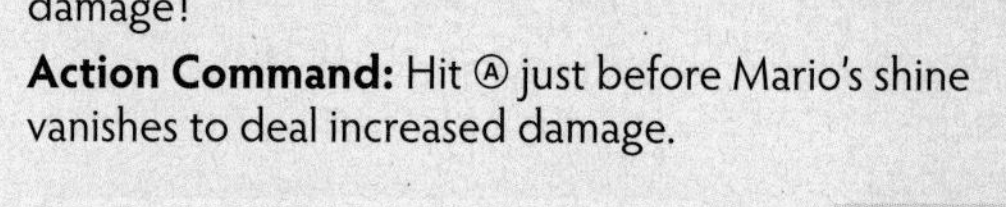

Action Command: Hit Ⓐ just before Mario's shine vanishes to deal increased damage.

BIG SHINY HAMMER

Attack Power: ✶✶✶✶

Attack Range: Ground/low altitude

Sticking Points: A big, shiny Hammer boasting big, shiny damage. Definitely do not miss your swing, or you'll be really bummed out.

Action Command: Hit Ⓐ just before Mario's shine vanishes to deal increased damage.

MEGAFLASH HAMMER

Attack Power: ✶✶✶✶✶

Attack Range: Ground/low altitude

Sticking Points: A Hammer with ultimate attack power. The main target and its neighbors get seriously *bonked*.

Action Command: Hit Ⓐ just before Mario's shine vanishes to deal increased damage.

SLAPHAMMER

Attack Power: ✶

Attack Range: Ground/low altitude

Sticking Points: An attack that strikes from the side. If swung with good timing, it sends enemies flying.

Action Command: Hit Ⓐ just before Mario's shine vanishes to deal increased damage.

HOW TO USE THIS GUIDE
HOW TO PLAY
STICKERS
ENEMIES
WALKTHROUGH
DECALBURG
SURFSHINE HARBOR
WORLD 1
WORLD 2
WORLD 3
WORLD 4
WORLD 5
WORLD 6
CHECKLISTS

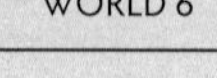

Shiny Slaphammer

Attack Power: ✶✶

Attack Range: Ground/low altitude

Sticking Points: A side-striking Hammer attack that has a chance of making an enemy dizzy, which could make its attacks miss.

Action Command: Hit Ⓐ just before Mario's shine vanishes to deal increased damage.

Flashy Slaphammer

Attack Power: ✶✶✶

Attack Range: Ground/low altitude

Sticking Points: An attack that hits only a single target, but it hits it really hard and might make it dizzy.

Action Command: Hit Ⓐ just before Mario's shine vanishes to deal increased damage.

Big Shiny Slaphammer

Attack Power: ✶✶✶✶

Attack Range: Ground/low altitude

Sticking Points: A big Hammer attack with big damage, but like all attacks, it's totally dependent on good timing.

Action Command: Hit Ⓐ just before Mario's shine vanishes to deal increased damage.

Megaflash Slaphammer

Attack Power: ✶✶✶✶✶

Attack Range: Ground/low altitude

Sticking Points: An attack whose mighty swing punishes foes, launching them dramatically and often making them dizzy.

Action Command: Hit Ⓐ just before Mario's shine vanishes to deal increased damage.

Eekhammer

Attack Power: ✶

Attack Range: Ground/low altitude

Sticking Points: A Hammer that really looks like a toy. Land up to five strikes for five times the annoyance. Squeaksqueaksqueak!

Action Command: Hit Ⓐ each time Mario shines to swing up to five times.

Shiny Eekhammer

Attack Power: ✶✶

Attack Range: Ground/low altitude

Sticking Points: A shiny attack that is regrettably still toylike. Still, five strikes should ease the shame of using it.

Action Command: Hit Ⓐ each time Mario shines to swing up to five times.

Flashy Eekhammer

Attack Power: ✶✶✶

Attack Range: Ground/low altitude

Sticking Points: A pretty flashy Hammer attack. Get in five hits so you can hear the squeaksqueaksqueak-squeaksqueak!

Action Command: Hit Ⓐ each time Mario shines to swing up to five times.

Big Shiny Eekhammer

Attack Power: ✶✶✶✶

Attack Range: Ground/low altitude

Sticking Points: Like other Eekhammers, its power gets stronger with each swing for a max of five strikes. This one's bigger, though.

Action Command: Hit Ⓐ each time Mario shines to swing up to five times.

Megaflash Eekhammer

Attack Power: ✶✶✶✶✶

Attack Range: Ground/low altitude

Sticking Points: A megasized attack that packs a serious wallop for a toy. Get in five strikes for perfection.

Action Command: Hit Ⓐ each time Mario shines to swing up to five times.

Hurlhamer

Attack Power: ✶

Attack Range: Ground/low altitude/air

Sticking Points: A hurlable Hammer that, with good timing, can damage all foes—even flying ones. Bad timing just ain't gonna cut it.

Action Command: Hit Ⓐ just before Mario's shine vanishes to hit multiple enemies.

Shiny Hurlhammer

Attack Power: ✶✶

Attack Range: Ground/low altitude/air

Sticking Points: An attack that, like other Hammers, fails if held too long. If you throw it too fast, it'll hit only one foe.

Action Command: Hit Ⓐ just before Mario's shine vanishes to hit multiple enemies.

Flashy Hurlhammer

Attack Power: ✶✶✶

Attack Range: Ground/low altitude/air

Sticking Points: A hurlable Hammer that, like others, damages enemies in front most but can also hit subsequent targets.

Action Command: Hit Ⓐ just before Mario's shine vanishes to hit multiple enemies.

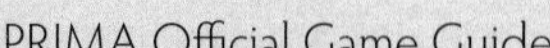

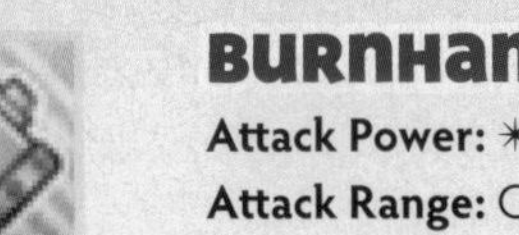

BIG SHINY HURLHAMMER

Attack Power: ✳✳✳✳

Attack Range: Ground/low altitude/air

Sticking Points: A decent-sized shiny Hammer that falls from above as its targets gaze in awe, helplessly watching doom approach.

Action Command: Hit Ⓐ just before Mario's shine vanishes to hit multiple enemies.

MEGAFLASH HURLHAMMER

Attack Power: ✳✳✳✳✳

Attack Range: Ground/low altitude/air

Sticking Points: A big, pretty, very hurlable Hammer. In fact, it's almost too pretty to hurl. Good thing you put it in here.

Action Command: Hit Ⓐ just before Mario's shine vanishes to hit multiple enemies.

BAAHAMMER

Attack Power: ✳

Attack Range: Ground/low altitude

Sticking Points: A Hammer that, with good timing, puts enemies to sleep. The fact that it deals damage is a bonus.

Action Command: Hit Ⓐ just before Mario's shine vanishes to increase the chance that enemies will sleep.

BIG SHINY BAAHAMMER

Attack Power: ✳✳✳✳

Attack Range: Ground/low altitude

Sticking Points: A Hammer that can knock even the most sleep-resistant enemy out. Of course, you've got to time it well.

Action Command: Hit Ⓐ just before Mario's shine vanishes to increase the chance that enemies will sleep.

MEGAFLASH BAAHAMMER

Attack Power: ✳✳✳✳✳

Attack Range: Ground/low altitude

Sticking Points: A Hammer attack with good power that also puts foes to bed. If you mess up the timing, though, that's baaaaaaaad.

Action Command: Hit Ⓐ just before Mario's shine vanishes to increase the chance that enemies will sleep.

BURNHAMMER

Attack Power: ✳

Attack Range: Ground/low altitude

Sticking Points: A Hammer whose tepid flames can fry a small fry. If your timing's off, though, you won't produce any flames.

Action Command: Hit Ⓐ just before Mario's shine vanishes to deal increased damage.

BIG SHINY BURNHAMMER

Attack Power: ✳✳✳✳

Attack Range: Ground/low altitude

Sticking Points: A hot, flaming Hammer attack that's nonetheless ineffective against the Buzzy Beetle family.

Action Command: Hit Ⓐ just before Mario's shine vanishes to deal increased damage.

MEGAFLASH BURNHAMMER

Attack Power: ✳✳✳✳✳

Attack Range: Ground/low altitude

Sticking Points: A flaming Hammer attack that damages all foes that it strikes equally. We just want to see you succeed, y'know?

Action Command: Hit Ⓐ just before Mario's shine vanishes to deal increased damage.

CHILLHAMMER

Attack Power: ✳

Attack Range: Ground/low altitude

Sticking Points: A Hammer that, if timed well, sends a freezing arctic blast howling into the faces of all enemies.

Action Command: Hit Ⓐ just before Mario's shine vanishes to deal increased damage.

BIG SHINY CHILLHAMMER

Attack Power: ✳✳✳✳

Attack Range: Ground/low altitude

Sticking Points: A Hammer attack that cold haters hate, but cold lovers love not hating. You know what I mean?

Action Command: Hit Ⓐ just before Mario's shine vanishes to deal increased damage.

MEGAFLASH CHILL-HAMMER

Attack Power: ✳✳✳✳✳

Attack Range: Ground/low altitude

Sticking Points: An attack that launches a really nasty cold wave boasting megaflash damage. Miss, and you hit zip.

Action Command: Hit Ⓐ just before Mario's shine vanishes to deal increased damage.

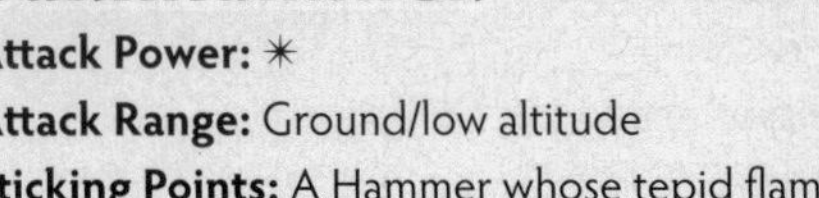

HOW TO USE THIS GUIDE
HOW TO PLAY
STICKERS
ENEMIES
WALKTHROUGH
DECALBURG
SURFSHINE HARBOR
WORLD 1
WORLD 2
WORLD 3
WORLD 4
WORLD 5
WORLD 6
CHECKLISTS

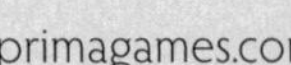

SUPER BOOT

Attack Power: —

Attack Range: —

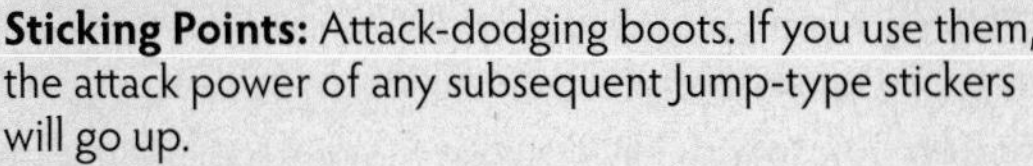

Sticking Points: Attack-dodging boots. If you use them, the attack power of any subsequent Jump-type stickers will go up.

Action Command: Hit Ⓐ just before an attack makes contact to dodge.

SHINY SUPER BOOT

Attack Power: —

Attack Range: —

Sticking Points: A defensive sticker that hugely boosts the attack power of subsequent jump stickers. Definitely stick this one first!

Action Command: Hit Ⓐ just before an attack makes contact to dodge.

TAIL

Attack Power: —

Attack Range: —

Sticking Points: A tail that repels attacks that come flying right at you. You've got to swing that tail with good timing, though!

Action Command: Hit Ⓐ to counter horizontal attacks just before they make contact.

SHINY TAIL

Attack Power: —

Attack Range: —

Sticking Points: A shiny tail that smacks onrushing enemies and straight-flying projectiles. When you connect, it feels good.

Action Command: Hit Ⓐ to counter horizontal attacks just before they make contact.

FROG SUIT

Attack Power: —

Attack Range: —

Sticking Points: A froggy dodge maneuver that ups attack power on subsequent stickers, too. Not too bad for a frog.

Action Command: Hit Ⓐ just before an attack makes contact to dodge.

SHINY FROG SUIT

Attack Power: —

Attack Range: —

Sticking Points: A shiny, froggy dodge that drastically boosts the attack power of subsequent stickers. Well done, frog.

Action Command: Hit Ⓐ just before an attack makes contact to dodge.

SPIKE HELMET

Attack Power: —

Attack Range: —

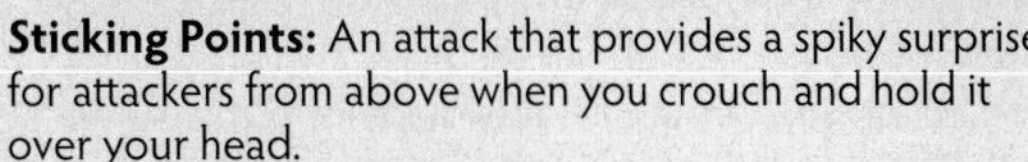

Sticking Points: An attack that provides a spiky surprise for attackers from above when you crouch and hold it over your head.

Action Command: Hit Ⓐ to counter horizontal attacks just before they make contact.

SHINY SPIKE HELMET

Attack Power: —

Attack Range: —

Sticking Points: A stronger spiked-helmet attack; this one hurts even more if you time your poke with the foe's landing.

Action Command: Hit Ⓐ to counter horizontal attacks just before they make contact.

FLASHY SPIKE HELMET

Attack Power: —

Attack Range: —

Sticking Points: A flashy spike attack that counters attacks from above with authority. Time it right, and *ow*!

Action Command: Hit Ⓐ to counter horizontal attacks just before they make contact.

FIRE FLOWER

Attack Power: ✶✶

Attack Range: Ground/low altitude

Sticking Points: An attack that launches one fireball per enemy but doesn't reach flying foes. Fireballs can't bounce that high.

Action Command: Hit Ⓐ just before Mario's shine vanishes to deal increased damage.

SHINY FIRE FLOWER

Attack Power: ✶✶✶

Attack Range: Ground/low altitude

Sticking Points: An attack that fires one shiny fireball per foe. Like others, this attack is a bit stronger if timed well.

Action Command: Hit Ⓐ just before Mario's shine vanishes to deal increased damage.

FLASHY FIRE FLOWER

Attack Power: ✶✶✶✶

Attack Range: Ground/low altitude

Sticking Points: An attack that greets each grounded and low-altitude foe with a strong, made-to-order fireball.

Action Command: Hit Ⓐ just before Mario's shine vanishes to deal increased damage.

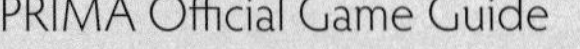

Ice Flower

Attack Power: ✱✱

Attack Range: Ground/low altitude

Sticking Points: A chilly attack that serves an ice ball to each enemy. These ice balls are the opposite of refreshing.

Action Command: Hit Ⓐ just before Mario's shine vanishes to deal increased damage.

Shiny Ice Flower

Attack Power: ✱✱✱

Attack Range: Ground/low altitude

Sticking Points: A stronger ice-ball attack that strikes ground-bound and low-altitude foes with shiny chill damage.

Action Command: Hit Ⓐ just before Mario's shine vanishes to deal increased damage.

Flashy Ice Flower

Attack Power: ✱✱✱✱

Attack Range: Ground/low altitude

Sticking Points: A flashy ice-ball attack that boasts boosted wintry power if you time your throws correctly.

Action Command: Hit Ⓐ just before Mario's shine vanishes to deal increased damage.

POW Block

Attack Power: ✱✱

Attack Range: Ground

Sticking Points: An attack that can crumple grounded foes. You get two chances at it, so time it well.

Action Command: Hit Ⓐ just as Mario starts each jump to increase the damage done and the chances of crumpling enemies.

Shiny POW Block

Attack Power: ✱✱✱

Attack Range: Ground

Sticking Points: An attack that offers higher damage and an elevated crumple rate if you time it well.

Action Command: Hit Ⓐ just as Mario starts each jump to increase the damage done and the chances of crumpling enemies.

Flashy POW Block

Attack Power: ✱✱✱✱

Attack Range: Ground

Sticking Points: A one-shot crumpler. As expected, its attack power is also higher due to extreme flashiness.

Action Command: Hit Ⓐ just as Mario starts each jump to increase the damage done and the chances of crumpling enemies.

Shell

Attack Power: ✱✱

Attack Range: Ground

Sticking Points: A shell that knocks around foes when stomped and kicked. Time it well for more power.

Action Command: Hit Ⓐ just as Mario starts his jump and when he lands to deal increased damage.

Shiny Shell

Attack Power: ✱✱✱

Attack Range: Ground

Sticking Points: A powerful shell that should remind you to pre-stomp Koopas in the field. Then you can use them to scatter other foes.

Action Command: Hit Ⓐ just as Mario starts his jump and when he lands to deal increased damage.

Flashy Shell

Attack Power: ✱✱✱✱

Attack Range: Ground

Sticking Points: A flashy shell that delivers big damage. The damage on this attack nearly doubles with good timing.

Action Command: Hit Ⓐ just as Mario starts his jump and when he lands to deal increased damage.

Mushroom

Attack Power: —

Attack Range: —

Sticking Points: An all-important HP-restoring sticker that can only be used during battle. Always, *always* carry one with you!

Action Command: Hit Ⓐ just before Mario drops his hands to increase the HP received.

Shiny Mushroom

Attack Power: —

Attack Range: —

Sticking Points: An item that increases HP more than a regular Mushroom. Wait until you're really flagging to use it!

Action Command: Hit Ⓐ just before Mario drops his hands to increase the HP received.

Flashy Mushroom

Attack Power: —

Attack Range: —

Sticking Points: A flashy mushroom that greatly restores HP with flashy mushroom goodness. You get bonus HP for good timing.

Action Command: Hit Ⓐ just before Mario drops his hands to increase the HP received.

HOW TO USE THIS GUIDE
HOW TO PLAY
STICKERS
ENEMIES
WALKTHROUGH
DECALBURG
SURFSHINE HARBOR
WORLD 1
WORLD 2
WORLD 3
WORLD 4
WORLD 5
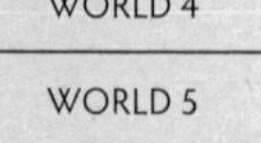
WORLD 6
CHECKLISTS

BIG 1UP

Attack Power: —

Attack Range: —

Sticking Points: A sticker that should teach you that big mushrooms are great for you. This one slowly restores HP over 10 turns.

Action Command: Hit Ⓐ just before Mario drops his hands to increase the HP received.

BIG SHINY 1UP

Attack Power: —

Attack Range: —

Sticking Points: A shiny HP restorer effective over 10 turns. Time it with Mario's hands in the air for extra restorative power!

Action Command: Hit Ⓐ just before Mario drops his hands to increase the HP received.

POISON MUSHROOM

Attack Power: —

Attack Range: —

Sticking Points: Oh no! An item that poisons you! But hang on... What if you touch an enemy while poisoned...?

Action Command: Hit Ⓐ just before Mario drops his hands.

LEAF

Attack Power: —

Attack Range: —

Sticking Points: A helpful sticker that automatically makes every attack Excellent and every block successful.

Action Command: None

SHINY LEAF

Attack Power: —

Attack Range: —

Sticking Points: A sticker with the exact same effects as an ordinary leaf sticker. But look! It's shiny! So it sells for more.

Action Command: None

Note: Leaf stickers do not ensure that you achieve 100 attacks while using an Infinijump sticker.

SECRET DOOR

Attack Power: —

Attack Range: —

Sticking Points: A door that opens the way to a secret place. This sticker can also be used to flee a battle.

Action Command: Mash Ⓐ to increase your chance of a successful retreat.

SNOWBALL

Attack Power: ✳✳✳

Attack Range: —

Sticking Points: An icy snowball yacked up by a Snow Spike that hits all grounded foes with a cold-blooded attack.

Action Command: Hit Ⓐ just before Mario's shine vanishes to deal increased damage.

SPIKE BALL

Attack Power: ✳✳✳

Attack Range: —

Sticking Points: A spiky steel ball horked up by a Spike. This bad boy deals bonus damage for a well-timed throw!

Action Command: Hit Ⓐ just before Mario's shine vanishes to deal increased damage.

BARREL

Attack Power: ✳✳✳

Attack Range: —

Sticking Points: A wooded barrel thrown by a Broozer. This thing is heavy, so be careful when tossing it.

Action Command: Hit Ⓐ just before Mario's shine vanishes to deal increased damage.

WRENCH

Attack Power: ✳✳✳

Attack Range: —

Sticking Points: A repair wrench tossed by Rocky Wrenches. Time your toss well, because it'll affect the power of the spin!

Action Command: Hit Ⓐ just before Mario's shine vanishes to deal increased damage.

BONE

Attack Power: ✳✳✳

Attack Range: —

Sticking Points: Part of a Dry Bones? Some kind of bone, anyway. It hits with a satisfying *donk* if thrown with enough force.

Action Command: Hit Ⓐ just before Mario's shine vanishes to deal increased damage.

BOOMERANG

Attack Power: ✳✳✳

Attack Range: —

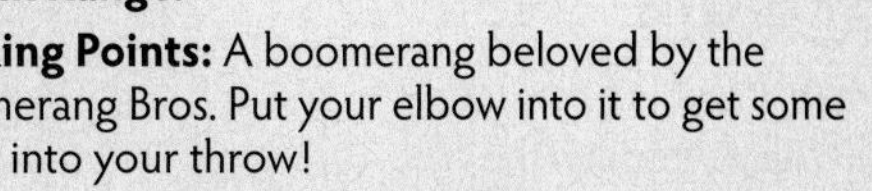

Sticking Points: A boomerang beloved by the Boomerang Bros. Put your elbow into it to get some force into your throw!

Action Command: Hit Ⓐ just before Mario's shine vanishes to deal increased damage.

BOMB

Attack Power: ✱✱✱

Attack Range: —

Sticking Points: An unused bomb dropped by a Bob-omb. This explosive has a dramatic effect if tossed properly.

Action Command: Hit Ⓐ just before Mario's shine vanishes to deal increased damage.

SOMBRERO

Attack Power: ✱✱✱

Attack Range: —

Sticking Points: A sombrero worn by Sombrero Guys. The angle of the throw affects how cool the attack turns out!

Action Command: Hit Ⓐ just before Mario's shine vanishes to deal increased damage.

THROWING STAR

Attack Power: ✱✱✱

Attack Range: —

Sticking Points: A throwing star favored by Ninjis. It's easy to time this attack if you concentrate.

Action Command: Hit Ⓐ just before Mario's shine vanishes to deal increased damage.

THING STICKERS

SEWING SCISSORS

Category: Cutting

Effect: Slices through the area, damaging all enemies.

Action Command: Mash Ⓐ while the environment is sliced apart.

HAIR SHEARS

Category: Cutting

Effect: Slices through the area, damaging all enemies.

Action Command: Mash Ⓐ while the environment is sliced apart.

SCISSORS

Category: Cutting

Effect: Slices through the area, damaging all enemies.

Action Command: Mash Ⓐ while the environment is sliced apart.

TAILOR SHEARS

Category: Cutting

Effect: Slices through the area, damaging all enemies.

Action Command: Mash Ⓐ while the environment is sliced apart.

BELLOWS

Category: Wind

Effect: Sweeps up enemies in a damaging cyclone.

Action Command: Mash Ⓐ while the wind is blowing.

PAPER FAN

Category: Wind

Effect: Sweeps up enemies in a damaging cyclone.

Action Command: Mash Ⓐ while the wind is blowing.

FAN

Category: Wind

Effect: Sweeps up enemies in a damaging cyclone.

Action Command: Mash Ⓐ while the wind is blowing.

MINI VACUUM

Category: Suction

Effect: Pulls enemies in for a damaging attack.

Action Command: Mash Ⓐ for the duration of the suction effect.

UPRIGHT VACUUM

Category: Suction

Effect: Pulls enemies in for a damaging attack.

Action Command: Mash Ⓐ for the duration of the suction effect.

VACUUM

Category: Suction

Effect: Pulls enemies in for a damaging attack.

Action Command: Mash Ⓐ for the duration of the suction effect.

WATERING CAN

Category: Flood

Effect: Floods the battlefield to cleanse poison and damage enemies. Has a slight chance to turn enemies soggy.

Action Command: Mash Ⓐ while the flood rises.

Faucet
Category: Flood
Effect: Floods the battlefield to cleanse poison and damage enemies. Has a slight chance to turn enemies soggy.
Action Command: Mash Ⓐ while the flood rises.

Teapot
Category: Flood
Effect: Floods the battlefield to cleanse poison and damage enemies. Has a slight chance to turn enemies soggy.
Action Command: Mash Ⓐ while the flood rises.

Trumpet
Category: Noise
Effect: Blaring music damages enemies and has a chance to wake sleeping targets.
Action Command: Mash Ⓐ while the instrument plays.

Violin
Category: Noise
Effect: Blaring music damages enemies and has a chance to wake sleeping targets.
Action Command: Mash Ⓐ after the quartet plays Mario's theme song.

Guitar
Category: Noise
Effect: Blaring music damages enemies and has a chance to wake sleeping targets.
Action Command: Mash Ⓐ during the intense guitar solo.

Newspaper
Category: Bat
Effect: Hits up to four enemies, causing damage. Has a chance to knock enemies out of the battlefield.
Action Command: Press Ⓐ when the Newspaper shakes.

Toy Bat
Category: Bat
Effect: Hits up to four enemies, causing damage. Has a chance to knock enemies out of the battlefield.
Action Command: Press Ⓐ when the Toy Bat shakes.

Bat
Category: Bat
Effect: Hits up to four enemies, causing damage. Has a chance to knock enemies out of the battlefield.
Action Command: Press Ⓐ when the Bat shakes.

Square Can
Category: Smashing
Effect: Falls to the ground, damaging a single enemy.
Action Command: Press Ⓐ at the instant the container hits an enemy.

Basin
Category: Smashing
Effect: Falls to the ground, damaging enemies.
Action Command: Press Ⓐ at the instant the container hits the enemies.

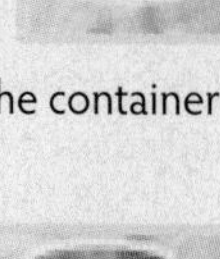

Drum
Category: Smashing
Effect: Falls to the ground, damaging enemies.
Action Command: Press Ⓐ at the instant the container hits the enemies.

Lightbulb
Category: Light
Effect: Blinds enemies, causing damage and making them dizzy.
Action Command: Press Ⓐ while the light is glowing.

Flashlight
Category: Light
Effect: Blinds enemies, causing damage and making them dizzy.
Action Command: Press Ⓐ while the light is glowing.

Searchlight
Category: Light
Effect: Blinds enemies, causing damage and making them dizzy.
Action Command: Press Ⓐ while the light is glowing.

Watch Battery
Category: Shocking
Effect: Damages enemies with lightning bolts.
Action Command: Press Ⓐ as the lightning strikes each enemy.

D-Cell Battery
Category: Shocking
Effect: Damages enemies with lightning bolts.
Action Command: Press Ⓐ as the lightning strikes each enemy.

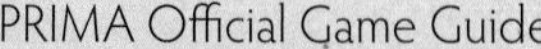

CAR BATTERY

Category: Shocking

Effect: Damages enemies with lightning bolts.

Action Command: Press Ⓐ as the lightning strikes each enemy.

BILLIARD BALL

Category: Thrown

Effect: Damages enemies with a heavy projectile.

Action Command: Press Ⓐ when Mario's hand is at the midpoint of his throwing motion.

CURLING STONE

Category: Thrown

Effect: Damages enemies with a heavy projectile.

Action Command: Press Ⓐ when Mario's hand is at the midpoint of his throwing motion.

BOWLING BALL

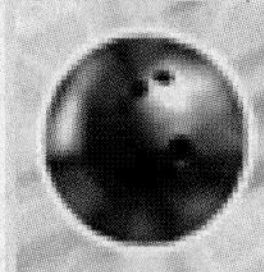

Category: Thrown

Effect: Damages enemies with a heavy projectile.

Action Command: Press Ⓐ when Mario's hand is at the midpoint of his throwing motion.

TROPHY

Category: Thrown

Effect: Damages enemies with a heavy projectile.

Action Command: Press Ⓐ when Mario's hand is at the midpoint of his throwing motion.

CELL PHONE

Category: Vibration

Effect: The ground shakes, damaging enemies.

Action Command: Mash Ⓐ when the phone's screen lights up.

JACKHAMMER

Category: Vibration

Effect: The ground shakes, damaging enemies.

Action Command: Mash Ⓐ when the Jackhammer's bit pierces the ground.

RADIATOR

Category: Heat

Effect: An intense heat damages enemies.

Action Command: Mash Ⓐ for the duration of the heat effect.

HAIR DRYER

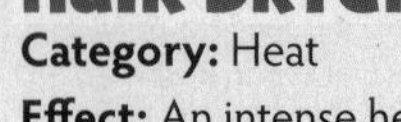

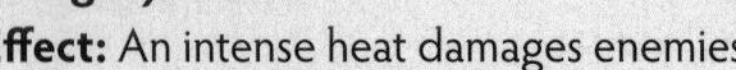

Category: Heat

Effect: An intense heat damages enemies.

Action Command: Mash Ⓐ for the duration of the heat effect.

OVEN

Category: Heat

Effect: An intense heat damages enemies.

Action Command: Mash Ⓐ for the duration of the heat effect.

MAGNIFYING GLASS

Category: Fire

Effect: Damages enemies with fire.

Action Command: Mash Ⓐ when the beam focuses to a tiny point.

MATCHES

Category: Fire

Effect: Damages enemies with fire.

Action Command: Press Ⓐ when the match is struck against the matchbox.

LIGHTER

Category: Fire

Effect: Damages enemies with fire.

Action Command: Mash Ⓐ while the flame burns.

SHAVED ICE

Category: Cold

Effect: An icy attack damages enemies.

Action Command: Mash Ⓐ for the duration of the cold effect.

AIR CONDITIONER

Category: Cold

Effect: An icy attack damages enemies.

Action Command: Mash Ⓐ for the duration of the cold effect.

REFRIGERATOR

Category: Cold

Effect: An icy attack damages enemies.

Action Command: Mash Ⓐ for the duration of the cold effect.

SODA

Category: Spray

Effect: Damages enemies and has a chance to turn them soggy.

Action Command: Mash Ⓐ when the can starts to shake.

SQUIRT GUN

Category: Spray

Effect: Damages enemies with a manually aimed stream of water. Has a chance to turn affected enemies soggy.

Action Command: Hold Ⓐ to spray water. Mash Ⓐ to pump the weapon while it reloads.

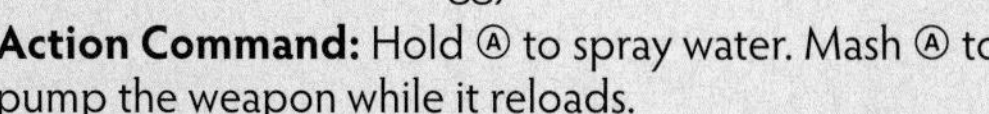

RUBBER DUCKY

Category: Miscellaneous

Effect: Ducks appear and damage enemies with a series of attacks.

Action Command: Press Ⓐ each time a duck attacks an enemy.

POWDER PUFF

Category: Defense

Effect: Absorbs incoming attacks, preventing damage.

Action Command: None

SPONGE

Category: Defense

Effect: Absorbs incoming attacks, preventing damage.

Action Command: None

CAR SPONGE

Category: Defense

Effect: Absorbs incoming attacks, preventing damage.

Action Command: None

PILLOW

Category: Sleep

Effect: Puts enemies to sleep and causes light damage. Has a chance to put Mario to sleep as well.

Action Command: Mash Ⓐ while the music plays to avoid falling asleep.

BED

Category: Sleep

Effect: Puts enemies to sleep and causes light damage. Has a chance to put Mario to sleep as well.

Action Command: Mash Ⓐ while the music plays to avoid falling asleep.

LUXURIOUS BED

Category: Sleep

Effect: Puts enemies to sleep and causes light damage. Has a chance to put Mario to sleep as well.

Action Command: Mash Ⓐ while the music plays to avoid falling asleep.

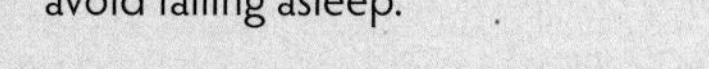

TAPE

Category: Immobilize

Effect: Prevents enemies from moving or attacking.

Action Command: Press Ⓐ when the first strip touches the battlefield.

THUMBTACK

Category: Immobilize

Effect: Prevents enemies from moving or attacking.

Action Command: Press Ⓐ when the first tack touches the battlefield.

STAPLER

Category: Immobilize

Effect: Prevents enemies from moving or attacking.

Action Command: Press Ⓐ when the first staple touches the battlefield.

FISHHOOK

Category: Miscellaneous

Effect: Grants a Jump-based sticker.

Action Command: Press Ⓐ the moment the line twitches to earn a higher quality sticker.

BALLOON

Category: Miscellaneous

Effect: Damages enemies if it bursts.

Action Command: Mash Ⓐ while the Balloon expands to make it burst.

POCKET WATCH

Category: Miscellaneous

Effect: Makes it more difficult for enemies to time their maneuvers. Mario can also be affected.

Action Command: Press Ⓐ when the hands reach 12 o'clock to avoid the negative effects.

CAT-O-LUCK

Category: Miscellaneous

Effect: Repeatedly slams down on enemies, causing damage.

Action Command: Press Ⓐ each time the statue hits the ground.

HIGH HEEL

Category: Miscellaneous

Effect: Damages a single enemy with a series of quick attacks.

Action Command: Mash Ⓐ while each heel grinds into its target.

Goat

Category: Miscellaneous

Effect: Chomps enemies up to eight times, causing damage.

Action Command: Press Ⓐ during each chomp to extend the attack. Successfully time eight chomps to earn a bonus attack.

Turkey

Category: Miscellaneous

Effect: A cooked Turkey dances around, damaging enemies.

Action Command: Press Ⓐ at the end of the song's countdown, when the Turkey strikes its final pose.

Cake

Category: Miscellaneous

Effect: Has a chance to replenish Mario's HP.

Action Command: Blow into the Nintendo 3DS System's microphone when the song ends and the candles ignite. Put out at least three candles to replenish some of Mario's HP.

Boom Box

Category: Miscellaneous

Effect: Has a chance to double Mario's attack power for a few turns.

Action Command: Mash Ⓐ while the music plays.

Additional Information

Megaflash Sticker Locations

COURSE	STICKER
World 2-2	Megaflash Hammer
World 4-6	Megaflash Line Jump
World 4-6	Megaflash Chillhammer
World 5-1	Megaflash Hurlhammer
World 5-3	Megaflash Infinijump
World 5-4	Megaflash Eekhammer
World 5-4	Megaflash Hurlhammer
World 5-4	Megaflash Baahammer
World 5-4	Megaflash Hopslipper
World 5-5	Megaflash Iron Jump
World 5-5	Megaflash Slaphammer
World 5-5	Megaflash Burnhammer
World 5-6	Megaflash Clone Jump
World 6-2	Megaflash Jump

Sticker Shop Inventory

BATTLE STICKER	PURCHASE PRICE	SELL VALUE	REQUIRED COURSE	DECALBURG	WORLD 1-5	WORLD 3-6	WORLD 4-4	WORLD 5-6
Baahammer	10	5	World 1-5	Sold	—	—	—	—
Barrel	—	15	—	—	—	—	—	—
Big 1UP	—	30	—	—	—	—	—	—
Big Shiny 1UP		30	—	—	—	—	—	—
Big Shiny Baahammer	20	10	World 3-12	Sold	—	—	Sold	Sold
Big Shiny Burnhammer	30	15	World 3-12	Sold	—	—	Sold	Sold
Big Shiny Chillhammer	30	15	World 3-12	Sold	—	—	Sold	Sold
Big Shiny Clone Jump	—	45	—	—	—	—	—	—
Big Shiny Eekhammer	35	18	World 3-6	Sold	—	—	—	—
Big Shiny Hammer	25	13	World 3-6	Sold	—	Sold	Sold	—
Big Shiny Hopslipper	35	18	World 5-6	Sold	—	—	—	Sold
Big Shiny Hurlhammer	55	28	World 3-6	Sold	—	—	—	—
Big Shiny Infinijump	—	30	—	—	—	—	—	—
Big Shiny Iron Jump	30	15	World 5-6	Sold	—	—	—	Sold
Big Shiny Jump	25	13	World 3-6	Sold	—	Sold	—	Sold

Continued

BATTLE STICKER	PURCHASE PRICE	SELL VALUE	REQUIRED COURSE	DECALBURG	WORLD 1-5	WORLD 3-6	WORLD 4-4	WORLD 5-6
Big Shiny Line Jump	55	28	World 3-6	Sold	—	—	—	—
Big Shiny Slaphammer	25	13	World 3-6	Sold	—	—	—	—
Bomb	—	15	—	—	—	—	—	—
Bone	—	15	—	—	—	—	—	—
Boomerang	—	15	—	—	—	—	—	—
Burnhammer	20	10	World 1-5	Sold	—	—	—	—
Chillhammer	20	10	World 1-5	Sold	—	—	—	—
Eekhammer	5	3	World 1-1	Sold	—	—	—	—
Fire Flower	20	10	World 1-5	—	Sold	—	—	—
Flashy Clone Jump	60	30	World 4-4	—	—	—	Sold	—
Flashy Eekhammer	—	13	—	—	—	—	—	—
Flashy Fire Flower	40	20	World 3-12	—	Sold	—	—	—
Flashy Hammer	20	10	World 5-6	—	—	—	—	Sold
Flashy Hopslipper	—	13	—	—	—	—	—	—
Flashy Hurlhammer	—	20	—	—	—	—	—	—
Flashy Ice Flower	40	20	World 3-12	—	Sold	—	—	—
Flashy Infinijump	—	30	—	—	—	—	—	—
Flashy Iron Jump	—	13	—	—	—	—	—	—
Flashy Jump	20	10	World 5-6	—	—	—	—	Sold
Flashy Line Jump	—	23	—	—	—	—	—	—
Flashy Mushroom	50	25	World 4-6	Sold	—	—	—	—
Flashy POW Block	—	30	—	—	—	—	—	—
Flashy Shell	—	30	—	—	—	—	—	—
Flashy Slaphammer	—	10	—	—	—	—	—	—
Flashy Spike Helmet	—	12	—	—	—	—	—	—
Frog Suit	20	10	World 3-6	—	—	Sold	—	—
Hammer	3	2	Introduction	Sold	Sold	—	—	—
Hopslipper	5	3	World 1-1	Sold	—	—	—	—
Hurlhammer	20	10	World 1-3	Sold	—	—	—	—
Ice Flower	20	10	World 1-5	—	Sold	—	—	—
Iron Jump	5	3	World 1-3	Sold	—	—	—	—
Jump	3	2	Introduction	Sold	Sold	—	—	—
Leaf	—	20	—	—	—	—	—	—
Line Jump	12	6	World 1-1	Sold	—	—	—	—
Megaflash Baahammer	—	15	—	—	—	—	—	—
Megaflash Burnhammer	—	20	—	—	—	—	—	—
Megaflash Chillhammer	—	20	—	—	—	—	—	—
Megaflash Clone Jump	—	60	—	—	—	—	—	—
Megaflash Eekhammer	—	23	—	—	—	—	—	—
Megaflash Hammer	—	18	—	—	—	—	—	—

Continued

BATTLE STICKER	PURCHASE PRICE	SELL VALUE	REQUIRED COURSE	DECALBURG	WORLD 1-5	WORLD 3-6	WORLD 4-4	WORLD 5-6
Megaflash Hopslipper	—	23	—	—	—	—	—	—
Megaflash Hurlhammer	—	35	—	—	—	—	—	—
Megaflash Infinijump	—	30	—	—	—	—	—	—
Megaflash Iron Jump	—	20	—	—	—	—	—	—
Megaflash Jump	—	18	—	—	—	—	—	—
Megaflash Line Jump	—	35	—	—	—	—	—	—
Megaflash Slaphammer	—	18	—	—	—	—	—	—
Mushroom	15	8	Introduction	Sold	Sold	—	—	—
Poison Mushroom	2	1	World 1-5	—	Sold	—	—	—
POW Block	30	15	World 1-3	Sold	—	—	—	—
Secret Door	80	40	World 3-6	—	—	Sold	—	—
Shell	20	10	World 1-3	Sold	—	—	—	—
Shiny Eekhammer	12	6	World 4-4	—	—	—	Sold	—
Shiny Fire Flower	30	15	World 1-6	—	Sold	—	—	Sold
Shiny Frog Suit	40	20	World 4-4	—	—	Sold	—	—
Shiny Hammer	10	5	World 4-4	—	—	—	Sold	Sold
Shiny Hopslipper	12	6	World 4-4	—	—	—	Sold	—
Shiny Hurlhammer	30	15	World 4-4	—	—	—	Sold	—
Shiny Ice Flower	30	15	World 1-6	—	Sold	—	—	—
Shiny Iron Jump	12	6	World 4-4	—	—	—	Sold	Sold
Shiny Jump	10	5	World 4-4	—	—	—	Sold	Sold
Shiny Leaf	—	50	—	—	—	—	—	—
Shiny Line Jump	28	14	World 4-4	—	—	—	Sold	—
Shiny Mushroom	30	15	World 1-6	Sold	—	Sold	Sold	Sold
Shiny POW Block	45	23	World 4-4	—	—	—	Sold	Sold
Shiny Shell	40	20	World 3-6	Sold	—	—	Sold	—
Shiny Slaphammer	10	5	World 4-4	—	—	—	Sold	—
Shiny Spike Helmet	16	8	World 4-4	—	—	—	Sold	—
Shiny Super Boot	40	20	World 4-4	—	—	Sold	—	—
Shiny Tail	40	20	World 4-4	—	—	Sold	—	—
Slaphammer	3	2	World 1-1	Sold	—	—	—	—
Snowball	—	15	—	—	—	—	—	—
Sombrero	—	15	—	—	—	—	—	—
Spike Ball	—	15	—	—	—	—	—	—
Spike Helmet	8	4	World 1-3	Sold	—	—	—	—
Super Boot	20	10	World 3-6	—	—	Sold	—	—
Tail	20	10	World 3-6	—	—	Sold	—	—
Throwing Star	—	15	—	—	—	—	—	—
Worn-Out Hammer	—	1	—	—	—	—	—	—
Worn-Out Jump	—	1	—	—	—	—	—	—
Wrench	—	15	—	—	—	—	—	—

PAPERIZATION BLOCK OUTCOMES

INPUT STICKER	POSSIBLE OUTCOMES
Worn-Out Jump	Jump
	Worn-Out Hammer x3
	5-Heart
	1-Coin
Jump	Shiny Jump
	Hammer, Hammer, Shiny Jump
	Iron Jump
	Hammer
Shiny Jump	Flashy Jump
	Hammer, Shiny Hammer, Flashy Jump
	Shiny Iron Jump
	Shiny Hammer
Flashy Jump	Flashy Clone Jump
	Shiny Hammer, Flashy Hammer, Flashy Jump
	Flashy Iron Jump
	Flashy Hammer
Iron Jump	Shiny Iron Jump
	Slaphammer, Slaphammer, Shiny Iron Jump
	Hopslipper
	Slaphammer
Shiny Iron Jump	Flashy Iron Jump
	Slaphammer, Shiny Slaphammer, Flashy Iron Jump
	Shiny Hopslipper
	Shiny Slaphammer
Flashy Iron Jump	Flashy Clone Jump
	Shiny Slaphammer, Flashy Slaphammer, Flashy Iron Jump
	Flashy Hopslipper
	Flashy Slaphammer
Hopslipper	Shiny Hopslipper
	Eekhammer, Eekhammer, Shiny Hopslipper
	Line Jump
	Eekhammer
Shiny Hopslipper	Flashy Hopslipper
	Eekhammer, Shiny Eekhammer, Flashy Hopslipper
	Shiny Line Jump
	Shiny Eekhammer
Flashy Hopslipper	Flashy Infinijump
	Shiny Eekhammer, Flashy Eekhammer, Flashy Hopslipper
	Flashy Line Jump
	Flashy Eekhammer
Line Jump	Shiny Line Jump
	Hurlhammer, Hurlhammer, Shiny Line Jump
	Shiny POW Block
	Hurlhammer

INPUT STICKER	POSSIBLE OUTCOMES
Shiny Line Jump	Flashy Line Jump
	Hurlhammer, Shiny Hurlhammer, Flashy Line Jump
	Flashy POW Block
	Shiny Hurlhammer
Flashy Line Jump	Flashy Infinijump
	Shiny Hurlhammer, Flashy Hurlhammer, Flashy Line Jump
	Flashy Clone Jump
	Flashy Hurlhammer
Flashy Clone Jump	
	Flashy Clone Jump
	Flashy Infinijump
Flashy Infinijump	
	Flashy Infinijump
	Flashy Clone Jump
Worn-Out Hammer	Hammer
	Worn-Out Jump x3
	5-Heart
	1-Coin
Hammer	Shiny Hammer
	Jump, Jump, Shiny Hammer
	Eekhammer
	Jump
Shiny Hammer	Flashy Hammer
	Jump, Shiny Jump, Flashy Hammer
	Shiny Eekhammer
	Shiny Jump
Flashy Hammer	Shiny Jump, Flashy Jump, Flashy Hammer
	Flashy Eekhammer
	Flashy Jump
Slaphammer	Shiny Slaphammer
	Iron Jump, Iron Jump, Shiny Slaphammer
	Eekhammer
	Iron Jump
Shiny Slaphammer	Flashy Slaphammer
	Iron Jump, Shiny Iron Jump, Flashy Slaphammer
	Shiny Eekhammer
	Shiny Iron Jump
Flashy Slaphammer	Flashy Slaphammer
	Shiny Iron Jump, Flashy Iron Jump, Flashy Slaphammer
	Flashy Eekhammer
	Flashy Iron Jump

Continued

INPUT STICKER	POSSIBLE OUTCOMES
Eekhammer	Shiny Eekhammer
	Hopslipper, Hopslipper, Shiny Eekhammer
	Hurlhammer
	Hopslipper
Shiny Eekhammer	Flashy Eekhammer
	Hopslipper, Shiny Hopslipper, Flashy Eekhammer
	Shiny Hurlhammer
	Shiny Hopslipper
Flashy Eekhammer	Flashy POW Block
	Shiny Hopslipper, Flashy Hopslipper, Flashy Eekhammer
	Flashy Hurlhammer
	Flashy Hopslipper
Hurlhammer	Shiny Hurlhammer
	Line Jump, Line Jump, Shiny Hurlhammer
	Burnhammer
	Line Jump
Shiny Hurlhammer	Flashy Hurlhammer
	Line Jump, Shiny Line Jump, Flashy Hurlhammer
	Shiny POW Block
	Shiny Line Jump
Flashy Hurlhammer	Flashy Fire Flower
	Shiny Line Jump, Flashy Line Jump, Flashy Hurlhammer
	Flashy POW Block
	Flashy Line Jump
Baahammer	Burnhammer, Chillhammer, Baahammer
	Burnhammer
	Chillhammer
	POW Block
Burnhammer	Chillhammer, Baahammer, Burnhammer
	Chillhammer
	Baahammer
	Fire Flower
Chillhammer	Baahammer, Burnhammer, Chill-hammer
	Burnhammer
	Baahammer
	Ice Flower
Super Boot	Shiny Super Boot
	Tail
	Frog Suit
	Shiny Fire Flower, Shiny Ice Flower, Flashy Spike Helmet
Shiny Super Boot	Flashy Fire Flower
	Shiny Tail
	Shiny Frog Suit
	Flashy Fire Flower, Flashy Ice Flower, Flashy Spike Helmet

INPUT STICKER	POSSIBLE OUTCOMES
Tail	Shiny Tail
	Super Boot
	Flashy POW Block
	Shiny Fire Flower, Shiny Ice Flower, Flashy Spike Helmet
Shiny Tail	Flashy Ice Flower
	Shiny Super Boot
	Shiny Frog Suit
	Flashy Fire Flower, Flashy Ice Flower, Flashy Spike Helmet
Frog Suit	Shiny Frog Suit
	Super Boot
	Flashy POW Block
	Shiny Fire Flower, Shiny Ice Flower, Flashy Spike Helmet
Shiny Frog Suit	Flashy Fire Flower
	Shiny Super Boot
	Shiny Tail
	Flashy Fire Flower, Flashy Ice Flower, Flashy Spike Helmet
Spike Helmet	Fire Flower, Ice Flower, Shiny Spike Helmet
	Super Boot
	Tail
	Frog Suit
Shiny Spike Helmet	Shiny Fire Flower, Shiny Ice Flower, Flashy Spike Helmet
	Shiny Super Boot
	Shiny Tail
	Shiny Frog Suit
Flashy Spike Helmet	Flashy Fire Flower, Flashy Ice Flower, Flashy Spike Helmet
	Flashy Fire Flower
	Flashy Ice Flower
	Flashy Shell
Fire Flower	Shiny Fire Flower
	Ice Flower, POW Block, Shiny Fire Flower
	Ice Flower
	Shell
Shiny Fire Flower	Flashy Fire Flower
	Ice Flower, POW Block, Flashy Fire Flower
	Shiny Ice Flower
	Shiny Shell
Flashy Fire Flower	Flashy POW Block
	Shiny Ice Flower, Shiny POW Block, Flashy Fire Flower
	Flashy Ice Flower
	Flashy Shell
Ice Flower	Shiny Ice Flower
	Fire Flower, POW Block, Shiny Ice Flower
	Fire Flower
	Shell

Continued

INPUT STICKER	POSSIBLE OUTCOMES
Shiny Ice Flower	Flashy Ice Flower
	Fire Flower, POW Block, Flashy Ice Flower
	Shiny Fire Flower
	Shiny Shell
Flashy Ice Flower	Flashy POW Block
	Shiny Fire Flower, Shiny POW Block, Flashy Ice Flower
	Flashy Fire Flower
	Flashy Shell
POW Block	Shiny POW Block
	Fire Flower, Ice Flower, Shiny POW Block
	Fire Flower
	Ice Flower
Shiny POW Block	Flashy POW Block
	Fire Flower, Ice Flower, Flashy POW Block
	Shiny Fire Flower
	Shiny Ice Flower
Flashy POW Block	Flashy Shell
	Shiny Fire Flower, Shiny Ice Flower, Flashy POW Block
	Flashy Fire Flower
	Flashy Ice Flower
Shell	Shiny Shell
	Burnhammer, Chillhammer, Shiny Shell
	Fire Flower
	Ice Flower
Shiny Shell	Flashy Shell
	Shiny Fire Flower, Shiny Ice Flower, Shiny Shell
	Shiny Fire Flower
	Shiny Ice Flower
Flashy Shell	Flashy POW Block
	Flashy Line Jump, Flashy Hurlhammer, Flashy Shell
	Flashy Fire Flower
	Flashy Ice Flower
Mushroom	Shiny Mushroom
	30-Heart, 10-Coin, Mushroom
	5-Heart x2, Mushroom
	5-Heart x3
Shiny Mushroom	Flashy Mushroom
	30-Heart, 10-Coin, Shiny Mushroom
	10-Heart x2, Shiny Mushroom
	10-Heart x3
Flashy Mushroom	Shiny Leaf
	30-Heart, 10-Coin, Flashy Mushroom
	30-Heart x2, Flashy Mushroom
	30-Heart x3

INPUT STICKER	POSSIBLE OUTCOMES
Poison Mushroom	Flashy Mushroom
	Shiny Mushroom
	Mushroom
	Shiny Leaf x3
Leaf	Shiny Leaf x3
	Shiny Leaf
	Leaf x3
	10-Coin x3
Shiny Leaf	Shiny Leaf x3
	Shiny Ice Flower, Shiny POW Block, Flashy Fire Flower
	Chillhammer, Baahammer, Burnhammer
	Shiny Line Jump, Shiny Hurlhammer, Flashy Shell
Snowball	Flashy Jump
	Flashy Hammer
	Shiny Leaf x3
	Leaf x3
Spike Ball	Shiny Jump
	Shiny Hammer
	Shiny Leaf x3
	Leaf x3
Barrel	Flashy Jump
	Flashy Hammer
	Shiny Leaf x3
	Leaf x3
Wrench	Flashy Jump
	Flashy Hammer
	Bomb
	Sombrero
Bone	Shiny Jump
	Shiny Hammer
	Shiny Leaf x3
	Leaf x3
Boomerang	Flashy Jump
	Flashy Hammer
	Shiny Leaf x3
	Leaf x3
Bomb	Shiny Jump
	Shiny Hammer
	Shiny Leaf x3
	Leaf x3
Sombrero	Shiny Jump
	Shiny Hammer
	Shiny Leaf x3
	Leaf x3
Throwing Star	Shiny Jump
	Shiny Hammer
	Shiny Leaf x3
	Leaf x3

Standard Enemies

Goomba

Goombas are among the most common enemies in the game. You won't need any special tactics to defeat these enemies—any stickers that deal damage will get the job done.

The game contains a wide variety of Goombas. Some of these creatures have a healthy supply of HP. As you encounter more powerful variations, consider using more powerful stickers.

Goomba Variations:

- **Goomba**
- **Shiny Goomba**
- **2-Fold Goomba**
- **2-Fold Shiny Goomba**
- **4-Fold Goomba**
- **4-Fold Shiny Goomba**
- **Mural Goomba**

Paper-Cone Goomba

Every so often, a Goomba transforms into a Paper-Cone Goomba. These creatures roll themselves into large spikes, protecting themselves from most Jump-based attacks. Iron Boots still work, but it's generally best to rely on Hammer attacks and any other stickers that deal damage.

Paper-Cone Goomba Variations:

- **Paper-Cone Goomba**
- **Shiny-Cone Goomba**

Paragoomba

Paragoombas are similar to Goombas, but they use their wings to fly just above the ground. Paragoombas can dodge most Hammer-based attacks, but they're vulnerable to shock waves produced by Hammer-based stickers used on nearby enemies. These enemies are vulnerable to Shells, Fire Flowers, and Ice Flowers, but Jump-based stickers usually get the job done..

Paragoomba Variations:

- **Paragoomba**
- **Shiny Paragoomba**
- **5-Fold Paragoomba**

Koopa Troopa

Koopa Troopas aren't quite as common as Goombas, but they patrol many of the same areas. Koopa Troopas attack by tucking into their shells and sliding toward you. If you stomp a Koopa before the battle begins, however, you can use a Jump sticker to kick it into its allies. If this isn't possible, virtually any sticker that causes damage will work well.

Koopa Troopa Variations:

- **Koopa Troopa**
- **Shiny Koopa Troopa**
- **Mural Koopa**

Paratroopa

Paratroopas are very similar to Koopa Troopas, but they use their wings to fly high above the ground. Jump stickers are very effective, but any attack that affects airborne enemies can be used.

Paratroopa Variations:

- **Paratroopa**
- **Shiny Paratroopa**

Buzzy Beetle

Buzzy Beetles are tough little guys. Their shells protect them from most heat-based attacks, so it's best to stick to the basics. As with Koopa Troopas, you can stomp Buzzy Beetles outside of battle and kick them into their allies when the fight starts. If that's not an option, use POW Blocks to flip or crumple these enemies and then finish them off with Jump-based attacks, or just use Shell Stickers or Ice Flowers to clear out entire groups.

Buzzy Beetle Variations:

- **Buzzy Beetle**
- **Shiny Buzzy Beetle**

Spike Top

Spike Tops are very similar to Buzzy Beetles. They're fairly tough, and they're protected from most heat-based attacks. Additionally, their spikes protect them from most Jump-based stickers. Standard Hammer stickers will get the job done, but powerful Shell stickers or Ice Flowers are usually more effective.

Bony Beetle

In most ways, Bony Beetles are very similar to Buzzy Beetles and Spike Tops—they're just a bit tougher. They're immune to most heat-based attacks, and their retractable spikes can counter most Jump-based attacks. Once again, POW Blocks and Shells are very useful when dealing with these enemies.

Spiny

A Spiny's spikes protect it from most Jump-based stickers, but it's vulnerable to your other attacks. Use Hammer stickers to take out a single Spiny, or any available multi-target stickers to deal with larger groups.

Bob-omb

Bob-ombs aren't the toughest enemies you'll face, but they tend to attack in groups, and they really pack a punch! Use multi-target stickers to clear out these little guys before they can attack.

Bob-omb Variations:

- **Bob-omb**
- **Shiny Bob-omb**

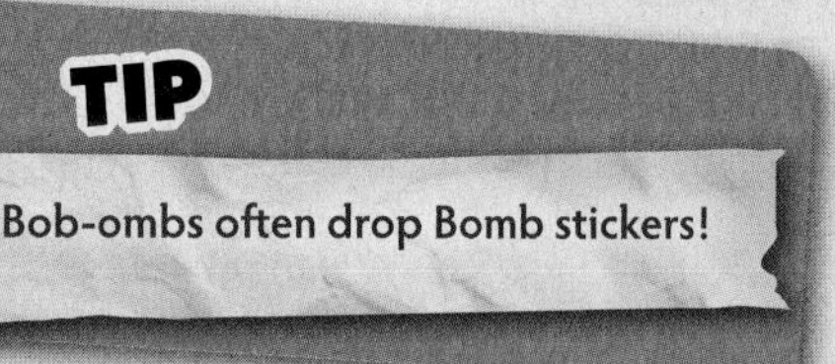

TIP

Bob-ombs often drop Bomb stickers!

Swoop

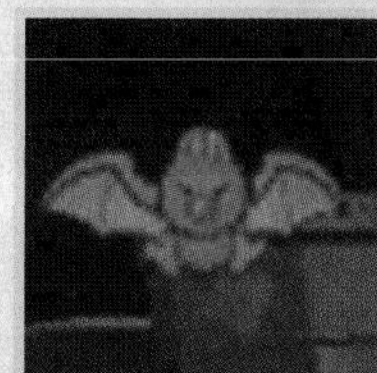

Swoops are high-flying enemies that hide in the shadows until you approach. When a Swoop moves in, jump up and stomp it to initiate the battle. Any attacks that reach airborne targets should be effective, but Jump-based stickers are always a good choice.

Pokey

Don't be fooled by a Pokey's smile—these enemies can be prickly! Green Pokeys are vulnerable to all attacks, but yellow Pokeys have thick spikes that protect them from most Jump-based stickers.

DRY BONES

Dry Bones are extremely resilient! Soon after you defeat one, it pulls itself together and resumes the fight. When you first encounter these enemies, Hopslipper stickers are probably your best option. Ice Flowers and Chill-hammers also work well. Once you defeat a Dry Bones, leave the area before it recovers.

Dry Bones Variations:

- Dry Bones
- Shiny Dry Bones

TIP

Dry Bones occasionally drop Bone stickers!

THE BROS

You'll encounter a variety of Bros as you progress through the game, but their colored shells and chosen weapons make it very easy to identify each type. Hammer Bros are green, Boomerang Bros are blue, Ice Bros are light blue, and Fire Bros are red. Ice Bros are resistant to cold attacks, and Fire Bros are resistant to heat attacks, but your basic stickers will usually prove effective.

Bro Variations:

Hammer Bro
Boomerang Bro
Ice Bro
Fire Bro

SHY GUY

Shy Guys aren't the toughest foes around, but they rarely attack alone. Lucky, these enemies don't have any special defenses, so any of your stickers should work well.

SOMBRERO GUY

Sombrero Guys won't attack you on their own, but they'll take every opportunity jump into existing battles. These enemies use their Sombreros to attack from a distance, but they're much more dangerous when they play their instruments. A Sombrero Guy's music can boost the HP and attack power of nearby enemies. Whenever you spot a Sombrero Guy, deal with him before you initiate any other battles.

Sombrero Guy Variations:

- Sombrero Guy
- Maraca Guy
- Accordion Guy

TIP

Defeated Sombrero Guys have a chance to drop Sombrero stickers.

PAINT GUY

Paint Guys use their buckets to cover the screen in paint, obscuring your view of the action. When a Paint Guy approaches, mash Ⓐ for a chance to defend against the attack. After a Paint Guy uses his bucket, he becomes a standard Shy Guy. Any stickers that deal damage should prove effective.

HOW TO USE THIS GUIDE
HOW TO PLAY
STICKERS
ENEMIES
WALKTHROUGH
DECALBURG
SURFSHINE HARBOR
WORLD 1
WORLD 2
WORLD 3
WORLD 4
WORLD 5
WORLD 6
CHECKLISTS

CLIP GUY

Clip Guys use paperclips to immobilize you for a few turns. When a Clip Guy approaches, mash Ⓐ for a chance to defend against the attack. After a Clip Guy uses his paperclip, he becomes a standard Shy Guy. Any stickers that deal damage should prove effective.

SPEAR GUY

Spear Guys use their spears not only to attack, but to defend against certain attacks. When a Spear Guy's weapon is pointed upward, it counters most Jump-based attacks. When the spear is pointed at Mario, the Spear Guy is immune to most Hammer-based attacks. As long as you account for the spear's position, most stickers can be used when battling a Spear Guy.

SNIFIT

Snifits are similar to Shy Guys in most regards, but they attack by shooting projectiles out of their masks. Despite this difference, any stickers that cause damage can be used against a Snifit.

SPIKE

Spikes attack by throwing spiked steel balls. This enemy must first spit a Spike Ball into its hands, and then it holds the weapon above its head until it has a chance to attack. While a Spike is holding a Spike Ball, it can counter most Jump-based attacks. Use Hammers and projectiles to damage this enemy for a chance to knock the Spike Ball out of its hands.

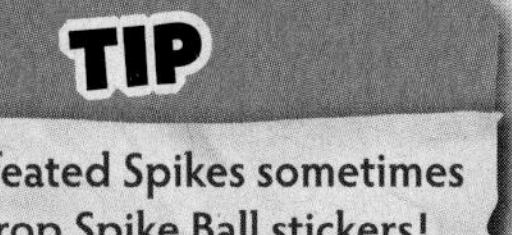

TIP

Defeated Spikes sometimes drop Spike Ball stickers!

SNOW SPIKE

In battle, Snow Spikes behave very much like their warm-weather counterparts, but they throw Snowballs instead of Spike Balls. If you don't have a sticker capable of finishing a Snow Spike in a single turn, you still have a chance to knock the Snowball out of its hands.

TIP

Defeated Snow Spikes sometimes drop Snowball stickers!

NINJI

Ninjis are very agile, and they're capable of dodging multiple attacks. If a Ninji is standing still, it will dodge any Jump-based attacks you attempt. When a Ninji is jumping up and down, it will dodge any Hammer-based attacks you attempt. As long as you keep these limitations in mind, any sticker can be used effectively against a nimble Ninji.

TIP

Ninjis sometimes drop Throwing Star stickers when they're defeated.

PIRANHA PLANT

Piranha Plants are fairly tough enemies, and they have a variety of attacks. They have relatively high HP, and their sharp teeth protect them from most Jump-based attacks. These enemies can attack with their jaws or by spitting projectiles, and they sometimes burrow underground to avoid taking damage.

Piranha Plant Variations:

- **Piranha Plant**
- **Fire Piranha**

SCUTTLEBUG

Scuttlebugs are spider-like creatures that are often found suspended above the ground. Depending on a Scuttlebug's position, it can be considered a ground target, a low-altitude target, or an air target. Any sticker that will reach a Scuttlebug can be used, but Jump-based attacks are always a safe bet.

POISON BLOOPER

As the name implies, a Poison Blooper's attack has a chance to poison you. While poisoned, you not only suffer damage, but your attacks have an increased chance to miss. These low-flying enemies are vulnerable to any attacks that can reach them, but Jump-based stickers always work well.

CHEEP CHEEP

Cheep Cheeps leap out of the water to launch surprise attacks, but they aren't particularly hard to handle once the battle begins. Use a Shell or any other multi-target attacks to clear groups of Cheep Cheeps with ease.

SCAREDY RAT

Scaredy Rats often appear in large groups. Each time a Scaredy Rat attacks, there's a chance it will steal one of your stickers. Luckily, these enemies are vulnerable to all types of damage.

BOO

Boos are low-flying enemies with relatively high HP. A Hopslipper is very effective against a single Boo, but they often appear in groups. These sneaky specters can even join forces to create a Boo Stack! Any sticker that can reach low-altitude enemies can be used against a Boo, and most multi-target stickers can be used to defeat them in groups.

Boo Variations:

- Boo
- Boo Stack

FUZZY

Fuzzies aren't very effective fighters, but they can certainly slow you down as you move through an area. Don't bother using your more powerful stickers—when you face one of these jittery creatures, even basic stickers can end the battle quickly.

ROCKY WRENCH

Rocky Wrenches peek out of their hiding spots just long enough to attack. When battling a group of Rocky Wrenches, use multi-target stickers to quickly clear them out. Be warned, though—your attacks won't have any effect on a Rocky Wrench while it's hiding.

TIP

Each time you defeat a Rocky Wrench, there's a chance it will drop a Wrench sticker!

Broozer

Broozers are excellent fighters, and when these short-tempered creatures get angry, they're capable of deflecting most attacks. Bombs, Boomerangs, Snowballs, and POW Blocks can break through their defenses, however.

TIP

Defeated Broozers sometimes drop Barrel stickers!

Lava Bubble

Lava Bubbles only appear in one of the Bowser battles during the game's finale. Use a cold-based Thing Sticker to freeze them, then sweep them up with a wind-based Thing Sticker to finish them off.

Chain Chomp

The Chain Chomp only appears as one of Bowser's allies during the game's finale. Use a bat-type Thing Sticker to knock this fierce enemy out of the area, or use a Tail Sticker to get the same result when it lunges at you.

Special Creatures

Wiggler Segment

Thanks to Kamek's magic, Wiggler Segments appear throughout World Three. You must defeat these enemies in battle before returning them to Wiggler's Tree House.

Whomp

The game's only Whomp appears as one of Bowser's allies during the finale. This massive creature can take quite a beating—unless you find its weak spot, that is. Land two hits with an Eekhammer to topple this mighty foe, then use a cutting Thing Sticker to finish it off while its back is exposed.

Mini-Bosses

Bowser Jr.

Bowser Jr. pesters you throughout the game, and he learns at least one new trick between each encounter. The first time you meet him, he can only be defeated by the Scissors Thing Sticker. In subsequent encounters, use Jump stickers and thrown weapons to take down this high-flying enemy.

Kamek

Kamek impedes your progress at multiple points in the game, and like Bowser Jr., he enters each battle with a new trick up his sleeve. The first time you battle Kamek, use Jump-based stickers to defeat him without breaking a sweat. In subsequent battles, however, Kamek transforms all of your stickers into Sandals.

Big Buzzy Beetle

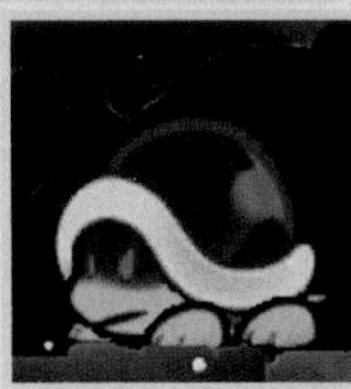

The Big Buzzy Beetle doesn't have many weaknesses, so it's essential you bring the proper stickers into battle. Use POW Blocks to flip this oversized enemy, then attack its exposed belly with high-damage stickers.

Big Scuttlebug

The Big Scuttlebug uses its web to stay out of your attack range.Use Boomerangs, Fire Flowers, or Pow Blocks to destroy the web, then take down the Big Buzzy Beetle with any stickers that deal damage.

Big Cheep Cheep

The Big Cheep Cheep uses the ocean to replenish its HP. When you face this crafty creature, make sure you bring a Fishhook Thing Sticker to pull it out of the water.

Big Boo

When the Big Boo takes too much damage, it turns invisible to avoid your attacks. Use a spray-type Thing Sticker to reveal the Big Boo, then resume your attacks.

Big Chain Chomp

The game contains multiple Big Chain Chomps, but you only have to battle two of them. Although you can't defeat these powerful enemies, you can trick them into leaving the battlefield. If the Big Chain Chomp is awake, use a Baahammer to put it to sleep, then run from the battle. If the enemy is asleep when you arrive, you can proceed right to the next step. Sneak behind the sleeping Big Chain Chomp and use your Hammer to hit the stake anchoring it to the ground. Battle the Big Chain Chomp until it wakes up and lunges right out of the area.

Bosses

The game contains six bosses, and each one holds one of the six Royal Stickers. Boss battles can be very challenging, and they generally require a good deal of preparation. For details about recommended Battle Stickers, Thing Stickers, and general tactics, please refer to the end of each world's walkthrough.

Megasparkle Goomba

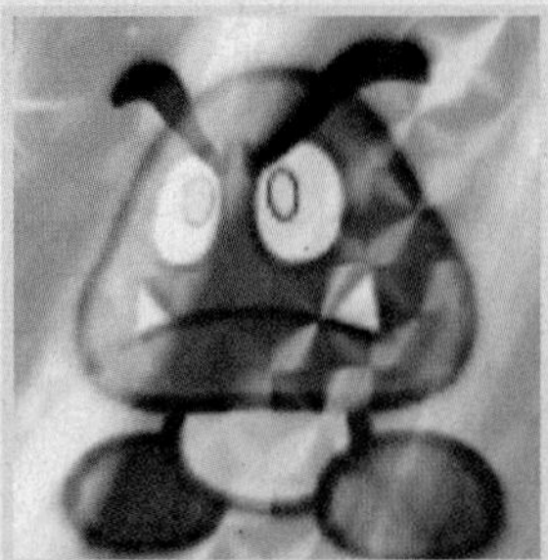

The Megasparkle Goomba is in the Goomba Fortress at the end of World One.

HOW TO USE THIS GUIDE
HOW TO PLAY
STICKERS
ENEMIES
WALKTHROUGH
DECALBURG
SURFSHINE HARBOR
WORLD 1
WORLD 2
WORLD 3
WORLD 4
WORLD 5
WORLD 6
CHECKLISTS

Tower Power Pokey

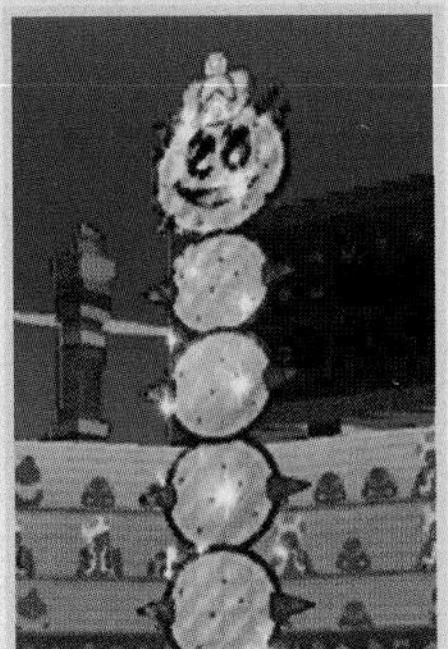

The Tower Power Pokey is in Drybake Stadium at the end of World Two.

Gooper Blooper

The Gooper Blooper is off the coast of Whitecap Beach at the end of World Three.

Bowser Snow Statue and Mizzter Blizzard

The Bowser Snow Statue and Mizzter Blizzard are perched atop Bowser's Snow Fort at the end of World Four.

Petey Piranha

Petey Piranha is inside the Rumble Volcano at the end of World Five.

Bowser

Bowser is waiting inside Bowser's Sky Castle at the end of World Six.

Decalburg is not only the site of Sticker Fest, it serves as a hub between World One, World Two, World Three, and Surfshine Harbor. Aside from a tutorial combat session during your first visit, Decalburg is a friendly location that offers important services, such as a Sticker Shop, Sticker Museum, and Sling-a-Thing Platform.

NOTE

Over the course of the game, Decalburg undergoes a series of changes. New services become available, and the damage caused during the Sticker Fest is repaired. The Course's basic layout, however, remains consistent.

Decalburg Town Layout

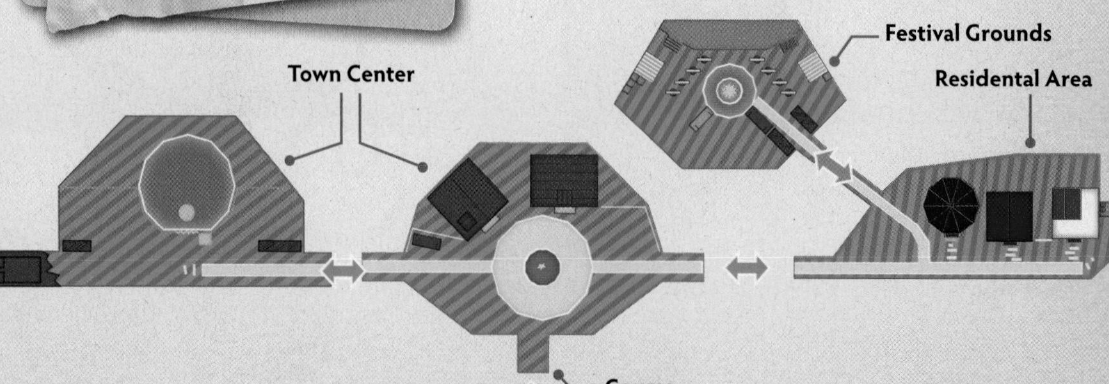

Overview

Your first visit to Decalburg serves as a tutorial about many of the game's basic elements. You'll find changes and additions as you revisit this Course. The Sticker Shop, Heart Block, and Save Block become available during your first visit. As you progress through the game, the Sticker Museum, Sling-a-Thing Platform, and Thing Shop all open for business.

Although the game begins in the festival grounds, the Course's entrance/exit is actually located in the town center. As a generally peaceful town, Decalburg is a great place to catch your breath now and again. You'll find several common (but essential!) Battle Stickers scattered around the town; swing by and grab a few whenever your Album is looking a little sparse.

IMPORTANT ITEMS AND LOCATIONS

DESCRIPTION	NOTES
Secret Door	None
HP-Up Heart	After you complete all five Toad rescues, return to Decalburg's residential area. Enter the house on the right and speak to the Toad inside.
Toad Rescue	None
Luigi Location	None
Wiggler Diary Entry	None
Things	None

Prerequisites

Decalburg is available when the game starts. Additional visits are needed to gain access to the Sticker Museum, fill the Sticker Museum, and collect the available HP-Up Heart.

Objectives

Decalburg contains several objectives, some of which require additional visits:

- **Gather the 27 missing Toads.**
- **Repair the town center.**
- **Unlock the Sticker Museum (requires an additional visit).**
- **Fill the Sticker Museum (requires additional visits).**
- **Collect the HP-Up Heart (requires extensive play).**
- **Unfurl all eight of the Super Flags (satisfy the conditions stated on each Super Flag).**

NOTE

As you play through this Course, you also receive the first two Album pages and Mario's Hammer.

Recommended Tactics

Outside of the game's cinematics, Decalburg contains only a single battle. The first time you attempt to exit the town, you're ambushed by three Goombas.

In addition to any stickers you collected during your time in Decalburg, Kersti supplies you with a selection of Jump, Hammer, and Mushroom stickers at the start of the battle. Virtually any combination of stickers can lead you to victory, but consider using a Hammer during your first turn. If you time your attack for a rating of "Great" or better, you'll defeat the first two enemies before they have a chance to react.

Festival Grounds

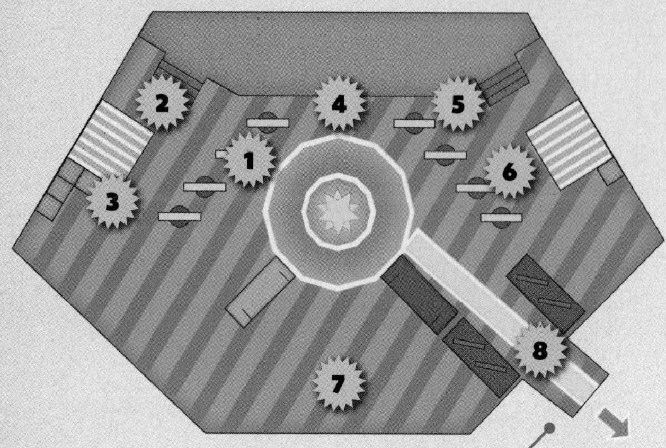

NOTE

Although the festival grounds are badly damaged during your first visit, this map reflects the area as it appears during the bulk of the game.

Not only was Sticker Fest ruined, but Mario's battle with Bowser doesn't go quite as well as he might have hoped. When the opening cinematic ends, tap Ⓐ repeatedly until Mario recovers. The voice calling out to you belongs to Kersti. Move to the nearby poster of Peach and hold Ⓐ to pry Kersti loose.

After you free Kersti, it's time to lend a hand to the citizens of Decalburg. There are 27 Toads trapped (or panicked) in various locations around the town, and you'll need to find them all to clear a path to the exit. Six of these Toads are located within the festival grounds—start your search with the two Toads to the left. Hop onto the crates and peel the Bowser tape to free the first Toad.

Before you can reach the Toad hanging from the pennants, you must peel the Bowser tape at Point 3. After the booth springs into place, jump up along the nearby crates and free your helpless friend.

When you free the Toad trapped at Point 4, he gives Mario an indispensable tool. Peel away the Bowser tape to receive the Hammer, along with one more citizen to help repair the town.

TIP

Mario's Hammer is a surprisingly versatile tool. It's not only effective in combat, it allows you to interact with the environment. Keep an eye out for flimsy objects that can be toppled or destroyed with a few strikes from the Hammer.

5

Locate the poster leaning against the front of the stage, then tap Ⓑ to slam the Hammer into the ground. The impact topples the poster, revealing yet another Toad. Peel away the Bowser tape to free him.

6

Near the right edge of the area, you'll find a Toad running around in a panic. Peel the Jump sticker off of his head to calm him down.

7

The remaining Toad is stuck on a crate in the foreground. Peel the Bowser tape from the top of the crate, then hop down and peel the tape from the front of the crate.

8

Search the area for any stickers you might like to place in your Album. When you're ready to continue, use the Hammer to smash the Block at Point 8, then peel the exposed Bowser tape. After the walkway springs into place, follow it into Decalburg's residential area.

TIP

As you play through the campaign, the festival grounds are whipped back into shape. Once repaired, the Super Flags in this area reflect your accomplishments. Visit this area whenever you'd like to check on your progress.

Residential Area

There are 21 Toads scattered throughout Decalburg's residential area. When you enter the area, look for the Toad hiding in the yard to the left. Hop over the fence, then use the Hammer to topple the flimsy bush. With his hiding place compromised, the Toad scurries off to the next area.

Hop back over the fence and use the Hammer to knock over the bush at Point 2. Peel the Bowser tape to free the revealed Toad, then continue to the right.

The area contains three houses. Enter the house on the left, then climb onto the cabinet and jump up to find a Hidden Block. Drop down and open the cabinet to reveal a stack of 10 Toads!

NOTE

As you progress through the game, articles about Luigi sightings appear in this house.

The house in the center of the row contains a Toad. Peel the Bowser tape from the front door, then head inside. Use the Hammer to knock the trash bin over, then wait for the crumpled Toad to recover.

After you leave the middle house, hop over the small fence to the right. Follow the path between the houses to find a Toad trapped in the back yard. Peel the Bowser tape to free the Toad. Don't forget to check the nearby ? Block before you leave!

Caution

When you revisit these houses later in the game, you may find a Toad in the yard behind them. This shifty fellow offers to sell you a special sticker—don't fall for his scheme! If purchased, the sticker turns out to be an overpriced Poison Mushroom!

When you try to enter the house on the right, a voice cries out from somewhere nearby. Stand near the porch, then use the Hammer to flip the doormat over. Peel the Bowser tape to free the revealed Toad, then head inside.

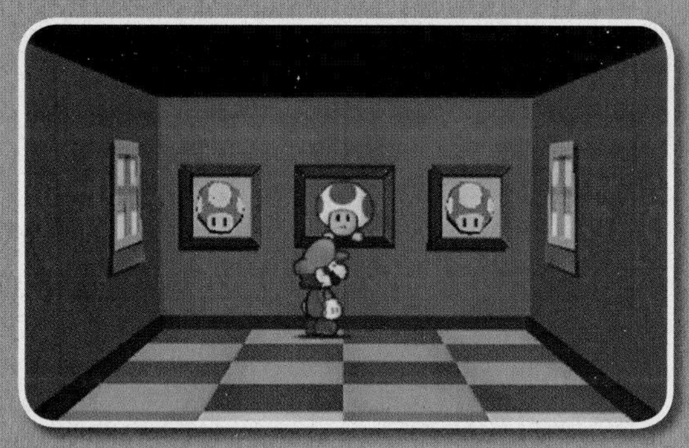

Approach the room's back wall, then examine the picture in the middle of the row to discover a stack of five Toads.

There's a tightly folded Toad trapped on the small structure to the right of the houses. Stand under the structure, then jump up to jostle the incapacitated Toad. Repeat the process until the poor fellow manages to flatten himself out.

TIP

There's a ? Block atop the house on the right. Use the Blocks stacked near the house to climb up to the roof!

Search the area for any stickers you'd like to add to your Album, then move to the path in the foreground. Follow the path to the left to find the town center.

MISSING TOAD LOCATIONS

Missing Toads within the festival grounds (6 total):

- Hanging above the crates on the left
- Hanging above the collapsed booth on the left
- Stuck to the center of the stage
- Stuck to the right side of the stage, hidden behind the poster
- Running along the right side of the area
- Stuck to the crate in the foreground

Missing Toads within the residential area (21 total):

- Hidden behind the bush to the left
- Stuck to the back of the bush near the path
- In the house on the left, within the cabinet (×10 Toads)
- In the house in the middle, within the trash bin
- In the yard behind the houses
- In front of the house on the right, under the doormat
- In the house on the right, in the picture frame (×5 Toads)
- On the structure on the area's right edge

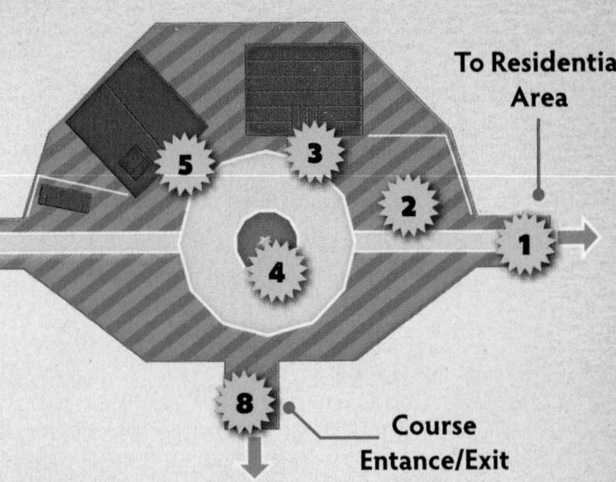

The chaos at the Sticker Fest seriously damaged the town center, and it will take every available Toad to fix it. After you gather the 27 missing Toads, enter the town center to initiate the repairs. Once the area has been smoothed out, you're free to explore the rest of Decalburg.

The building to the right contains a Sticker Museum. The building is locked during your first visit. Before you can access the Sticker Museum, you must find a way to rescue its founder. Return to Decalburg after you complete World 1-1.

NOTE

It takes all 27 missing Toads to unroll the town center. If you left any Toads in the previous areas, you must head back and find them before you can continue.

The town center contains a Heart Block and a Save Block. Remember to head back to Decalburg whenever you feel a little run down.

The Toad near the fountain claims to have heard a mysterious cry for help. You're not able to do anything about it during your first visit, but return to this location after you complete World 1-1.

5

The Decalburg Sticker Shop is a great place to stock up on essential stickers. This location offers a fairly limited selection at the start of the game, but new stickers will become available as you progress through the campaign.

7

The Thing Shop is located behind the suspicious door just left of the Sling-a-Thing Platform. This shop sells all of the Things you've managed to collect during your adventure. Any Things (or resulting Thing Stickers) currently in your Album, however, will be excluded from the shop's inventory.

NOTE

The Secret Door located in World 4-3 opens an alternative path back to the Decalburg Thing Shop.

6

The path to the left of the fountain leads to the Decalburg Sling-a-Thing Platform. After you complete World 1-3, you can use this platform to turn any collected Things into powerful stickers.

8

When you're finished exploring the town and collecting stickers, return to the fountain and attempt to exit the Course. When you do, three Goombas jump out and accost you. This is a fairly straightforward battle, so take this opportunity to experiment with the various Battle Stickers in your Album. After the battle, use the nearby Heart Block to refill any lost health, then exit the Course.

ADDITIONAL VISITS

With all of the services this town offers, you're likely to make regular visits to Decalburg. You should visit whenever you need to update the Sticker Museum, convert Things into stickers, review the Super Flags, or replenish your stickers and health. Aside from these common tasks, however, there are three major objectives that cannot be completed during your first visit.

RECOMMENDED VISIT #2

After you complete World 1-1, return to Decalburg's town center. Use Kersti's paperization ability to peel the fountain and free the trapped Toad (press Ⓨ to initiate paperization, move Mario's shadow onto the fountain, then press Ⓐ to peel the loose scrap). Use paperization to replace the scrap, then follow the grateful Toad to discover the Sticker Museum.

RECOMMENDED VISIT #3

As you play through the game, you'll occasionally encounter a group of enemies bullying a Toad. After you complete all five Toad rescues, return to Decalburg to claim a well deserved HP-Up Heart. Walk to the residential area, enter the house on the right, and examine the green postcard to the right.

HP-UP HEART: DECALBURG

To collect the HP-Up Heart in Decalburg, rescue the bullied Toad in World 1-2, World 2-1, World 3-11, World 4-6, and World 5-2. After you resolve all five conflicts, return to Decalburg's residential area. Examine the green postcard to receive your prize.

SURFSHINE HARBOR

Surfshine Harbor is a small, friendly area that eventually provides passage to World Four, World Five, and World Six. While Surfshine Harbor cannot be made fully functional until you've progressed through much of the game, it can be explored any time after you leave Decalburg.

SURFSHINE HARBOR TOWN LAYOUT

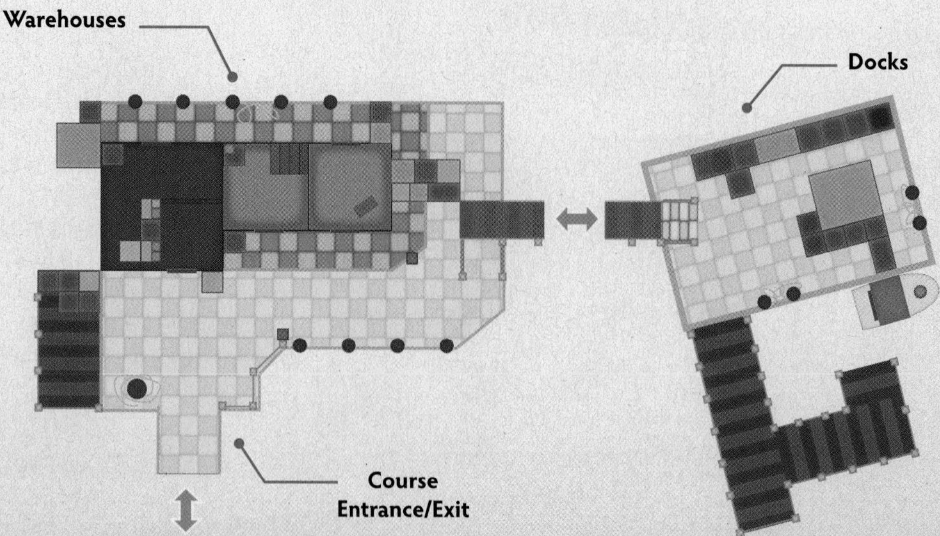

Overview

Like Decalburg, Surfshine Harbor is a generally friendly area. It will, however, take some work to transform it into a functioning port. You can postpone your first visit for quite a while, but consider making early visits to collect stickers, Things, and a helpful HP-Up Heart as you progress through the game's early levels. Before you can travel to World Four (and beyond), you must free the boat from the dock, replace the missing Ship's Wheel, and overcome the unseen enemy lurking just offshore.

Prerequisites

Surfshine Harbor is available from the moment you leave Decalburg. To complete all available objectives, you must either make multiple trips or postpone your first visit until you've completed the bulk of the first three worlds.

ESSENTIAL THING STICKERS

NAME	THING LOCATION	NOTES
Scissors	World 1-1	Needed to free the boat from the dock.
Lightbulb	World 2-2	Needed to recover the Ship's Wheel scrap from the basement.
Fishhook	World 3-6	Needed to defeat the Big Cheep Cheep.

Objectives

Surfshine Harbor contains several objectives. These objectives can be completed over multiple visits, or during a single visit much later in the course of the game:

- **Cut the boat free from the dock.**
- **Collect the Vacuum.**
- **Collect the HP-Up Heart.**
- **Collect the Ship's Wheel scrap.**
- **Use the Ship's Wheel scrap to repair the boat.**
- **Defeat the Big Cheep Cheep.**
- **Retrieve the fleeing Wiggler segment.**

NOTE

Before the Wiggler segment appears in Surfshine Harbor, you must locate the segment in World 3-11, follow it to World 3-12, defeat it in battle, and return to the Map Screen.

IMPORTANT ITEMS AND LOCATIONS

DESCRIPTION	NOTES
Secret Door	None
HP-Up Heart	Reposition the Warehouse Door scrap, then follow the path to the upper floor.
Toad Rescue	None
Luigi Location	None
Wiggler Diary Entry	This entry is automatically earned when you collect the Wiggler segment from Surfshine Harbor.
Things	Reposition the Warehouse Door scrap, then follow the path to the upper floor to find the Vacuum.

Recommended Tactics

Surfshine Harbor contains only one battle. Before you can use the boat, you'll need to deal with the Big Cheep Cheep that arrives when you complete the repairs.

The Big Cheep Cheep is a formidable opponent, but the proper strategy can end the battle fairly quickly. By the time the Cheep Cheep appears, you should have access to a variety of stickers. Before you initiate the battle, consider stocking your Album with a supply of Hopslippers, a Fishhook, a Spike Helmet, and a Mushroom or two. It's also important to collect any available HP-Up Hearts as you play through the first few worlds.

RECOMMENDED VISIT #1

1

You won't be able to collect the Vacuum and HP-Up Heart until you've gained the paperization ability, but an early visit does give you a chance to speak with more Toads and grab some extra stickers before you head into hostile areas. Aside from the stickers posted around the area, you'll find two ? Blocks in front of the warehouses.

TIP

Use the Block on the ground to reach the nearby ? Block, as well as the sticker above the crate to the left.

2

When you're ready to explore the inside of the warehouses, enter the door on the left to find a single sticker within an enclosure. The Vacuum is above you, but you'll need the paperization ability before you can reach it.

3

Enter the door in the middle to find the basement stairs. The basement is too dark to navigate at this time. Return to the area after you collect the Lightbulb from World 2-2.

The door on the right is askew, but it eventually provides access to the rest of the warehouse area. After you acquire the paperization ability, return to this location and realign the Warehouse Door scrap.

As you approach the walkway that leads to the docks, look for the ? Block in the background. Slip under the walkway to find a small area behind the shipping containers. Use the crates to reach the ? Block, then follow the path back out to the main area.

Follow the walkway to the docks to find a Heart Block and a few more stickers. Follow the path between the shipping containers to find the rope securing the boat to the dock. After you collect the Scissors from World 1-1, you can use them to free the boat.

When you first visit Surfshine Harbor, the boat is malfunctioning. You'll need to retrieve the Ship's Wheel from the warehouse basement before you can repair it. Return to Surfshine Harbor after you've collected the Lightbulb from World 2-2.

RECOMMENDED VISIT #2

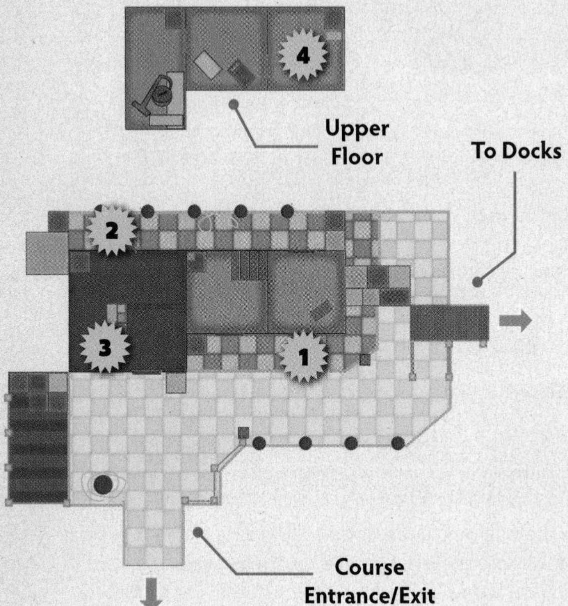

Once inside, you can see the HP-Up Heart on the upper floor. After you've searched the room for stickers, exit through the door on the back wall.

Follow the path behind the building to find a row of Blocks. After you search the Blocks, use the nearby door to head back inside.

After you complete World 1-1, return to Surfshine Harbor. Approach the warehouses and use the paperization ability to adjust the Warehouse Door scrap. Simply peel the scrap, then reapply it. When the door is in place, head into the building.

After you pass through the door, move to the foreground and climb the stacked crates. Reach the upper floor to collect the Vacuum!

Thing: Vacuum

To collect the Vacuum, use paperization to reposition the Warehouse Door scrap.

Enter the door and follow the path to the building's upper floor.

Recommended VISIT #3

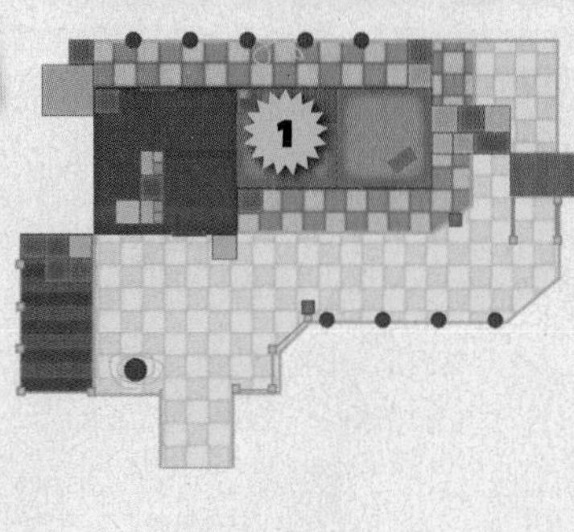

After you collect the Vacuum, explore the rooms to the right to find a ? Block and HP-Up Heart.

By the time you complete World 3-6, you should have everything you need to get the boat up and running. Return to Surfshine Harbor with the Lightbulb, Scissors, and Fishhook stickers in your Album. Enter the warehouses through the middle door and head down to the basement.

HP-Up Heart: Surfshine Harbor

To collect the Surfshine Harbor HP-Up Heart, use paperization to reposition the Warehouse Door scrap.

Enter the door and follow the path to the building's upper floor.

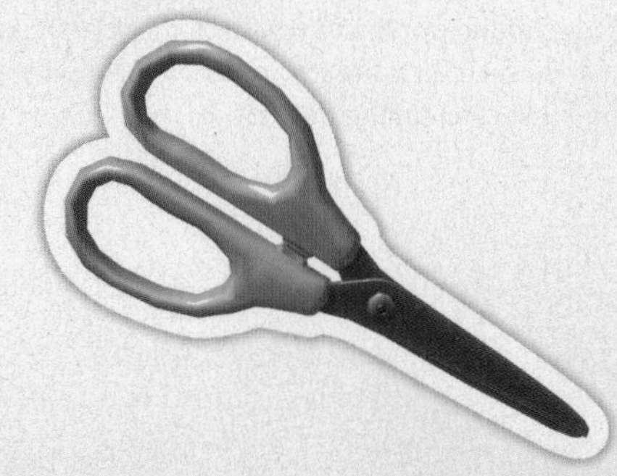

2

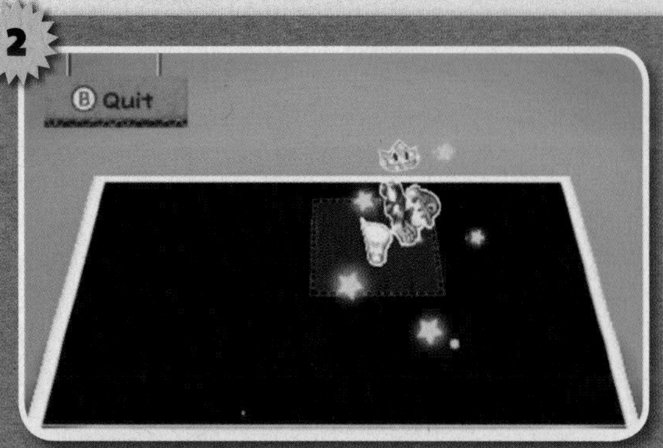

When you reach the bottom of the basement steps, activate the Paperize ability. Place the Lightbulb sticker in the indicated space to illuminate the area. Climb up and wake the sleeping Toad, then grab the Ship's Wheel scrap.

3

Cross over to the docks and return to the rope holding the boat in place. Activate the paperization ability, then use the Scissors to cut the boat loose.

4

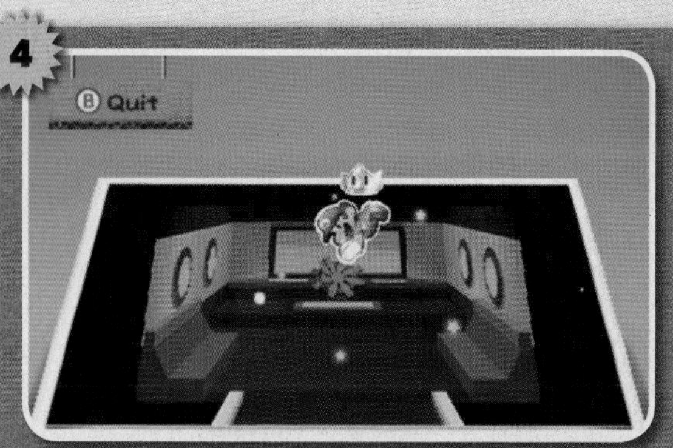

Walk back around the shipping containers and hop onto the back of the boat. Enter the cabin, then use the paperization ability to place the Ship's Wheel in the appropriate spot. Wait for the captain to board the vessel, then confirm that you'd like to shove off.

5

When the captain attempts to shove off, a Big Cheep Cheep swims into the area. Before the boat can leave the harbor, you'll need to deal with this oversized enemy. Make sure you're happy with your sticker supply, and use the nearby Heart Block to top off your health. When you're ready, head to the end of the pier. When the Big Cheep Cheep leaps from the water, back away to avoid taking damage. Dash in to begin the battle before the big bully returns to the water.

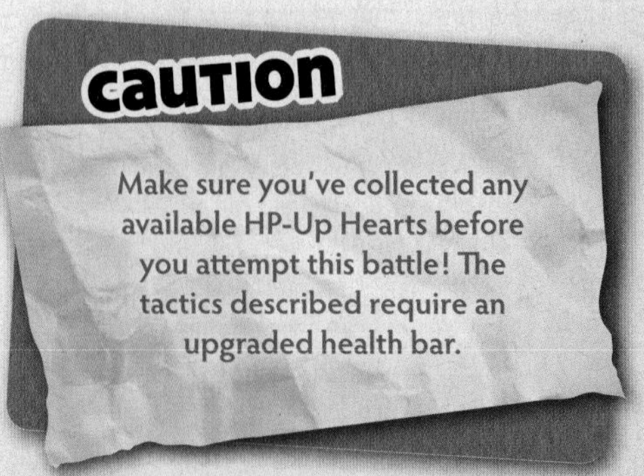

CAUTION

Make sure you've collected any available HP-Up Hearts before you attempt this battle! The tactics described require an upgraded health bar.

MINI-BOSS: BIG CHEEP CHEEP

When the battle starts, use Jump-type stickers to deal reliable damage to your enemy. If you use the Battle Spinner to earn (or purchase) a second attack, you can use two Hopslippers to deal up to 40 points of damage. This is enough to complete the battle's first phase before your enemy has a chance to attack. Otherwise, simply attack and defend until you deal the required damage.

When the Big Cheep Cheep suffers enough damage, it retreats to the water. Not only does this allow your enemy to replenish its health, it prevents you from launching effective attacks. Defend yourself from the Big Cheep Cheep's water spray and await your next turn.

Use the Fishhook to pull the Big Cheep Cheep back onto the pier. Any additional attacks granted by the Battle Spinner should be carefully considered. You have the opportunity to end the battle in one stroke, but you'll need to take some precautions.

The most effective tactic is to equip a Spike Helmet immediately after you use the Fishhook. When you defend yourself from the next attack, you'll deplete the Big Cheep Cheep's entire health bar. Unfortunately, you'll take 40 points of damage in the process! If you don't have enough health to survive the impact, make sure you use a Mushroom before attempting this attack.

After you defeat the Big Cheep Cheep, you can use the boat to reach World Four, World Five, and World Six.

RECOMMENDED VISIT #4

You're likely to pass through Surfshine Harbor on many occasions, but there's one piece of business that demands a visit. The Wiggler segment found in World 3-11 eventually leads you back to Surfshine Harbor. When it does, retrieve the segment from the docks and deliver it to World 3-3. The relevant entry will automatically be added to Wiggler's diary.

WORLD ONE

WORLD ONE COURSES

NUMBER	NAME
World 1-1	Warm Fuzzy Plains
World 1-2	Bouquet Gardens
World 1-3	Water's Edge Way
World 1-4	Hither Thither Hill
World 1-5	Whammino Mountain
World 1-6	Goomba Fortress

World One is filled with rolling hills, lovely gardens, and grassy plains. Unfortunately, it's also home to a fair number of nasty critters. Goombas and Koopa Troopas are both common sights, but you find some Spinies and Bob-ombs along the way. Of course, these battles pale in comparison to what awaits in the Goomba Fortress. If you want to claim the first Royal Sticker, you'll have to take it from the power-mad Megasparkle Goomba!

WORLD 1-1: Warm Fuzzy Plains

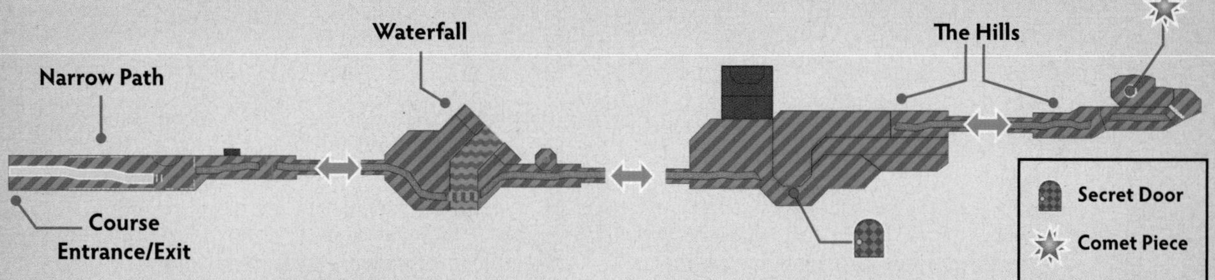

Overview

Prerequisites

World 1-1 is available from the moment you leave Decalburg. Aside from the Secret Door sticker that can be purchased in World 3-6, this Course contains everything needed to complete the available objectives.

Objectives

This Course contains several objectives, most of which can be completed during your first visit:

- **Acquire the Scissors sticker.**
- **Defeat Bowser Jr.**
- **Replace the Wooden Bridge scrap.**
- **Collect the Scissors.**
- **Collect the Comet Piece to unlock World 1-2.**
- **Collect the Thumbtack from the Secret Door.**

IMPORTANT ITEMS AND LOCATIONS

DESCRIPTION	NOTES
Secret Door	The marked location is on one of the hills beyond the waterfall.
HP-Up Heart	None
Toad Rescue	None
Luigi Location	None
Wiggler Diary Entry	None
Things	Peel the Bowser tape within the hills to find the Scissors. Enter the Secret Door to find the Thumbtack.

NOTE

During the course of this Course, you also acquire Kersti's Paperize ability.

Recommended Tactics

Most of this Course's battles are fairly simple, but you'll also face Bowser Jr. and a group of particularly nasty Goombas. Luckily, the Course provides all of the stickers you're likely to need!

During most battles, you'll face off against one or two Goombas. You don't have access to the Battle Spinner during your first visit, so efficiency is important. You shouldn't have any trouble facing a single Goomba—virtually any Battle Sticker can be used—but multiple Goombas are another matter. Use Hammer stickers to damage both opponents with one hit. A properly timed Hammer attack can defeat two Goombas in a single turn. This not only preserves Mario's HP, it allows you to earn a Perfect Bonus!

WORLD 1-1

During your first encounter with Bowser Jr., your Battle Stickers aren't enough to defeat him. Use the Scissors sticker dropped by the fleeing Toad to end the battle in a single attack.

At the end of the Course, you must face three Paper-Cone Goombas. These nasty characters are immune to most Jump-based attacks, so make sure you save a few Hammer stickers for this battle.

NARROW PATH

This Course contains several common stickers, so make sure you stock up. Search every ? Block along the path, and keep an eye out for stickers posted throughout each area. You'll also find helpful signs and talkative Toads on your way through the Course.

There's a hidden coin stash at Point 2! Peel the Bowser tape on the background to reveal a secret area.

WATERFALL

As you approach the waterfall, a panicked Toad crashes into you, dropping a Scissors sticker in the process. When you recover, collect this powerful sticker.

Soon after the Scissors sticker is safely in your Album, Bowser Jr. arrives. After a brief speech, he attacks. Use your newly acquired sticker to bring the battle to an early end.

MINI-BOSS: BOWSER JR.

During your first turn, use the Scissors sticker you just collected to knock Bowser Jr. out of the fight before he makes his first move!

Outraged at his defeat, Bowser Jr. uses the power of paperization to rip the Wooden Bridge scrap out of the environment. After crumpling the scrap into a ball, he tosses it up to the ledge at Point 2.

The ledge is much too high for Mario to reach on his own. Luckily there are plenty of friends hiding nearby. Follow the path back to the left to find a group of Toads along the narrow path at the start of the Course. Speak to the Toad hiding in the bushes to recruit the group, then return to the waterfall.

When you approach the ledge, the Toads join together to create a set of stairs. After they do, climb up and collect the Wooden Bridge scrap.

After you collect the scrap, return to the hole Bowser Jr. created when he tore it from the environment. Follow Kersti's instructions to learn the Paperize ability. Drop the Wooden Bridge into place, then smooth it down to complete the repair. Follow the path across the bridge and continue exploring the area.

NOTE

Once you've completed Kersti's tutorial, you can press Ⓨ to activate the Paperize ability.

When you reach the HP Block at Point 4, activate the Paperize ability to discover a Paperization Block location above the nearby tree stump. To take advantage of this location, simply place a sticker from your Album in the indicated spot.

TIP

The game contains several Paperization Block locations, and most of them are above tree stumps or near pink flowers.

The Hills

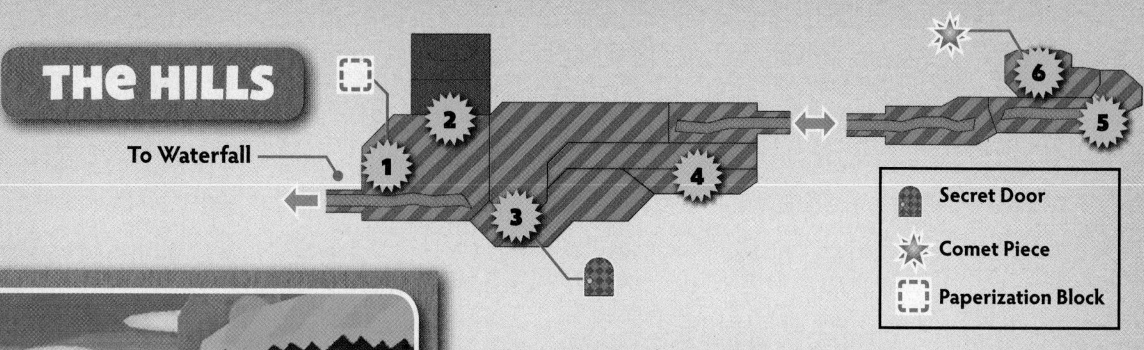

When you reach the hills past the waterfall, look for the ring of green circles at Point 1. Use the Hammer to flip each of the circles and reveal a ring of pink flowers. This flower arrangement usually indicates a Paperization Block location. Activate the Paperize ability to find it.

Thing: Scissors

When you reach the hills beyond the waterfall, peel the Bowser tape on the background. When the panel falls out of the way, head into the secret area to find the Scissors.

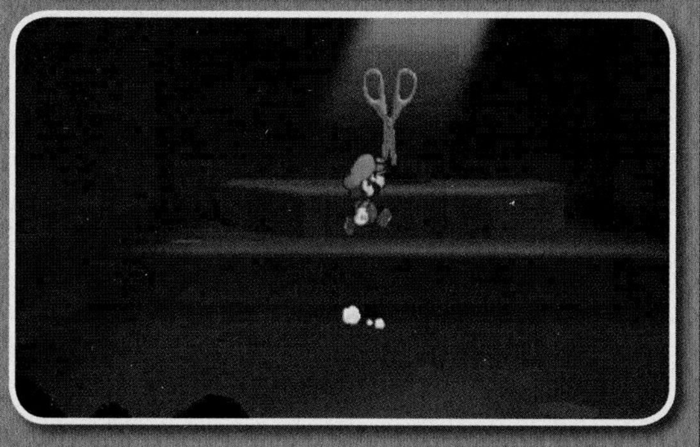

There's a Thing behind a loose panel at Point 2. Peel the Bowser tape to reveal a hidden area, then head inside to find the Scissors.

As you follow the path through the hills, look for the Secret Door location at Point 3. You cannot use the Secret Door at this time. After you reach World 3-6, however, you can purchase a Secret Door sticker and return to this location.

There are several ? Blocks within the area, and it's well worth searching them all. When it isn't possible to hit a Block from below, use the Hammer to strike it from above.

As you approach the Comet Piece at the end of the Course, you're accosted by the three Goombas you encountered in Decalburg. After demanding a rematch, these poor sports transform into Paper-Cone Goombas.

Paper-Cone Goombas can counter most Jump-based attacks, so it's best to use Hammer-based stickers. If you have a Baahammer handy, you can use it to put them to sleep during your first turn. If your HP Bar is relatively full, however, it's simpler to attack with a standard Hammer sticker. An "Excellent" attack will take care of the first two enemies. Defend yourself from any remaining enemies, then use another Hammer or two to finish the fight.

After you defeat the Paper-Cone Goombas, grab the Comet Piece at the top of the hill to complete the Course.

Sticker Comet Piece: Unlocking World 1-2

This Course contains only one piece of the Sticker Comet. To unlock World 1-2, simply collect the Comet Piece at the end of World 1-1.

Recommended Visit #2

After you gain access to the World 3-6 Sticker Shop, purchase a Secret Door sticker and revisit this Course. Apply the Secret Door to the marked location in the hills, then head through the door to find the Thumbtack.

Thing: Thumbtack

After you acquire a Secret Door sticker, use it at the marked location in the hills near the end of the Course. Pass through the Secret Door to find the Thumbtack within the hidden area.

WORLD 1-2: BOUQUET GARDENS

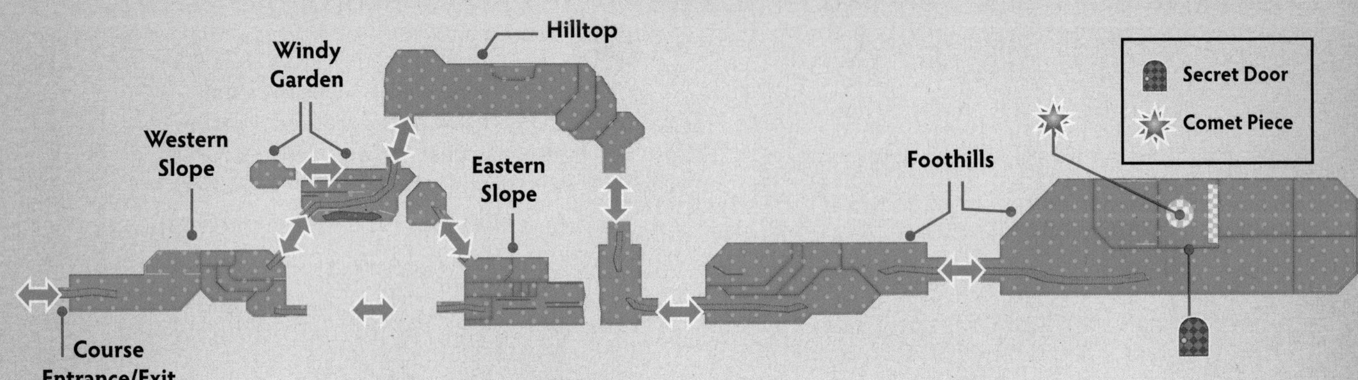

OVERVIEW

PREREQUISITES

This Course becomes available when you collect the Comet Piece from World 1-1. Aside from the Secret Door sticker, everything you need to complete the available objectives can be found in the Course.

OBJECTIVES

This Course contains several objectives, most of which can be completed on your first visit:

- **Collect the Fan.**
- **Earn the HP-Up Heart.**
- **Rescue the bullied Toad.**
- **Collect the Cat-o-Luck.**
- **Collect the Comet Piece to unlock World 1-3.**
- **Collect the flashy stickers from the Secret Door.**

NOTE

As you play through this Course, you'll also gain access to Kersti's Battle Spinner.

IMPORTANT ITEMS AND LOCATIONS

DESCRIPTION	NOTES
Secret Door	The marked location is in the foothills toward the end of the Course.
HP-Up Heart	Replace the ruined flowers in the windy garden.
Toad Rescue	Two Goombas are bullying a Toad on the hilltop.
Luigi Location	None
Wiggler Diary Entry	None
Things	Enter the windy garden by way of the eastern slope to find the Fan. Complete the Toad rescue on the hilltop to find the Cat-o-Luck.

RECOMMENDED TACTICS

In addition to plenty of Goombas and Koopa Troopas, this Course contains a few special encounters. You'll find a nice variety of stickers in the environment, and it probably won't take long to fill your Album to capacity. Try to maintain a good balance of Jump-based stickers and Hammer-based stickers, and save a total of three Flower-based stickers (Fire Flowers or Ice Flowers) to use outside of combat.

When it comes to Koopa Troopas, it's important to take the initiative. If you stomp a Koopa Troopa outside of combat, it starts the battle tucked inside of its shell. Use a Jump sticker to kick the Koopa Troopa off of the screen. This tactic also damages any foes caught in the shell's path!

The Goombas in this Course use a variety of tactics, so it's important to keep a balanced selection of stickers. Use Hammers when you're outnumbered, or when you're facing Paper-Cone Goombas. When you're up against enemies like the 2-Fold Goomba, however, use Jump-based stickers to deliver maximum damage to a single opponent.

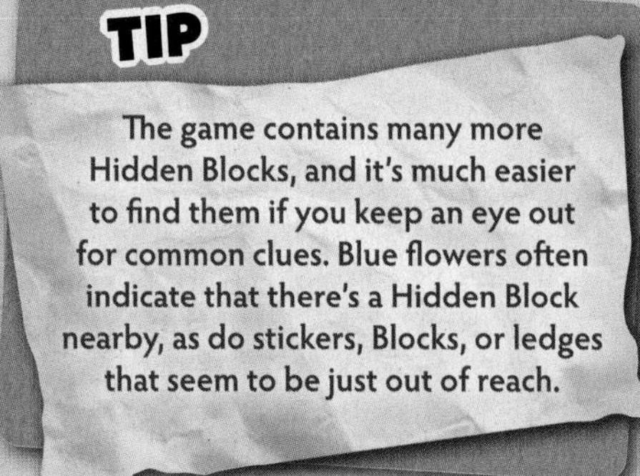

TIP

The game contains many more Hidden Blocks, and it's much easier to find them if you keep an eye out for common clues. Blue flowers often indicate that there's a Hidden Block nearby, as do stickers, Blocks, or ledges that seem to be just out of reach.

Western Slope

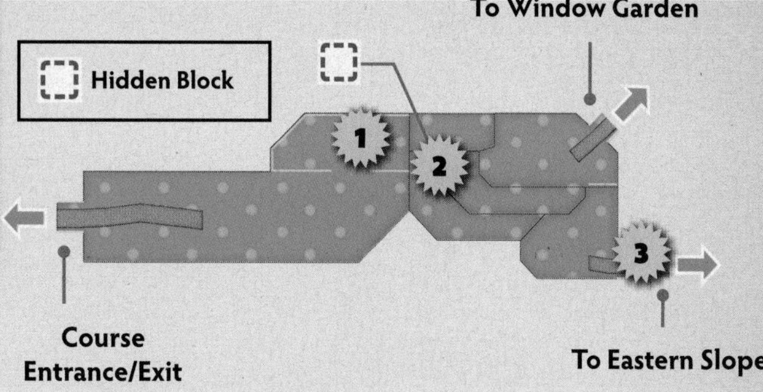

There's an extra ? Block floating high above Point 1. Before you smash the lower Blocks, use them to reach the higher ? Block.

To collect the Hopslipper at Point 2, you must first locate the nearby Hidden Block. Use the Hammer to smack the ground just to the right, then climb up and peel the sticker.

Eastern Slope

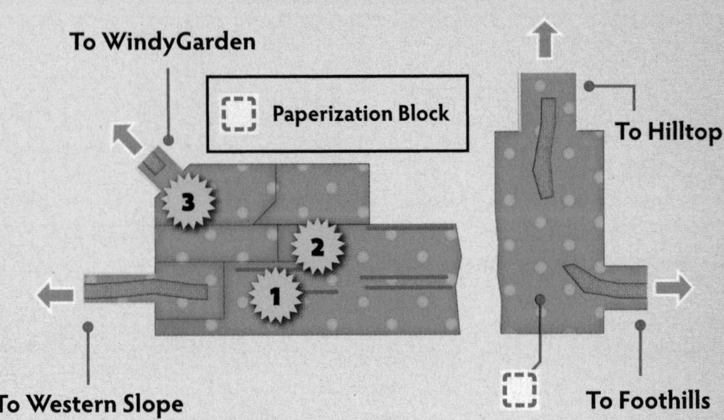

There's a large gap in the middle of the eastern slope. To cross this gap, you must follow the main path as it winds up the hill and back through the area.

The main path leads up the hill, but you need to take care of some business before you can pass through the windy garden. When you're finished exploring the western slope, follow the path to the eastern slope.

The eastern slope is packed with enemies, and it's not always easy to spot them before they attack. Watch out for the patrolling Koopa Troopas, and use the Hammer to expose any enemies that might be hiding behind the bushes. You'll find a Goomba hiding at Point 1 and a Koopa Troopa hiding behind a bush to the right.

HOW TO USE THIS GUIDE
HOW TO PLAY
STICKERS
ENEMIES
WALKTHROUGH
DECALBURG
SURFSHINE HARBOR
WORLD 1
WORLD 2
WORLD 3
WORLD 4
WORLD 5
WORLD 6
CHECKLISTS

Windy Garden

When you first enter the area, the ledge in the background is too high to reach. Use your Hammer to topple the bush at Point 2, then peel the Bowser tape to reveal some steps.

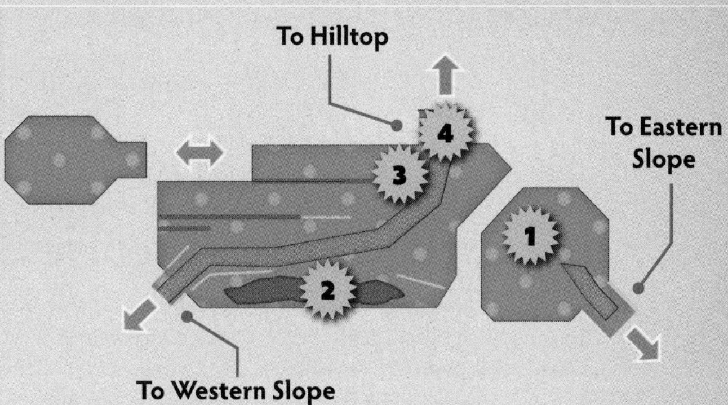

When you're finished exploring the area, take the alternative path to the windy garden.

When you enter the windy garden from the western slope, the wind pushes you off of the path. When you enter the area from the eastern slope, however, you appear near the source of the wind. Approach the Fan without stepping in front of the blades to avoid being blown away, then add it to your Album and calm the air.

NOTE

Much like the eastern slope, the windy garden is divided by a large gap. The main path runs through one section, while the alternative path leads to the other.

Thing: Fan

To collect the Fan, follow the alternative path through the eastern slope and into the windy garden.

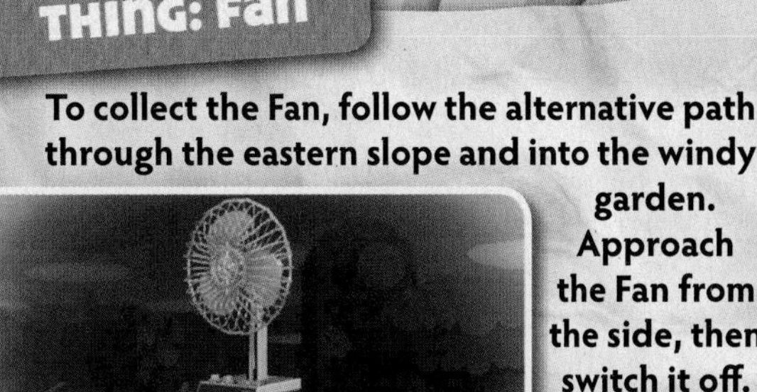

Approach the Fan from the side, then switch it off.

After you collect the Fan, return to the western slope and follow the main path back into the windy garden. The Toad at Point 2 is weeping over the loss of his flowers. After you collect a few of the Ice Flowers and Fire Flowers scattered throughout this Course, return to this area and use them to replant the Toad's garden.

Paperize the flower patch, then place either a Fire Flower or Ice Flower in each of the three indicated spots. When you finish, each flower you planted produces two copies of the original sticker. Additionally, the relieved Toad rewards you with an HP-Up Heart.

HP-UP HEART: BOUQUET GARDENS

Use Ice Flowers and Fire Flowers to replace the ruined flowers in the windy garden. Aside from a significant sticker reward, you receive an HP-Up Heart for your hard work!

TIP

If you want to replant the garden on a separate visit, make sure your Album doesn't contain the Fan or the Fan sticker when you enter the Course. If the Fan isn't back at its original location, the garden won't need to be replanted.

Before you move on, move toward the background, then step into the gap between the hedges. Follow the path to the left to find a secret area with a ? Block and a stack of coins.

When you're ready, follow the path to the hilltop.

HILLTOP

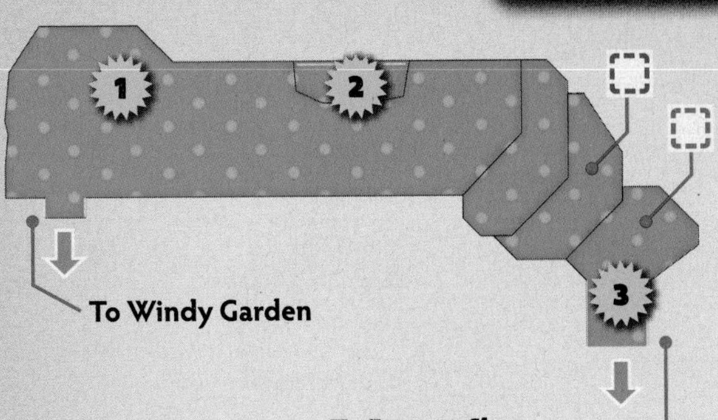

As you explore the hilltop for stickers and enemies, use the HP Block at Point 1 to top off your HP Bar. There are plenty of enemies left on the path to the Comet Piece, so make sure you're prepared.

Two Goombas are bullying a Toad at Point 2. When you investigate the situation, the Goombas give you a choice. To rescue the Toad, you must either pay the Goombas 20 coins or defeat them in battle. Choose an option and complete the Toad rescue to earn the Cat-o-Luck for your trouble. After revealing the reward, the Toad runs off to continue his travels.

As you follow the path back down from the hilltop, look for the blue and pink flowers that mark the Hidden Block and the Paperization Block near the end of the area. When you're ready, follow the path down through the right half of the eastern slope and into the foothills.

Toad Rescue: Bouquet Gardens

The first available Toad rescue is located in the hillside area of World 1-2. Pay the Goombas 20 coins to stop bullying the Toad, or simply defeat them in battle. Once you've resolved the conflict, the grateful Toad rewards you with a Cat-o-Luck and leaves the area.

WORLD 1-2

To collect the Cat-o-Luck, complete the Toad rescue in the hilltop area.

FOOTHILLS

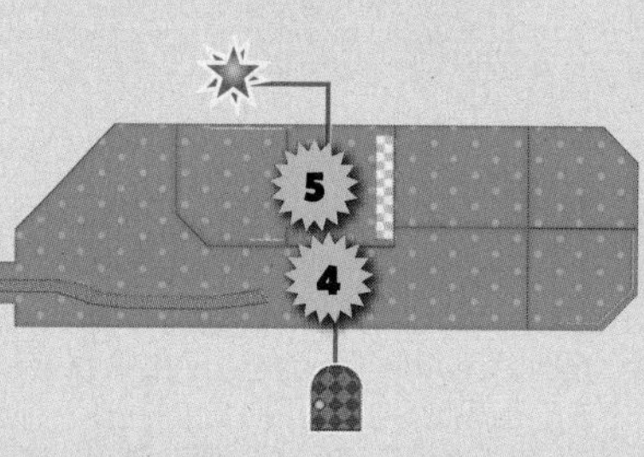

HOW TO USE THIS GUIDE
HOW TO PLAY
STICKERS
ENEMIES
WALKTHROUGH
DECALBURG
SURFSHINE HARBOR
WORLD 1
WORLD 2
WORLD 3
WORLD 4
WORLD 5
WORLD 6
CHECKLISTS

When you reach Point 1, peel the strips of Bowser tape on the hill in the background. When you do, a panel falls open to reveal a stash of coins and stickers.

As you approach Point 2, five Goombas spring an ambush. Kersti decides to even the odds by introducing the Battle Spinner. Follow Kersti's instructions to complete the tutorial, then turn your attention to the battle. Kersti ensures that you can use three stickers on your first turn.

Any number of sticker combinations can lead to victory, but consider selecting three Hammer stickers. The collateral damage resulting from a properly timed attack will clear most of your enemies on the first hit, and the remaining Hammers should be more than enough to finish off any stragglers.

3

Search the area for stickers, then follow the path to the right.

4

As you pass by Point 4, look for the Secret Door location on the small hill in the background. After you acquire a Secret Door sticker, return to this area and apply it to the marked location.

5

Follow the path as it curves around the edge of the area, and collect the Comet Piece to complete the Course.

STICKER COMET PIECE: UNLOCKING WORLD 1-3

This Course contains only one piece of the Sticker Comet. To unlock World 1-3, collect the Comet Piece at the end of World 1-2.

RECOMMENDED VISIT #2

After you gain access to the World 3-6 Sticker Shop, purchase a Secret Door sticker and revisit this Course. Apply the Secret Door to the marked location in the foothills, then head inside.

There are three ? Blocks behind the Secret Door. The first time you search them, the contain flashy stickers!

WORLD 1-3: Water's Edge Way

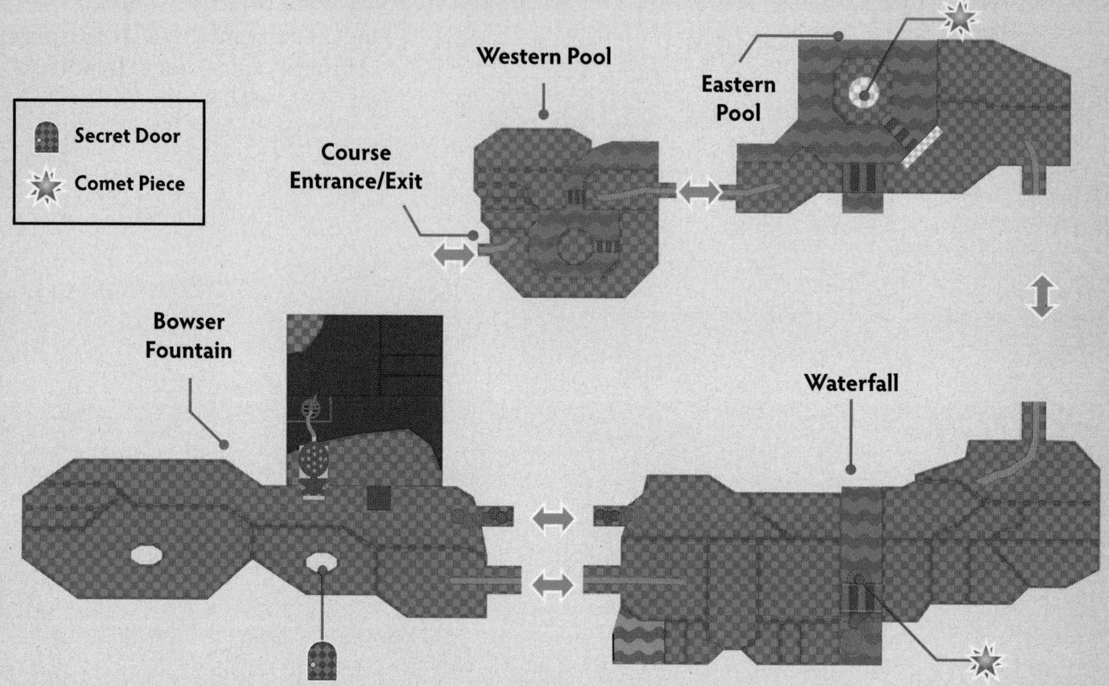

Overview

Prerequisites

This Course becomes available when you collect the Comet Piece from World 1-2. Aside from the Secret Door sticker, everything you need to complete the available objectives can be found in the Course.

Objectives

This Course contains several objectives, some of which require additional visits:

- **Defeat Kamek.**
- **Collect the hidden Comet Piece to unlock World 1-5.**
- **Shut off the Bowser fountain.**
- **Collect the Faucet.**
- **Recover the Comet Piece scrap.**
- **Collect the Comet Piece to unlock World 1-4.**
- **Collect the Bed from the Secret Door.**

IMPORTANT ITEMS AND LOCATIONS

DESCRIPTION	NOTES
Secret Door	The marked location is in the drain below the Bowser fountain.
HP-Up Heart	None
Toad Rescue	None
Luigi Location	None
Wiggler Diary Entry	None
Things	The Faucet is in the room behind the Bowser fountain. Enter the Secret Door below the Bowser fountain to find the Bed.

NOTE

This Course contains two Comet Pieces. After you collect one, make sure you return to collect the other.

Recommended Tactics

Most of the battles in this Course involve familiar enemies, but you will have to face a particularly nasty character. You should find all the stickers you need within the Course, but consider bringing a Hopslipper or two with you.

By this point, you should be fairly comfortable battling Koopa Troopas and Goombas. These enemies attack in a wide variety of formations, but a decent supply of Hammers, Jumps, and Shell stickers will allow you overcome any combination of these common enemies—particularly if you opt to use the Battle Spinner at the beginning of each round.

During your first visit, you must defeat the troublesome Kamek. This broom-riding Magikoopa is most vulnerable to Jump-based stickers, and a properly utilized Hopslipper will finish him off in one shot. Kamek won't be facing you on his own, however, so make sure you bring at least one multi-target sticker to take care his allies.

Western Pool

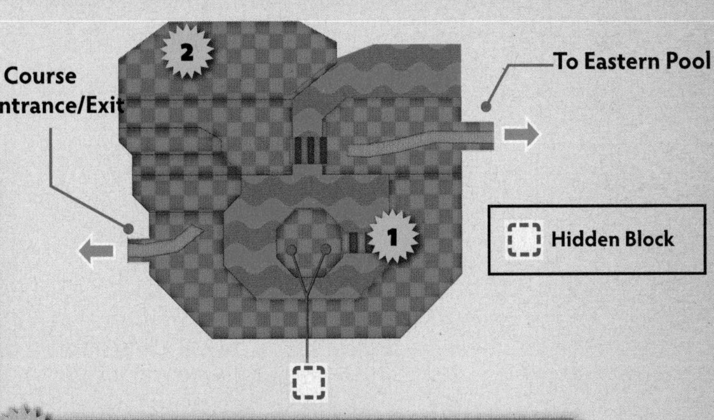

Peel the Bowser tape at Point 1 to create a bridge. Walk across to the island, then jump up to find the Hidden Block directly above each of the blue flowers.

There's a Koopa Troopa hiding behind the Blocks at Point 2. Try to stomp it before it leaps out to attack. When you're finished collecting stickers, follow the path to the eastern pool.

Eastern Pool

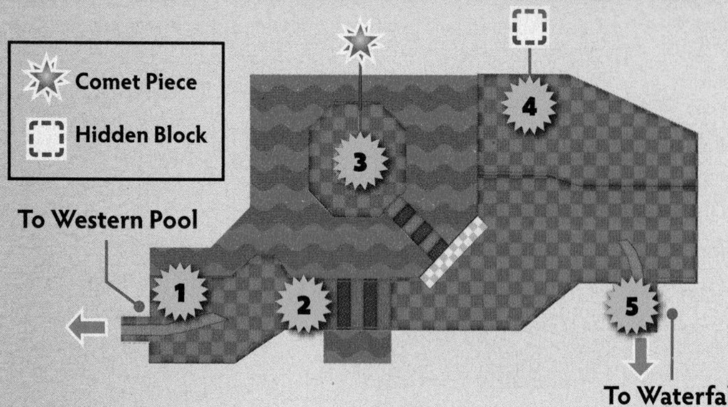

Before you move past Point 1, take advantage of the HP Block and Save Block. Kamek is about to make his first appearance, so make sure you're prepared.

Mini-Boss: Kamek

As you play through the game, you have to defeat Kamek a few times. Although he introduces some pretty dirty tricks in later encounters, this battle is fairly straightforward. Use a Hammer, Shell, or any multi-target attack to clear away the two Goombas. Kamek's broomstick keeps him out of range of most attacks, but Jump stickers will prove very effective.

A properly utilized Hopslipper will do just enough damage to defeat Kamek. If you earn a second attack with the Battle Spinner, you can easily defeat all three enemies on your first turn. Otherwise, just defeat the Goombas on your first turn, defend yourself from Kamek's attack, and finish him off on your second turn.

As you approach Point 2, a Toad comes charging across the nearby bridge. After you finish the conversation, continue across the bridge to face Kamek and two Goombas.

Kamek doesn't handle his defeat particularly well. After the battle, he paperizes the Comet Piece and tosses the scrap to the other end of the Course. To unlock World 1-4, you must recover the scrap and return it to Point 3.

There's a Hidden Block between the two ? Blocks at Point 4. As you approach the area, however, watch out for the Goomba that springs out from behind the bush. If you react quickly, you can foil the attempted ambush with a stomp or a Hammer strike.

When you're ready to move on, follow the path down to the waterfall.

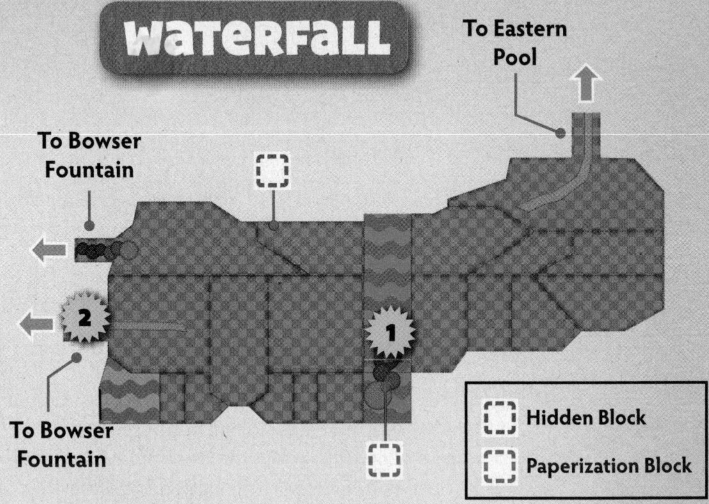

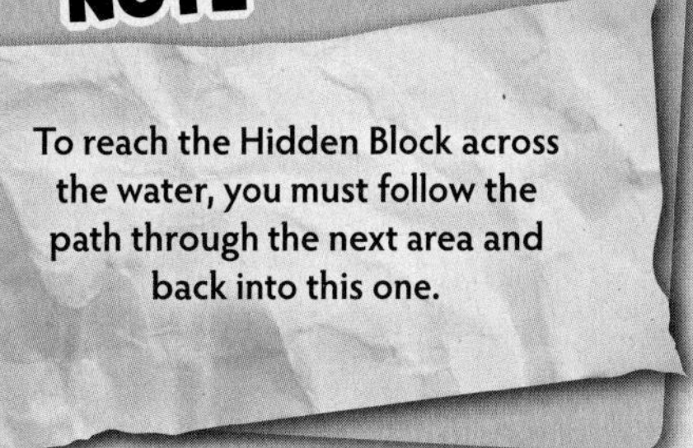

You'll find a number of ? Blocks, stickers, and enemies scattered around the waterfall. When you reach the bridge at Point 1, move toward the waterfall to drop into a secret area.

The secret area contains one of the Course's two Comet Pieces. You can grab it now to end your first visit, but consider dealing with the Comet Piece scrap first. Leave the secret area to emerge at the base of the waterfall, then paperize the area to find a Paperization Block location.

Bowser Fountain

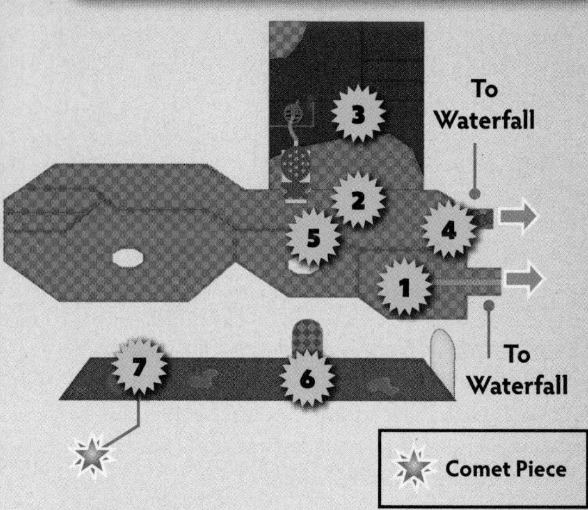

When you're finished searching the area for stickers, follow the path to the Bowser fountain.

NOTE

Before you can reach the underground area, you must stop the water flowing out of the Bowser fountain.

The water spilling out of the Bowser fountain is causing the nearby geyser. Before you can collect the Comet Piece scrap, you must find a way to shut off the water.

HOW TO USE THIS GUIDE
HOW TO PLAY
STICKERS
ENEMIES
WALKTHROUGH
DECALBURG
SURFSHINE HARBOR
WORLD 1
WORLD 2
WORLD 3
WORLD 4
WORLD 5
WORLD 6
CHECKLISTS

2

Follow the path around the left edge of the area and climb up to the ledge that runs along the back wall. After you pass under the fountain, peel the Bowser tape to reveal a hidden room.

Thing: Faucet

Enter the room behind the Bowser fountain to find the Faucet. Climb up the steps and jump up and down on the Faucet until it pops loose.

3

After you pass through the opening, cross the room and climb to the top of the steps. Hop onto the Faucet and jump up and down until the water shuts off and the Faucet breaks loose. Grab the Faucet, then head back outside.

4

Before you head down to collect the Comet Piece scrap, follow the upper path back toward the waterfall. Aside from the ? Blocks and posted stickers, this ledge contains a Hidden Block. When you're finished, move back to the Bowser fountain.

When you're ready, drop through one of the holes below the Bowser fountain and explore the underground area.

The underground area contains a marked location for a Secret Door. The area is fairly dark, but the paperization ability makes it much easier to find the exact spot. After you acquire a Secret Door sticker, return to this location to apply it.

Move to the left edge of the underground area to collect the Comet Piece scrap, then follow the path to the right. After you shut down the Bowser fountain, this passage leads back to the waterfall.

Make your way back up to the eastern pool and put the Comet Piece scrap back in its proper place. After you finish the repair, collect the Comet Piece to complete your first visit.

RECOMMENDED VISIT #2

After you complete your first visit, you must still collect the Course's remaining Comet Piece. Return to the bridge halfway down the waterfall, then walk toward the background to fall into the secret area. After you land, collect the Comet Piece and complete the Course.

STICKER COMET PIECE: UNLOCKING WORLD 1-5

The Course's second Comet Piece is located in a secret area. Revisit the bridge in the waterfall area and move toward the background until you drop into the water. To unlock World 1-5, collect the Comet Piece near your landing spot.

RECOMMENDED VISIT #3

After you gain access to the World 3-6 Sticker Shop, purchase a Secret Door sticker and return to the Bowser fountain. Shut off the water, then drop down through one of the drainage holes. Place the Secret Door sticker in the marked spot, then head inside to find the Bed and a stash of coins.

THING: BED

After you acquire a Secret Door sticker, return to the Bowser fountain. Shut off the water and drop into the underwater area. Apply the sticker to the marked location, then pass through the Secret Door to find the Bed.

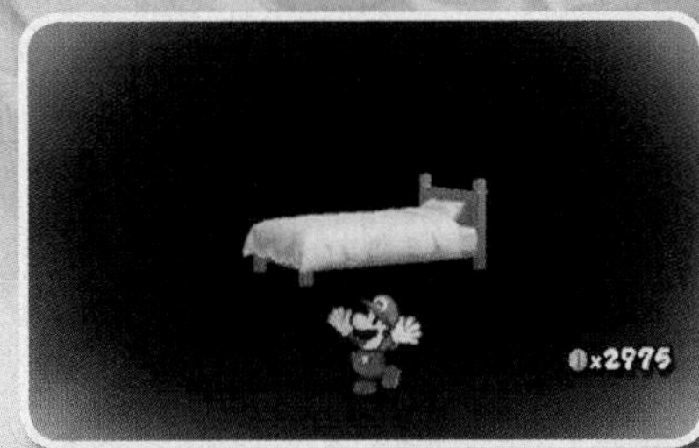

TIP

Before you collect the bed, you can use it to replenish Mario's HP! Hop onto the Bed and press Ⓐ to take a quick nap!

WORLD 1-4: HITHER THITHER HILL

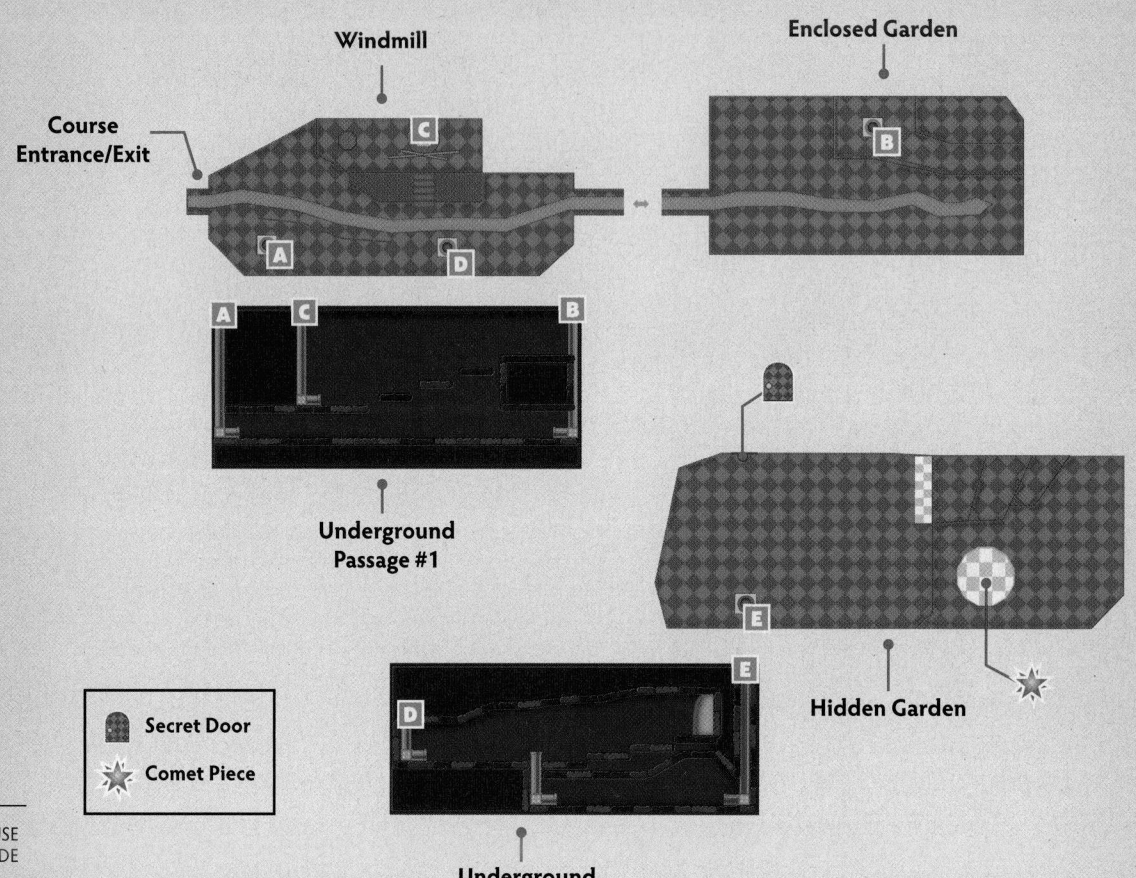

Overview

Prerequisites

To unlock this Course, you must collect the corresponding Comet Piece from World 1-3. Recover the scrap created by Kamek, then return it to its proper location. Collect the resulting Comet Piece to reveal the path to World 1-4.

This Course also requires a number of stickers, a supply of coins, and an extra visit once you've purchased a Secret Door sticker from the World 3-6 Sticker Shop.

NOTE

This Course contains several warp pipes, some of which must be unlocked or repaired before they can be used.

ESSENTIAL THING STICKERS

NAME	THING LOCATION	NOTES
Fan	World 1-2	Needed to adjust the windmill blades.

TIP

It's best to bring a supply of coins and Jump-based stickers for the mini-boss battle.

OBJECTIVES

This Course contains several objectives, some of which require additional visits to complete:

- **Lead the stranded Toad back to Decalburg.**
- **Decipher the windmill code.**
- **Use the Fan sticker to gain access to the windmill.**
- **Enter the windmill code.**
- **Recover and replace the Green Warp Pipe scrap.**
- **Defeat the Big Buzzy Beetle.**
- **Collect the Comet Piece to unlock a path to World 1-6.**
- **Collect the Matches from the Secret Door.**

IMPORTANT ITEMS AND LOCATIONS

DESCRIPTION	NOTES
Secret Door	The marked location is in the hidden garden at the end of the Course.
HP-Up Heart	Defeat the Big Buzzy Beetle to earn an HP-Up Heart.
Toad Rescue	None
Luigi Location	None
Wiggler Diary Entry	None
Things	The Matches are located through the Secret Door.

RECOMMENDED TACTICS

In addition to Goombas and Koopa Troopas, this Course also contains several Buzzy Beetles. These shelled critters are considerably tougher than Koopa Troopas, but most of the same tactics apply. You'll find plenty of useful stickers around the environment, but you'll want to bring some specific stickers for the mini-boss encounter.

Buzzy Beetles are immune to fire attacks, so it's best to stick to the basics. Stomp a Buzzy Beetle before the battle starts, then use a Jump sticker to kick it into its allies.

Unless the Big Buzzy Beetle is on its back, it's immune to all damage. A properly timed Jump sticker is enough to flip this mini-boss over, but it always recovers on its next turn. To damage the Big Buzzy Beetle, use the Battle Spinner to earn (or purchase) at least one extra attack on each turn. Use a Jump sticker to flip the oversized enemy, then follow up with a Hopslipper to deal heavy damage.

RECOMMENDED VISIT #1

WINDMILL

Course Entrance/Exit
To Enclosed Garden
To First Underground Passage
To First Underground Passage

As you search the area for stickers, investigate the tree at Point 1. Strike the tree with your Hammer to collect some hidden coins.

When you first visit the Course, one of the windmill's blades is blocking the door. Use paperization to place the Fan on the nearby stump. After the blade moves out of the way, head into the windmill.

The first time you enter the windmill, there are four strange Blocks inside. Each Block displays a number, and each time you hit a Block, the number changes. To reveal the hidden warp pipe, you must enter the correct sequence of numbers. Return to this location after you learn the code.

TIP

The path to the right of the windmill leads straight to the enclosed garden. This route leads to the area outside of the enclosure, but consider exploring the path before you take the described route.

When you're ready, enter the warp pipe at Point 4 to emerge in the first underground passage.

FIRST UNDERGROUND PASSAGE

After you exit the pipe, follow the path to the right. There are a few Buzzy Beetles along the way; stomp them or avoid them as you see fit. When you reach Point 1, look for the warp pipe on the ledge. After you input the windmill code, you can use this pipe to explore the platforms above you. For now, enter the pipe to the right to find the enclosed garden.

ENCLOSED GARDEN

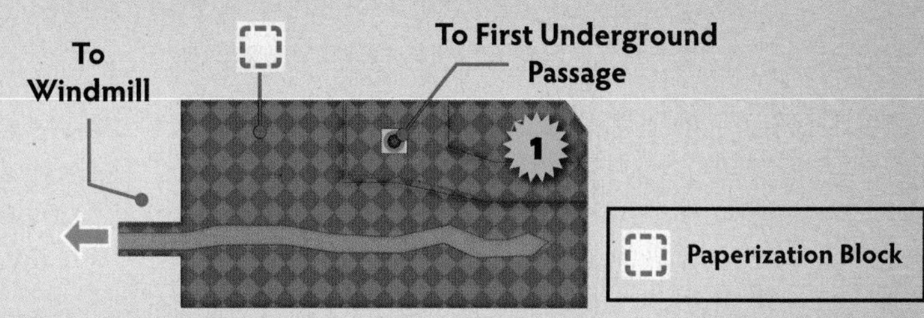

After you reach the enclosed garden, move right to find a weeping Toad. Collect any nearby stickers you might like to add to your Album, then lead the Toad back into the pipe. Escort the Toad back to Decalburg to learn the windmill code.

TIMID TOAD ESCORT

As you lead the Toad back to the World-Map, take the time to defeat each enemy along the way. If you allow an enemy to get too close, the panicky Toad runs back to the enclosed garden.

Lead the Toad through the first underground passage, up to the windmill, and through the Course entrance/exit. After you return to the World-Map, allow the Toad to follow you back to Decalburg. When you enter the towm, the Toad asks you to visit him in his home.

Return to the residential area and enter the house in the middle. The Toad rewards you with a Mushroom sticker and describes something he overheard near the windmill. Use the story to determine the windmill code, then head back to World 1-4.

RECOMMENDED VISIT #2

WINDMILL

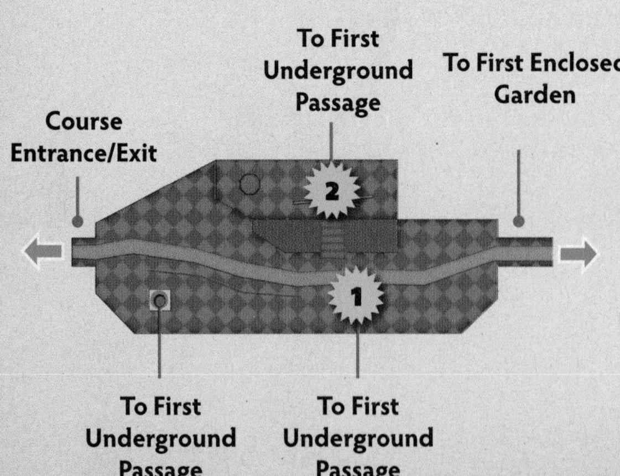

The pipe at Point 1 leads to the second underground passage. You have some business to take care of before you head down, but you'll be returning to this location shortly.

Enter the windmill and hit the Blocks until they display the code you learned from the timid Toad (4123). When you input the proper code, the Blocks vanish and a warp pipe emerges from the floor. Enter the pipe to emerge on the upper platforms in the first underground passage.

First Underground Passage

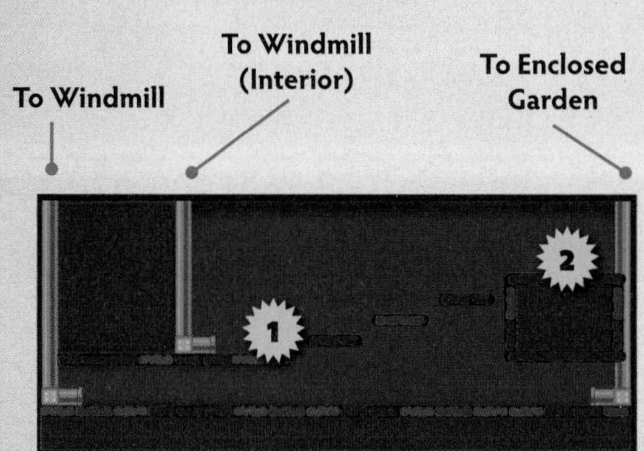

After you emerge from the pipe, hop along the platforms to the right. Watch out for the Buzzy Beetles along the path! Time your jumps to avoid each enemy or to initiate a battle with a well-aimed stomp.

When you reach the last ledge, collect the Green Warp Pipe scrap. Once the scrap is in your Album, head back to the windmill and enter the warp pipe that connects to the second underground passage.

Second Underground Passage

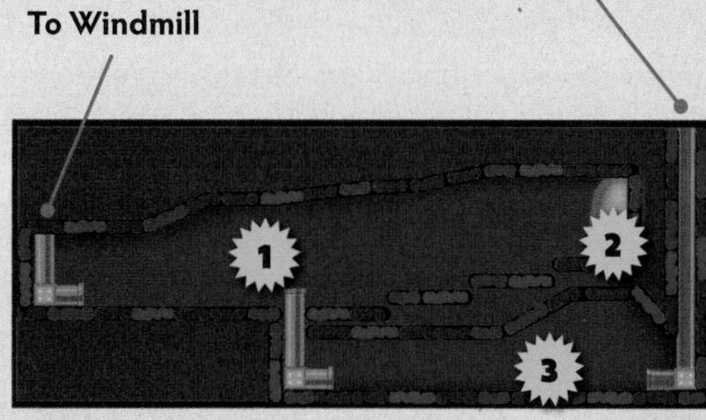

After you emerge from the pipe, move to the incomplete warp pipe to the right. Use the paperization ability to place the Green Warp Pipe scrap in the indicated spot. Before you enter the repaired pipe, search the area to the right.

2

Use the HP Block to top off your HP Bar, then head through the arch to the right to find a small nook below the hidden garden. After you collect the coins and stickers return to the repaired pipe.

3

Pass through the repaired pipe to enter the cavern below you, then move right until a Big Buzzy Beetle drops into your path. Defeat this mini-boss, collect the HP-Up Heart you receive as an award, and enter the red warp pipe to the right.

Mini-Boss: Big Buzzy Beetle

The key to defeating the Big Buzzy Beetle is to take advantage of the Battle Spinner. Unless you have a supply of POW Blocks, you must perform at least two attacks during each turn. If you haven't mastered the Battle Spinner's timing, consider paying for a double-match. Select a Jump sticker for your first attack, then select Hopslipper stickers for any remaining attacks.

The Jump sticker doesn't deal any damage, but it does flip the Big Buzzy Beetle onto its back. Follow up with a properly timed Hopslipper to deplete half of your enemy's HP Bar. If you managed to earn a third attack, you can finish the battle on your first turn.

If the battle continues beyond your first turn, simply defend against the Big Buzzy Beetle's attack, then repeat the process as many times as needed. When you defeat your enemy, an HP-Up Heart appears in its place.

HP-UP HEART: HITHER THITHER HILL

Defeat the Big Buzzy Beetle in the second underground area to receive an HP-Up Heart.

STICKER COMET PIECE: UNLOCKING WORLD 1-6

The game contains two Comet Pieces that unlock separate paths to World 1-6. Collect the Comet Piece at the end of World 1-4 to unlock the first available path to World 1-6.

HIDDEN GARDEN

1

After you exit the red warp pipe, move toward the background to find the marked Secret Door location. Revisit this area when you acquire a Secret Door sticker.

2

Search the hidden garden for stickers, then follow the steps down to the right. Collect the Comet Piece to end the Course.

RECOMMENDED VISIT #3

After you gain access to the World 3-6 Sticker Shop, purchase a Secret Door sticker and return to the hidden garden at the end of World 1-4. Apply the sticker to the marked location, then head through the secret door to find the Matches.

THING: MATCHES

After you acquire a Secret Door sticker, apply it to the marked location in the hidden garden. Head through the door to add the Matches to your collection.

WORLD 1-5: WHAMMINO MOUNTAIN

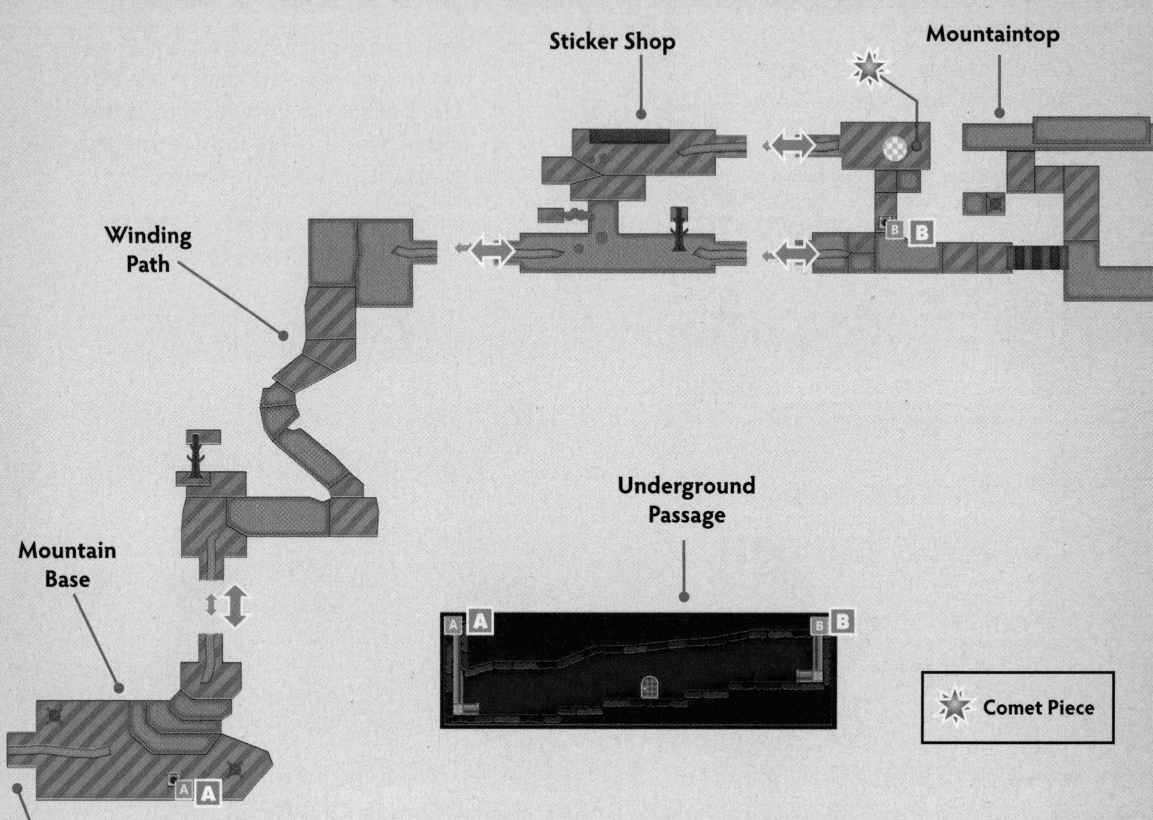

NOTE

This Course undergoes a few changes during your first visit. This map shows World 1-5 as it appears after these changes occur.

Overview

Prerequisites

To unlock this Course, you must collect the Comet Piece hidden behind the waterfall in World 1-3. Other than the Secret Door sticker, this Course contains everything you need to meet the available objectives.

Objectives

This Course contains several objectives, most of which can be completed during your first visit:

- **Roll the boulder off of the mountaintop.**
- **Open the path through the underground passage.**
- **Recover and replace the White Gate scrap.**
- **Gain access to the Sticker Shop.**
- **Collect the Comet Piece.**
- **Enter the Secret Door and collect the Bellows.**

IMPORTANT ITEMS AND LOCATIONS

DESCRIPTION	NOTES
Secret Door	The marked location is in the underground passage.
HP-Up Heart	None
Toad Rescue	None
Luigi Location	None
Wiggler Diary Entry	None
Things	The Bellows are through the Secret Door.

Mountain Base

To Winding Path

Course Entrance/Exit

1

To Underground Passage

NOTE

Once activated, this Course's Sticker Shop is a convenient source of Ice Flowers, Fire Flowers, and a variety of Mushroom stickers.

Recommended Tactics

This Course is filled with Spinies, and a troublesome Lakitu makes sure it stays that way. You'll also find a few Goombas and Koopa Troopas, so use your preferred tactics to defeat them.

Since Spinies can counter virtually all Jump attacks, it's important to maintain a supply of Hammer stickers. These little guys are fairly tough, so try to soften them up with a Hammer strike just before the battle begins.

The Iron Jump stickers scattered around the Course are also effective, but you might find it simpler to avoid most enemies. Your sticker supply won't last long if you battle every Spiny the Lakitu drops in your path!

1

On your first visit, there's a big plug in the warp pipe at the beginning of the Course. To open this route, you must enter the underground passage by way of the mountaintop. Once you do, you can clear the plug from this warp pipe to create a shortcut between the mountain base and the mountaintop! For now, however, search the area for stickers and continue to the winding path.

The dead trees scattered around the Course can be knocked down to form bridges. To do so, simply strike a dead tree with a Hammer until it topples over. Knock down the tree at Point 1 to bridge the gap to a small platform. The nearby White Gate scrap is sitting just out of reach, but that will change soon enough. For now, just note the location and continue along the winding path.

As you continue along the path, a Lakitu drops an endless supply of Spinies in front of you. Try to avoid the enemies on your way to Point 2, then grab the Super Star to gain temporary invincibility. Collect any nearby stickers you'd like to add to your Album, then continue to the end of the path before the power-up wears off.

If you took any damage on your way through the area, make sure you take advantage of the HP Block at the end of the winding path.

STICKER SHOP

To Mountaintop

To Winding Path

To Mountaintop

Paperization Block

MOUNTAINTOP

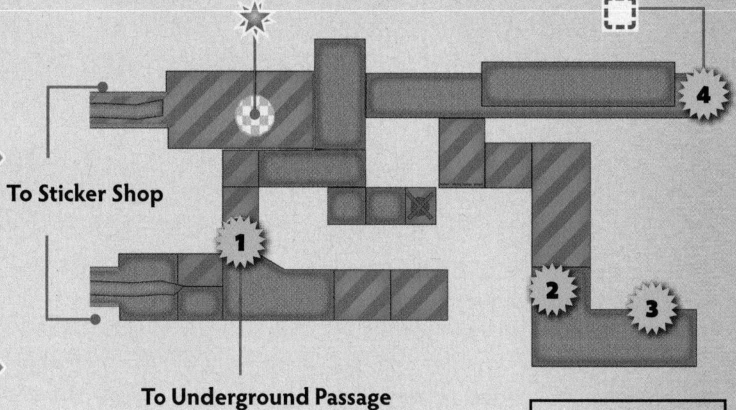

Comet Piece

Hidden Block

NOTE

This area undergoes a significant change during your first visit. After you trigger the change, the warp pipe appears and many of the platforms vanish.

Before you can take advantage of this Course's Sticker Shop, you must return the White Gate scrap to its proper place. The path beyond the gate also leads to this Course's Comet Piece, so it's essential that you recover the scrap, whether or not you intend to purchase stickers.

There's a warp pipe under the platform at Point 1. The platform flips over when you trigger the environmental change.

Follow the path as it curves around the area. Peel the Bowser tape at Point 2 to create a bridge across the nearby gap.

When you're ready, use your Hammer to knock down the dead tree at Point 3. When the tree falls, it causes a chain reaction of disappearing platforms and toppled scenery. After the cinematic ends, the mountaintop warp pipe has flipped into position, a Toad appears near the Sticker Shop, and the White Gate scrap drops into a more accessible location.

Before you leave the mountaintop, explore the area around Point 4. After you find the Hidden Block, use it to reach the coins on the upper platform.

When you're ready, return to Point 1 and enter the newly available mountaintop warp pipe.

Underground Passage

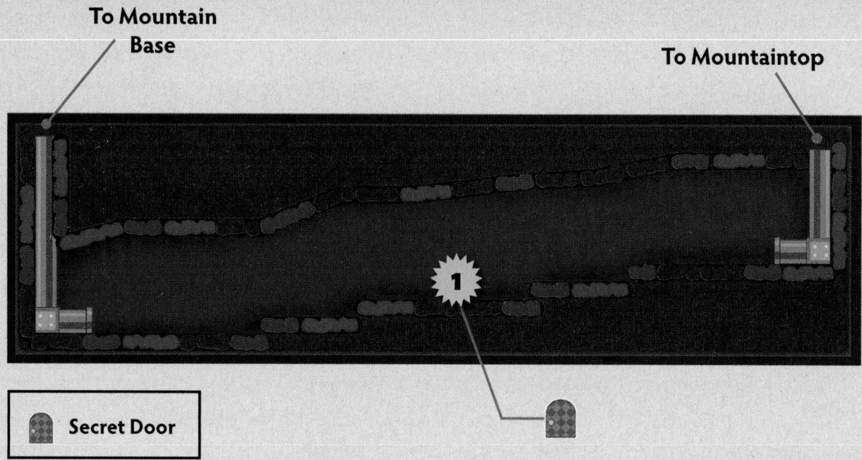

The underground passage serves as a convenient shortcut through the Course, but it also contains the Secret Door location. As you follow the path to the left, look for the marked location on the rock cluster at Point 1.

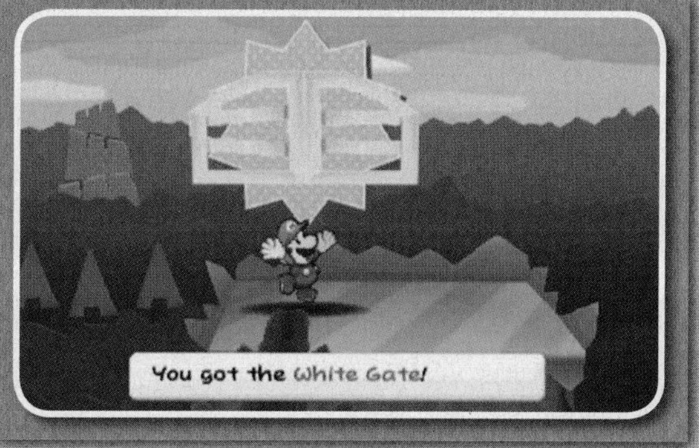

Continue into the winding path and collect the White Gate scrap beyond the toppled tree. Unless you're itching for a fight, head back through the underground passage and return to the Sticker Shop by way of the mountaintop.

Enter the pipe on the left end of the underground passage to emerge at the mountain base. Now that the plug has popped loose, you can use this shortcut whenever you like.

OPENING THE STICKER SHOP

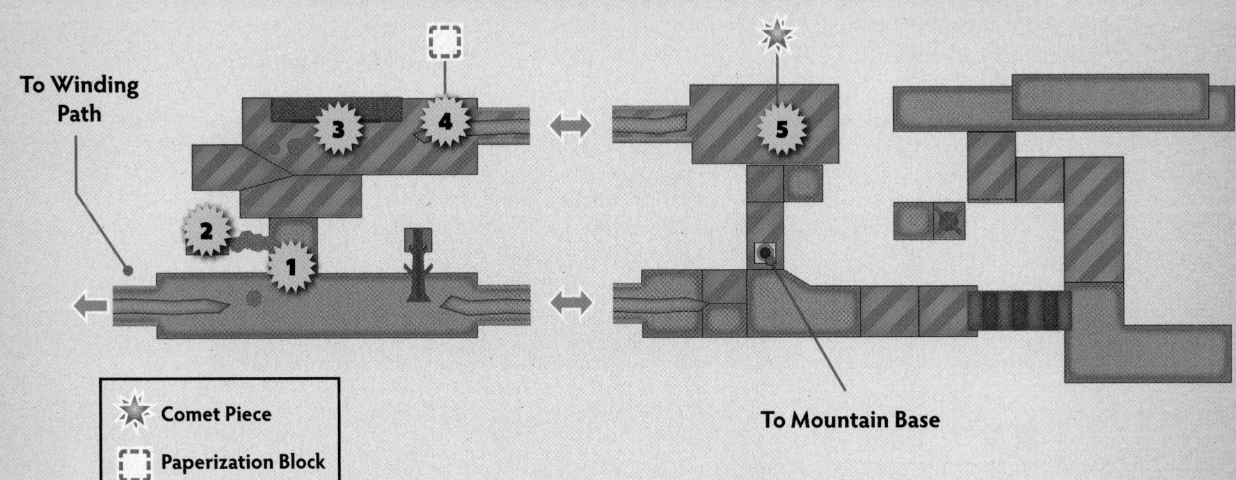

After you collect the White Gate scrap, return to the Sticker Shop. Apply the scrap to the indicated spot and wait for the gate to swing open.

Pass through the open gate and approach the Toad to the left. Peel the Bowser Tape to free the Toad, then follow him up to the Sticker Shop board.

Once the Toad is in position, the World 1-5 Sticker Shop is open for business. The shop stocks additional stickers as you progress through the game, so you may want to check back every so often.

When you finish exploring the area around the shop, move to the background and follow the path to the mountaintop.

When you're ready, collect the Comet Piece at Point 5 to end the Course.

STICKER COMET PIECE: UNLOCKING WORLD 1-6

The game contains two Comet Pieces that unlock separate paths to World 1-6. Collect the Comet Piece at the end of World 1-5 to unlock one of the available paths.

RECOMMENDED VISIT #2

After you gain access to the World 3-6 Sticker Shop, purchase a Secret Door sticker and revisit the underground passage. Place the sticker on the marked rock cluster, then head though the Secret Door to find the Bellows.

THING: BELLOWS

After you acquire a Secret Door sticker, apply it to the marked location in the underground passage. Pass through the door to find the Bellows.

WORLD 1-6: GOOMBA FORTRESS

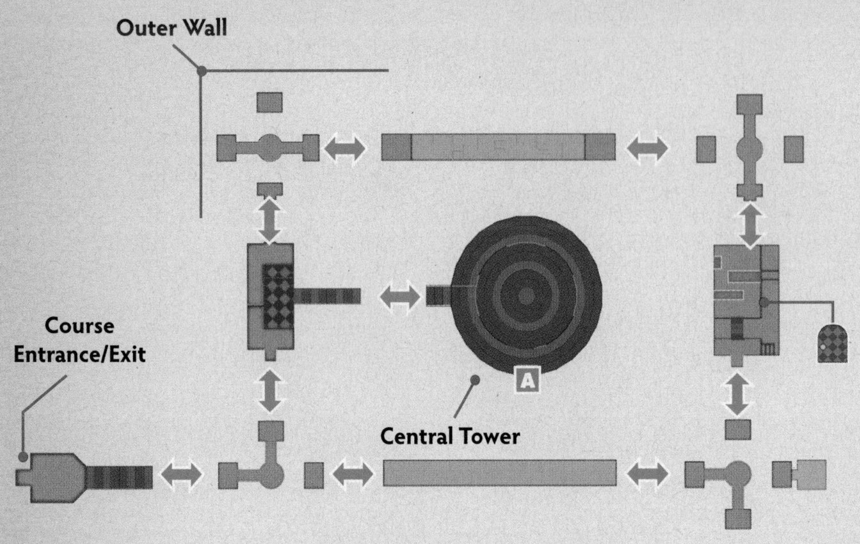

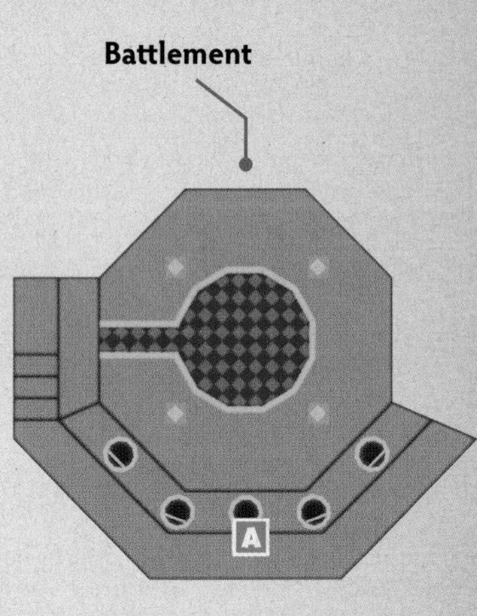

OVERVIEW

PREREQUISITES

To unlock this Course, you must collect either the Comet Piece at the end of World 1-4 or the Comet Piece at the end of World 1-5. There's a boss battle at the end of the Course, so plan ahead! A supply of powerful stickers can make the battle much easier. Once again, you must revisit this area after you acquire a Secret Door sticker.

ESSENTIAL THING STICKERS

NAME	THING LOCATION	NOTES
Scissors	World 1-2	Recommended for the boss battle.
Cat-o-Luck	World 1-2	Recommended for the boss battle.

NOTE

Although the Thing Stickers will make the boss battle much easier, you'll also need a good supply of Battle Stickers. Consider bringing some Hopslippers, a few Iron Jumps, and some POW Block stickers.

OBJECTIVES

This Course contains several objectives, most of which can be completed during your first visit:

- **Cover the spikes on the western wall.**
- **Find Luigi.**
- **Climb the central tower.**
- **Collect the Trumpet.**
- **Defeat the Megasparkle Goomba.**
- **Collect the Royal Sticker.**
- **Collect the Squirt Gun from the Secret Door.**

IMPORTANT ITEMS AND LOCATIONS

DESCRIPTION	NOTES
Secret Door	The marked location is near the middle of the eastern wall.
HP-Up Heart	None
Toad Rescue	None
Luigi Location	As you approach the central tower, look for Luigi in the background.
Wiggler Diary Entry	None
Things	The Trumpet is at the top of the central tower. The Squirt Gun is beyond the Secret Door.

Bob-ombs play a large role in the fortress's defenses, and they'll swarm you at every opportunity. It's often best to simply avoid these explosive enemies, but when you're drawn into a fight, Shells and Fire Flowers are very useful.

Make sure you bring a few Jump-type stickers in case you run into a Paragoomba along the way. Paragoombas are low-altitude enemies, so they tend to dodge targeted Hammer attacks.

Recommended Tactics

During your first visit to this Course, you'll find most areas are packed with enemies. After you collect the Royal Sticker, however, very few foes remain to guard the fortress.

The Megasparkle Goomba is actually a group of several Goombas united through the power of a Royal Sticker. This boss is one tough customer, so it's important to bring some powerful stickers. The Cat-o-Luck and Scissors are very effective when used at the appropriate times, but you'll need some Battle Stickers to deal reliable damage throughout the fight. Bring a supply of Hopslippers, Iron Jumps, and POW Block stickers.

As always, you should keep a Mushroom or two in your Album.

OUTER WALL

The fortress's outer wall is composed of four wall segments connected by small towers. To reach the large tower in the center of the Course, you must follow the outer wall all the way around the perimeter.

WESTERN WALL—PART 1

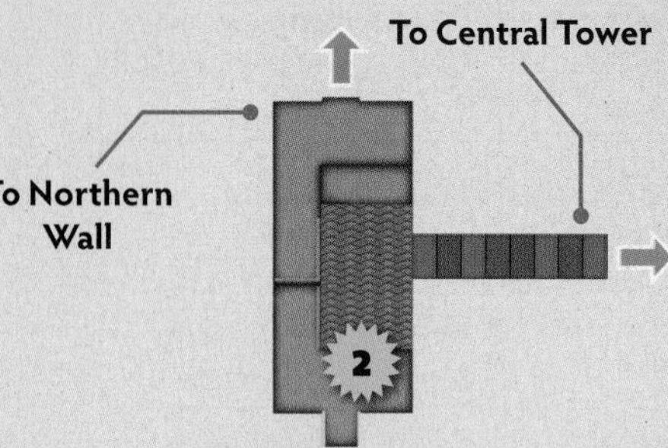

Course Entrance/Exit

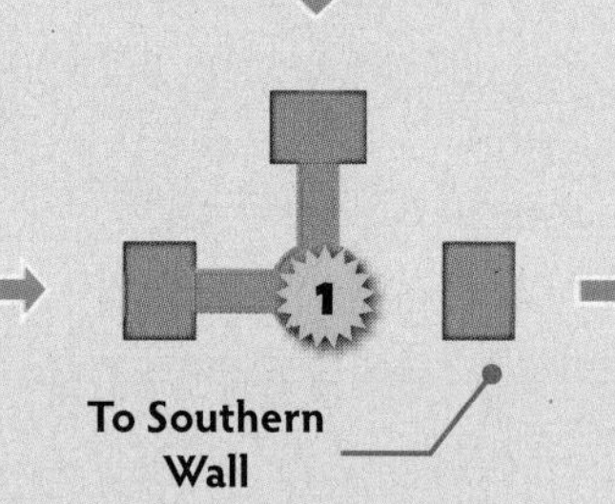

Defeat or avoid the Goombas guarding the main gate, then head into the first tower. Hit the Block Switch in the middle of the room to rotate the walkway, then head through the doorway on the back wall to find the western wall.

On your first visit, the path to the central tower is blocked by deadly spikes. Pull the Bowser tape at Point 2 to cover half of the spikes with a red carpet. Use the nearby HP Block if needed, then head back into the first tower. Follow the walkway to the southern wall.

TIP

Each of the smaller towers along the outer wall contains a Block Switch. Use these devices to control the rotating walkways.

HOW TO USE THIS GUIDE
HOW TO PLAY
STICKERS
ENEMIES
WALKTHROUGH
DECALBURG
SURFSHINE HARBOR
WORLD 1
WORLD 2
WORLD 3
WORLD 4
WORLD 5
WORLD 6
CHECKLISTS

Southern Wall

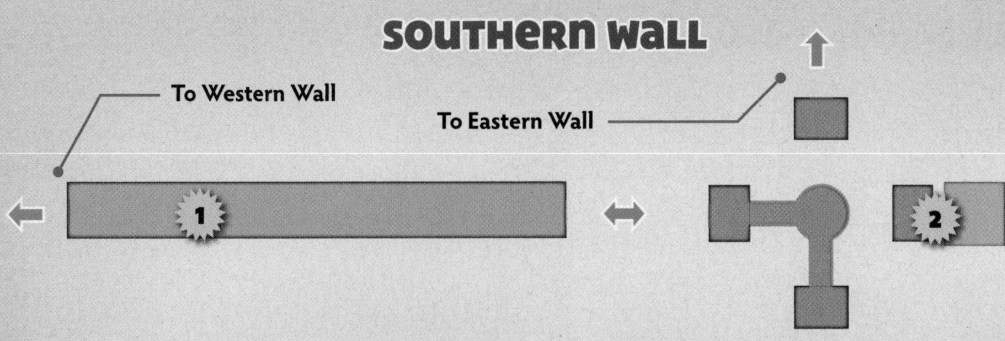

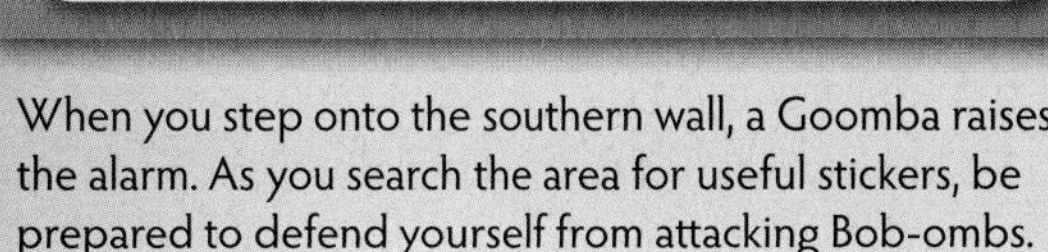

When you step onto the southern wall, a Goomba raises the alarm. As you search the area for useful stickers, be prepared to defend yourself from attacking Bob-ombs.

When you reach the second tower, strike the wall to the right with your Hammer. When the loose panel falls away, it reveals a secret area with a ? Block and a stash of coins. When you're ready, leave the secret area and continue to the eastern wall.

Eastern Wall

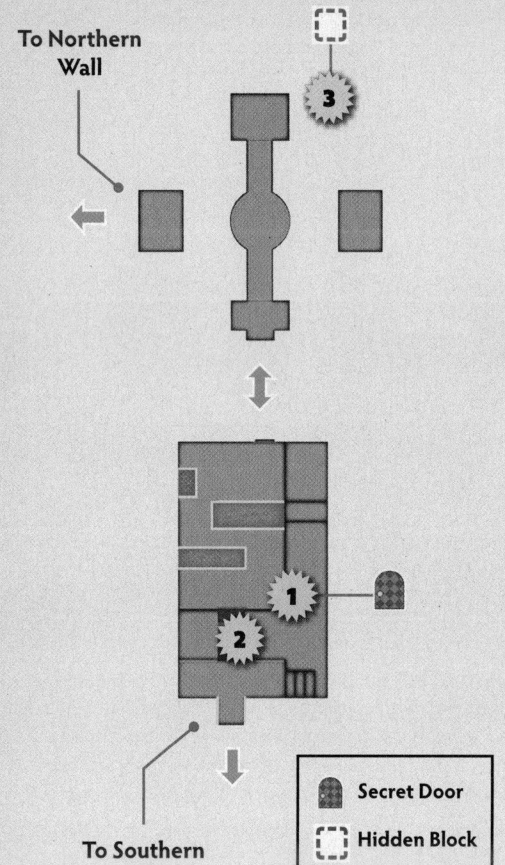

When you're finished searching the area, climb the steps back up to the walkway. When you move across the nearby bridge, a hidden switch activates the two large vents in the background. The resulting gusts are powerful enough to knock you right off the walkway!

After this happens, activate the Paperize ability, then place a sticker from your Album in each of the two indicated spots. The stickers only stop the exhaust for a short time, so move quickly! Navigate around the spikes and head into the next tower.

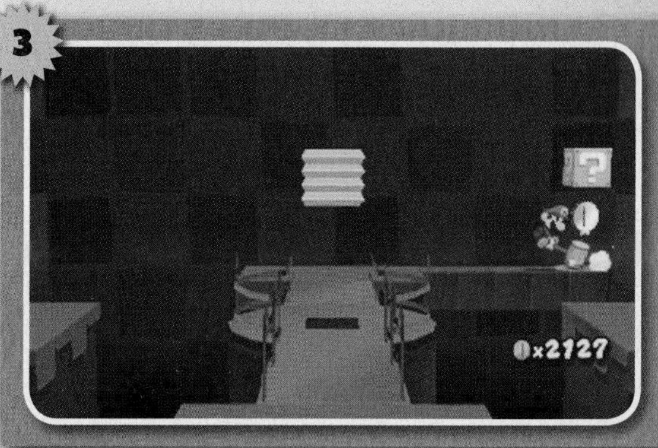

To reach the ? Block at Point 3, use your Hammer to reveal the row of Hidden Blocks along the back wall. When you're ready, continue to the northern wall.

When you reach the eastern wall, move to the right and drop down from the walkway. As you search the area for stickers, look for the Secret Door location at Point 1. Return to this area after you acquire a Secret Door sticker.

Northern Wall

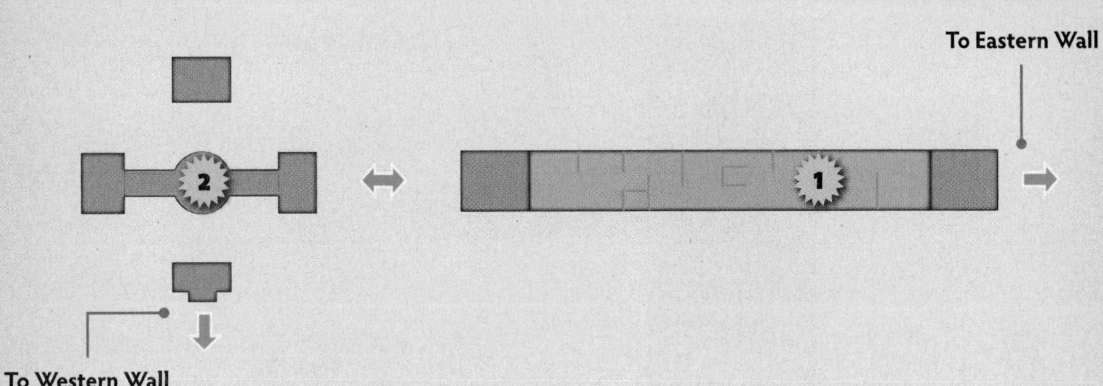

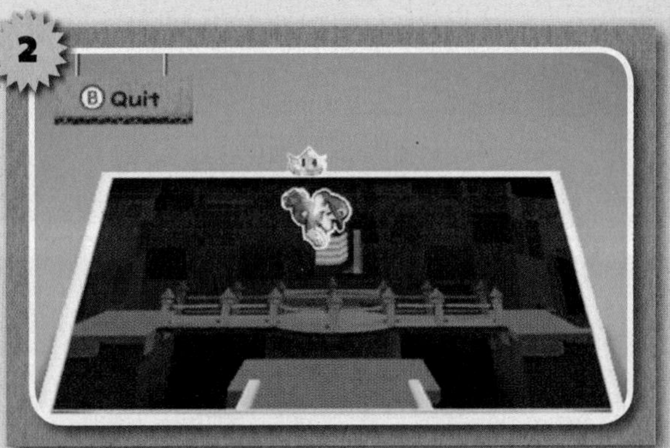

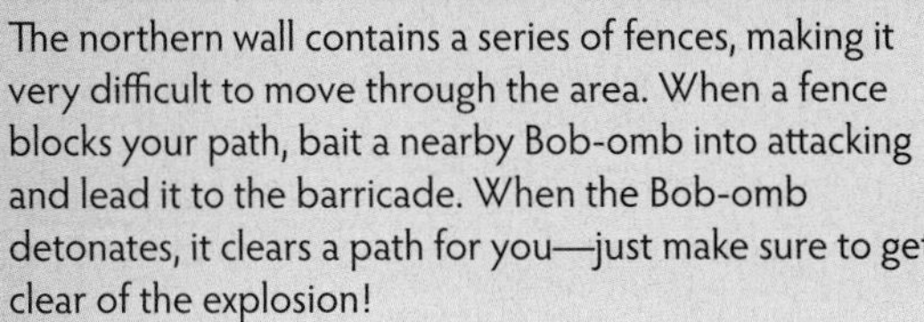

The northern wall contains a series of fences, making it very difficult to move through the area. When a fence blocks your path, bait a nearby Bob-omb into attacking and lead it to the barricade. When the Bob-omb detonates, it clears a path for you—just make sure to get clear of the explosion!

The Block Switch in the next tower is turned on its side. Activate the Paperize ability, then peel the scrap and realign the Block Switch. Move the walkway into position, then head back out to the western wall.

Western Wall—Part 2

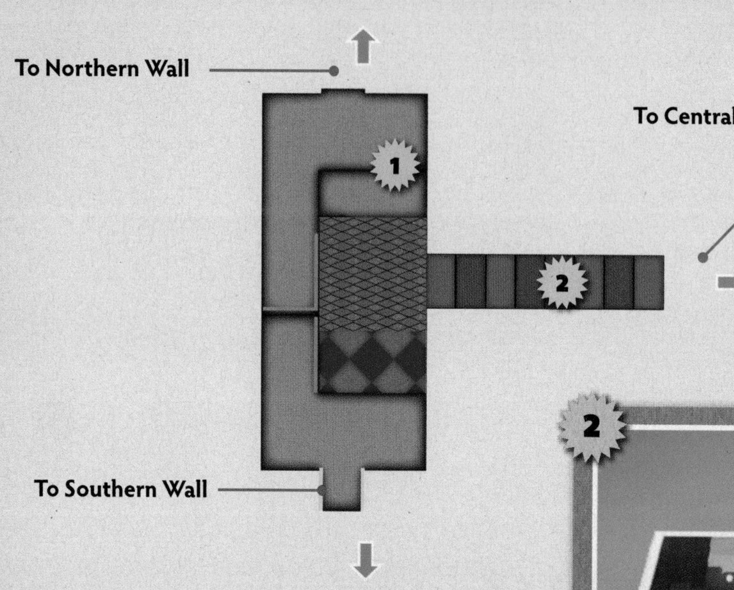

When you return to the western wall, peel the Bowser tape near the spikes to unroll the second half of the red carpet. Now that the spikes are completely covered, you can reach the central tower. Search the area for stickers, take advantage of the nearby HP Block and Save Block, and then follow the walkway to the right.

As you approach the central tower, watch the background for Luigi. When you spot him, activate the paperization ability and pull him off of the wall. When you're ready, follow the walkway into the central tower.

Luigi Location: Goomba Fortress

As you approach the central tower, Luigi can be seen on the wall in the background.

Central Tower

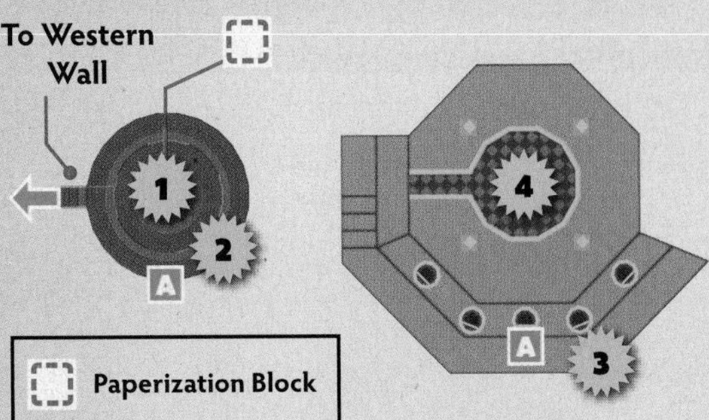

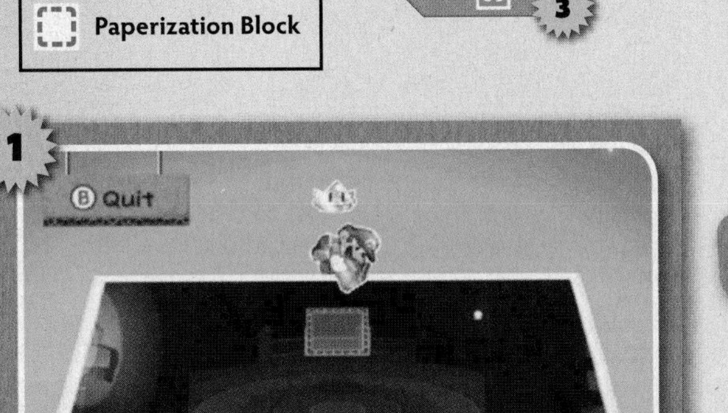

There's a Paperization Block hidden on the ground floor of the central tower. Before you head up the stairs, move to the center of the area and activate the Paperize ability.

As you climb up to the battlement, you'll find a few enemies and ? Blocks within the tower. You're not far from the boss battle, so make sure you're satisfied with your sticker selection.

When you reach the battlement, follow the path to the right to collect the Trumpet and to search one last ? Block before the big battle.

Thing: Trumpet

Climb to the top of the central tower. When you reach the battlement, move to the right to find the Trumpet.

When you're ready, move to the center of the battlement to confront the Megasparkle Goomba.

BOSS FIGHT!

Megasparkle Goomba

When the battle starts, the Megasparkle Goomba is actually a group of Goombas. These enemies act as one, however, and they'll stay in this form for two turns, or until they've suffered significant damage. If you brought a Cat-o-Luck sticker, consider using it now. Doing so is almost guaranteed to trigger the first transformation.

Once the Megasparkle Goomba reveals its true form, it gains several new abilities. When it rolls into a cone, make sure you adjust your tactics accordingly. Use the Battle Spinner to earn at least one extra attack, and consider using a POW Block sticker to crumple your opponent, followed by the Scissors sticker for heavy damage. If you're limited to a single attack, use an Iron Jump and try to earn an extra attack on your next turn.

The Megasparkle Goomba has several attacks, and all of them deal significant damage. It might stomp you, roll over you, or throw multiple Goombas at you. Try to defend against each attack at the moment of impact, but keep an eye on your HP Bar. Remember to use a Mushroom sticker if you take too much damage.

As the battle continues, use Hopslippers to deal reliable damage to your wilting opponent. When the Megasparkle Goomba's HP Bar is completely empty, a single Goomba summons up the strength for one more round. Use a Jump sticker to defeat the Megasparkle Goomba once and for all.

After you defeat the Megasparkle Goomba, collect the Royal Sticker to exit the Course.

HOW TO USE THIS GUIDE
HOW TO PLAY
STICKERS
ENEMIES
WALKTHROUGH
DECALBURG
SURFSHINE HARBOR
WORLD 1
WORLD 2
WORLD 3
WORLD 4
WORLD 5
WORLD 6
CHECKLISTS

TIP

If you combine the Scissors with a Fan Thing Sticker, you can deal massive damage to the Megasparkle Goomba! For this method to be effective, however, you must use these Thing Stickers after the enemy turns around, revealing the individual Goombas that form the Megasparkle Goomba. There's no way to predict when this will happen, but consider bringing a Fan sticker in case the opportunity presents itself.

Recommended Visit #2

After you gain access to the World 3-6 Sticker Shop, purchase a Secret Door sticker and return to the eastern wall. Apply the sticker to the marked location, then head through the door to find the Squirt Gun.

Thing: Squirt Gun

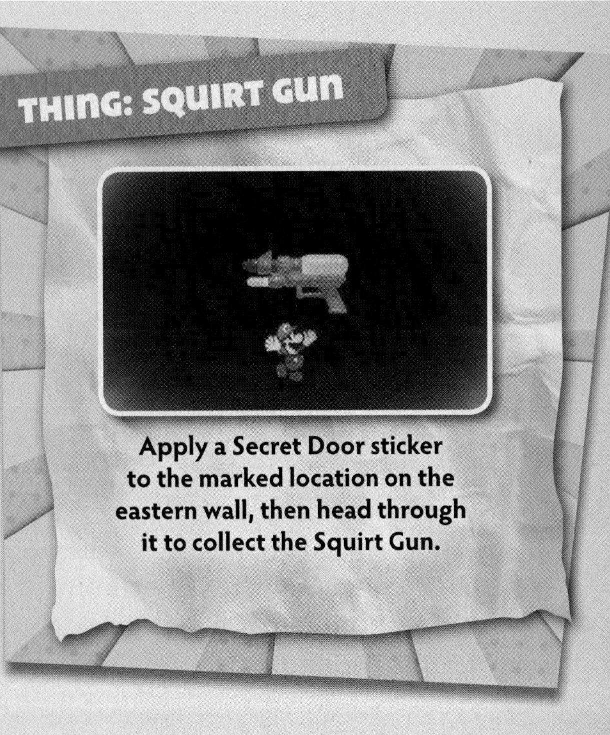

Apply a Secret Door sticker to the marked location on the eastern wall, then head through it to collect the Squirt Gun.

HOW TO USE THIS GUIDE

HOW TO PLAY

STICKERS

ENEMIES

WALKTHROUGH

DECALBURG

SURFSHINE HARBOR

WORLD 1

WORLD 2

WORLD 3

WORLD 4

WORLD 5

WORLD 6

CHECKLISTS

WORLD COURSES

NUMBER	NAME
World 2-1	Drybake Desert
World 2-2	Yoshi Sphinx
World 2-3	Sandshifter Ruins
World 2-4	Damp Oasis
World 2-5	Drybake Stadium

World Two is filled with arid deserts, flowing quicksand, and crumbling ruins. As you explore each Course, you'll find a few new foes peppered among familiar enemies. These new creatures are fairly durable, so adjust your tactics accordingly. Take advantage of the Battle Spinner, and look for the increasingly common shiny stickers scattered throughout most Courses.

There's a Royal Sticker waiting in the ancient Drybake Stadium, but you'll have to defeat the Tower Power Pokey before you can claim it!

NOTE

World Two contains three Tablet Piece scraps. Before you can reach the Tower Power Pokey, you must collect all three scraps.

WORLD 2-1: DRYBAKE DESERT

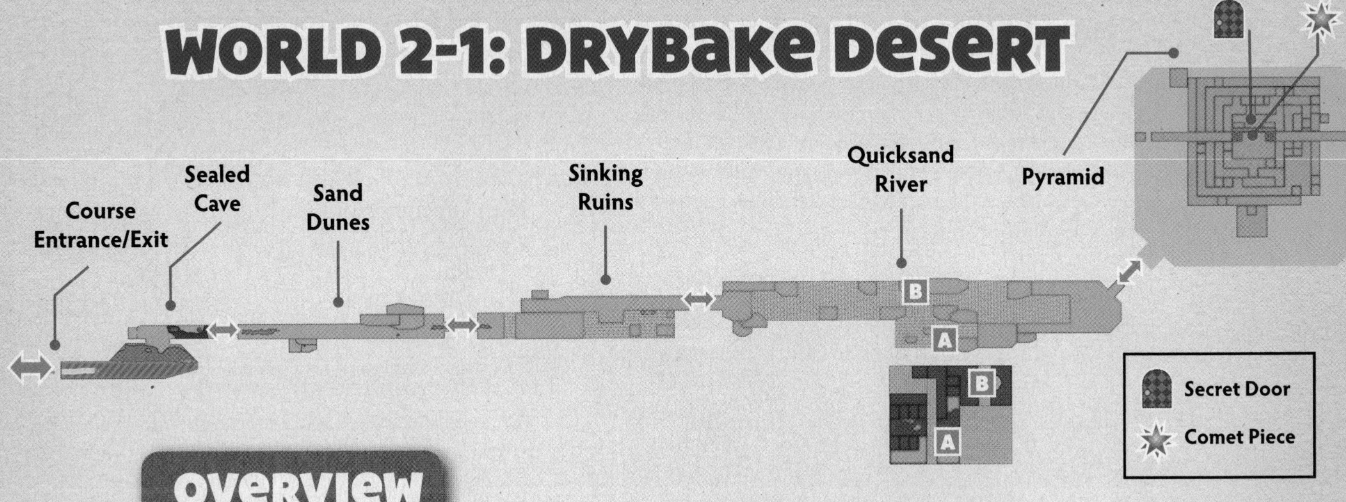

OVERVIEW

PREREQUISITES

This Course is available as soon as you leave Decalburg. Make sure your Album contains the stickers needed to open the sealed cave: Jump, Hammer, Mushroom, Poison Mushroom, Spike Helmet, and Fire Flower (or Ice Flower).

Once again, you must revisit this Course after you acquire a Secret Door.

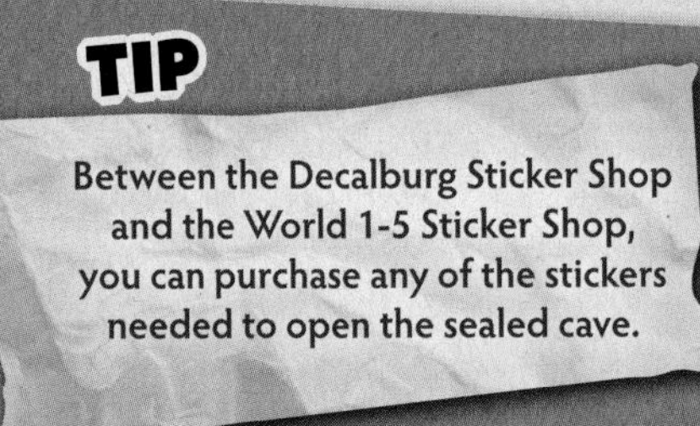

TIP

Between the Decalburg Sticker Shop and the World 1-5 Sticker Shop, you can purchase any of the stickers needed to open the sealed cave.

NOTE

This Course contains the first available Tablet Piece scrap. Although clues to the scraps' locations aren't introduced until later Courses, you can collect the scrap during your first visit.

OBJECTIVES

This Course contains several objectives, most of which can be completed during your first visit:

- **Open the sealed cave.**
- **Rescue the bullied Toad.**
- **Collect the Big 1UP sticker.**
- **Collect the first Tablet Piece.**
- **Collect the Soda.**
- **Collect the HP-Up Heart.**
- **Collect the Comet Piece to unlock World 2-2.**
- **Collect the Car Battery from the Secret Door.**

IMPORTANT ITEMS AND LOCATIONS

DESCRIPTION	NOTES
Secret Door	The marked location is at the top of the pyramid.
HP-Up Heart	The HP-Up Heart is on a platform near the pyramid.
Toad Rescue	The bullied Toad is on a platform among the sand dunes.
Luigi Location	None
Wiggler Diary Entry	None
Things	The Soda is near the end of the quicksand river. The Car Battery is through the Secret Door.

WORLD 2-1

Recommended Tactics

This Course contains some new enemies, but the most dangerous addition is the Sombrero Guy. This devious enemy uses music to heal his allies or increase their attack power. A Sombrero Guy will jump into any and all nearby battles, so it's best to deal with these enemies as soon as you spot them.

Swoops are airborne enemies, making them immune to many stickers. Use Jump-based stickers to deal with these fast-moving enemies, or select a Spike Helmet and take care of them while you defend yourself from their attacks.

You're bound to face some diverse groups of enemies, so you'll want to keep a variety of stickers in your Album. Jumps and Hammers can be combined to overcome most groups—especially if you take advantage of the Battle Spinner—but you'll want to bring a few Hopslippers, Slaphammers, and Spike Helmets.

TIP

Green Pokeys are vulnerable to most attacks, but yellow Pokeys are covered with dangerous spikes. Keep your Album stocked with plenty of Hammer-based stickers.

SEALED CAVE

To open the doors to the sealed cave, you must apply the six stickers indicated by the markings. The left door requires a Jump sticker, a Mushroom, and a Spike Helmet. The right door requires a Hammer sticker, a Poison Mushroom, and a Fire Flower (or Ice Flower).

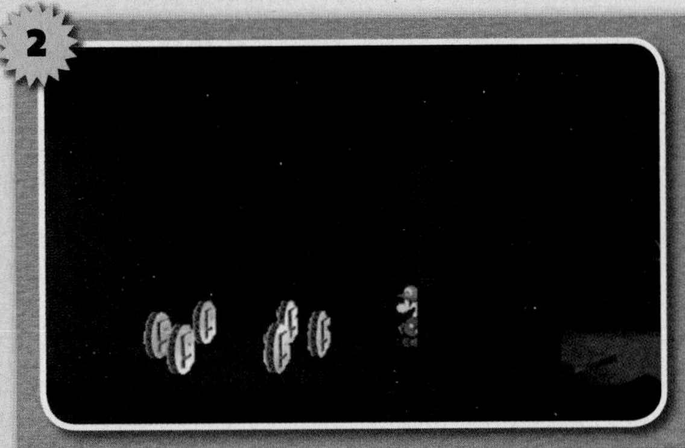

When you enter the cave, look for the hidden area to the left. Head through the small opening in the wall to find a stash of coins.

One of the ? Blocks in the cave is floating just out of reach. Jump into the tube at Point 3 to discover a secret passage. Follow the coins up the ramp, then jump through the panel above you.

When the panel lands, hop on and use it to reach the ? Block.

Sand Dunes

Sombrero Guys don't attack on their own, but they'll join in any battle that takes place near them. These enemies not only make combat considerably more difficult, they often flee from battle before you finish them off. When you spot a Sombrero Guy, it's almost always best to deal with him then and there.

There's a cluster of hidden platforms at Point 2. Look for the fences along the edge of the main path, then drop down to find a ? Block.

3

Before you initiate the Toad rescue, look for the Sombrero Guy hiding behind the rocks at Point 3. Make sure you eliminate this lurking enemy before you pick another fight.

If you completed the Toad rescue in World 1-2, you'll find some Paragoombas bullying a Toad at Point 4. You can either defeat them in battle or pay them 25 coins to walk away. Make your choice and complete the rescue. The grateful Toad rewards you with a Shiny Mushroom sticker before heading off for his next adventure.

HOW TO USE THIS GUIDE
HOW TO PLAY
STICKERS
ENEMIES
WALKTHROUGH
DECALBURG
SURFSHINE HARBOR
WORLD 1
WORLD 2
WORLD 3
WORLD 4
WORLD 5
WORLD 6
CHECKLISTS

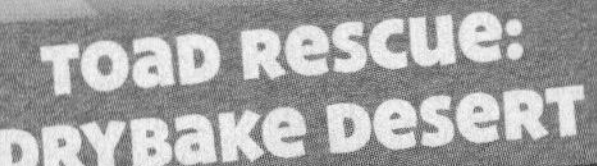

The second available Toad rescue takes place on a platform among the sand dunes of World 2-1. Pay the Paragoombas 25 coins to stop bullying the Toad, or engage them in battle. If you choose to fight, the enemies combine into a 5-Fold Paragoomba. This enemy has a fairly large HP Bar, but a couple of Hopslippers should end the battle without issue.

Sinking Ruins

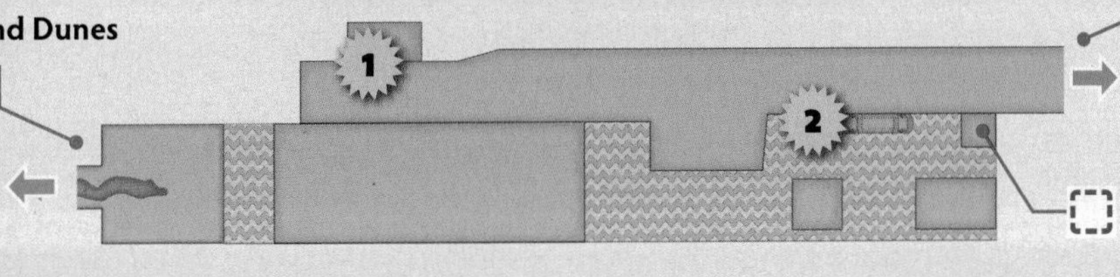

There's a hidden stash of coins at Point 1! Peel the Bowser tape from the structure to clear the panel from the opening.

Caution

Beware of the quicksand patches located throughout the area! Keep jumping to prevent yourself from sinking into this unstable terrain.

In addition to the ? Block and Hidden Block at Point 2, there's a shiny sticker behind the toppled column. To collect it, stand near the column and allow yourself to sink into quicksand. When you're low enough, slip into the alcove and peel the sticker from the back wall. Once you have the sticker, resume jumping to climb back out of the quicksand as you exit the alcove.

QUICKSAND RIVER

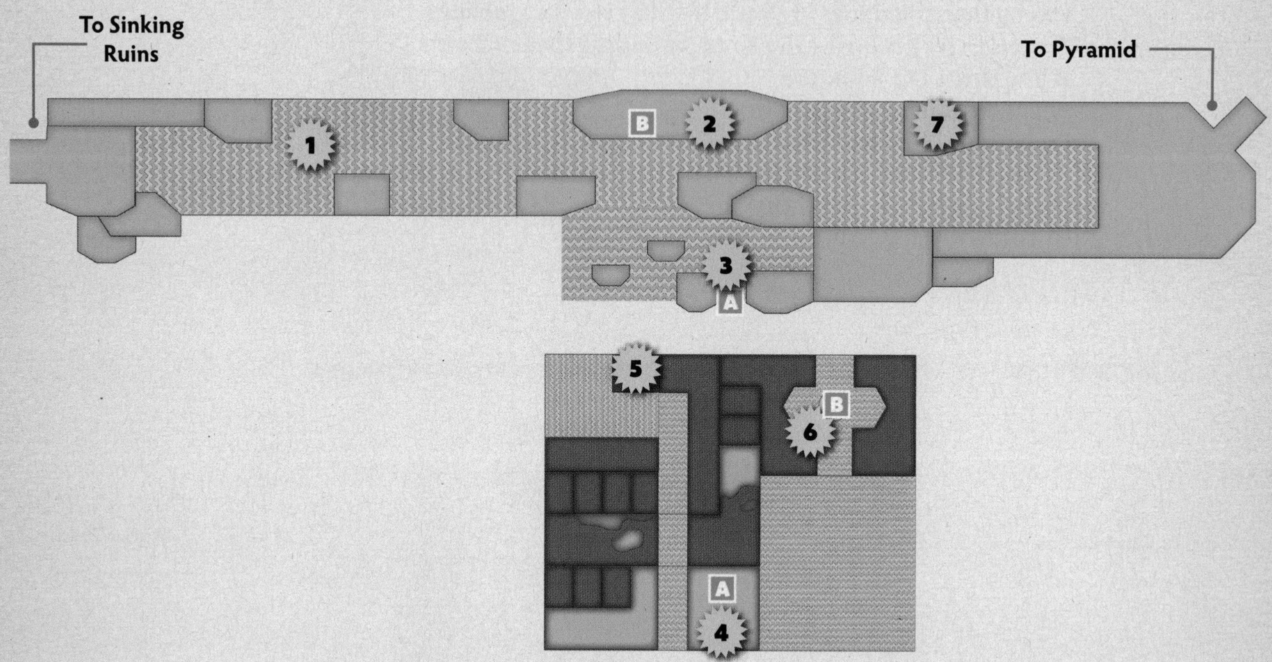

As you fight the current of the quicksand river, try to avoid the Pokeys flowing toward you—a Sombrero Guy is likely to join any battle you initiate. The platforms along the path offer relatively safe spots to catch your breath, but continue to dodge incoming Pokeys.

When you reach the top of the hill, slip through the small gap at the center of the rock formation to find a hidden area.

Collect the coins on the ground, then search the ? Block to find the Big 1UP sticker.

After you leave the hidden area, move toward the foreground to find a hidden series of platforms. As you explore the area, look for the two platforms holding striped cacti. Jump into the stream of quicksand between the cacti, move into the foreground, and allow yourself to sink into the quicksand to find a hidden chamber.

When you land, search the ? Blocks to the right, then head up the stairs to the left. There are several useful items in the chamber, so take the time to fully search the area. You find a few Pokeys in your path. Try to initiate each battle with a Hammer strike.

Follow the path up to the top of the area and locate the chest at Point 5. Open the chest to find the first Tablet Piece scrap, then move across to the chamber's right wall.

When you're ready, hop onto the sand geyser to return to the main path.

As you continue along the quicksand river, move toward the background. Collect the Soda from the platform near the bottom of the slope, search the area for any remaining stickers, and continue to the pyramid.

THING: SODA

The Soda is near the end of the quicksand river. Collect it from the platforms near the bottom of the decline.

PYRAMID

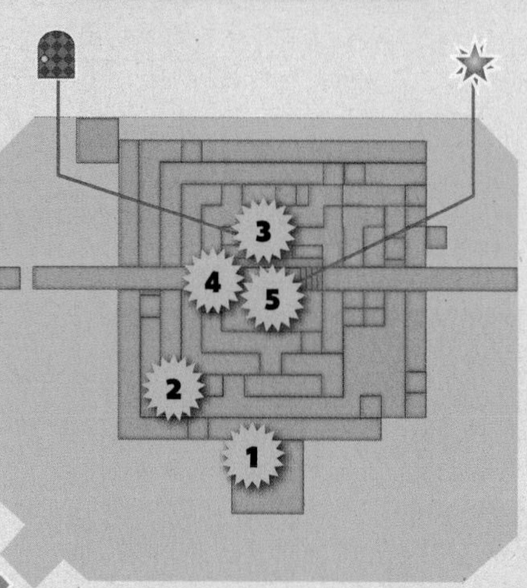

Before you begin climbing the pyramid, search the surrounding area for stickers. When you're ready, use the platforms at Point 1 to begin your ascent.

The pyramid is essentially a series of ledges and platforms, many of which are too tall for you to reach. To climb the pyramid, you must find the shorter platforms scattered around the structure. When there aren't any accessible platforms in sight, move to the other half of the pyramid.

As you move along the north side of the pyramid, look for the Secret Door location behind the Sombrero Guy near the top of the structure. After you acquire a Secret Door sticker, return to the area and apply it to the marked location.

The Comet Piece is at the top of the pyramid, but don't collect it just yet. Hop on the ramp to the left and slide down the side of the structure.

When you land, look for the HP-Up Heart on the platform to the left.

HP-UP HEART: DRYBAKE DESERT

Climb to the top of the pyramid, then slide down the ramp to the left. After you land, jump over the gap to the left and collect the HP-Up Heart.

5

When you're finished exploring the area, return to the top of the pyramid and collect the Comet Piece.

STICKER COMET PIECE: UNLOCKING WORLD 2-2

This Course contains only one piece of the Sticker Comet. To unlock World 2-2, simply collect the Comet Piece at the end of World 2-1.

RECOMMENDED VISIT #2

After you gain access to the World 3-6 Sticker Shop, purchase a Secret Door sticker and return to the pyramid. Climb to the Sombrero Guy near the top of the structure. Clear the enemy out of your way, then apply the sticker to the marked location. Pass through the door and collect the Car Battery.

THING: CAR BATTERY

Apply a Secret Door sticker to the marked location near the top of the pyramid, then head through it to find the Car Battery.

WORLD 2-2: YOSHI SPHINX

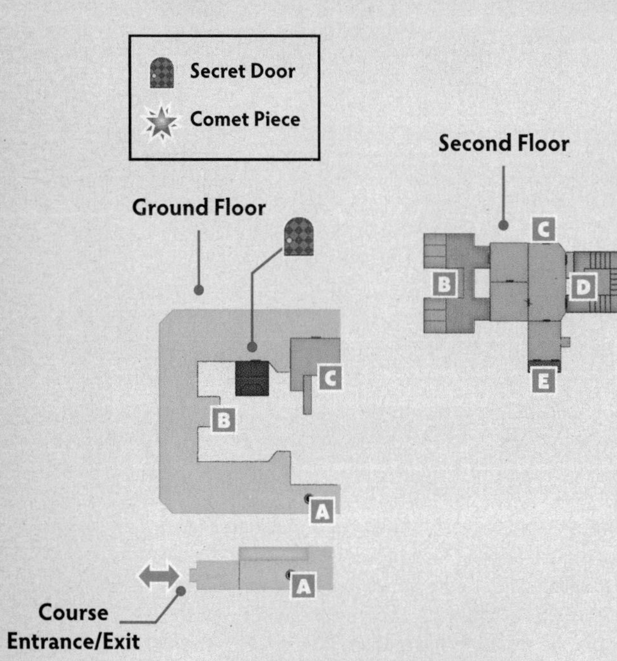

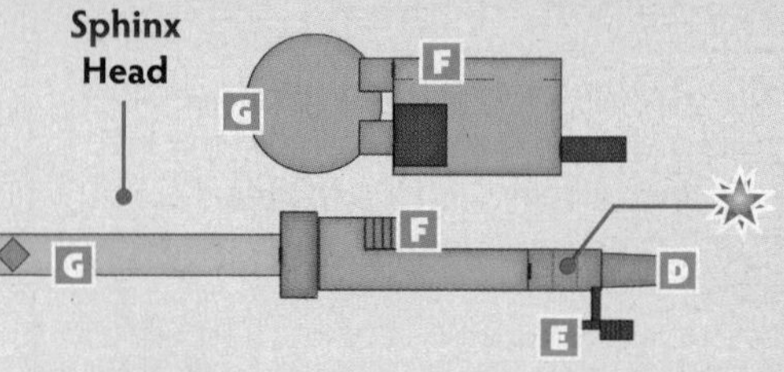

IMPORTANT ITEMS AND LOCATIONS

DESCRIPTION	NOTES
Secret Door	The marked location is on the ground floor, on the north edge of the sphinx.
HP-Up Heart	The HP-Up Heart is on the sphinx's north side, on the right rear foot.
Toad Rescue	None
Luigi Location	None
Wiggler Diary Entry	None
Things	The Lightbulb is mounted on a wall inside of the sphinx's head. The Paper Fan is through the Secret Door.

OVERVIEW

PREREQUISITES

This Course becomes available when you collect the Comet Piece from World 2-1. Aside from the Secret Door sticker, everything you need to complete the available objectives can be found in the Course.

OBJECTIVES

This Course contains several objectives, most of which can be completed during your first visit:

- **Collect the Megaflash Hammer sticker.**
- **Gain Access to the sphinx's head.**
- **Collect the HP-Up Heart.**
- **Collect the Lightbulb.**
- **Collect the Tablet Piece scrap.**
- **Collect the Comet Piece to unlock World 2-3.**
- **Collect the Paper Fan from the Secret Door.**

> **NOTE**
>
> This Course contains the second available Tablet Piece scrap.

RECOMMENDED TACTICS

This Course contains plenty of familiar enemies, but you'll find some particularly tough newcomers as well. Keep an eye out for troublesome Sombrero Guys, and try to clear them out of the area before you pick any fights.

Dry Bones are immune to fire damage, so don't bother attacking with Fire Flowers or Burnhammers. If you stomp a Dry Bones before the battle begins, a Shiny Jump should be enough to end the fight. It won't take long for a defeated Dry Bones to recover, however, so it's often best to avoid direct combat.

You also find a few Hammer Bros in this Course. A Hammer Bro can absorb a good amount of damage, so it's very helpful to land a Hammer strike before the battle begins. This allows you to finish a Hammer Bro with a single Hopslipper. If a Hammer Bro has a full HP Bar when the battle starts, consider using the Battle Spinner to earn at least one extra attack.

Paratroopas can be troublesome in battle, particularly when you're facing more than one. These airborne enemies are not only immune to ground attacks, they attack head on, rendering the Spike Helmet useless. Use the Battle Spinner to combine multiple Jump-based stickers or Hurlhammers.

Kamek also makes an appearance in this Course. Thanks to one of his tricks, however, your sticker selection isn't particularly important. Just make sure your Album stays relatively full.

GROUND FLOOR—PART 1

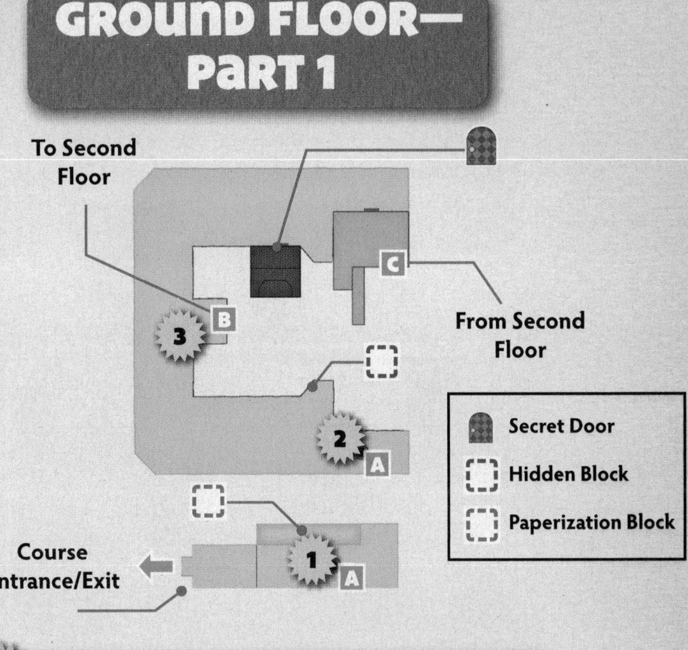

1

The starting area contains some stickers and a Paperization Block. When you're done searching the area, enter the warp pipe at Point 1 to reach the sphinx in the background.

2

After you emerge from the warp pipe, locate the Hidden Block floating above the nearby blue flower. There are plenty of stickers scattered around the area, but there are several enemies as well. As you search for useful items, keep an eye out for incoming Spinies.

WORLD 2-2

TIP

To reach the Shy Guy band and the ? Block on the sphinx's left leg, you must drop down from the second floor.

Before you explore the rest of the ground floor, you'd do well to take care of a couple of particularly sneaky Sombrero Guys. When you reach the front of the sphinx, climb the stairs to the second floor.

Second Floor—Part 1

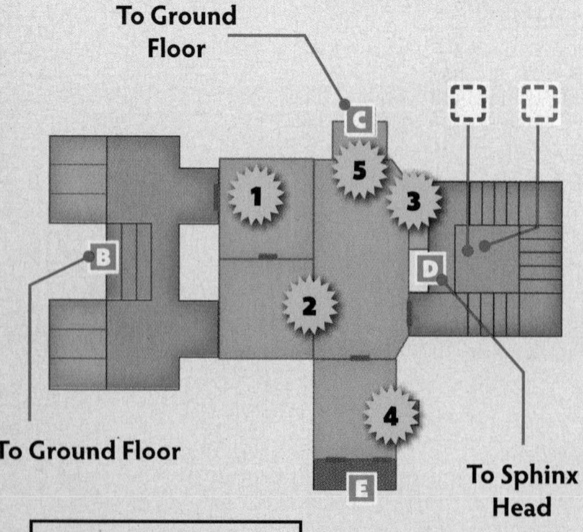

Search the ? Blocks past the steps, then enter the sphinx through the door to the left. The first room is fairly dark. You can activate the unlit torch by hitting it from below, but the Dry Bones on the floor will attack if you linger. Head through the door to the right.

The back wall contains a rotating panel. Move to Point 2, then strike the wall with your Hammer to reveal the path to the central room.

The central room contains a Spiny and a Pokey, but you'll also see a Sombrero Guy peeking out from a hole in the back wall. Before you take on either of the patrolling enemies, make sure you deal with the Sombrero Guy! Run through the door at Point 3, then follow the ramp up to initiate the battle.

After you defeat the Sombrero Guy, continue to the right, then use your Hammer to strike the back of the wall. A panel falls to the ground, making it possible to collect the previously unreachable sticker.

If you're running low on HP, look for the hidden Heart Block at Point 4. Enter the room to the right, then peel the Bowser tape from the back wall. After the panel falls away from the wall, use the Heart Block to top off your HP Bar. The two doors to the right lead to some steps, but you have some work to do before they can be used.

When you're ready, move back across the central room, then pass through the doorway on the left wall to find another Sombrero Guy on a small balcony. Defeat the Sombrero guy, then hop over the railing to drop back down to the ground floor.

Caution

The room the balcony overlooks contains a Dry Bones and two Hammer Bros, all of which are sure to attack you. If you aren't happy with your current sticker selection, you may want to remain on the second floor.

Ground Floor—Part 2

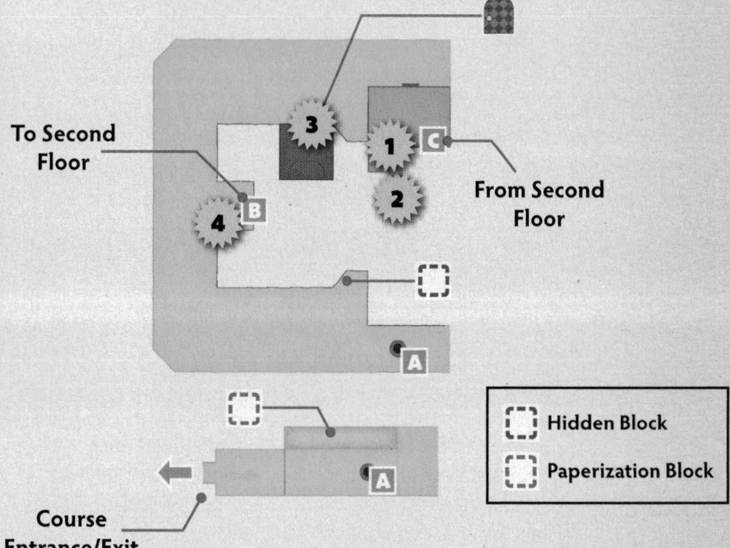

After you jump down from the balcony, you must deal with the Hammer Bros and the Dry Bones on the ground floor. Clear out your attackers, then search the room for useful stickers. Use your Hammer to strike the wall at Point 1. After it falls, head into the secret area below the balcony.

A Hammer Bro lurks in the hidden area, so try to close in before he attacks. After you deal with the enemy, peel the Megaflash Hammer sticker from the wall. This powerful sticker is very rare, so make sure you add it to your Album.

When you're ready, exit the room and head back toward the front of the sphinx to find the Secret Door location. After you acquire a Secret Door sticker, return to this area and apply it to the marked location.

When you're finished exploring the area, return to the front of the sphinx and head back up to the second floor.

SECOND FLOOR—PART 2

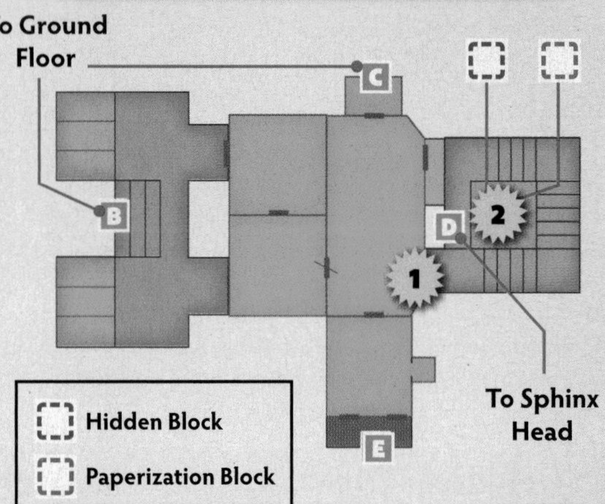

Enter the sphinx and return to the central room. Move behind the column on the room's right side to find a hidden doorway, then follow the path to find a darkened staircase.

When you reach the top of the stairs, activate the torches on the back wall. There's a ? Block floating at the top of the room. To reach it, you must reveal the Paperization Block and the Hidden Block floating just above the central platform. When you're ready, head through the door to the left.

SPHINX HEAD

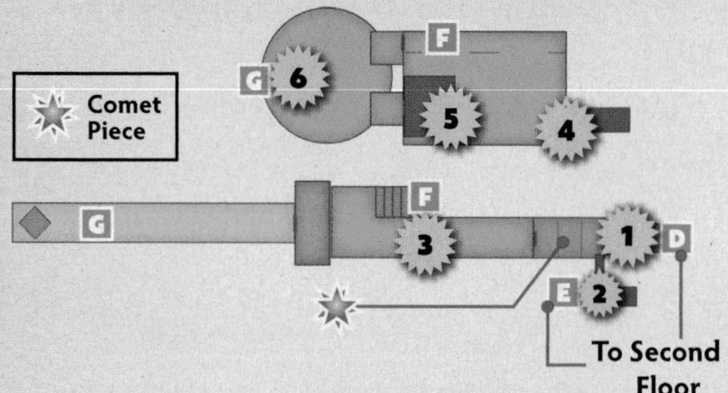

Walk past the Comet Piece and continue toward the background. Drop down from the edge of the sphinx to find the HP-Up Heart on one of the sphinx's legs.

When you leave the staircase, three Paratroopas swoop in and attack. Use the Battle Spinner to earn some extra attacks, then select high-damage Jump stickers to clear out the enemies. After the battle, peel the Bowser tape at Point 1 to reveal a set of stairs. The ledge to the left is too high to hop over, so you must find an alternative route to the Comet Piece and the sphinx's head.

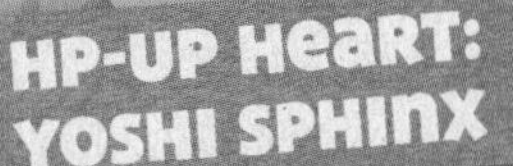

HP-UP HEART: YOSHI SPHINX

Before you collect the Comet Piece, walk toward the background until you drop from the ledge. When you land, collect the HP-Up Heart from the sphinx's foot.

Head back into the staircase and return to the second floor. When you reach the central room, follow the path to the right until you reach the balcony running along the south side of the sphinx. Climb up the stairs, but don't collect the Comet Piece just yet.

Climb back up to the Comet Piece, then follow the path to the left and enter the sphinx's head. Defeat or avoid the Swoops and Dry Bones on your way through the area. When you reach Point 3, look for the Lightbulb mounted on the wall.

CAUTION

There's plenty left to do. Don't collect the Comet Piece until you're ready to leave the Course!

THING: LIGHTBULB

The Lightbulb is in the sphinx's head, mounted in place of a torch. To collect it, move under the fixture and hit it until the Lightbulb comes loose.

Climb the stairs to the next floor, then continue moving right to find a few enemies patrolling what seems to be an empty room. Use your Hammer to strike the loose panel on the wall to the right, then enter the hidden area to find some ? Blocks.

Cross to the room's left side, then strike the wall with your Hammer to knock it over.

Using the toppled wall as a ramp, approach the arches to the left. These panels are actually the sphinx's eyes! Use your Hammer to knock them loose, then step through the openings and onto the sphinx's nose.

Now it's time to take a leap of faith. Walk to the edge of the sphinx's nose, then drop down to land on the tongue below you. After you land, take a moment to sort your Album, and try to remember the stickers on your current page. When you're ready, approach the nearby treasure chest to initiate a battle with Kamek.

Sticker Comet Piece: Unlocking World 2-3

This Course contains only one piece of the Sticker Comet. To unlock World 2-3, simply collect the Comet Piece at the end of World 2-2.

Mini-Boss: Kamek

When the battle begins, Kamek uses magic to transform all of your stickers into Sandals! Each sticker maintains its original size and quality, but all of the other properties are changed. The effect wears off when the battle ends, so avoid using your rare stickers at this time.

Higher-quality stickers do more damage, so if you have shiny stickers to spare, consider using them. If you press Ⓐ each time the spark appears, you can land up to five hits with a single Sandal. If you earn extra attacks with the Battle Spinner, you can deal significant damage during your first turn.

After you defeat Kamek, open the chest to claim the second Tablet Piece scrap. Once the scrap is in your Album, the tongue retracts into the sphinx.

As the battle continues, Kamek uses his broomstick to move out of your effective range. When this happens, select a low-quality sticker and wait for him to move back into range.

Kamek has a variety of attacks, so it's important to stay on your toes. Block each attack just before the impact to minimize the damage you take. Depending on the attack, a successful defense might even grant a new sticker. Protect yourself, and chip away at Kamek's HP Bar until you defeat him.

Ride the tongue back into the sphinx's head. Search the ? Block on the ledge, then drop and follow the path to the right to return to the Comet Piece. When you're ready, collect the Comet Piece to exit the Course.

Recommended Visit #2

After you gain access to the World 3-6 Sticker Shop, purchase a Secret Door sticker and apply it to the marked location on the ground floor, along the north edge of the sphinx. Head through the door to find the Paper Fan.

Thing: Paper Fan

After you acquire a Secret Door sticker, apply it to the marked location along the sphinx's north edge. Pass through the door to find the Paper Fan.

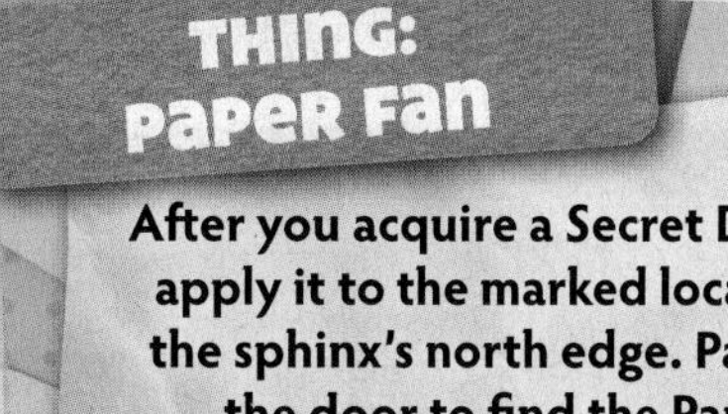

WORLD 2-3: SANDSHIFTER RUINS

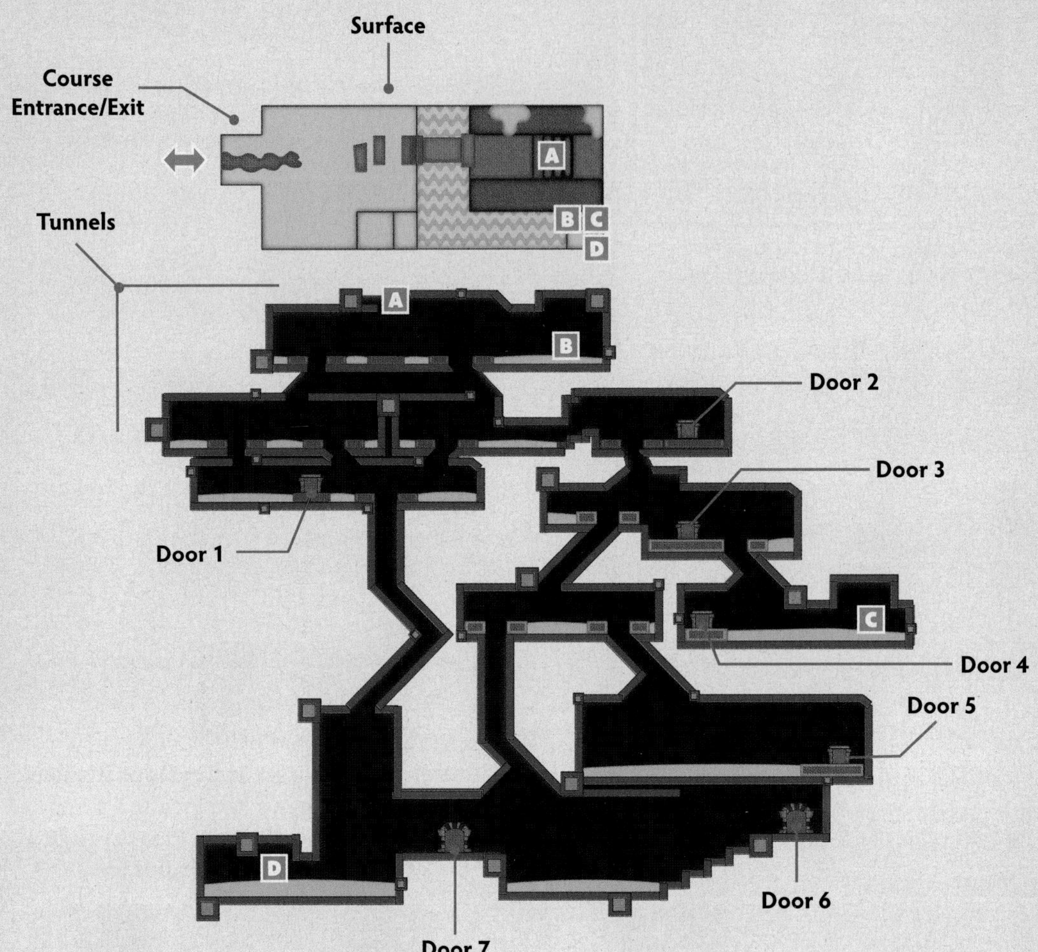

OVERVIEW

PREREQUISITES

This Course becomes available when you collect the Comet Piece from World 2-2. Aside from the Secret Door sticker, everything you need to complete the available objectives can be found in the Course.

OBJECTIVES

This Course contains several objectives, a few of which require additional visits to complete:

- **Collect the Jackhammer.**
- **Collect the Magnifying Glass.**
- **Collect the HP-Up Heart.**
- **Collect the Bat.**
- **Collect the Comet Piece to unlock World 2-5.**
- **Collect the Comet Piece to unlock World 2-4.**
- **Collect the Lighter from the Secret Door.**

IMPORTANT ITEMS AND LOCATIONS

DESCRIPTION	NOTES
Secret Door	The marked location is through Door 4 (or Door 5).
HP-Up Heart	The HP-Up Heart is in a sarcophagus through Door 3.
Toad Rescue	None
Luigi Location	None
Wiggler Diary Entry	None
Things	The Jackhammer is near the geyser to the left of Door 7. The Magnifying Glass is in a sarcophagus through Door 2. The Bat is through Door 6. The Lighter is through the Secret Door.

This Course can be confusing! Keep your objective in mind as you plot a route through the tunnels. Aside from containing a variety of stickers, each door contains at least one noteworthy item or feature:

- Door 1: One-way passage to Door 3
- Door 2: Magnifying Glass
- Door 3: HP-Up Heart
- Door 4: Secret Door; Lighter; connected to Door 5
- Door 5: Connected to Door 4 (Secret Door; Lighter)
- Door 6: Bat; Comet Piece to unlock World 2-5
- Door 7: Comet Piece to unlock World 2-4

RECOMMENDED TACTICS

The Course is packed with enemies, and the narrow tunnels make it very difficult to avoid most battles. Luckily, you'll find plenty of stickers scattered around each area.

In addition to familiar foes like Paragoombas, Paratroopas, Swoops, and Sombrero Guys, you'll find plenty of Spikes in this Course. Spikes are burly Koopa-like critters that use Spike Balls to attack from a distance. Dodge these attacks, or use your Hammer to knock them out of the air. During the battle, the Spike's behavior determines which stickers you should use. When a Spike is holding its weapon, attack with projectiles or Hammer-based stickers. When a Spike is unarmed, however, Jump-based stickers can also be used.

Most battles involve at least one airborne enemy, so you'll want a reasonable supply of stickers that can reach them. Jump-based stickers and Hurlhammers are very effective, particularly if you take advantage of the Battle Spinner.

WORLD 2-3

The sarcophagi in this Course can actually help you avoid battles! If you lure a Dry Bones in front of a sarcophagus just as you pry the lid off, the impact will prevent the Dry Bones from recovering. Unfortunately, sarcophagi can also contain enemies. Before you open a sarcophagus, make sure you're prepared to defend yourself.

SURFACE

Course Entrance/Exit

To Tunnels

1

2

A

B

C

D

Hidden Block

From Tunnels

Two Spikes guard the bridge at Point 1. They may start attacking before they're in sight, so watch out for incoming Spike Balls. The nearby Sombrero Guy makes early battles more difficult, so don't hold back!

TIP

To reach the ? Block at Point 1, you must first reveal the Hidden Block directly below it.

When you're done searching the area for stickers, use the Heart Block to top off your HP Bar and then follow the stairs down to the tunnels.

TUNNELS

TIP

As you search the tunnels for important items, try to keep track of which doors you've visited. If you make a wrong turn—or if you simply reach the end of your intended route—use one of the tunnel's sand geysers to return to the surface.

HOW TO USE THIS GUIDE
HOW TO PLAY
STICKERS
ENEMIES
WALKTHROUGH
DECALBURG
SURFSHINE HARBOR
WORLD 1
WORLD 2
WORLD 3
WORLD 4
WORLD 5
WORLD 6
CHECKLISTS

DOOR 1

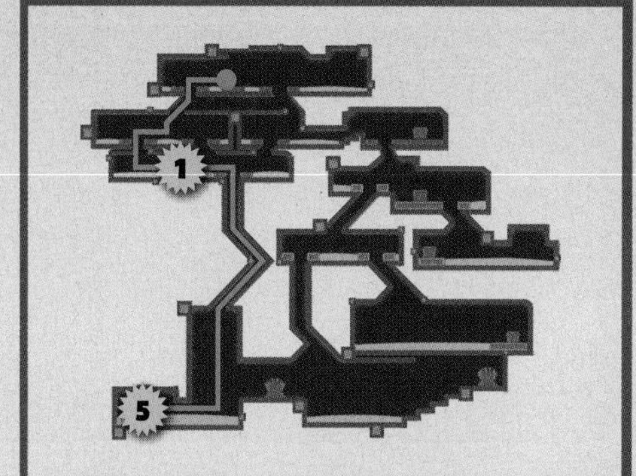

Door 1 is the only door on the left half of the tunnels. It leads to a room that contains a few stickers, a couple of enemies, and a one-way passage leading to Door 3.

The sarcophagus at Point 2 contains a Sombrero Guy, and the Dry Bones heaped on the floor reassembles itself soon after you enter the room. Try to draw the Dry Bones over to Point 2, then open the sarcophagus. As the lid falls to reveal the Sombrero Guy, it also pins the Dry Bones to the ground.

After you search the room for useful items, head through the opening on the right wall.

If you drop down from the ledge at Point 4, you must return to the tunnels through Door 3. During your first visit, however, consider sticking to the left half of the tunnels. Collect the stickers on the wall, then return to Door 1.

After you exit through Door 1, follow the path to the right and drop down through the gap. You land near one of the geysers that return you to the surface. Wait for the geyser to die down, then jump over it to collect the Jackhammer near the wall.

THING: JACKHAMMER

The Jackhammer is in the lower-left corner of the tunnels. To find it, simply make your way down the left half of the tunnels.

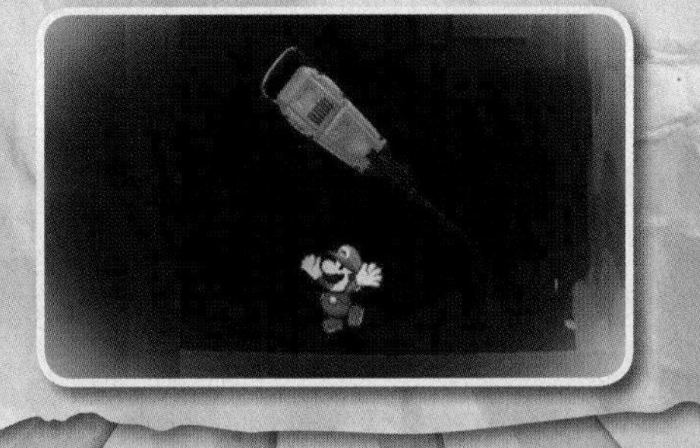

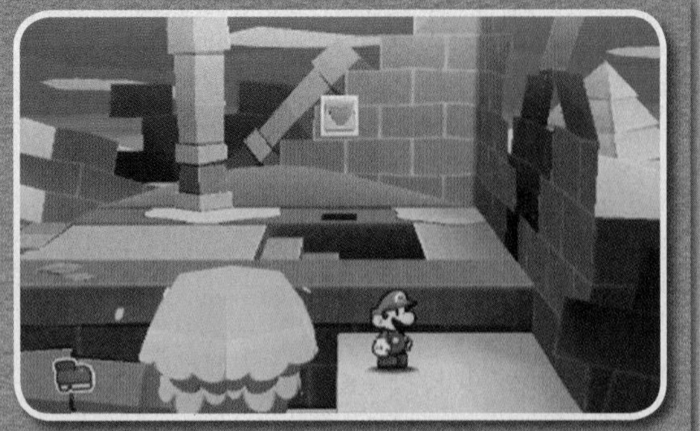

After you collect the Jackhammer, hop onto the geyser and let it carry you to the surface. After you land, use the Heart Block to recover any lost HP, then head back down the stairs.

DOOR 2

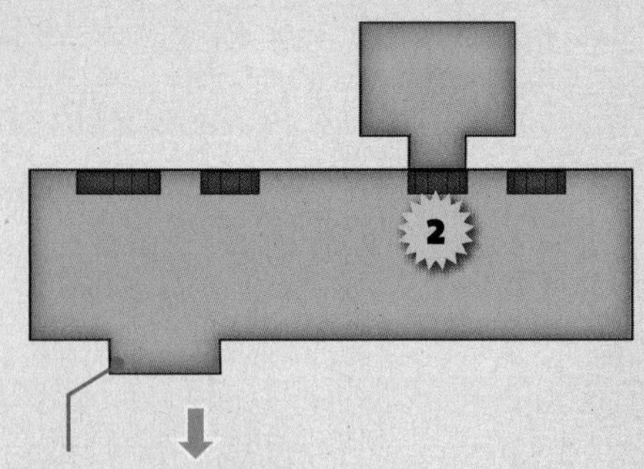

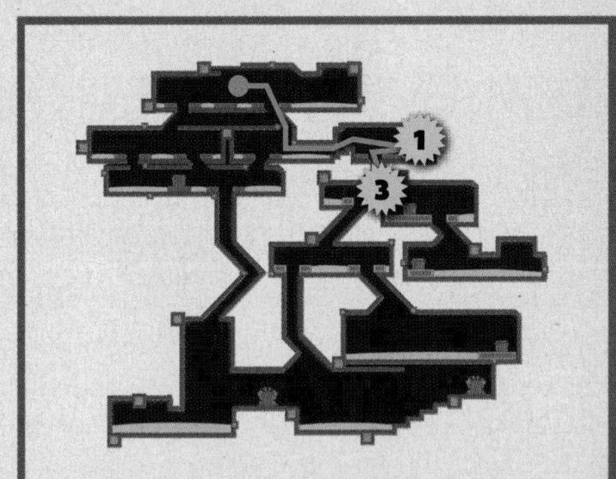

Like most of the tunnel doors, Door 2 is in the right half of the tunnels. This makes it very easy to explore several doors without returning to the surface. Door 2 leads to a room that contains a few stickers, a hidden enemy, and the Magnifying Glass.

The room contains three sealed sarcophagi. The sarcophagus on the left contains a sticker. The sarcophagus on the right contains a Dry Bones. The sarcophagus in the middle, however, contains a hidden area! After you unravel the bandages, step into the sarcophagus to find the Magnifying Glass.

Thing: Magnifying Glass

The Magnifying Glass is in a hidden area. To find it, enter through Door 2, search the middle sarcophagus, and step inside.

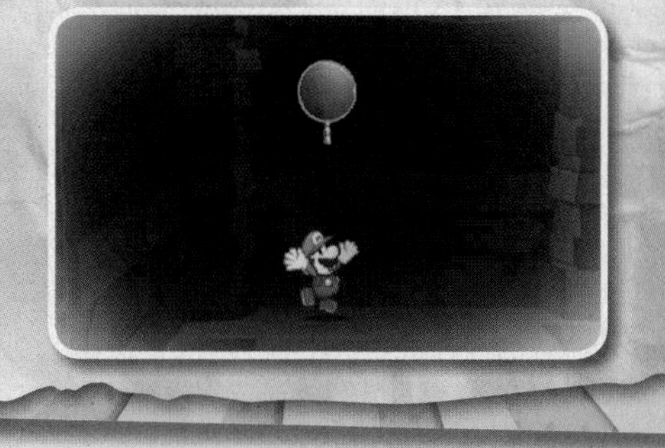

When you're ready, leave the room and return to the tunnels. Drop through the gap to your left to land near Door 3.

Door 3

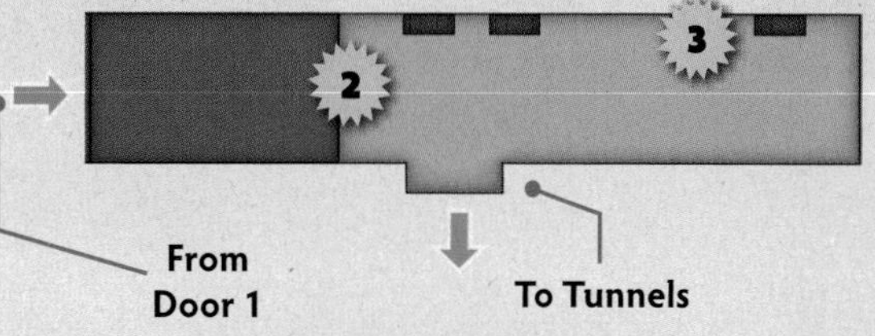

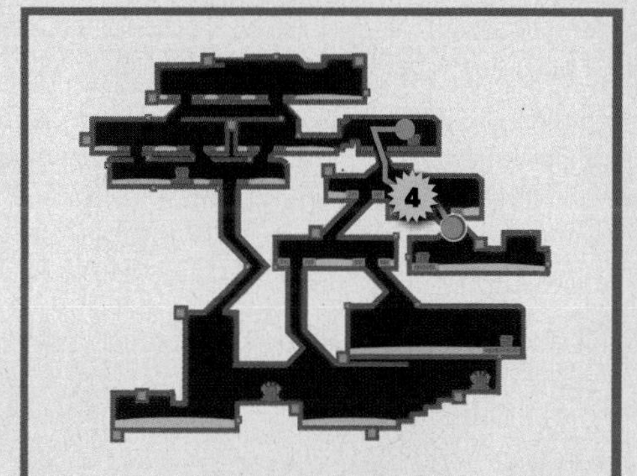

Door 3 is in the right half of the tunnels, just below Door 2. This room contains, among other things, an HP-Up Heart and a one-way passage from Door 1.

Caution

As you approach Door 3, watch out for incoming attacks from the Spike to the right.

Step through the open sarcophagus on the left wall to find the hidden passage from Door 1. The area contains several stickers, so make sure you search it before moving on.

The sarcophagus at Point 3 contains an HP-Up Heart. There are plenty of other items in this room, though, so make sure you search it all.

HP-UP HEART: SANDSHIFTER RUINS

The HP-Up Heart is hidden in a sarcophagus behind Door 3. After you enter the room, search the sarcophagi along the back wall.

When you're ready, leave the room and search the area to the right. Clear out the Spike and search the ? Block to the right, then drop down the nearby gap to land near Door 4.

CAUTION

There's another Spike waiting near your landing spot. Be ready to defend yourself!

DOORS 4 AND 5

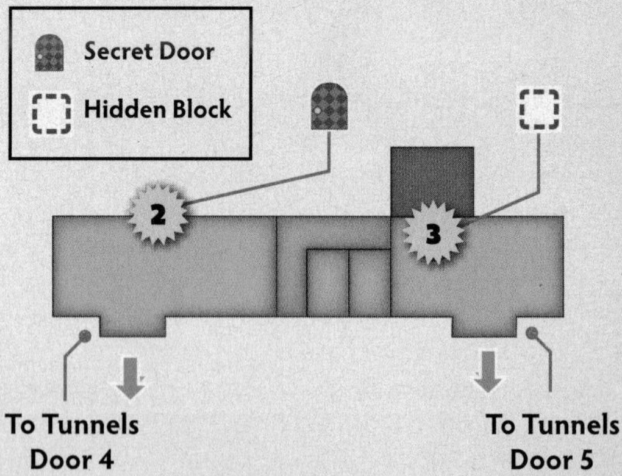

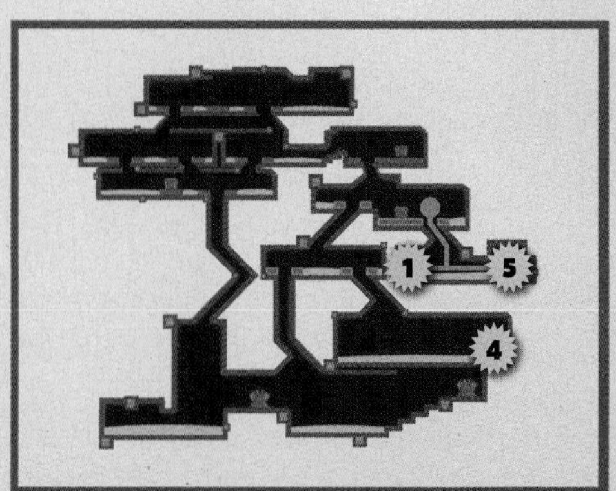

Door 4 is just under Door 3. This room contains the Secret Door location and hidden stash of stickers. Since Door 5 also leads to this room, this area serves as a passage of sorts. The room contains a few enemies, so be prepared to defend yourself!

When you step through Door 4, look for the Secret Door location on the back wall. After you acquire a Secret Door sticker, return to this area and apply it to the marked location.

There's a row of Hidden Blocks on the room's right side. After you find them, climb up the steps and peel the Bowser tape on the rear wall. The loose panel falls away to reveal a stash of stickers.

If you pass through the exit on the room's right side, you emerge from Door 5. A few enemies lurk in the area, but the path leads to a dead end.

After you collect the Course's first Comet Piece, revisit the level and make your way down to Door 7.

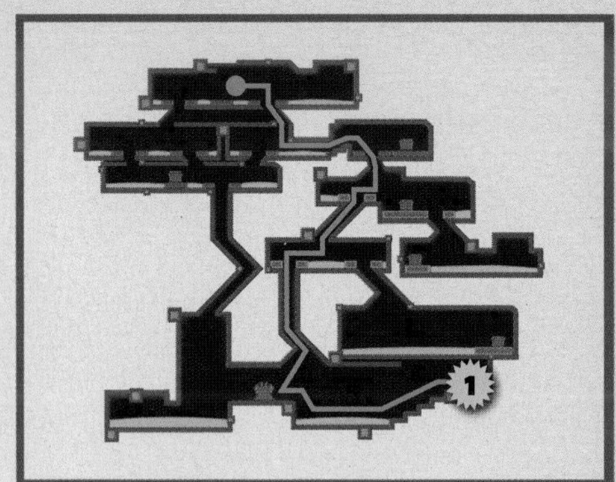

DOOR 6

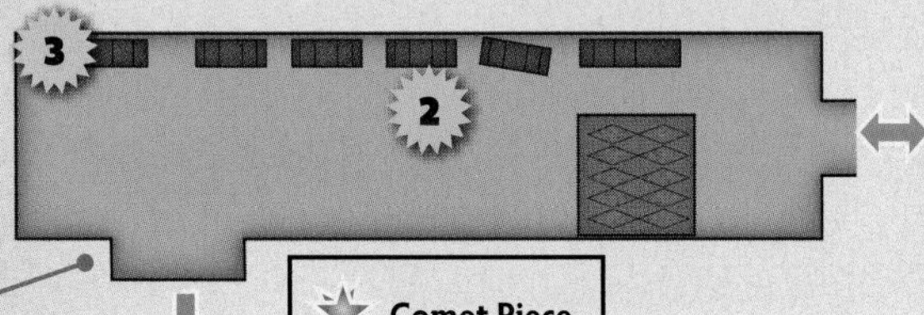

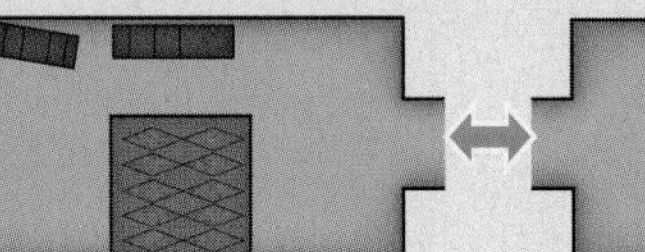

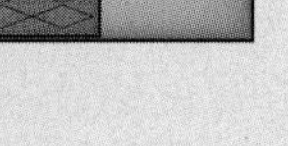

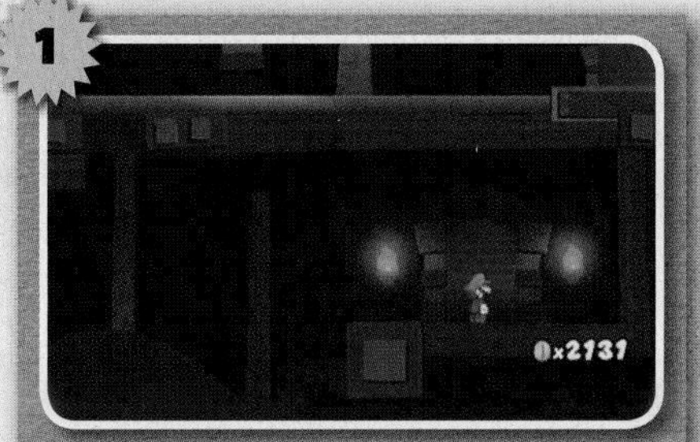

After you explore the room connecting Door 4 and Door 5, it's time to collect the Course's first Comet Piece. Enter the tunnels and make your way down to Door 6. This room contains a few stickers, the Bat, and one of the Course's Comet Pieces.

THING: BAT

To collect the Bat, enter Door 6 and search the sarcophagi along the back wall.

Head through the door and search the sealed sarcophagi along the back wall. The sarcophagus on the right contains a suspiciously thin object. Unravel the bandages to find the Bat.

To get past the spikes, jump onto the toppled sarcophagus near the left wall. Hop along the tops of the sarcophagi until you're safely past the spikes, then continue to the next room.

As you traverse the quicksand, try to avoid the Dry Bones that drop into your path.

When you reach the end of the path, collect the Comet Piece to end your first visit.

ADDITIONAL VISITS

RECOMMENDED VISIT #2

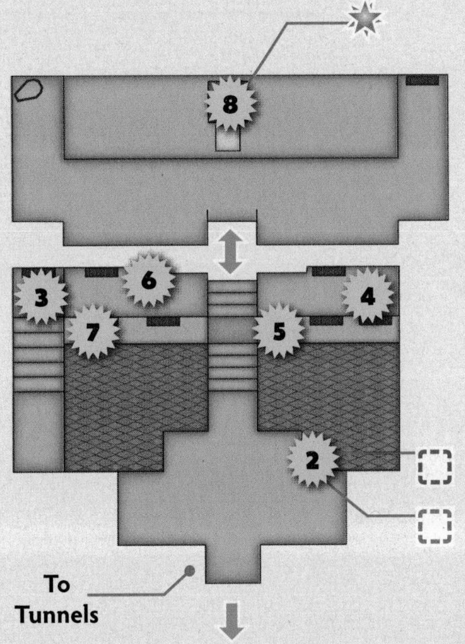

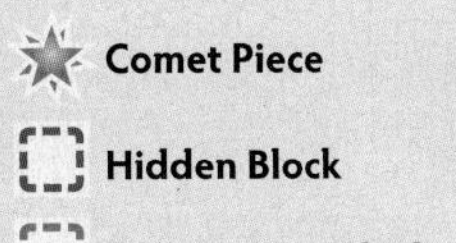

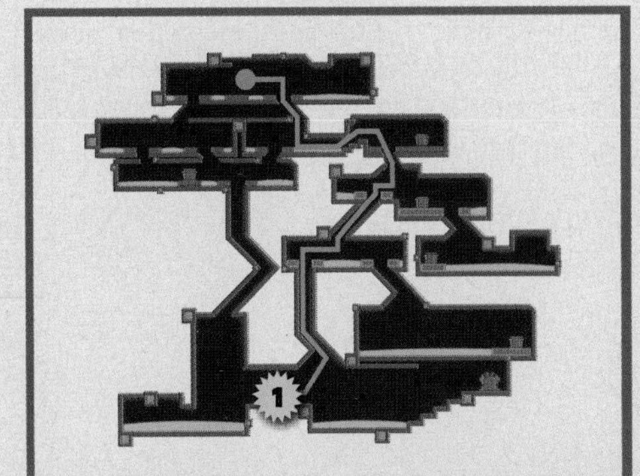

WORLD 2-3

1

Drop back to the tunnels and make your way down to Door 7. This room contains one of the Course's two Comet Pieces.

2

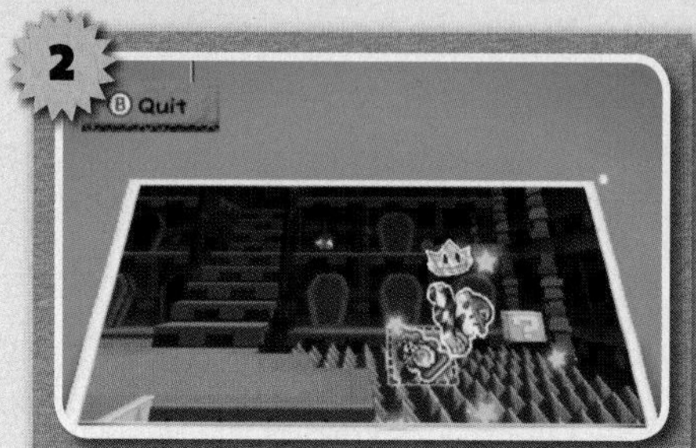

When you first enter the room, there's a ? Block floating above the spikes to the right. Activate the Paperize ability and use a sticker to reveal the nearby Paperization Block. Carefully hop over to the floating ? Block, then jump up to find a flashy sticker inside a Hidden Block.

3

The Comet Piece is floating above a platform at the top of the chamber. Before you can collect it, you must find a way to move the platform into reach. To do that, you must navigate the hidden passages between the room's sarcophagi. Climb to the top of the stairs, then move to the left wall. Move toward the foreground and drop from the ledge. Step into the sarcophagus, then follow the hidden path to the right.

4

The hidden path leads to a sarcophagus to the right of the stairs. Move the lid out of your way and search the area for stickers. When you're ready, hop into the toppled sarcophagus to the right.

5

A hole in the sarcophagus allows you to drop down to the three sarcophagi on the next floor. The sarcophagus to the right contains a Dry Bones, the sarcophagus in the center contains a sticker, and the sarcophagus on the left holds a hidden passage.

6

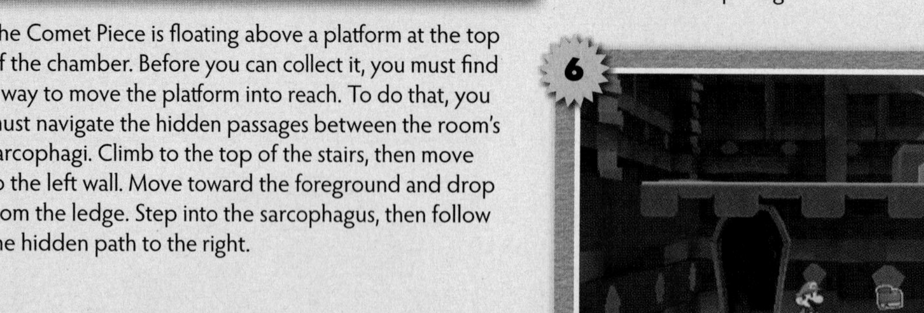

Follow the passage to emerge from a sarcophagus on the left side of the stairs. There's a panel to the right. Peel the sticker on the front of the panel, then slip behind the panel to drop to the next floor.

7

After you land, move left and open the sarcophagus to flood half of the room with sand. This not only covers the spikes to the left of the stairs, it lowers the platform at the top of the chamber.

8

When you're finished exploring the chamber, climb back up the stairs. Hop onto the platform and collect the Comet Piece to exit the Course.

STICKER COMET PIECE: UNLOCKING WORLD 2-4

This Course contains two pieces of the Sticker Comet. To unlock World 2-4, collect the Comet Piece located through Door 7.

RECOMMENDED VISIT #3

After you gain access to the World 3-6 Sticker Shop, purchase a Secret Door sticker, return to the tunnels, and enter Door 4. Apply the Secret Door to the marked location, then head inside to find the Lighter.

THING: LIGHTER

After you acquire a Secret Door sticker, apply it to the marked location through Door 4. Once the sticker is in place, pass through the door to find the Lighter.

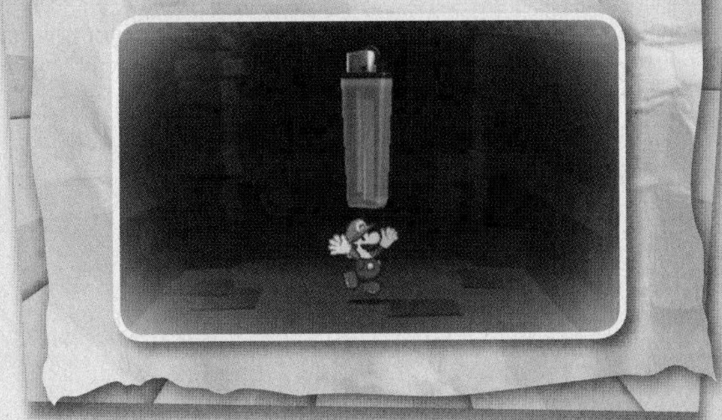

WORLD 2-4: DAMP OASIS

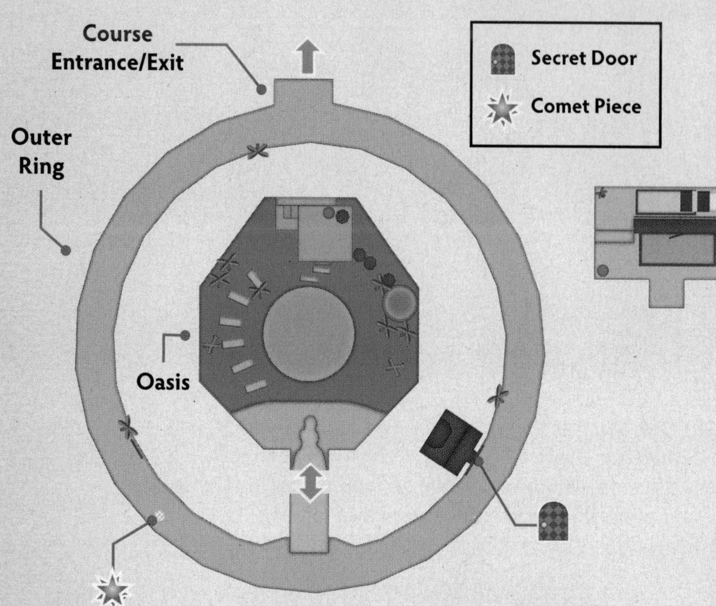

NOTE

This map shows the Course as it appears by the end of your first visit. Although there are some major changes to the environment, the Course layout remains fairly consistent.

OVERVIEW

PREREQUISITES

To unlock this Course, you must collect the corresponding Comet Piece from Door 7 in World 2-3. You'll need to bring a Vacuum sticker and a Faucet sticker to make the most of your first visit. As usual, you must also revisit this Course after you acquire a Secret Door sticker.

ESSENTIAL THING STICKERS

NAME	THING LOCATION	NOTES
Vacuum	Surfshine Harbor	Required to settle the sandstorm.
Faucet	World 1-3	Required to refill the oasis.

NOTE

This Course also contains the third and final Tablet Piece scrap.

OBJECTIVES

This Course contains several objectives, most of which can be completed during your first visit:

- **Settle the sandstorm.**
- **Refill the oasis.**
- **Collect the Tablet Piece scrap.**
- **Collect the Shaved Ice.**
- **Collect the Comet Piece to open a path to World 2-1.**
- **Collect the Hair Shears from the Secret Door.**

IMPORTANT ITEMS AND LOCATIONS

DESCRIPTION	NOTES
Secret Door	The marked location is on the outer ring, near the path to the oasis.
HP-Up Heart	None
Toad Rescue	None
Luigi Location	None
Wiggler Diary Entry	None
Things	The Shaved Ice is on the house near the oasis. The Hair Shears are located through the Secret Door.

Recommended Tactics

This compact Course doesn't contain many hostile creatures, but you will find a few Pokeys patrolling the outer ring.

You have plenty of room to maneuver past the wandering Pokeys, and since this Course doesn't contain any stickers, it's usually best to do so. Still, make sure you bring a few Hammers or Iron Jump stickers in case you stumble into a battle.

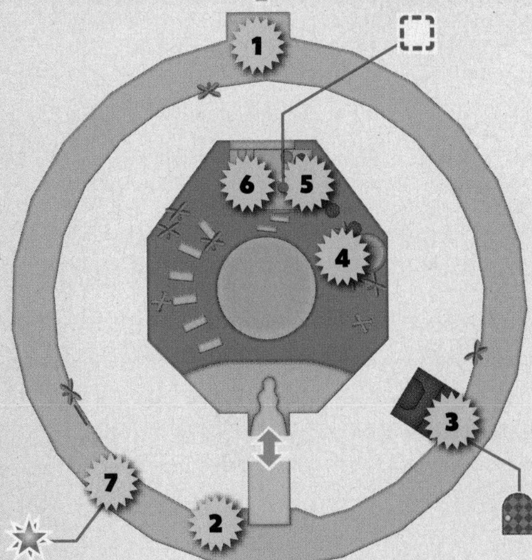

NOTE

The plaque along the outer ring holds a clue about the Tablet Piece scrap in World 2-1.

When you first enter the Course, a whirlwind is causing a violent sandstorm. Move left and follow the outer ring until you find the source of the storm.

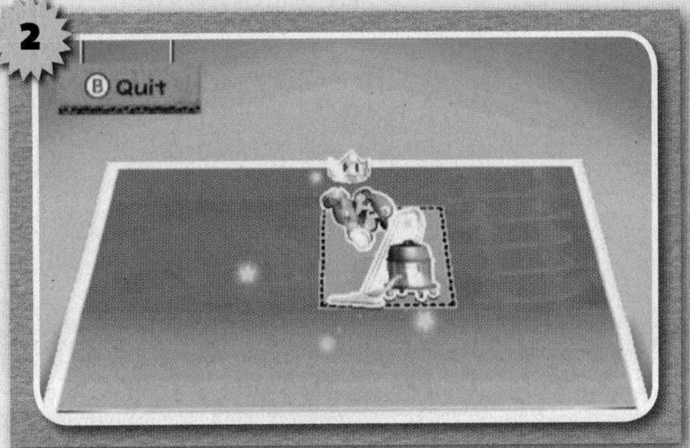

When you reach the whirlwind, locate the large outlet to the left. Activate the Paperize ability ability and apply the Vacuum sticker to the indicated spot.

After the Vacuum settles the sandstorm, the whirlwind falls over and becomes a path to the oasis. Before you head into the oasis, however, locate the Secret Door's marked location along the outer ring. You'll find the Comet Piece just to the left of the outlet, but avoid collecting it until you're ready to leave the Course.

The Secret Door location is on a cluster of rocks at Point 3. After you acquire a Secret Door sticker, return to this area and apply it to the marked location.

The area is in pretty bad shape during your first visit. Approach the large blue jug and activate the paperization ability. Apply the Faucet sticker to the indicated spot. Once the oasis has been restored, enter the nearby house.

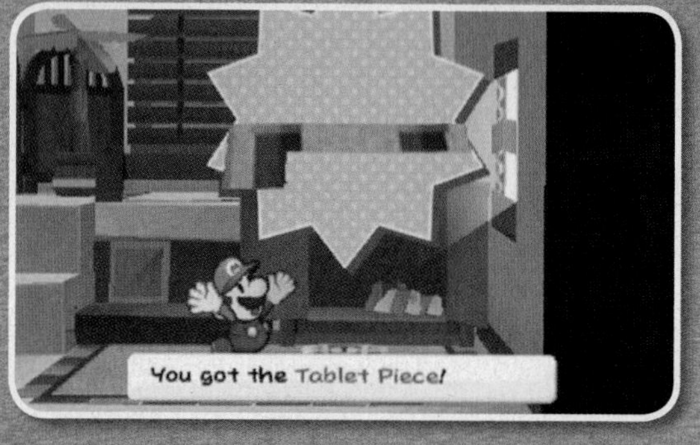

Search the cabinets in the house to find a treasure chest, then open the chest to collect the last Tablet Piece scrap. When you're ready, open the blinds on the back wall and hop out the window.

Follow the walkway to the side of the house, then climb the steps to the roof to find the Shaved Ice. Before you hop down, look for the Hidden Block above the nearby barrel.

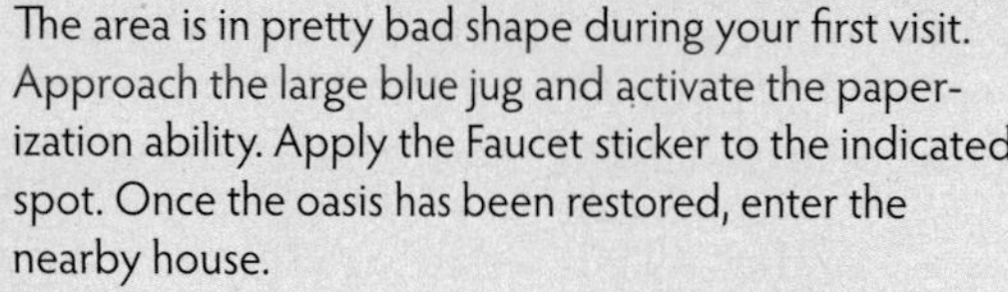

THING: SHAVED ICE

To collect the Shaved Ice, you must refill the oasis, pass through the house, and climb up to the roof.

7

When you're ready, return to the outer ring and follow the path to the left. Collect the Comet Piece to end your first visit.

STICKER COMET PIECE: UNLOCKING THE PATH TO WORLD 2-1

Rather than unlocking a new Course, this Course's Comet Piece unlocks a new path to World 2-1. After you settle the sandstorm, collect the Comet Piece to the left of the outlet.

RECOMMENDED VISIT #2

After you gain access to the World 3-6 Sticker Shop, purchase a Secret Door sticker and apply it to the marked location along the outer ring. Head through the door to find the Hair Shears.

THING: HAIR SHEARS

After you acquire a Secret Door sticker, apply it to the marked location along the outer ring. Open the door and head inside to collect the Hair Shears.

WORLD 2-5: DRYBAKE STADIUM

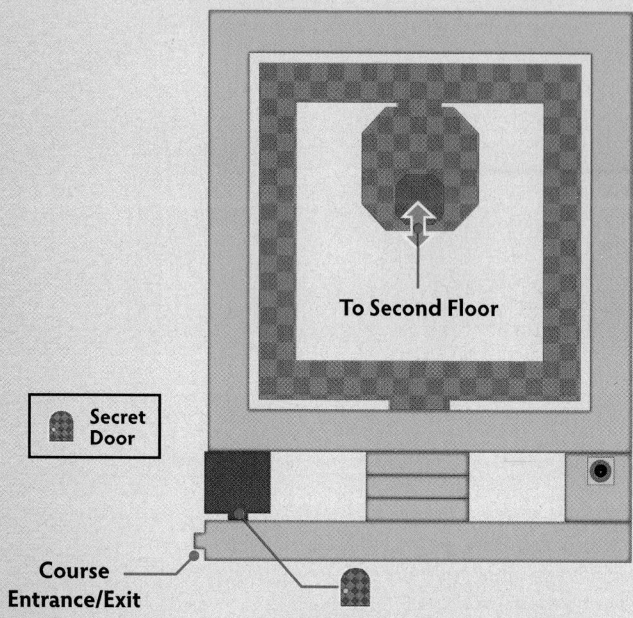

OBJECTIVES

This Course contains several objectives, most of which can be completed during your first visit:

- **Assemble the Tablet Piece scraps.**
- **Solve the first sticker puzzle.**
- **Recover and replace the Stone Entry scrap.**
- **Solve the second sticker puzzle.**
- **Find Luigi.**
- **Clear the path to the warp pipe shortcut.**
- **Reposition the Tower Outer Wall scrap.**
- **Solve the third sticker puzzle.**
- **Defeat the Tower Power Pokey.**
- **Collect the Royal Sticker.**
- **Collect the flashy stickers from the Secret Door.**

OVERVIEW

PREREQUISITES

To unlock this Course, you must collect the corresponding Comet Piece from Door 6 in World 2-3. Before you can accomplish much within the Course, however, you must collect the Tablet Piece scraps from World 2-1, World 2-2, and World 2-4. This Course also contains several sticker puzzles and a boss battle, so make sure you stock up on essential stickers.

ESSENTIAL THING STICKERS

NAME	THING LOCATION	NOTES
Bat	World 2-3	Needed for boss battle.

TIP

Although the Course provides everything you'll need for the sticker puzzles, you might want to bring a few duplicates. Make sure your Album always contains plenty of Jumps and Hammers, as well as a few Spike Helmets, POW Blocks, and Fire/Ice Flowers.

IMPORTANT ITEMS AND LOCATIONS

DESCRIPTION	NOTES
Secret Door	The marked location is at the Course entrance.
HP-Up Heart	None
Toad Rescue	None
Luigi Location	Luigi is on the tower's fourth floor, along the outer walkway.
Wiggler Diary Entry	None
Things	None

RECOMMENDED TACTICS

This Course is packed with enemies, so you'll want to initiate each battle on your own terms. In addition to familiar critters, you'll find some unique enemies like the Mural Goomba, Mural Koopa, and the Royal Sticker–wielding Tower Power Pokey.

The Spikes in this Course tend to appear in groups, so keep plenty of Hammers on hand.

Mural Goombas and Mural Koopas are tougher than their standard counterparts. You'll find the same basic tactics just as effective, as long as you use higher-quality stickers and/or the Battle Spinner.

The Tower Power Pokey uses its spiked segments to counter your Hammer stickers, and its massive HP Bar allows it to absorb a lot of damage. Jump-based stickers, POW Block stickers, and Mushrooms should all prove very useful, but the Bat sticker is the key to an early victory—just make sure you don't use it too early!

GROUND FLOOR

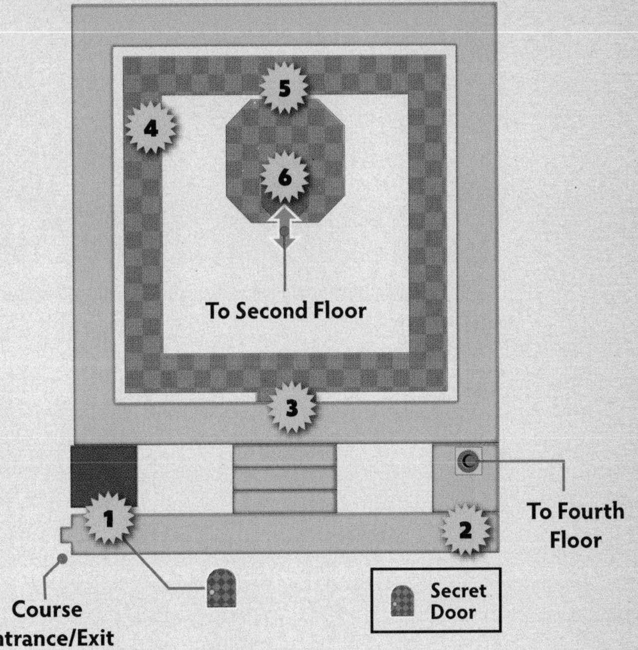

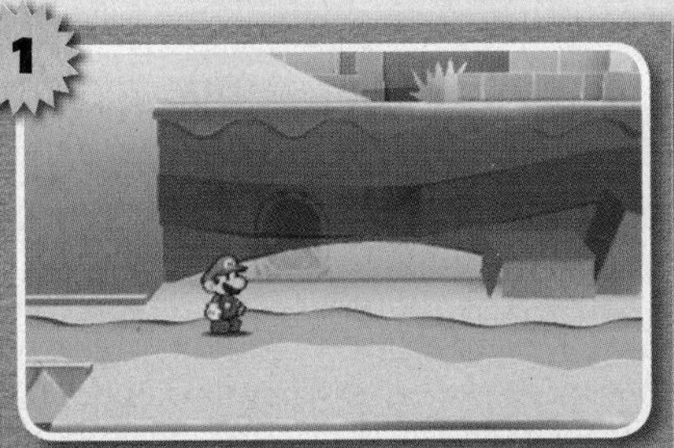

The Secret Door location is just next to the Course entrance/exit. Return to this location after you acquire a Secret Door sticker.

There's a warp pipe hidden behind a panel at Point 2. Before you can access this shortcut, you must enter the warp pipe on the tower's fourth floor and knock the panel loose from the other side.

When you first visit this area, the tower is missing. Approach the marked location at the top of the steps and activate the Paperize ability. Apply the Tablet Piece scraps from World 2-1, World 2-2, and World 2-4 to the indicated areas.

WORLD 2-5

When the cinematic ends, enter the tower and begin your ascent.

Search the ? Blocks near the rear wall, then hop onto the platform and ride up to the second floor.

The tower's first sticker puzzle is on the ground floor. To solve this puzzle, you must decipher the nearby clues. After you clear the enemies from the corridor, examine the murals on the walls. The figure at Point 4 has one arm extended and is holding what looks like a Jump sticker. A figure on the other side of the area is using the opposite arm to hold a Hammer.

SECOND FLOOR

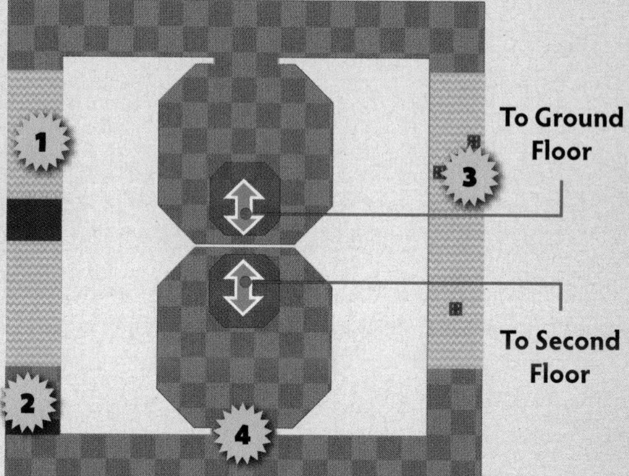

Move to the sealed door at Point 5 and activate the Paperize ability. Apply a Jump sticker to the slot on the left, and place a Hammer sticker in the slot on the right. When both stickers are in place, the door rises to reveal a small chamber.

Step out of the chamber, then move to the right. Follow the corridor around the corner to find one of this floor's quicksand pits. After you search the ? Block at Point 1, move toward the spiked wall and allow yourself to sink into the quicksand. Once you've sunk low enough, slip under the wall and jump back up to the surface.

Continue across the quicksand to find the Stone Entry scrap near two ? Blocks. Collect the scrap and any stickers you find useful, then slip back under the spiked wall and follow the corridor to the other side of the area.

There are three Spikes at the edge of the quicksand, so approach with caution. Deal with these enemies, then continue along the corridor.

When you reach Point 4, activate the Paperize ability. Place the Stone Entry scrap in the indicated spot to reveal a new chamber. When you're ready, enter the chamber and continue to the third floor.

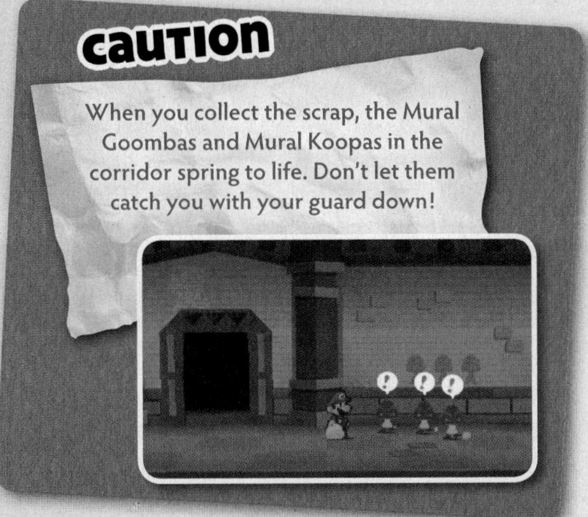

THIRD FLOOR

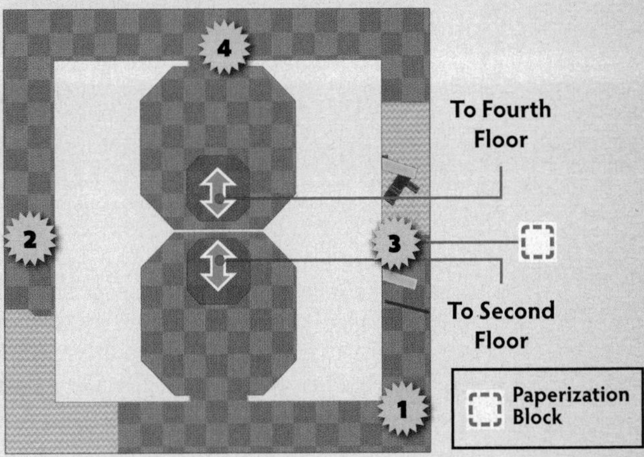

As you approach Point 3, watch out for incoming Spike Balls. As you continue across the quicksand, use your Hammer to knock away the projectiles in your path.

Step out of the chamber and search the area to the right. A small barricade prevents you from continuing along the corridor, but there are some stickers posted on the walls. When you're done, turn back and follow the corridor to the left.

This floor contains another sticker puzzle. As you deal with enemies and explore the area, remember to check the murals for clues.

Make sure you locate the Paperization Block at Point 3. It not only provides the typical rewards, but also it serves as a platform between the damaged pillars.

After you decipher the clues, use them to solve the sticker puzzle at Point 4. Activate the paperization ability, then place a Hammer in the left slot, a Spike Helmet in the middle slot, and a Jump sticker in the right slot. When you're ready, enter the chamber and ride up to the fourth floor.

FOURTH FLOOR

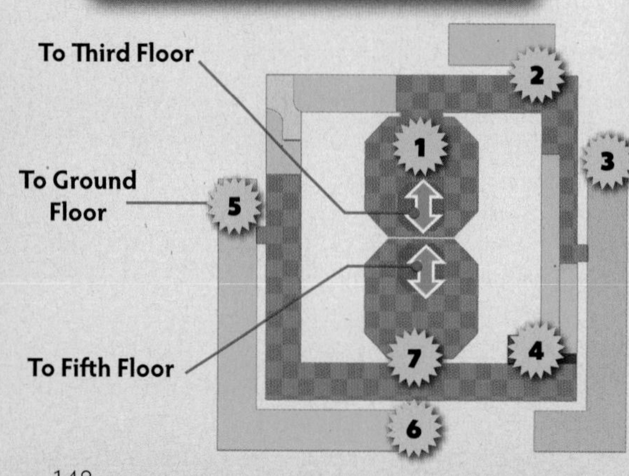

When you reach fourth floor, the chamber is filled with Buzzy Beetles. If you choose to engage one, you'll face all five enemies in a single battle. Stomp one before the battle and kick its shell through its allies, or combine a POW Block with a Line Jump to deal heavy damage to the overturned Buzzy Beetles.

On this floor, most of the important elements are located on the three walkways running along the outside of the tower. As you search the fourth-floor corridor, watch the narrow passages that appear in the foreground. Pass through the opening at Point 2 to find a Parakoopa and a ? Block on the first walkway.

Follow the corridor to the next opening, then search the walkway for stickers. Before you head back inside, move to Point 3. Activate the Paperize ability and pull Luigi out of the window.

HOW TO USE THIS GUIDE
HOW TO PLAY
STICKERS
ENEMIES
WALKTHROUGH
DECALBURG
SURFSHINE HARBOR
WORLD 1
WORLD 2
WORLD 3
WORLD 4
WORLD 5
WORLD 6
CHECKLISTS

LUIGI LOCATION: DRYBAKE STADIUM

Luigi is on the tower's fourth floor, in a window at the end of the second walkway.

After you emerge on the ground floor, use your Hammer to create a path through the enclosure. Once the shortcut is fully functional, use it to return to the fourth floor.

4

When you reach the wall at Point 4, look for the small opening hidden behind the piled sand. Slip through the tiny passage to emerge in the second half of the corridor.

6

Search the rest of the walkway for stickers, then investigate the wall at Point 6. Activate the Paperize ability and peel the Tower Outer Wall scrap off of the wall.

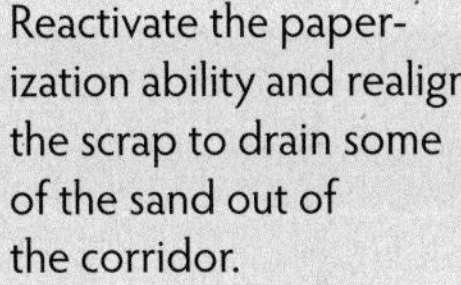

Reactivate the paperization ability and realign the scrap to drain some of the sand out of the corridor.

5

When you reach the third walkway, hop into the warp pipe to the left.

7

Head back into the corridor to find the newly revealed chamber at Point 7. When you're ready, head inside and ride up to the fifth floor.

WORLD 2-5

FIFTH FLOOR

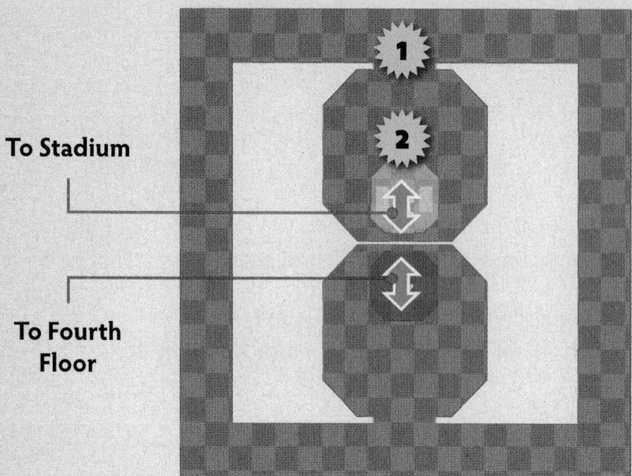

STADIUM

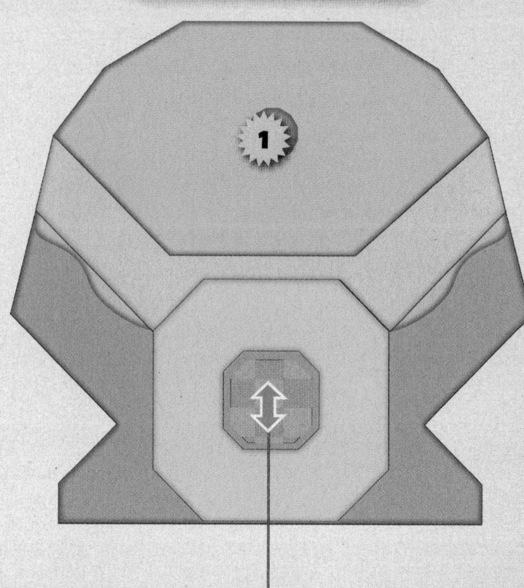

The fifth floor holds the third sticker puzzle. Unfortunately, the surrounding murals contain conflicting clues. Rather than trying sticker combinations until you find the correct one, activate the Paperize ability and place a Fire Flower (or Ice Flower) in the left slot, then place a POW Block sticker in the slot on the right.

After you solve the third sticker puzzle, step into the open chamber. Take care to avoid stepping on the platform until you've used the Heart Block and the Save Block. When you're ready, ride up to the stadium.

When the platform stops, approach the Royal Sticker in the center of the stadium. As you do, the Tower Power Pokey springs out of the ground. If you intend to recover the Royal Sticker, you must defeat this massive enemy.

BOSS FIGHT!

TOWER POWER POKEY

When the battle starts, the Tower Power Pokey sinks back into the ground. Use your more powerful Jump-based stickers—such as Flashy Jumps or Hopslippers—and defend yourself from incoming attacks.

The Tower Power Pokey can dish out significant damage, even if you properly defend yourself. Keep an eye on your HP Bar, and use a Mushroom if it drops too low.

As the battle continues, more and more of the Tower Power Pokey's body segments emerge from the ground. The spikes on each of the four body segments protect the creature from Hammer stickers, so just keep using your Jump attacks. When the entire Tower Power Pokey is exposed, use the Bat sticker to knock all four body segments out of the park.

The creature's head has plenty of fight left, but its HP Bar is now much smaller. TTake advantage of the Battle Spinner to combine POW Blocks with any high-damage stickers in your Album. The Tower Power Pokey can summon allies and recover HP, so make the most of each turn!

After you defeat the Tower Power Pokey, collect the Royal Sticker to complete your first visit.

RECOMMENDED VISIT #2

After you gain access to the World 3-6 Sticker Shop, purchase a Secret Door sticker and revisit this Course. Apply the sticker to the marked location near the Course entrance/exit.

Once the door is in place, head inside to find some ? Blocks. The first time you search them, the ? Blocks contain flashy stickers!

WORLD 3-1

WORLD THREE

WORLD 3-12 WORLD 3-6

WORLD 3-11 WORLD 3-4 WORLD 3-5

WORLD 3-9 WORLD 3-3 WORLD 3-2 WORLD 3-1

WORLD 3-10 WORLD 3-7 WORLD 3-8

HOW TO USE THIS GUIDE
HOW TO PLAY
STICKERS
ENEMIES
WALKTHROUGH
DECALBURG
SURFSHINE HARBOR
WORLD 1
WORLD 2
WORLD 3
WORLD 4
WORLD 5
WORLD 6
CHECKLISTS

WORLD THREE COURSES	
NUMBER	NAME
World 3-1	Leaflitter Path
World 3-2	The Bafflewood
World 3-3	Wiggler's Tree House
World 3-4	Strike Lake
World 3-5	Loop Loop River
World 3-6	Outlook Point
World 3-7	Rustle Burrow
World 3-8	Tree Branch Trail
World 3-9	Gauntlet Pond
World 3-10	Stump Glade
World 3-11	Holey Thicket
World 3-12	Whitecap Beach

World Three's sprawling forests have not only been overrun by enemies, they've been corrupted by the poisonous Gooper Blooper. You'll face several new enemies, such as Snifits, Ninjis, Piranha Plants, and Poison Bloopers, but due to toxic pools and poison gas, the environment is almost as dangerous as hostile creatures. Luckily, this world also contains a powerful ally—as long as you can get the frustrated Wiggler back on his many feet!

WORLD 3-1: LEAFLITTER PATH

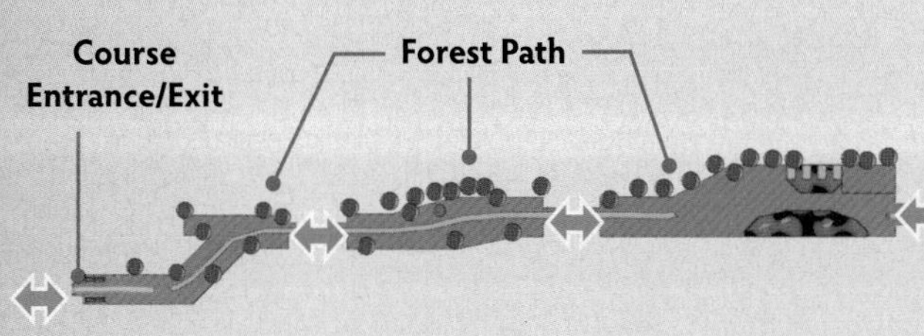

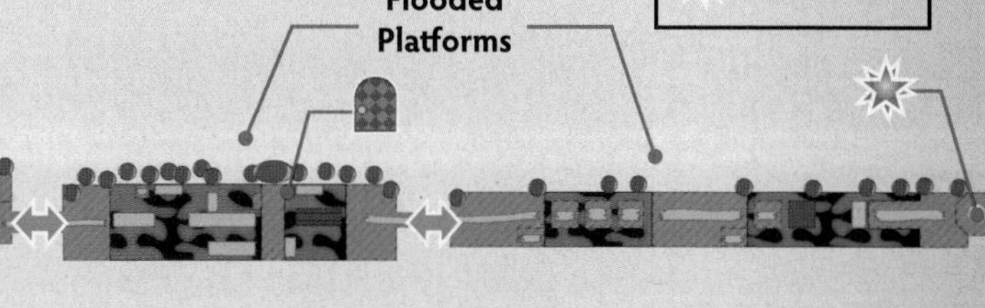

OVERVIEW

PREREQUISITES

This Course is available from the moment you leave Decalburg; however, you'll need a Trumpet sticker to reach the end of the Course. You must also acquire a Secret Door sticker before you can apply it to the marked location.

ESSENTIAL THING STICKERS		
NAME	THING LOCATION	NOTES
Trumpet	World 1-6	Needed to wake the sleeping Wiggler.

OBJECTIVES

This Course contains multiple objectives, some of which require additional visits:

- **Wake Wiggler.**
- **Collect the Comet Piece to unlock World 3-2.**
- **Collect the Searchlight from the Secret Door.**
- **Collect the HP-Up Heart from the cleansed forest.**

IMPORTANT ITEMS AND LOCATIONS	
DESCRIPTION	NOTES
Secret Door	The marked location is on a large tree among the flooded platforms.
HP-Up Heart	After the forest is cleansed, the HP-Up Heart appears at the end of the Course.
Toad Rescue	None
Luigi Location	None
Wiggler Diary Entry	None
Things	The Searchlight is through the Secret Door.

Recommended Tactics

This Course contains some new enemies, but the stickers scattered around each area should help you deal with most situations. As you navigate the flooded platforms, keep an eye out for a pesky pair of Boomerang Bros!

The Snifits in this Course usually team up with Clip Guys or Paint Guys. These enemies can absorb a fair amount of damage, but they're vulnerable to most attacks. Try to initiate each battle with a preemptive Hammer strike, then use the Battle Spinner to earn an extra attack or two.

If a Snifit battle lasts past your first turn, make sure you defend against the Clip Guys and Paint Guys. These pesky enemies use their weapons to immobilize you or obscure your vision. When one of these enemies attacks, rapidly tap Ⓐ until the turn ends. The faster you tap, the better your chances of fending off the attack.

Ninjis are very agile, and while most well-timed attacks will deal reliable damage, a Ninji will occasionally avoid taking damage. Make sure you keep a variety of Battle Stickers in case a Ninji proves resistant to a particular attack.

There's a pair of Boomerang Bros lurking near the end of the Course. These enemies are very durable, so consider combining a POW Block with projectile attacks or some of your more powerful Jump stickers. One of the most important things to keep in mind during this battle, however, is that you must defend yourself from each Boomerang not only when it's thrown but also when it returns to your attacker.

Forest Path

The forest path is fairly straight-forward, but the ? Block at Point 1 is easy to miss. As you follow the main path, watch the background for this small nook.

When you reach Point 2, a sleeping Wiggler is blocking the path. Use the Trumpet sticker to wake Wiggler and begin a short conversation. When the exchange ends, follow Wiggler toward the flooded platforms.

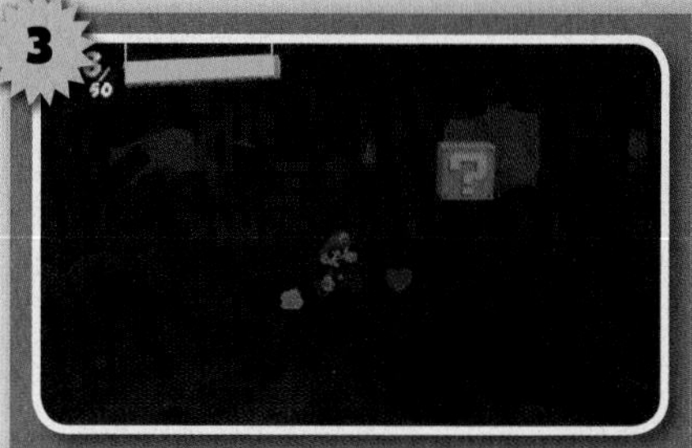

As you approach Point 3, the forest grows dark and Wiggler is yanked out of sight. As you search for useful items, take care to avoid the toxic puddles scattered around the area. When you're ready, follow the path to the flooded platforms.

TIP

Poison is hazardous, but it's not necessarily fatal. If you step into a toxic puddle or fall into a pool of poison, leap to dry ground to minimize the damage you suffer.

Flooded Platforms

To Forest Path

The platform at Point 1 is rotating in place. Wait for it to pivot toward you, then hop on and ride through the area.

Peel the Bowser tape at Point 2 to break the small platform loose. Ride the platform out to the ? Block, then ride back to continue through the area.

TIP

This platform not only allows you to reach the main path, it allows you to reach a ? Block hidden in the background.

WORLD 3-1

The Secret Door is at Point 3. After you acquire a Secret Door sticker, apply it to the marked location on the large tree in the background.

As you approach the platforms at Point 4, look for the shadowy figures lurking in the background. Time your jumps to avoid the Boomerangs they throw at you.

There's a Paperization Block between the HP Block and the Save Block at Point 5. There's a potentially difficult battle coming up, so make sure you're prepared before you move on.

As you approach the Comet Piece, the Boomerang Bros finally reveal themselves. These two enemies make a pretty formidable team, so take advantage of the Battle Spinner. Use high-damage stickers to chip away at their health until the battle ends.

When you're ready, collect the Comet Piece to end your first visit.

Sticker Comet Piece: Unlocking World 3-2

This Course contains only one piece of the Sticker Comet. To unlock World 3-2, simply collect the Comet Piece at the end of World 3-1.

ADDITIONAL VISITS

RECOMMENDED VISIT #2

After you gain access to the World 3-6 Sticker Shop, purchase a Secret Door sticker and return to the large tree among the flooded platforms. Apply the sticker to the marked location, then head inside to collect the Searchlight.

THING: SEARCHLIGHT

After you acquire a Secret Door sticker, apply it to the marked location among the flooded platforms. Head through the door to find the Searchlight.

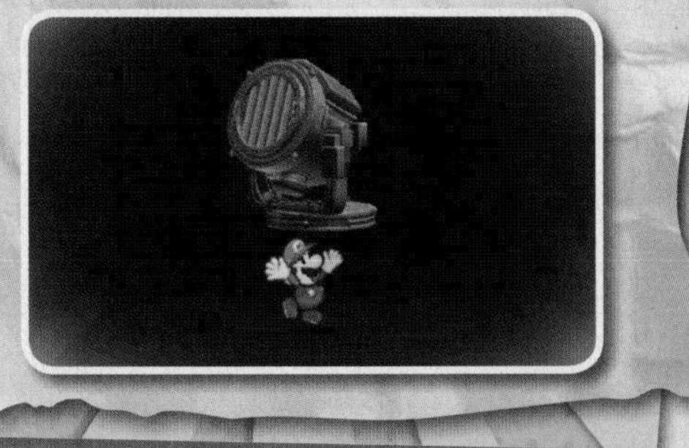

RECOMMENDED VISIT #3

After you defeat the Gooper Blooper and cleanse the forest, play through this Course to find an HP-Up Heart near the Comet Piece.

HP-UP HEART: LEAFLITTER PATH

After you cleanse the forest, an HP-Up Heart appears at the end of this Course. After you defeat the Gooper Blooper, revisit this Course to collect it.

WORLD 3-2: THE BAFFLEWOOD

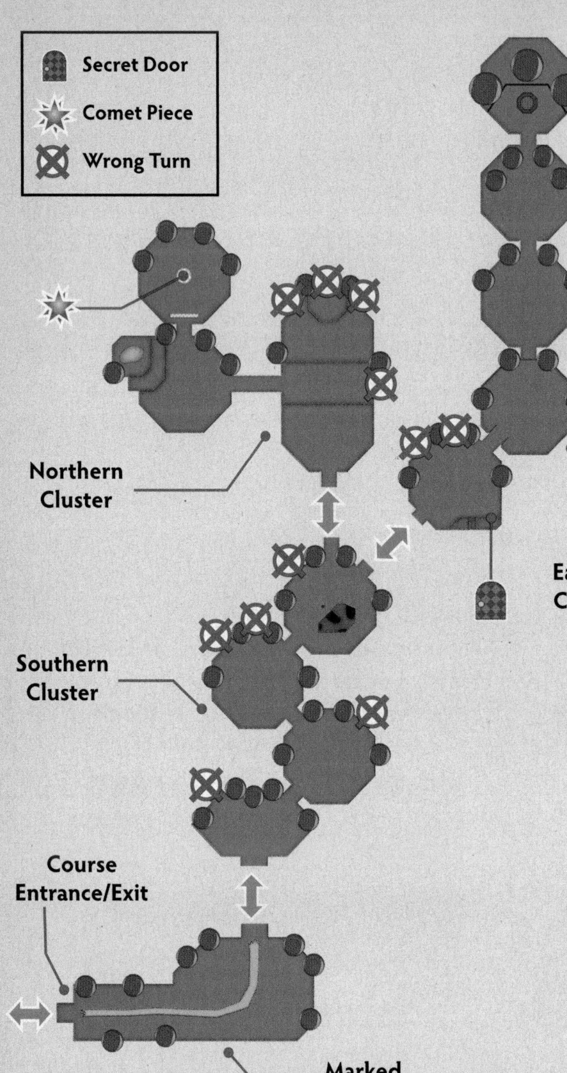

OVERVIEW

PREREQUISITES

To unlock this Course, you must collect the Comet Piece from World 3-1. Aside from a Secret Door sticker, the available objectives don't require any additional items.

OBJECTIVES

This Course contains several objectives, most of which require additional visits:

- **Determine the Course's valid paths.**
- **Collect the Comet Piece to unlock World 3-3.**
- **Collect the Violin from the Secret Door.**
- **Subdue the fleeing Wiggler Segment.**
- **Collect the Bowling Ball.**
- **Inspire a Wiggler Diary Entry.**
- **Collect the Trophy.**

IMPORTANT ITEMS AND LOCATIONS

DESCRIPTION	NOTES
Secret Door	The marked location is near the steps in the eastern cluster.
HP-Up Heart	None
Toad Rescue	None
Luigi Location	None
Wiggler Diary Entry	Walk through the dandelion in the northern cluster.
Things	The Violin is through the Secret Door. The Bowling Ball is at the end of the eastern cluster. The Trophy appears at the end of the eastern cluster after the Bowling Ball is used in World 3-4.

NOTE

This Course is essentially a maze in which each wrong turn sends you back to the beginning. To simplify this walkthrough, we've combined the Course's many small areas into a few distinct clusters.

NOTE

The Wiggler Segment that appears in this Course only does so after you find it in World 3-9 and chase it through World 3-10.

Recommended Tactics

This Course contains a few Snifits and Shy Guy variations, but the Piranha Plants are likely to prove your biggest concern.

Piranha Plants are surprisingly tricky enemies. Their sharp teeth counter most Jump attacks, and their sudden attacks can be difficult to predict. Additionally, they can burrow underground. This defensive maneuver protects a Piranha Plant from virtually all of your attacks for the duration of your next turn.

Marked Trail

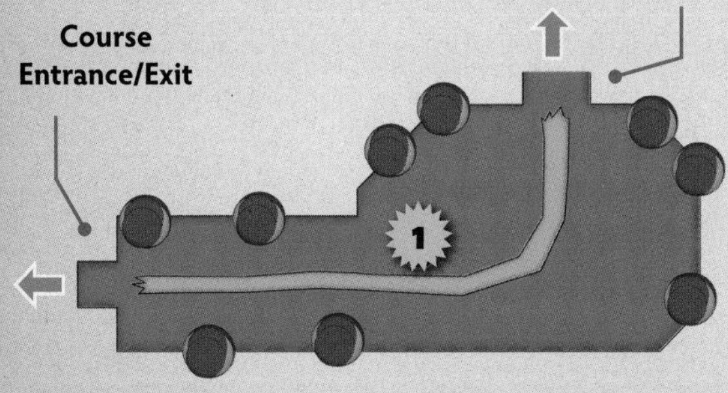

At the beginning of the Course, the forest trail is clearly marked. Unfortunately, this convenience doesn't extend beyond the first area. Follow the path into the southern cluster.

Southern Cluster

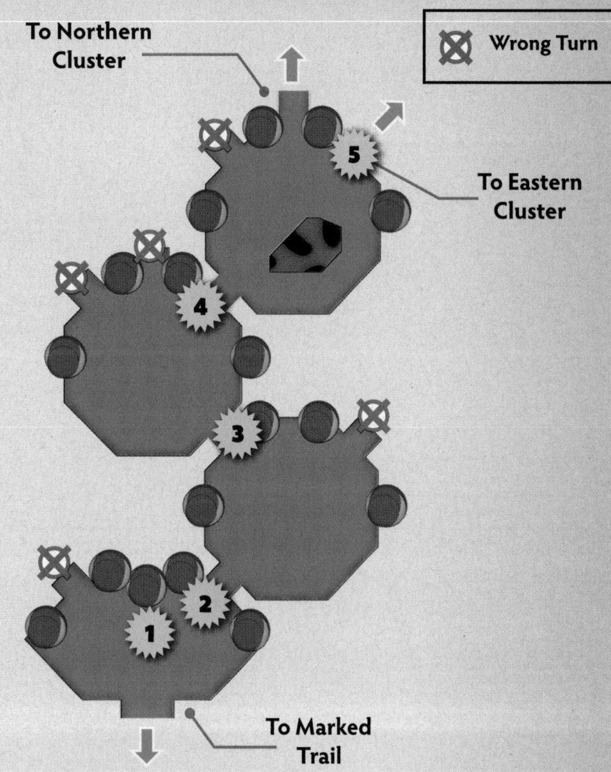

TIP

The maze begins at the area we've designated as the southern cluster. From this point on, a wrong turn brings you back to this area. There are plenty of enemies, stickers, and ? Blocks scattered throughout this Course, so remember to search each area before you move on.

As you explore the first clearing, examine the signs on either side of the HP Block. Similar signs are located throughout the maze. As you determine each valid turn, use stickers to mark the corresponding signs. This makes it much easier to navigate the maze during subsequent visits.

The valid path out of the first clearing is to the right, so place a sticker on the appropriate sign and continue to the next area.

TIP

If you wish to return to a previously explored area, simply leave the clearing the same way you entered it.

The valid path out of the second clearing is to the left. When you finish exploring the area, mark the appropriate path and continue to the next area.

There are three potential paths out of the third clearing. The path on the right, however, is the only valid option. When you're ready, mark the appropriate sign with a sticker and head into the next clearing.

TIP

Much of the eastern cluster can only be accessed after the Wiggler Segment appears in this Course. The first two clearings, however, are available during your first visit.

The fourth clearing features a poison pond, which is a very important landmark. This clearing serves as a junction between the northern cluster and the eastern cluster. Of the three potential paths, the path in the center leads to the northern cluster, and the path to the right leads to the eastern cluster.

Mark both of the corresponding signs, then follow the path to the right to explore the eastern cluster.

Eastern Cluster

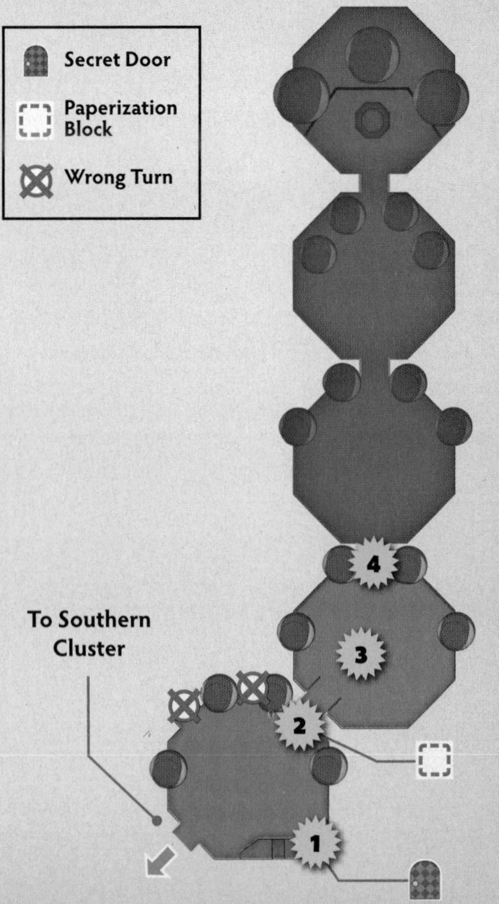

1

The eastern cluster's first clearing contains the Secret Door location. After you acquire a Secret Door sticker, apply it to the marked location at the bottom of the steps.

2

The first clearing doesn't contain any signs, but the correct path is easy to spot. Use your Hammer to reveal the ring of pink flowers at Point 2. These flowers mark the nearby Paperization Block and serve as a landmark for the correct path. When you're ready, follow the path on the right to find the next clearing.

3

The eastern cluster's second clearing is packed with stickers, so grab anything you think might be useful.

4

When the Wiggler Segment flees to this Course, it attempts to hide in this clearing. Once this happens, you can jump over the fence between the two trees along the north edge of the clearing. Until the Wiggler Segment arrives, however, the rest of the eastern cluster is inaccessible. After you collect the desired stickers, follow the path back to the southern cluster.

When you return to the poison pond, use the path in the middle to reach the northern cluster.

NORTHERN CLUSTER

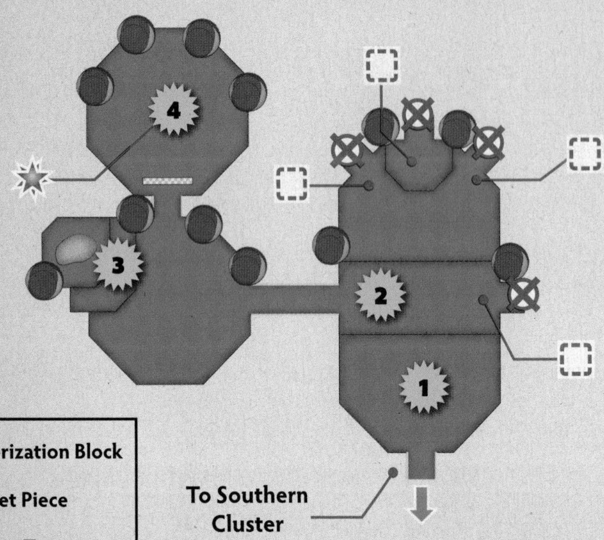

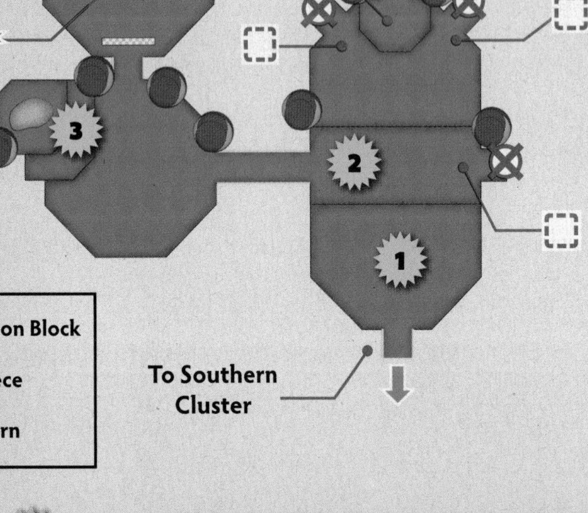

1

The northern cluster's first clearing is much larger than the others, so watch out for creatures that might be hiding behind bushes or lurking in the darkness.

2

Of the five potential paths, only the path on the far left is valid. You can mark the correct path with a sticker, but the clearing already has its own useful indicators; if you activate the Paperize ability, you'll find a Paperization Block near each of the four invalid paths. When you're ready, follow the path on the far left to the next clearing.

3

This area features a suspiciously located dandelion. After you subdue a Wiggler Segment, bring it to this area to inspire a diary entry.

4

When you're ready, follow the path to the final clearing, then collect the Comet Piece to end your first visit.

STICKER COMET PIECE: UNLOCKING WORLD 3-3

This Course contains only one piece of the Sticker Comet. To unlock World 3-3, simply collect the Comet Piece at the end of the Course.

THING: VIOLIN

After you acquire a Secret Door sticker, apply it to the marked location in the eastern cluster. Once the sticker is in place, head inside to collect the Violin.

ADDITIONAL VISITS

RECOMMENDED VISIT #2

After you reach World 3-6, purchase a Secret Door sticker and revisit this Course. Make your way back to the eastern cluster and apply the sticker to the marked location at the bottom of the steps. Enter the door to find the Violin.

RECOMMENDED VISIT #3

EASTERN CLUSTER

After you find the Wiggler Segment in World 3-9, chase it to World 3-10. When you lead the Wiggler Segment back to the World-Map, it flees to this Course. Enter the Course, then make your way to the eastern cluster's second clearing to find the Wiggler Segment.

When the Wiggler Segment attempts to flee, it reveals a path to the rest of the eastern cluster. When you're ready, approach the Wiggler Segment to initiate a battle.

The Wiggler Segment has two Piranha Plant allies, so take advantage of the Battle Spinner, and try to select high-damage, multi-target attacks such as Burnhammers.

After you subdue the Wiggler Segment, hop over the nearby fence and explore the rest of the eastern cluster. When you reach the last clearing, collect the Bowling Ball from the stump.

THING: BOWLING BALL

The Bowling Ball is located in the eastern cluster. After the Wiggler Segment reveals the path, hop over the fence and explore the rest of the cluster. The Bowling Ball is on a large stump in the center of the last clearing.

NORTHERN CLUSTER

When you're finished exploring the eastern cluster, lead the Wiggler Segment to the northern cluster. Approach the dandelion in the northern cluster's second clearing to get the Wiggler Segment's interest, then walk through the flower to inspire a diary entry.

Wiggler Diary Entry: The Bafflewood

After you subdue the Wiggler Segment in World 3-2, take it to the northern cluster's second clearing. Walk through the dandelion to inspire a diary entry. To read the new entry, visit World 3-3 and examine the book in Wiggler's bedroom.

Recommended Visit #4

A Bowling Ball sticker is required to collect one of the Comet Pieces within World 3-4. After you use the Bowling Ball for this purpose, return to this Course to find a Trophy in the eastern cluster's last clearing.

Tip

Before you return to World 3-3, take the Wiggler Segment to World 3-10 to inspire another diary entry.

Thing: Trophy

Use the Bowling Ball on the lane in World 3-4, then return to this Course. Revisit the clearing at the end of the eastern cluster to find a Trophy on the stump that originally held the Bowling Ball.

WORLD 3-3: WIGGLER'S TREE HOUSE

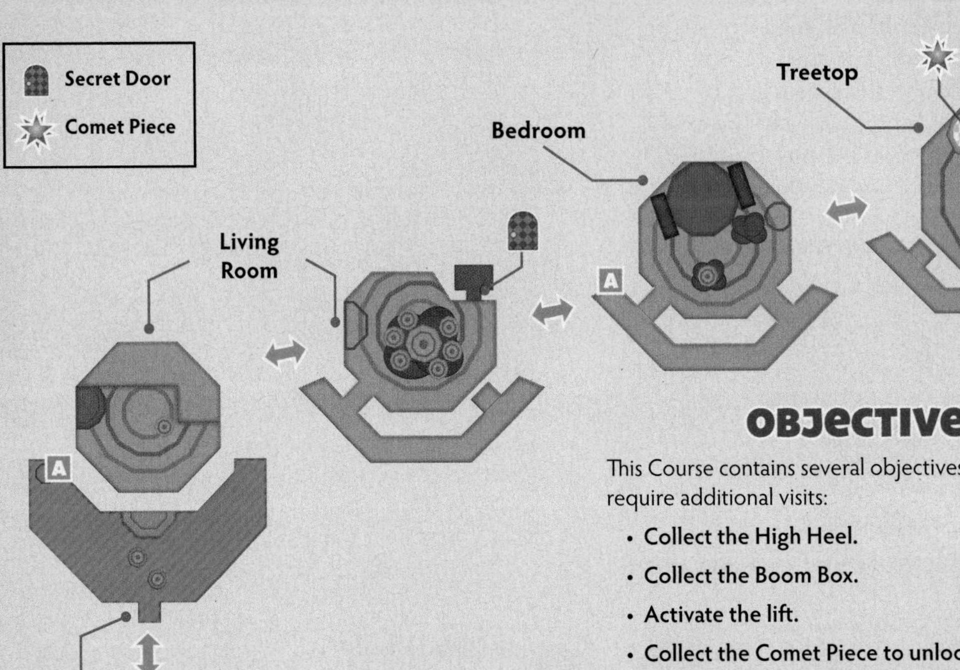

OVERVIEW

PREREQUISITES

To unlock this Course, you must collect the Comet Piece at the end of World 3-2. To complete all of the available objectives, you must acquire a Secret Door sticker, recover the Tree Stump scraps from World 3-5 and World 3-8, and wrangle the Wiggler Segments scattered around World Three.

NOTE

Progressing through World Three requires frequent visits to Wiggler's Tree House.

OBJECTIVES

This Course contains several objectives, many of which require additional visits:

- Collect the High Heel.
- Collect the Boom Box.
- Activate the lift.
- Collect the Comet Piece to unlock World 3-4.
- Return the first Wiggler Segment.
- Collect the HP-Up Heart from the Secret Door.
- Collect the Comet Piece to unlock World 3-7.
- Return the second Wiggler Segment.
- Collect the Comet Piece to unlock World 3-9.
- Return the third Wiggler Segment.
- Return the fourth Wiggler Segment.
- Reassemble Wiggler.
- Send Wiggler to World 6-2.

IMPORTANT ITEMS AND LOCATIONS

DESCRIPTION	NOTES
Secret Door	The marked location is in the living room, at the top of the ramp.
HP-Up Heart	The HP-Up Heart is through the Secret Door.
Toad Rescue	None
Luigi Location	None
Wiggler Diary Entry	None
Things	The High Heel is on the living room's first floor. The Boom Box is in the bedroom.

TIP

The bedroom also contains Wiggler's diary. Remember to read the entries your adventures have inspired!

RECOMMENDED TACTICS

This Course contains no hostile creatures, so combat is not a concern.

LIVING ROOM

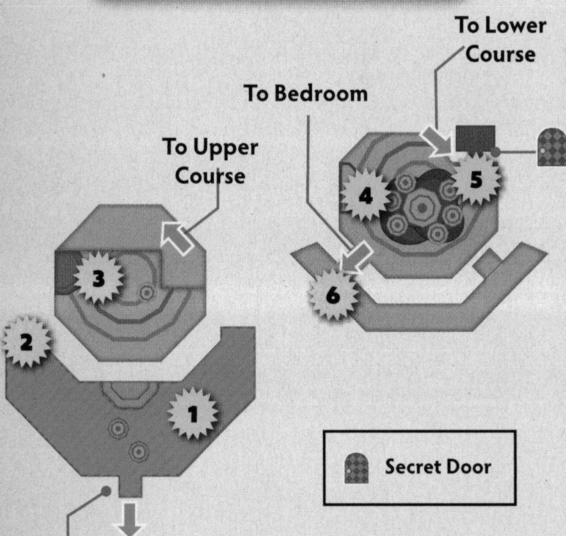

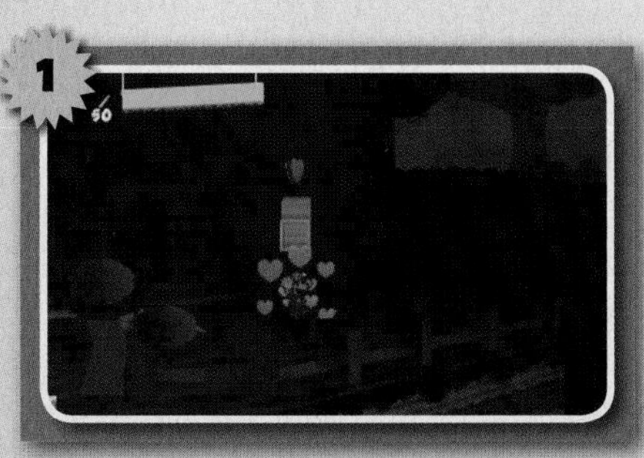

Before you enter the tree house, take a moment to explore the front yard. There's an HP Block to the right of the door, so use it to replace any lost health.

When you first visit this Course, the tree house lift is stuck to the ramp outside the bedroom. After you free the lift, however, it drops to the ground at Point 2. When you revisit this Course, return to this area to take advantage of the lift.

Enter the tree house to find the High Heel on the living room shelves. To reach the top shelf, you must drop down from the living room's upper Course.

Climb the ramp to the upper Course and approach the fireplace along the left wall. Use your Hammer to put out the flame, then hop through the opening to drop down to the High Heel.

THING: HIGH HEEL

Use your Hammer to extinguish the fire on the living room's upper Course, then drop through the fireplace to land near the High Heel.

Bedroom

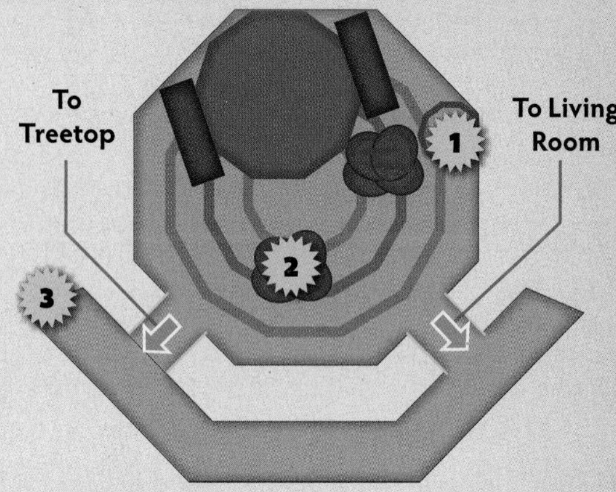

The Secret Door location is on the living room's upper Course. Move toward the right wall to find the marked location in the corner of the room. After you acquire a Secret Door sticker, apply it to this spot.

When you're finished exploring the living room, exit through the doorway near the fireplace and follow the ramp up to the bedroom.

1

The Boom Box is on a shelf at Point 1. Make sure you grab it when you reach the bedroom.

THING: BOOM BOX

When you enter the bedroom, jump onto the shelf near the right wall and examine the Boom Box to collect it.

The platform in the center of the bedroom holds Wiggler's diary. The pages are blank when you first visit this Course, but your actions can inspire new entries.

When you're ready, head through the doorway on the left side of the bedroom. Before you climb the ramp, peel the Bowser tape holding the lift in place. Now that the lift is functional, you'll find it waiting on the ground each time you revisit the Course.

TREETOP

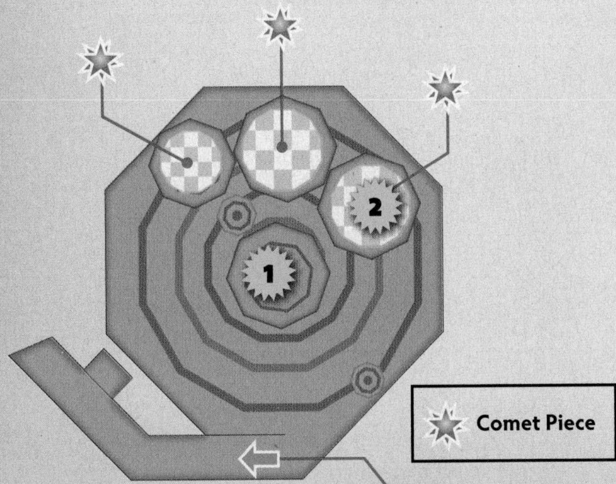

When you reach the treetop, you learn that Kamek has scattered Wiggler's body segments across World Three. As you progress through the game, you must find, subdue, and return each of the four Wiggler Segments to the treetop.

There are three stumps on the treetop, and each one has a Comet Piece floating above it. Unfortunately, two of the stumps are incomplete. Before you can collect the related Comet Pieces, you must locate the Tree Stump scraps located in World 3-5 and World 3-8. For now, collect the Comet Piece on the left to end your first visit.

STICKER COMET PIECE: UNLOCKING WORLD 3-4

This Course contains three pieces of the Sticker Comet, but only one can be reached during your first visit. To unlock World 3-4, collect the Comet Piece floating above the stump to the right.

ADDITIONAL VISITS

RECOMMENDED VISIT #2

After you subdue the first Wiggler Segment, revisit the treetop and return it to Wiggler.

Return to the treetop and use the Tree Stump scrap from World 3-5 to complete the stump on the left.

After the scrap is in place, climb onto the stump and collect the Comet Piece floating above you.

RECOMMENDED VISIT #3

After you collect the Tree Stump scrap from World 3-5, purchase a Secret Door sticker from the World 3-6 Sticker Shop. Return to Wiggler's Tree House and apply the Secret Door to the marked location on the living room's upper Course. Head inside to find an HP-Up Heart.

STICKER COMET PIECE: UNLOCKING WORLD 3-7

This Course contains three pieces of the Sticker Comet, all of which are located in the treetop. To unlock World 3-7, use the Tree Stump scrap from World 3-5 to complete the stump on the left, then climb up and grab the Comet Piece floating above it.

HP-UP HEART: WIGGLER'S TREE HOUSE

After you gain access to the World 3-6 Sticker Shop, purchase a Secret Door sticker and return to this Course. Apply the sticker to the marked location on the living room's upper Course, then head inside to collect the HP-Up Heart.

RECOMMENDED VISIT #4

You should find the Tree Stump scrap from World 3-8 just after you subdue the second Wiggler Segment. Once you've accomplished both tasks, return to the treetop and deliver the second Wiggler Segment.

Use the Tree Stump scrap to repair the stump in the middle, then collect the remaining Comet Piece.

STICKER COMET PIECE: UNLOCKING WORLD 3-9

This Course contains three pieces of the Sticker Comet, all of which are located in the treetop. To unlock World 3-9, use the Tree Stump scrap from World 3-8 to complete the stump in the middle, then climb up and grab the Comet Piece floating above it.

WIGGLER SEGMENT LOCATIONS

To reach the Gooper Blooper off the coast of Whitecap Beach, you must get Wiggler back on his feet. To do so, recover all four of the Wiggler Segments scattered throughout World Three:

- The first Wiggler Segment starts in World 3-4 and flees to World 3-5.
- The second Wiggler Segment starts in World 3-7 and flees to World 3-8.
- The third Wiggler Segment starts in World 3-9, flees to World 3-10, then flees to World 3-2.
- The fourth Wiggler Segment starts in World 3-11, flees to World 3-12, then flees to Surfshine Harbor.

Each Wiggler Segment eventually puts up a fight and must be subdued by force.

RECOMMENDED VISIT #5

After you subdue the third Wiggler Segment, lead it back to the treetop and deliver it to Wiggler.

RECOMMENDED VISIT #6

After you subdue the forth Wiggler Segment, lead it back to the treetop and reassemble Wiggler. Once Wiggler's back in one piece, he storms off to World 3-12 to await your arrival.

CAUTION

Before you bring the fourth Wiggler Segment back to the treetop, make sure you've inspired all possible Wiggler Diary Entries!

NOTE

Spoiler alert! You must revisit this Course toward the end of the game. When you're ready to enter World 6-2, return to the treetop and speak to Wiggler.

WORLD 3-4: STRIKE LAKE

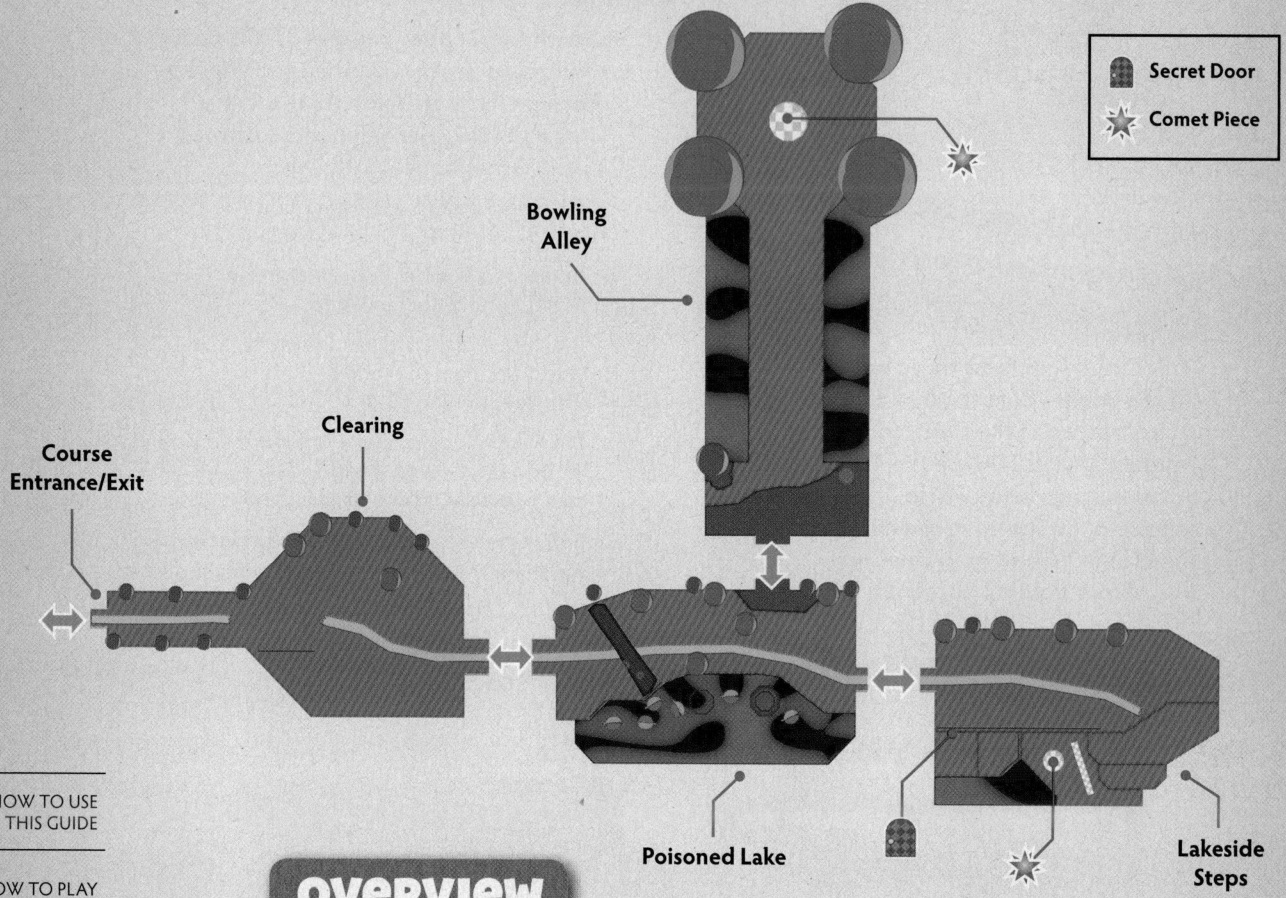

Secret Door
Comet Piece

Bowling Alley

Clearing

Course Entrance/Exit

Poisoned Lake

Lakeside Steps

OVERVIEW

PREREQUISITES

To unlock this Course, you must collect the corresponding Comet Piece from World 3-3. When you reach the top of Wiggler's Tree House, collect the Comet Piece from the stump on the right. To complete all of the available objectives, you need to acquire the Bowling Ball and a Secret Door sticker.

ESSENTIAL THING STICKERS

NAME	THING LOCATION	NOTES
Bowling Ball	World 3-2	Needed to clear the bowling pins.

OBJECTIVES

This Course contains several objectives, some of which require additional visits:

- **Chase the Wiggler Segment from the Course.**
- **Collect the Billiard Ball.**
- **Collect the Comet Piece to unlock World 3-5.**
- **Collect the Drum from the Secret Door.**
- **Use the Bowling Ball to clear the pins.**
- **Collect the Comet Piece to unlock World 3-11.**

IMPORTANT ITEMS AND LOCATIONS

DESCRIPTION	NOTES
Secret Door	The marked location is near the lakeside steps.
HP-Up Heart	None
Toad Rescue	None
Luigi Location	None
Wiggler Diary Entry	None
Things	The Billiard Ball is in a tree near the poisoned lake. The Drum is through the Secret Door.

Recommended Tactics

This Course contains a variety of enemies, but a standard selection of stickers should allow you to overcome any combat situations.

Most of this Course's battles involve Snifits and/or Ninjis, but you might find the odd Boomerang Bro appearing as a secondary attacker. Try to keep a nice selection of Hammer stickers, Jump stickers, and multi-target stickers. When you're facing a particularly durable opponent, make sure you take advantage of the Battle Spinner.

Clearing

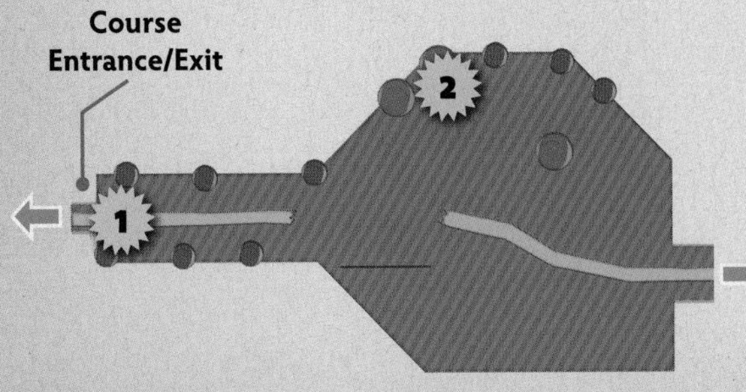

TIP

Most of the trees in this Course contain stickers and coins. Use your Hammer to knock these items to the ground, but watch out for any creatures that might be hiding among the leaves!

When you enter the Course, the first Wiggler Segment dashes away from you. As you explore each area, check any potential hiding spots for the cowering segment.

The Wiggler Segment attempts to hide in a tree at Point 2. Clear out any nearby enemies, then strike the tree with your Hammer to knock the segment out of the tree. Finish searching the area, then follow the Wiggler Segment to the next area.

POISONED LAKE

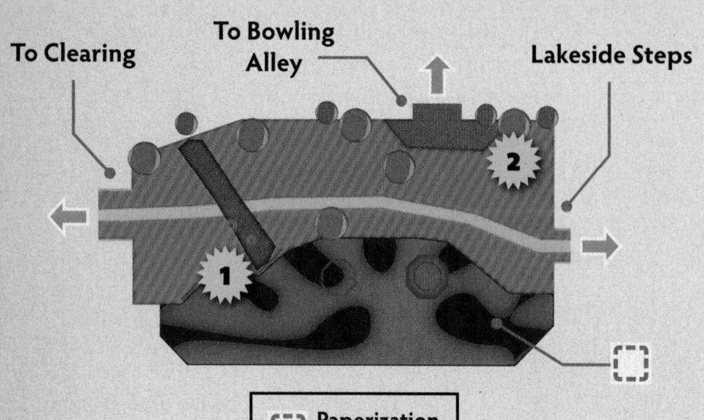

When you approach the Wiggler Segment, it flees across the poisoned lake. Hop along the floating leaves to get past the fallen tree, then use the HP Block to top off Mario's HP.

Follow the path to the right edge of the area and examine the tree in the background. Use your Hammer to shake the Wiggler Segment out of the branches. After it lands, the segment flees to the next area. Rather than follow it, continue to strike the tree until the Billiard Ball falls to the ground. Collect the Billiard Ball, then follow the nearby path to the bowling alley.

THING: BILLIARD BALL

The Billiard Ball is in a tree near the poisoned lake. Strike the tree along the area's right edge until the Billiard Ball falls to the ground.

BOWLING ALLEY

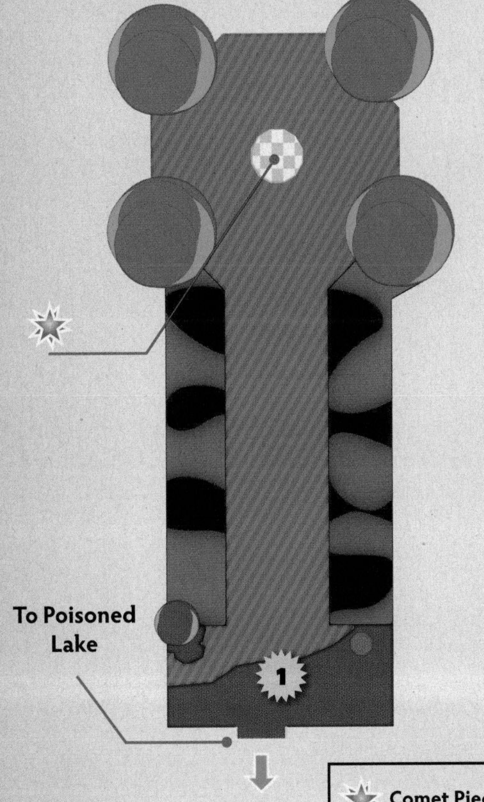

LAKESIDE STEPS

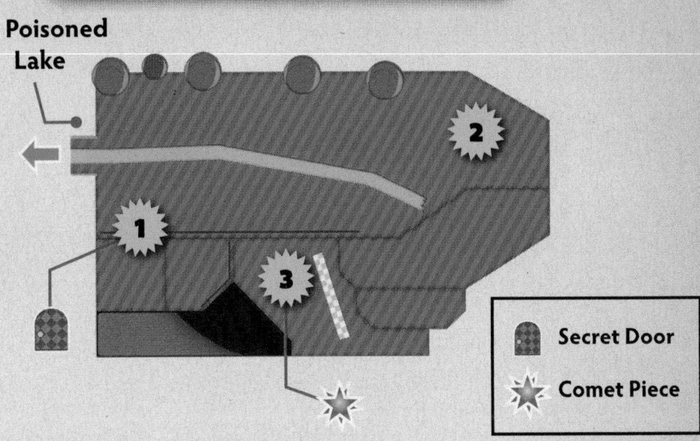

When you enter the area, jump over the fence in the foreground to find the Secret Door location. Return to this hidden enclosure after you acquire a Secret Door sticker.

This giant, single-lane bowling alley contains one of the Course's two Comet Pieces, but the wall of pins prevents you from reaching it. Return to this area after you acquire a Bowling Ball sticker. For now, leave the bowling alley, return to the main path, and continue to the lakeside steps at the end of the Course.

By the time you reach this area, the Wiggler Segment should be hiding behind the bush at Point 2. Strike the bush with your Hammer, then chase the Wiggler Segment back to the clearing at the start of the Course. Approach the bush near the clearing's right edge, and hit it with your Hammer until the Wiggler Segment leaves the Course. Once it does, follow the path back to the lakeside steps.

After the Wiggler Segment leaves the Course, collect the Comet Piece near the lakeside steps to end your first visit.

STICKER COMET PIECE: UNLOCKING WORLD 3-5

This Course contains two pieces of the Sticker Comet. To unlock World 3-5, collect the Comet Piece near the lakeside steps.

ADDITIONAL VISITS

RECOMMENDED VISIT #2

After you acquire a Secret Door sticker, return to the lakeside steps and hop over the fence in the foreground. Apply the sticker to the marked location, then head inside to collect the Drum.

THING: DRUM

After you acquire a Secret Door sticker, return to the lakeside steps and apply it to the marked location. Head through the door to find the Drum.

RECOMMENDED VISIT #3

After you collect the Bowling Ball from World 3-2, convert it to a Thing Sticker and return to the bowling alley. Approach the stump to the right of the lane and activate the Paperize ability. Place the Bowling Ball sticker in the indicated spot to trigger a cinematic.

When the path is clear, collect the Comet Piece at the end of the lane.

After the Bowling Ball crashes through the pins, it appears in the tree to the left. From now on, the Bowling Ball can be found in this location.

STICKER COMET PIECE: UNLOCKING WORLD 3-11

This Course contains two pieces of the Sticker Comet. To unlock World 3-11, collect the Comet Piece from the bowling alley.

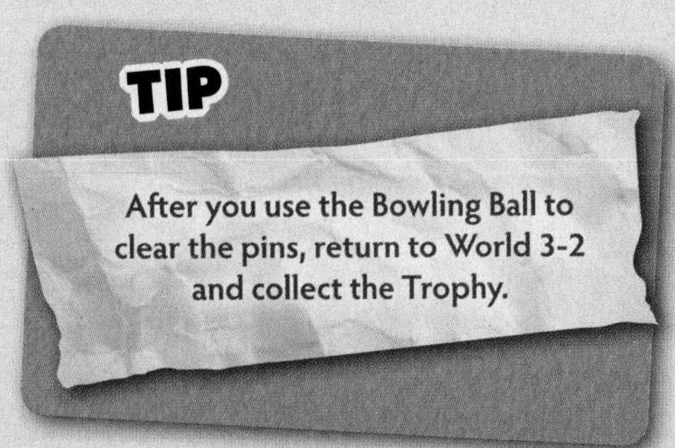

TIP

After you use the Bowling Ball to clear the pins, return to World 3-2 and collect the Trophy.

WORLD 3-5: LOOP LOOP RIVER

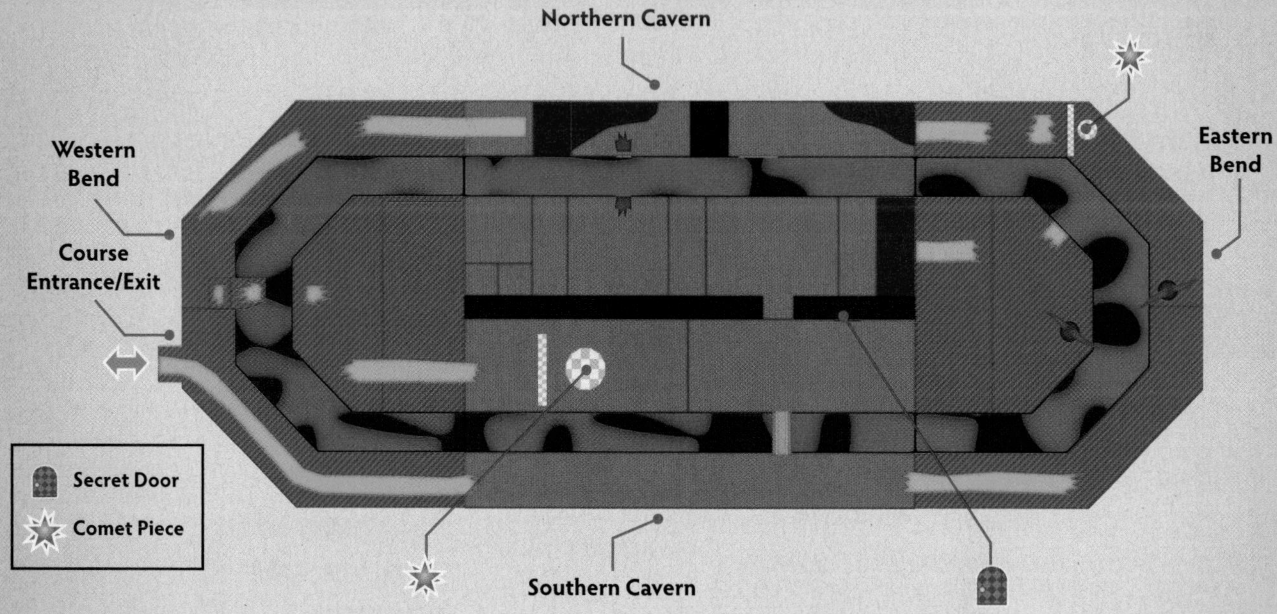

OVERVIEW

PREREQUISITES

To unlock this Course, you must collect the Comet Piece near the lakeside steps in World 3-4. You must acquire a Secret Door sticker before your second visit, but you should gain access to the World 3-6 Sticker Shop when you collect this Course's first Comet Piece.

OBJECTIVES

This Course contains several objectives, some of which require an additional visit:

- **Knock the first leaf into the stream.**
- **Subdue the Wiggler Segment.**
- **Knock the second leaf into the stream.**
- **Collect the Comet Piece to unlock World 3-6.**
- **Collect the Pillow from the Secret Door.**
- **Collect the Tree Stump scrap.**

Collect the Comet Piece to unlock an alternative path to World 3-2.

> **NOTE**
>
> The Wiggler Segment appears in this Course only after you chase it from World 3-4.

IMPORTANT ITEMS AND LOCATIONS	
DESCRIPTION	**NOTES**
Secret Door	The marked location is near the Boomerang Bro in the southern cavern.
HP-Up Heart	None
Toad Rescue	None
Luigi Location	None
Wiggler Diary Entry	None
Things	The Pillow is through the Secret Door.

RECOMMENDED TACTICS

This Course contains some new combinations of familiar enemies, such as a Boomerang Bro with a Paint Guy.

You'll find plenty of useful stickers scattered around the Course, but consider bringing a good selection of Hammer stickers, Jump stickers, and multi-target stickers.

This Course contains the first available Wiggler Segment battle. Wiggler Segments tend to dodge most Jump-based and Hammer-based attacks. Use Fire Flowers and Ice Flowers to deal reliable damage.

There's an HP Block at the start of the Course. If you fall into the toxic stream or take damage during a battle, circle back to this spot and refill Mario's HP.

Enter the southern cavern and head across the small bridge. After you acquire a Secret Door sticker, apply it to the marked location behind the Boomerang Bro. For now, however, simply defeat the enemy and search the area for nearby stickers. When you're ready, head through the nearby doorway to enter the northern cavern.

Recommended Visit #1

	Secret Door		Hidden Block
	Comet Piece		Paperization Block

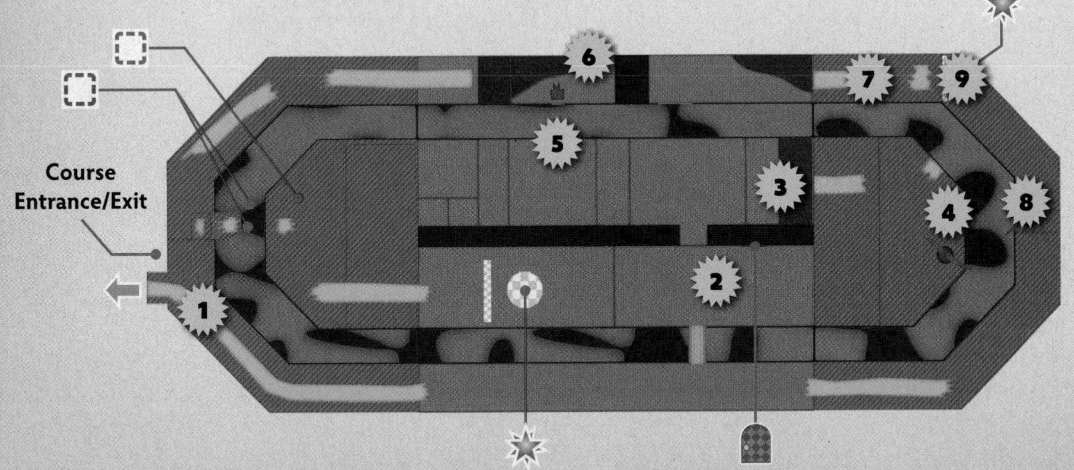

WORLD 3-5

After you step into the northern cavern, move up the steps to the right and head out to the eastern bend.

Continue to the right to find a plant at the edge of the platform. Strike the plant with your Hammer to knock a leaf into the stream, then hop onto the leaf and drift along with the current.

The leaf carries you back into the northern cavern. Jump up to reveal the Hidden Block between the floating coins.When you reach Point 5, jump onto the ledge in the foreground. Approach the wall to the left, then follow the path up toward the cavern ceiling.

Peel the Bowser tape at Point 6 to create some steps, then follow the path back out to the eastern bend.

The Wiggler Segment you chased from World 3-4 is now sitting at Point 7. The Wiggler Segment attacks as you approach it, so be prepared to defend yourself. Use one or two high-damage stickers to end the fight quickly. The defeated Wiggler Segment now follows you around.

Before you collect the nearby Comet Piece, strike the plant at Point 8 to knock another leaf into the stream.

When you're ready, collect the Comet Piece at Point 9 to complete your first visit.

STICKER COMET PIECE: UNLOCKING WORLD 3-6

This Course contains two pieces of the Sticker Comet. To unlock World 3-6, collect the Comet Piece along the stream's eastern bend.

TIP

Before you take the segment back to Wiggler's Tree House, lead it to World 3-6. Take the Wiggler Segment to the overlook near the entrance to inspire a diary entry!

RECOMMENDED VISIT #2

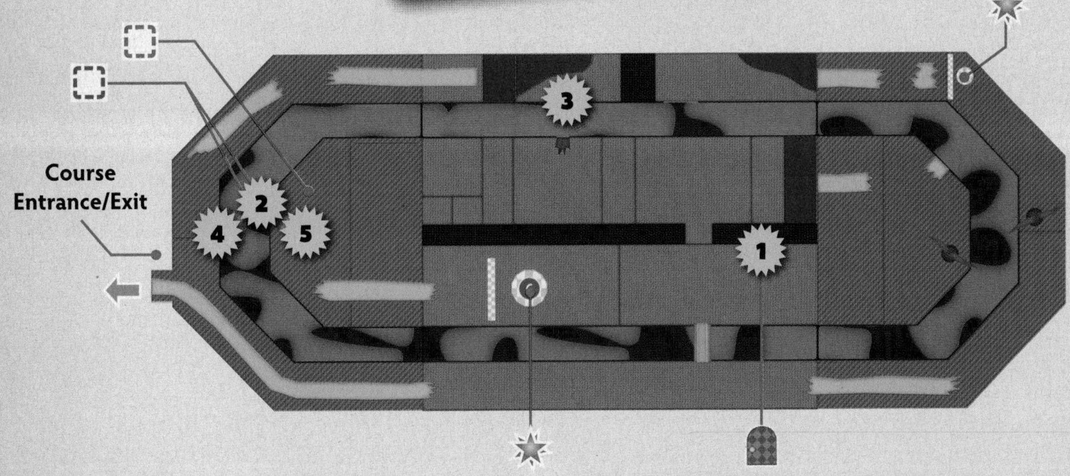

Secret Door	Comet Piece	Hidden Block	Paperization Block

You should have unlocked World 3-6 at the end of your first visit. Before you start your second visit, make sure you purchase a Secret Door sticker from the World 3-6 Sticker Shop.

After you purchase a Secret Door sticker, apply it to the marked location in the southern cavern. Head through the door to find the Pillow.

THING: PILLOW

Apply the Secret Door sticker to the marked location in the southern cavern, then head inside to find the Pillow.

Ride a leaf into the northern cavern. When you reach Point 3, hop onto the ledge in the background, then climb up the steps to the left.

Hop on one of the floating leaves and ride through the stream's western bend. When the leaf reaches the boards at Point 2, it slows down. Jump up to reveal the Hidden Blocks just above you.

After you emerge from the northern cavern, follow the path through the western bend. The Hidden Blocks you discovered earlier now serve as a small platform. Hop over to the platform just across the stream.

HOW TO USE THIS GUIDE
HOW TO PLAY
STICKERS
ENEMIES
WALKTHROUGH
DECALBURG
SURFSHINE HARBOR
WORLD 1
WORLD 2
WORLD 3
WORLD 4
WORLD 5
WORLD 6
CHECKLISTS

When you land, collect the Tree Stump scrap from the ground. This scrap allows you to collect one of the Comet Pieces in World 3-3, so make sure you grab it!

When you're ready, follow the path to the right and collect the Comet Piece in the southern cavern.

STICKER COMET PIECE: UNLOCKING THE PATH TO WORLD 3-2

This Course contains two pieces of the Sticker Comet, one of which opens an alternative route to a previously visited Course. Collect the Comet Piece from the southern cavern to reveal the shortcut between World 3-2 and World 3-5.

TIP

After you complete your visit, remember to take the Tree Stump scrap to World 3-3!

WORLD 3-6: OUTLOOK POINT

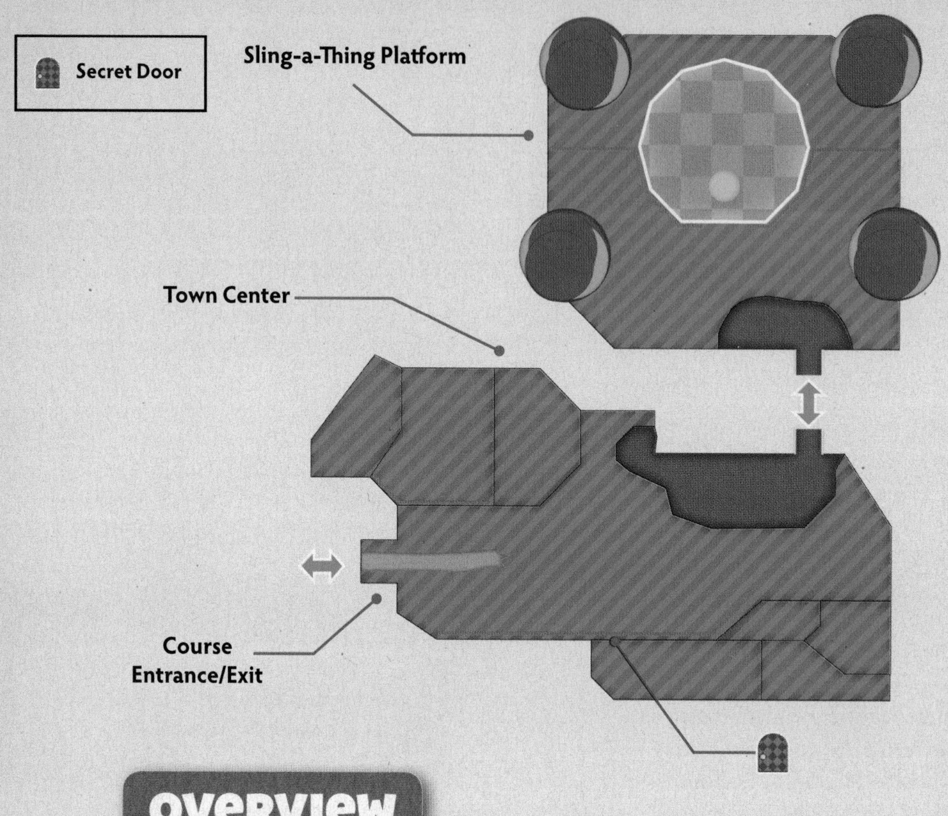

OVERVIEW

PREREQUISITES

To unlock this Course, you must collect the Comet Piece from the east bend in World 3-5. If you lead a Wiggler Segment to this area, you can inspire a diary entry. Aside from that, the Course contains everything you need to meet the available objectives.

OBJECTIVES

This Course contains a few objectives, all of which can be completed in a single visit:

- **Inspire a Wiggler Diary Entry.**
- **Purchase a Secret Door sticker.**
- **Collect the Fishhook from the Secret Door.**

TIP

This area also contains a secondary Thing-slinging platform.

IMPORTANT ITEMS AND LOCATIONS

DESCRIPTION	NOTES
Secret Door	The marked location is below the Sticker Shop.
HP-Up Heart	None
Toad Rescue	None
Luigi Location	None
Wiggler Diary Entry	Bring a Wiggler Segment to the overlook near the Course entrance.
Things	The Fishhook is through the Secret Door.

RECOMMENDED TACTICS

This is a friendly area, so combat is not a concern. However, the Sticker Shop provides an excellent opportunity to supplement your current stickers.

RECOMMENDED VISIT

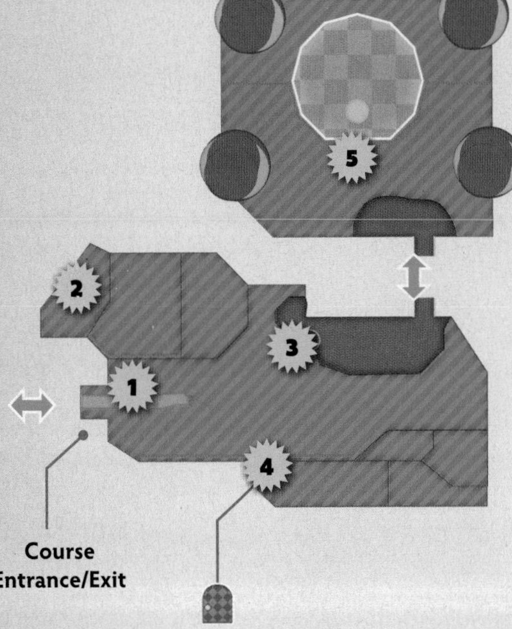

You should have subdued the first Wiggler Segment moments before this Course becomes available. Before you return the segment to World 3-3, lead it to the overlook near the Course's entrance to inspire a diary entry.

WIGGLER DIARY ENTRY: OUTLOOK POINT

Lead a Wiggler Segment to the overlook in World 3-6. When the segment sees the wrecked ship off of the coast, it inspires a new diary entry.

This Course contains an HP Block and a Save Block, making it another great spot to catch your breath between hostile Courses.

TIP

If you delivered the first Wiggler Segment before you visited this Course, you can earn this diary entry during a future visit. Simply lead one of the three remaining Wiggler Segments to the overlook before you reassemble Wiggler.

Apply a Secret Door sticker to the marked location at Point 4, then head inside to find the Fishhook.

This Course's Sticker Shop is the only establishment that sells Secret Door stickers. You can now purchase Secret Doors to use in previously visited Courses, thereby gaining access to several new Things. Buy at least one Secret Door to use in this Course and continue your exploration.

TIP

Almost every Course in the game contains a Secret Door. As a rule, it's best to purchase a Secret Door sticker before you visit a new Course.

THING: FISHHOOK

The Fishhook is located through the Secret Door below the Sticker Shop.

This Course contains a secondary Sling-a-Thing Platform! If you have a few extra Things in your Album, consider converting them to stickers at this convenient location.

TIP

After you collect the Fishhook, convert it to a Thing Sticker. You should now be ready to defeat the Big Cheep Cheep at Surfshine Harbor.

NOTE

Although it's possible to complete this Course's objectives in one visit, you'll find plenty of reasons to return. The HP Block, Save Block, and Sling-a-Thing Platform are all useful, and the Sticker Shop's inventory expands as you progress through the game. Most importantly, however, you must maintain a supply of Secret Door stickers.

WORLD 3-7: RUSTLE BURROW

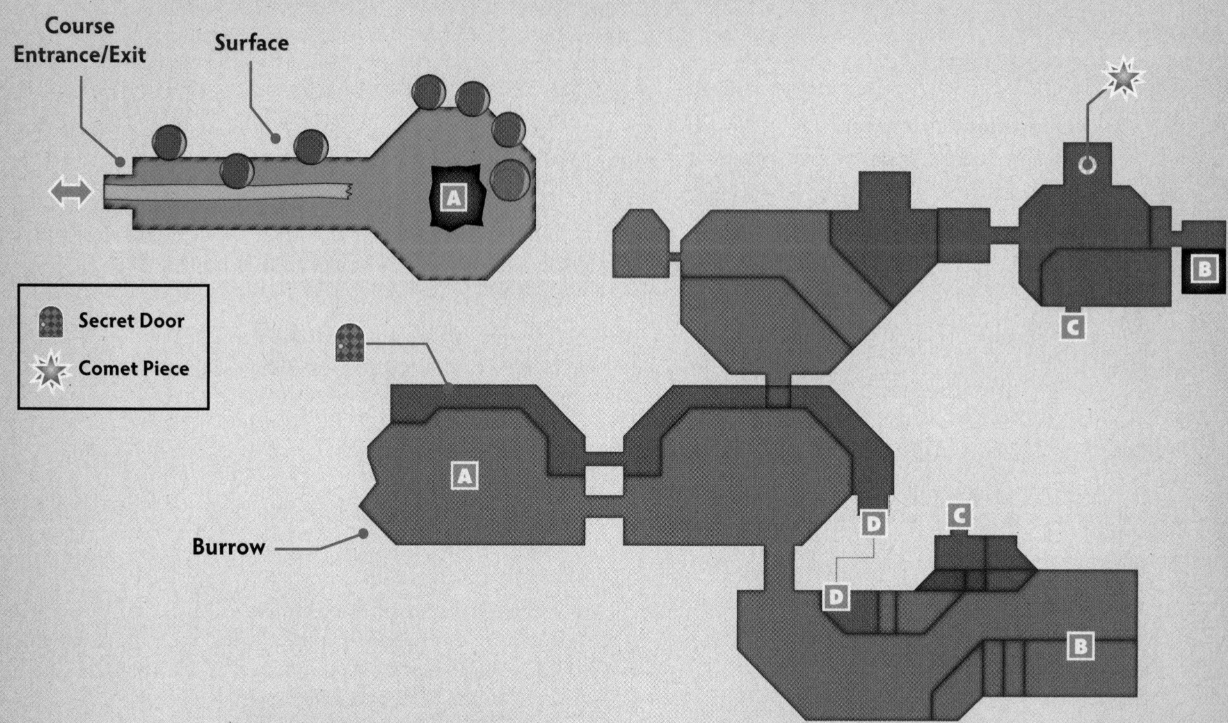

OVERVIEW

PREREQUISITES

To unlock this Course, you must collect the corresponding Comet Piece from the treetop in World 3-3. Before you enter the Course, purchase a Secret Door sticker from the World 3-6 Sticker Shop.

OBJECTIVES

This Course contains a number of objectives, all of which can be completed in a single visit:

- **Recover your stickers.**
- **Defeat the Big Scuttlebug.**
- **Free Kersti.**
- **Reposition the Burrow Door scrap.**
- **Recover the Hammer.**
- **Collect the Upright Vacuum from the Secret Door.**
- **Free the Wiggler Segment.**
- **Collect the Comet Piece to unlock World 3-8.**

TIP

Sell your Leaf stickers before you enter the Course! When you drop into the burrow, you lose all of your stickers. While most of your stickers can be recovered as you explore the Course, any Leaf stickers that were in your Album will be lost for good.

IMPORTANT ITEMS AND LOCATIONS

DESCRIPTION	NOTES
Secret Door	The marked location is behind the Hammer, on the ledge in the burrow's first chamber.
HP-Up Heart	None
Toad Rescue	None
Luigi Location	None
Wiggler Diary Entry	None
Things	The Upright Vacuum is through the Secret Door.

Recommended Tactics

When you enter the burrow, you lose Kersti, your Hammer, and all of your stickers. Obviously, you must recover at least a few of your stickers before you're ready for combat, but your tactical options are extremely limited until you find Kersti and recover your Hammer.

The burrow is filled with Scuttlebugs, and nearly every encounter will involve at least one of these creatures. Depending on the length of their threads, suspended Scuttlebugs must be considered low-flying or airborne enemies. Stock up on plenty of Jump-based stickers, and make recovering them your priority.

This Course also contains several Spike Tops. Spike Tops' natural defenses counter virtually all Jump-based stickers, and until you recover your missing Hammer, your Hammer-based stickers are useless. Shell stickers can be very effective, but only if you're lucky enough to recover them before stumbling onto one of these enemies. If you haven't recovered the appropriate items, it's best to retreat from any battle involving a Spike Top.

The burrow also contains a Big Scuttlebug. You'll face this enemy before you recover your Hammer, and its web allows it to counter all of your Jump-based attacks. Use thrown items, Fire Flowers, or POW Blocks to destroy the web, then use Jump-based stickers to deal heavy damage to the Big Scuttlebug.

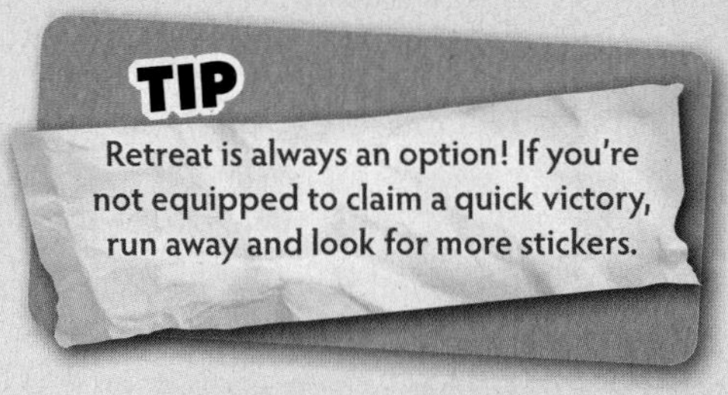

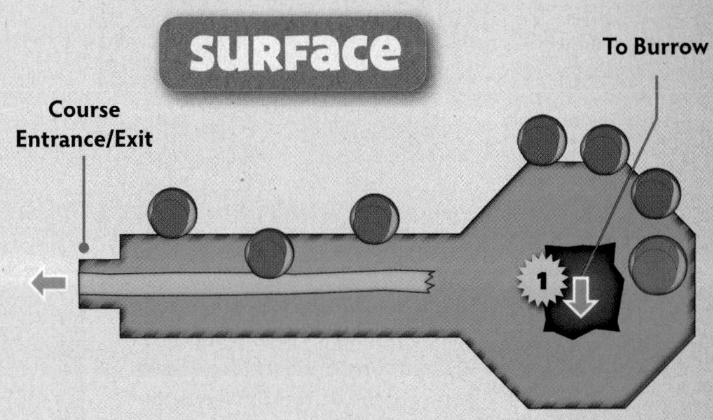

When you first enter the Course, a Wiggler Segment attempts to flee. Follow the path to the right to find the segment trapped in a giant web. When you approach, the web breaks apart. When you're ready, follow the Wiggler Segment into the burrow.

BURROW

Recommended Route—Part 1

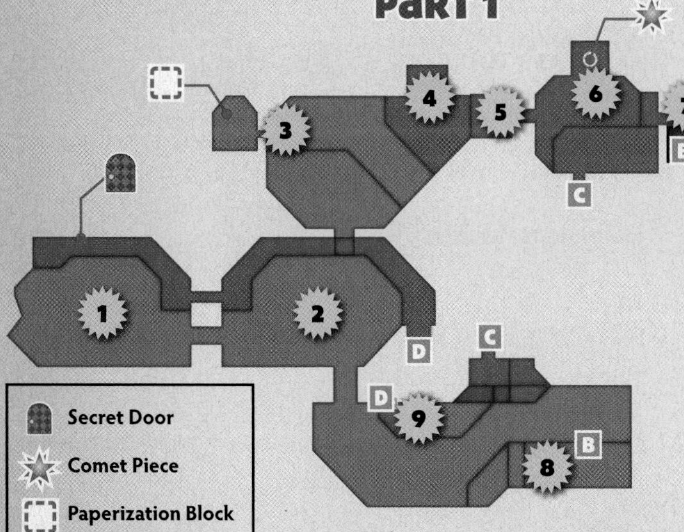

> **NOTE**
>
> During the fall, you lose Kersti, your Hammer, and all of your stickers. Without Kersti, you no longer have access to the Battle Spinner or the Paperize ability. Without your Hammer, you can't use Hammer-based stickers or destroy Scuttlebug webs. Without stickers, you have no way to defend yourself from attackers.

When you land in the first chamber, Kersti is carried off by Scuttlebugs, your Hammer is on a nearby ledge, and your stickers are scattered throughout the burrow. Your first task is to rebuild your sticker supply, but doing so requires a fair amount of exploration. Be careful to avoid combat until your Album contains a reasonable selection of stickers.

The second chamber is swarming with enemies, but the Super Star in the middle of the area makes it fairly easy to clear out the room. Collect the temporary power-up, then dash from enemy to enemy as quickly as possible. Search the area for stickers, then head through the doorway along the back wall.

> **TIP**
>
> They can be a nuisance, but tiny Scuttlebugs are too weak to initiate combat. Just walk across them until they disappear.

As you search the third chamber for stickers, look for the opening in the left wall.

Hop through the opening to find a hidden room. After you find Kersti, you can take advantage of the Paperization Block hidden in this room. For now, however, search the ? Block and return to the chamber.

4

The Wiggler Segment is trapped behind the web at Point 4. Unfortunately, you can't free the segment without the Hammer. The Big Scuttlebug is just to the right, so use the HP Block to top off your health, and then make sure you have a good selection of stickers before you continue.

5

When you're ready, approach the door to the right. The Big Scuttlebug drops down and begins a battle.

MINI-BOSS: BIG SCUTTLEBUG

Your Hammer-based stickers aren't usable at this point, and using Jump-based stickers will only get you caught in the Big Scuttlebug's web. Use stickers like Boomerangs, POW Blocks, or Fire Flowers to damage the web. The Battle Spinner isn't available, so it can take several turns before the web is completely destroyed.

Defend yourself from incoming attacks, and continue to attack the web until it disintegrates. After the Big Scuttlebug falls to the ground, attack it with Jump-based stickers. With the web out of the way, you shouldn't have any trouble finishing the battle.

6

After you defeat the Big Scuttlebug, head through the door and into the next chamber. As you follow the trail of stickers on the ground, look for the Comet Piece along the back wall. Like the Wiggler Segment, the Comet Piece is trapped behind a web. For now, search the chamber for stickers and head through the door in the right wall.

7

To find Kersti, hop on the web at Point 7 and jump in place until it gives way. After a short fall, you land to find Kersti stuck to another web. Peel Kersti free to break through the web and regain some of your lost abilities.

When you're ready, step out of the enclosure and explore the remaining chamber. Climb the steps to the left and search the area for the last of your lost stickers.

When you finish searching the chamber, move to Point 9 and peel the Burrow Door scrap from the wall.

Reapply the scrap so that it's properly aligned, then pass through the door to return to the second chamber.

Recommended Route—Part 2

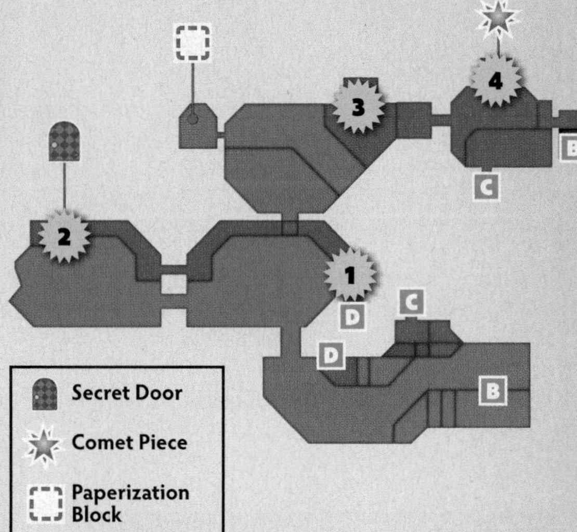

Once the Burrow Door scrap is in place, it creates a path to your Hammer. Follow the ledge along the wall and back into the first chamber.

Your Hammer is sitting at the end of the ledge, near the Secret Door location.

PAPER MARIO
Sticker Star
POW

After you recover the Hammer, apply a Secret Door sticker to the marked location and head inside to collect the Upright Vacuum.

Use your Hammer to destroy the web at Point 4. When you're ready, collect the Comet Piece to complete your visit.

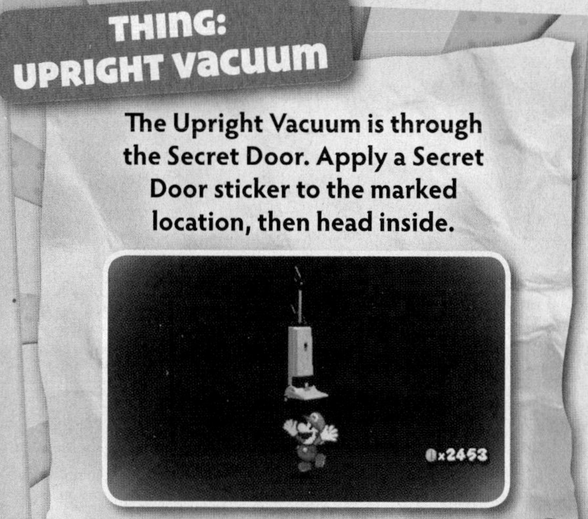

THING: UPRIGHT VACUUM

The Upright Vacuum is through the Secret Door. Apply a Secret Door sticker to the marked location, then head inside.

STICKER COMET PIECE: UNLOCKING WORLD 3-8

This Course contains a single piece of the Sticker Comet. To unlock World 3-8, simply collect the Comet Piece at the end of World 3-7.

Return to the Wiggler Segment and use your Hammer to destroy the web. After it joins you, lead the segment through the door to the right.

NOTE

When you return to the World-Map, the Wiggler Segment flees to World 3-8.

WORLD 3-8: TREE BRANCH TRAIL

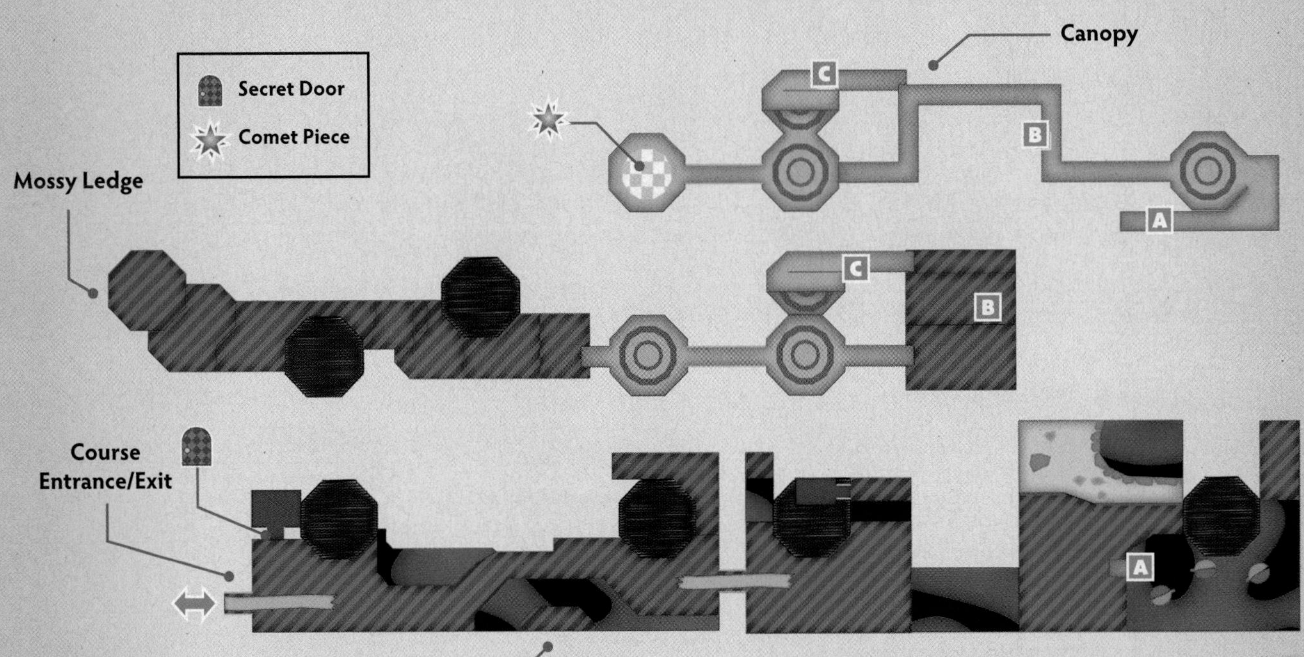

HOW TO USE THIS GUIDE
HOW TO PLAY
STICKERS
ENEMIES
WALKTHROUGH
DECALBURG
SURFSHINE HARBOR
WORLD 1
WORLD 2
WORLD 3
WORLD 4
WORLD 5
WORLD 6
CHECKLISTS

OVERVIEW

PREREQUISITES

To unlock this Course, you must collect the Comet Piece at the end of World 3-7. Before you enter the Course, purchase a Secret Door sticker from the World 3-6 Sticker Shop.

OBJECTIVES

This Course contains several objectives, most of which can be completed during a single visit:

- **Collect the Tape from the Secret Door.**
- **Collect the HP-Up Heart.**
- **Free the Wiggler Segment.**
- **Subdue the Wiggler Segment.**
- **Collect the Tree Stump scrap.**
- **Inspire the Wiggler Diary Entry.**
- **Collect the Comet Piece to unlock an alternative path to World 3-2.**
- **Collect the Watch Battery.**

IMPORTANT ITEMS AND LOCATIONS

DESCRIPTION	NOTES
Secret Door	The marked location is just inside the Course entrance.
HP-Up Heart	The HP-Up Heart is hidden on the forest floor, behind one of the large trees.
Toad Rescue	None
Luigi Location	None
Wiggler Diary Entry	Lead the Wiggler Segment to the poisoned hot springs.
Things	The Tape is through the Secret door. The Watch Battery is hidden under the first pool of poison.

> **NOTE**
>
> **The Wiggler Segment that appears in this Course does so only after you lead it out of World 3-7.**

Recommended Tactics

Most of this Course's encounters involve some combination of Snifits, Ninjis, and Scuttlebugs.

Many of the Scuttlebugs you encounter will be suspended above the ground. In addition to your standard selection of stickers, consider bringing a few Line Jumps to damage groups of airborne enemies.

After you free the Wiggler Segment, it attacks you. This segment is surprisingly agile, and it tends to dodge most Hammer-based attacks and Jump-based attacks. Thrown weapons, however, can be very effective. Try to save a few Throwing Stars or Boomerangs for this battle.

Forest Floor

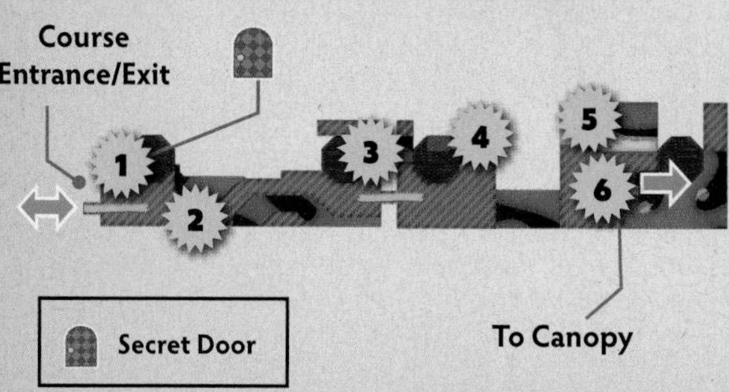

1

The Secret Door is just inside the Course's entrance. Apply a Secret Door sticker to the marked location, then head inside to find the Tape.

Thing: Tape

The Tape is behind the Secret Door. Apply a Secret Door sticker to the marked location, then head inside.

2

The Watch Battery is hidden under the poison at Point 2. Return to this location after you cleanse the forest.

There's a small ramp hidden behind the tree at Point 3. Hop on the step just past the tree, then follow the path to the left to find a ? Block.

There's a hidden room behind the tree at Point 4. To find it, cross the poisoned stream to the right of the tree and follow the path to the left. The hidden room contains an HP-Up Heart, so make sure you grab it before you move on.

HP-UP HEART: TREE BRANCH TRAIL

There's an HP-Up Heart behind one of the Course's large trees. When you reach the web on the floor, look for the poisoned stream in the background. Cross the stream, then head behind the tree to the left.

Investigate Point 5 to find an HP Block and the poisoned hot springs. After you subdue the Wiggler Segment, return to this area to inspire a Wiggler Diary Entry. For now, just use the HP Block to replace any lost health.

When you're finished exploring the forest floor, use the ramp at Point 6 to climb up to the canopy.

CANOPY—PART 1

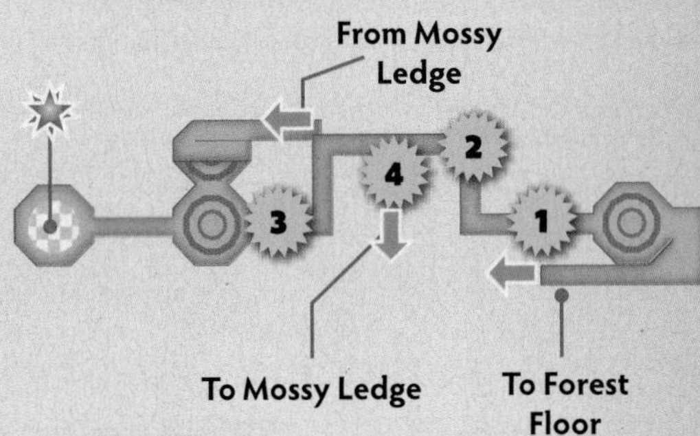

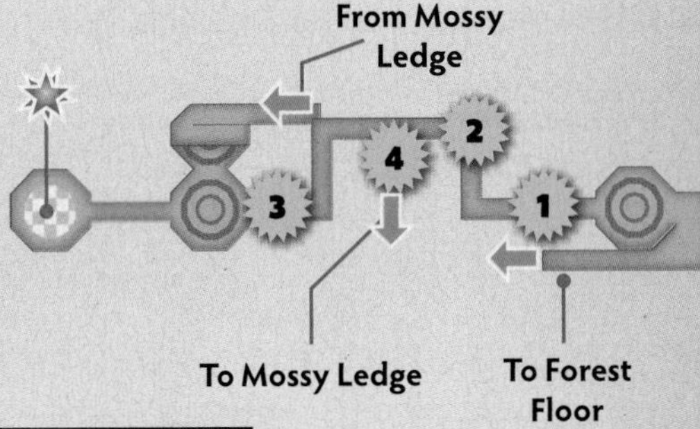

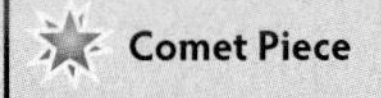

As you move along the ramps, watch out for Scuttlebugs that drop into your path. The canopy is filled with unseen enemies!

There are several Scuttlebugs hiding above the Blocks at Point 2. These enemies only reveal themselves when you're within striking distance, so be prepared to defend yourself!

The path ends just past the web. To reach the second half of the canopy, you must climb up from the mossy ledge.

When you're ready, step onto the web and hop in place. Destroy the web to drop down to the mossy ledge.

MOSSY LEDGE

When you land, take a moment to inspect your surroundings. The path to the second half of the canopy is hidden behind the bushes in the background, and the poisoned hot spring is just to the right. Once you have your bearings, follow the path to the left.

Follow the mossy ledge until you find the Wiggler Segment at Point 2, and then use your Hammer free it from the web. When the Wiggler Segment attacks, use thrown weapons like Throwing Stars and Boomerangs to defeat it.

After you subdue the Wiggler Segment, climb the steps to the left and continue along the mossy ledge.

The Tree Stump scrap is at the end of the mossy ledge. Follow the path until you reach it.

This Tree Stump scrap is needed to unlock World 3-9, so make sure you collect it!

After you collect the Tree Stump scrap, head back to the right. Return to the spot where you first landed on the mossy ledge, then jump down to the poisoned hot spring to inspire a Wiggler Diary Entry.

Wiggler Diary Entry: Tree Branch Trail

After you subdue the Wiggler Segment, drop to the forest floor and return to the poisoned hot spring to inspire a new diary entry.

After you inspire the Wiggler Diary Entry, lead the segment back to the mossy ledge. Climb the nearby ramp to the canopy, then drop back down to the mossy ledge. Step behind the bush in the background to find a hidden path.

Canopy—Part 2

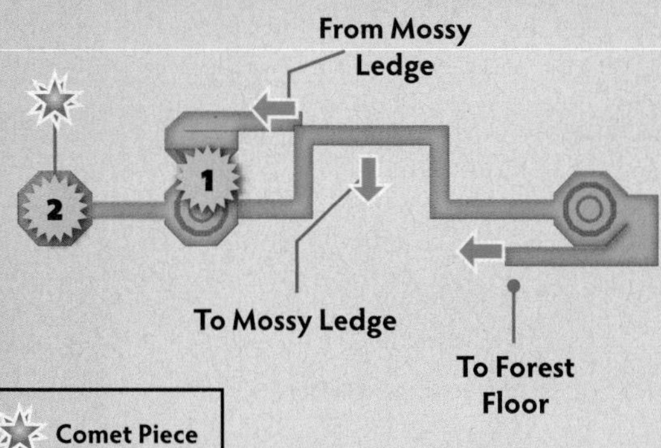

Comet Piece

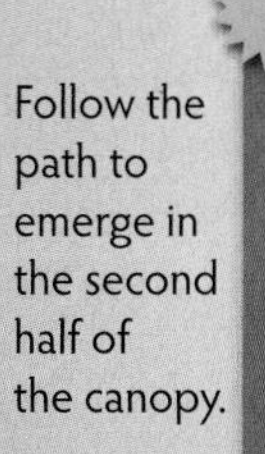

1 Follow the path to emerge in the second half of the canopy.

2 Follow the path to the left and collect the Comet Piece to complete your first visit.

Sticker Comet Piece: Unlocking the Path to World 3-2

This Course contains only a single piece of the Sticker Comet. Collect the Comet Piece from the canopy to reveal a path between World 3-8 and World 3-2.

TIP

After you complete your first visit, remember to deliver the Wiggler Segment and the Tree Stump scrap to World 3-3.

Recommended Visit #2

After you defeat the Gooper Blooper and cleanse the forest, revisit this Course and collect the Watch Battery.

Thing: Watch Battery

During your first visit, the Watch Battery is hidden in the first pool of poison. After you cleanse the forest, return to the pool and collect the exposed battery.

WORLD 3-9: GAUNTLET POND

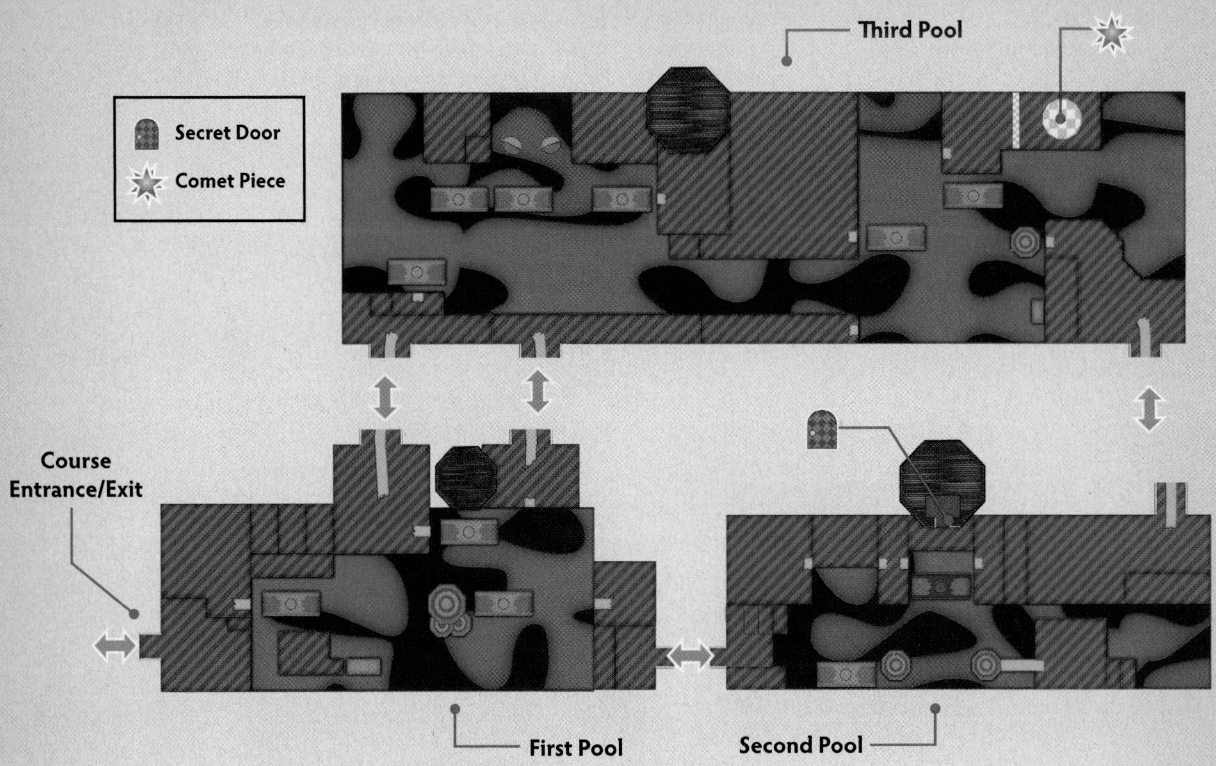

OVERVIEW

PREREQUISITES

To unlock this Course, you must collect the corresponding Comet Piece from World 3-3. To do so, you must first collect the Tree Stump from World 3-8. Before you enter the Course, make sure your Album contains a Secret Door sticker.

OBJECTIVES

This Course contains several objectives, all of which can be completed during a single visit:

- **Chase the Wiggler Segment through the Course.**
- **Collect the HP-Up Heart.**
- **Collect the shiny stickers through the Secret Door.**
- **Collect the Sponge.**
- **Free the Wiggler Segment.**
- **Collect the Comet Piece to unlock World 3-10.**

IMPORTANT ITEMS AND LOCATIONS

DESCRIPTION	NOTES
Secret Door	The marked location is beside the second pool, below the poison gas.
HP-Up Heart	The HP-Up Heart is hidden under the steps at the left edge of the second pool.
Toad Rescue	None
Luigi Location	None
Wiggler Diary Entry	None
Things	The Sponge is in the third pool, near the Comet Piece.

RECOMMENDED TACTICS

Most of the enemies in this Course are lurking in or around the poison pools. Whenever possible, avoid initiating combat in toxic areas.

In addition to Snifits and Ninjis, this Course contains several Poison Bloopers. As the name implies, these creatures use poison attacks to damage you over several turns. Block each attack to avoid the poison's effects, and use Jump-based stickers or thrown weapons to take them down quickly.

FIRST POOL

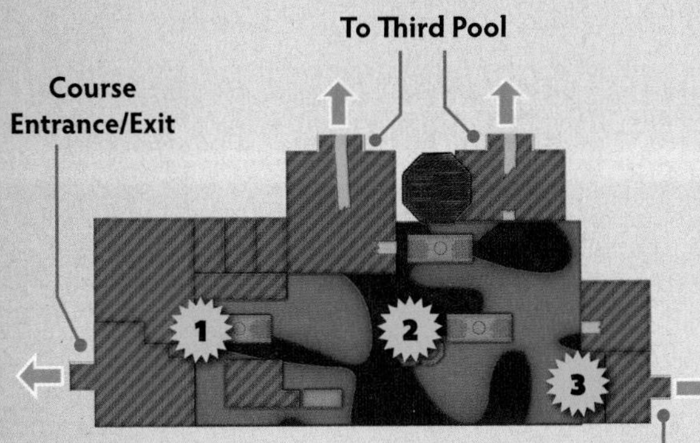

When you first enter the Course, the Wiggler Segment is standing on a platform in the first pool. Hop on the swinging platform at Point 1 and ride it to the stumps in the center of the pool.

When you reach the stumps, look for the poison gas spewing out of the tree in the background. Activate the Paperize ability, then select a sticker from your Album. Apply the sticker to the indicated spot to stop the flow of poison, then use the next swinging platform to cross the rest of the pool.

Peel the Bowser tape at the pool's right edge to free the floating platform, then hop on before it drifts out of range.

The platform carries you toward the Wiggler Segment. When you're in range, hop onto the platform to chase the segment out of the area. Return to the floating platform and ride back to the pool's right edge. When you're ready, follow the path to the second pool.

Second Pool

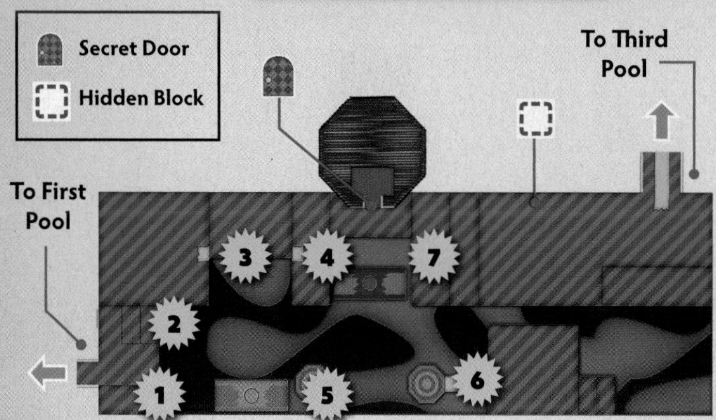

HP-Up Heart: Gauntlet Pond

The HP-Up Heart is hidden under the steps along the second pool's left edge. Drop into the poison, then dash under the steps to find the hidden area.

To make the most of this visit, you have to spend some time running around in the poison. Use the HP Block at Point 1 to refill Mario's HP between each dip in the pool.

Stop by the HP Block to top off your health, then climb up to Point 3. Wait for the platform to swing into position, then hop over to the next ledge. Peel the Bowser tape near the poison gas to free the poison-stained platform from the ledge.

2

There's a hidden area under the steps at Point 2. Climb to the top of the steps, then drop into the poison and dash to the left to find an HP-Up Heart surrounded by coins.

The Secret Door is located at Point 4, just under the poison gas. Apply a Secret Door sticker to the marked location, then drop down and head through the door. Search the ? Blocks for shiny stickers, then dash through the poison pool and return to the HP Block.

5

After you top off Mario's HP, climb back up to the swinging platforms. You can't block the gas flowing from this tree, so use the swinging platforms to move across the stumps in the center of the pool.

6

When you reach the second stump, follow the ramp down to the Wiggler Segment. When the segment flees, head back up the ramp and ride the poison-stained platform toward the background.

TIP

There's a Super Star near the pool's right edge. This power-up can be very useful if you accidentally fall into the poison.

7

When the poison-stained platform reaches the background, jump to the ledge to the right and follow the Wiggler Segment to the third pool.

TIP

Stand between the Blocks near Point 7, then jump up to find the Hidden Block between them.

THIRD POOL

WORLD 3-9

1

Peel the Bowser tape at Point 1 to free the floating platform, then hop up to the nearby stump and move across the swinging platforms. Although you can ride these platforms straight to the Comet Piece, you have some unfinished business to see to.

THING: SPONGE

The Sponge is on a platform near the third pool's rear-left corner. Before you collect it, use your Hammer to clean the poison off of the Sponge.

2

Ride over to the large cluster of platforms near the center of the pool. After you search the area for stickers, jump down to the small platform just past the large tree.

3

Follow the leaves to the left to find the Sponge. Before you collect the Sponge, strike it with your Hammer to clean it.

4

Follow the leaves back to the center of the pool, then continue along the swinging platforms. When you reach the pool's left edge, move to the foreground and make a quick detour back to the first pool.

The path leads to a previously unreachable ledge. Peel the Bowser tape at the end of the path to reveal a set of steps. This path is now accessible from the first pool!

Hop onto the nearby swinging platform and ride over to the next ledge. Follow the path back toward the third pool.

5

The path takes you to a narrow platform near the trapped Wiggler Segment. Hop on the drifting stump and pull the segment loose. Once it's free, the Wiggler Segment automatically joins you.

6

Hop off of the stump and follow the path to the right. Wait for the floating platform to drift into range, then hop on and ride to the pool's right edge.

NOTE

The floating platform appears only if you freed it upon entering the area.

7

Use the swinging platforms to reach Point 7. When you're ready, collect the Comet Piece to end your visit.

Sticker Comet Piece: Unlocking World 3-10

This Course contains a single piece of the Sticker Comet. To unlock World 3-10, collect the Comet Piece from the third pool.

NOTE

When you return to the World-Map, the Wiggler Segment flees to World 3-10.

WORLD 3-10: STUMP GLADE

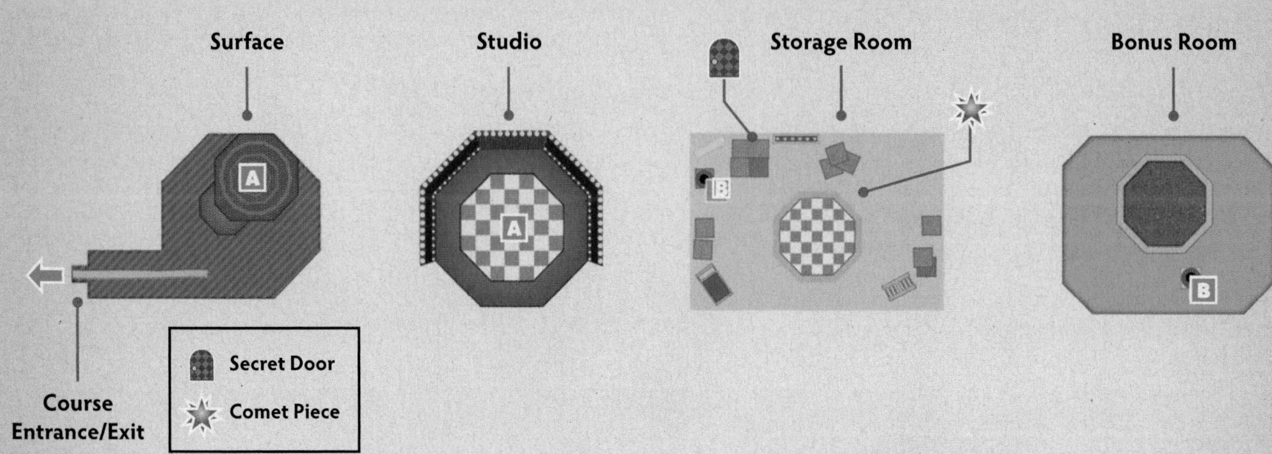

OVERVIEW

PREREQUISITES

To unlock this Course, you must collect the Comet Piece from World 3-9. Before you enter this Course, make sure your Album contains a Secret Door sticker.

> **NOTE**
>
> The Wiggler Segment appears in this Course only after you free it from World 3-9.

OBJECTIVES

This Course contains several objectives, some of which require additional visits:

- Complete the quiz show to rescue the Wiggler Segment.
- Complete the special challenge to collect the Radiator.
- Collect the Square Can from the Secret Door.
- Collect the Comet Piece to unlock the path to World 3-7.
- Inspire the Wiggler Diary Entry.
- Collect the HP-Up Heart.

IMPORTANT ITEMS AND LOCATIONS

DESCRIPTION	NOTES
Secret Door	The marked location is in the storage room.
HP-Up Heart	After you cleanse the forest, the HP-Up Heart appears in the storage room.
Toad Rescue	None
Luigi Location	None
Wiggler Diary Entry	Complete the quiz show a second time while the Wiggler Segment watches.
Things	The Radiator is in the bonus room. The Square Can is through the Secret Door.

RECOMMENDED TACTICS

If you perform well in the quiz show, you can complete the Course without fighting a single battle. If you stumble along the way, however, you may be forced to defend yourself.

If you're forced to fight, the encounter is sure to involve a Snifit and a cloud of poison gas. Bring a few high-damage stickers to ensure you can end any battles quickly.

SURFACE

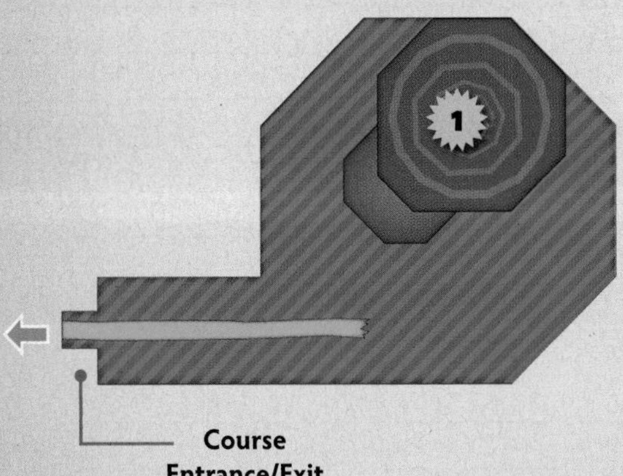

When you start the Course, follow the path to find a large stump. Drop through the hole in the center of the stump to trigger a brief cinematic.

STUDIO

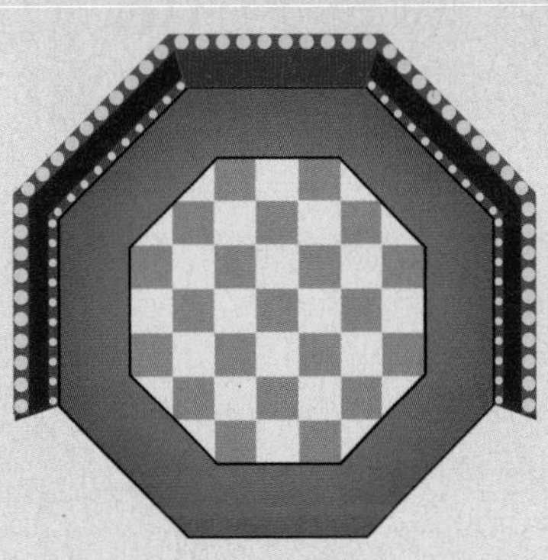

Each round of the quiz show takes place on a separate floor. As you progress through the game, you automatically transition between each room.

WORLD 3-10

ROUND 1: PICK-AND-CHOOSE PANIC

The Snifits have captured the Wiggler Segment. To free it, you must successfully complete their quiz show. Accept the challenge to begin the Pick-and-Choose Panic.

During this round you must answer a series of true-or-false questions. If the host's statement is true, hit the green Check Block on the left. If the statement is false, hit the red X Block on the right. To complete the round, you must correctly answer three questions before you succumb to the poison gas.

QUIZ SHOW QUESTIONS

STATEMENT	TRUE OR FALSE?
You're at Decalburg's Sticker Shop. A Mushroom sticker costs 15 coins.	True
Some Toads were locked up inside a cupboard in Decalburg. There were nine Toads inside that cupboard.	False
Straight up, Bowser's cooler than Mario!	True
If you get all Poison Mushrooms in the Battle Spinner, all foes get poisoned.	False
A Jump sticker will cost you 3 coins. You can sell one for 2.	True
Koopas, Paratroopas, and Lakitus can all fly.	False
When Mario and Kersti first met, Kersti was stuck to a sign.	True
If you use a Mushroom sticker, your HP will be restored.	True
My dinner last night was a delicious mushroom steak.	True
Kamek, Lakitu, and Bowser Jr. all wear glasses.	False
Kamek can fly through the sky. He rides a broom.	True
This doesn't leave this room, but…Princess Peach is actually a man.	False
Your host's name is Snifit.	True
To swing the Hammer, you press Ⓨ.	False
To swing the Hammer, you press Ⓑ.	True
This doesn't leave the room but…King Bowser actually loathes Princess Peach.	False
If you get a Super Star, you temporarily become invincible.	True
If you get a Super Star, you temporarily become invisible.	False
If you have an Iron Jump sticker, you can jump on enemies with spikes.	True
Mario has no siblings.	False
To use the Battle Spinner, you need 5 coins.	False
If you use a Mushroom sticker, Mario's body gets big.	False
Right now there are 30 Snifits in the studio audience.	True
If you're low on HP, you can't use the Paperize ability.	False
Mario, Toads, and Koopa Troopas all wear shoes.	True
Bowser Jr.'s father is King Bowser, and his mother is Princess Peach.	False
Wiggler's body has four segments, not counting the head.	True
A Hammer sticker has a more powerful attack than a Shiny Hammer sticker.	False
A Shiny Jump sticker is more expensive than a Jump sticker.	True
If you use a Spike Helmet sticker, you can also stomp enemies with spikes.	False

Score three correct answers to win the round and drop to the next floor.

Round 2: Big Bonking Snifit Bash

During the second round, you must use your Hammer to strike Snifits as they poke their heads out of the studio floor. Watch the four holes in the floor for signs of emerging Snifits. When you spot a potential target, get into position and whack it with your Hammer.

To complete the round, you must strike 20 Snifits before you succumb to the poison gas.

Round 3: Unrelentingly Exciting Shuffle Game

During the third round, you're shown three special Blocks. One Block is identified as the correct answer, and the two remaining Blocks—which contain Snifits—are identified as wrong answers. After a brief explanation, the Blocks are sealed and shuffled. When they stop, you must hit the Block you believe to be the correct answer.

There are three phases to this challenge. If you choose correctly, you move onto the next phase. If you chose the wrong Block, you're attacked by a Snifit. Your task becomes more difficult during each phase. After one correct answer, the shuffle speed increases. After your second correct answer, an extra Block enters the mix.

Choose the correct Block three times to complete the quiz show and free the Wiggler Segment. After a moment, the floor falls away, dropping you to the storage room.

Post Show

After you complete the quiz show, the host meets you in the storage room and offers you the chance to participate in a special challenge.

Accept the challenge to participate in the Big-Bonking-Panic-Pick-and-Choose Snifit Bash. This round combines elements of earlier rounds. You must correctly answer three true-or-false questions before you succumb to the poison gas, but before you're allowed to answer each question, you must hit five Snifits with your Hammer.

WORLD 3-10

2

When you complete the challenge, you're dropped into a bonus room that contains your reward. Open the gift to collect the Radiator, then use the nearby Warp Pipe to return to the storage room.

THING: RADIATOR

To collect the Radiator, complete the special challenge, then open the gift in the bonus room.

3

The Secret Door is on the back wall, just above the stacked crates. Apply a Secret Door sticker to the marked location. Climb the crates to the right, then jump over to the Secret Door and head inside to find the Square Can.

THING: SQUARE CAN

To collect the Square Can, apply a Secret Door sticker to the marked location in the storage room and head inside.

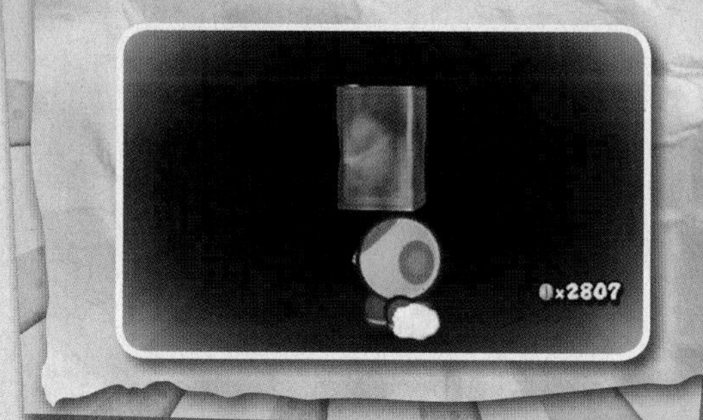

4

When you're ready, collect the Comet Piece in the storage room to complete your first visit.

STICKER COMET PIECE: UNLOCKING THE PATH TO WORLD 3-7

This Course contains a single piece of the Sticker Comet. Collect the Comet Piece in the storage room to unlock the path between World 3-10 and World 3-7.

NOTE

When you reach the World-Map the Wiggler Segment flees to World 3-2.

ADDITIONAL VISITS

RECOMMENDED VISIT #2

After you subdue the Wiggler Segment in World 3-2, lead it back to this Course. Drop through the large stump and complete the quiz show for a second time.

WIGGLER DIARY ENTRY: STUMP GLADE

Lead a Wiggler Segment back to World 3-10 and agree to participate in the quiz show. Complete the quiz show while the segment watches from the audience to inspire a new diary entry.

RECOMMENDED VISIT #3

After you defeat the Gooper Blooper and cleanse the forest, return to this Course and decline to participate in the quiz show. After the host drops you into the storage room, move to the foreground to collect an HP-Up Heart.

HP-UP HEART: STUMP GLADE

After you cleanse the forest, return to this Course and decline to participate in the quiz show. The HP-Up Heart is in the foreground of the storage room.

WORLD 3-11: HOLEY THICKET

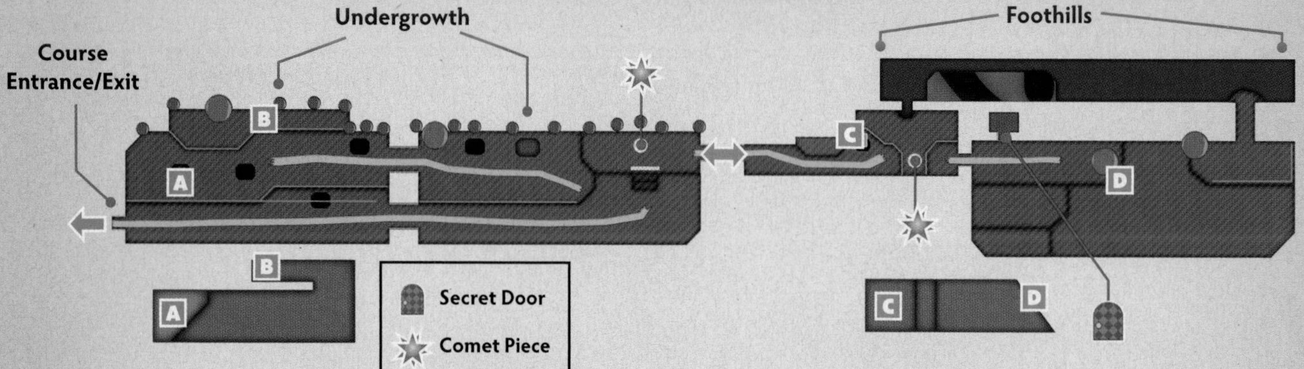

OVERVIEW

PREREQUISITES

To unlock this Course, you must collect the Comet Piece from the bowling alley in World 3-4. Before you enter this Course, make sure your Album contains a Secret Door sticker.

OBJECTIVES

This Course contains several objectives, at least one of which requires an additional visit:

- **Locate the Wiggler Segment.**
- **Recover and apply the Bowser Tape scrap.**
- **Collect the Comet Piece to unlock the path to World 3-9.**
- **Rescue the bullied Toad.**
- **Collect the Balloon from the Secret Door.**
- **Collect the Comet Piece to unlock World 3-12.**

NOTE

Although most of these objectives can be completed during your first visit, it's simpler to address the second half of the Course during your second visit.

IMPORTANT ITEMS AND LOCATIONS

DESCRIPTION	NOTES
Secret Door	The marked location is near the center of the foothills.
HP-Up Heart	None
Toad Rescue	The bullied Toad is on the left edge of the foothills.
Luigi Location	None
Wiggler Diary Entry	None
Things	The Balloon is through the Secret Door.

RECOMMENDED TACTICS

This Course contains most of the enemies you've encountered throughout World Three.

In addition to Ninjis and Poison Bloopers, you're likely to encounter Boomerang Bros, Piranha Plants, and Spike Tops. Make sure you have a good selection of Jump-based stickers, Hammers, and multi-target attacks. As always, the Battle Spinner can simplify any encounter.

RECOMMENDED VISIT #1

CAUTION

Watch your step! This Course contains a lot of toxic puddles, some of which can be very hard to see.

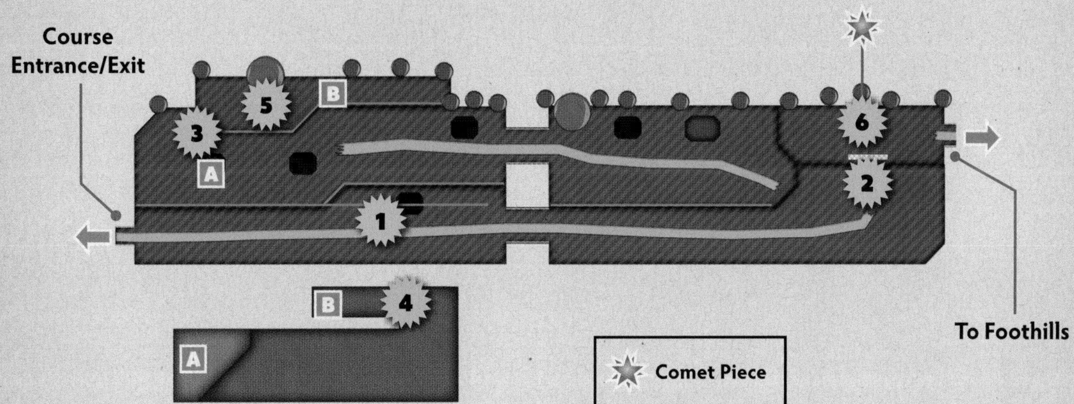

The Wiggler Segment is behind the hedge at Point 1. To reach it, continue along the path until you reach the end of the hedge, then slip behind it and double back to Point 1.

As you approach the Wiggler Segment, two Poison Bloopers grab it and carry it off to World 3-12.

After the Wiggler Segment leaves the Course, return to the main path and follow it to Point 2. The Course's first Comet Piece is floating nearby. Before you can reach it, however, you must track down a missing scrap.

When you peel the Bowser tape on the ground, it creates a hole in the ground. Drop down to find an underground passage.

Hop on the small ledge to the left, then follow the path through the undergrowth's back half. As you do, peel the Bowser tape scattered throughout the area.

When you land, follow the path to the right, then move toward the background and climb back up to the surface.

Clear out the Boomerang Bro at Point 3, search the area for stickers, then peel the nearby strips of Bowser tape.

The passage leads to a small area with a single tree surrounded by a hedge. Strike the tree with your Hammer to knock the Bowser Tape scrap loose.

Collect the Bowser Tape scrap, then hop over the hedge and follow the path to the right.

Return to Point 2 and apply the Bowser Tape scrap to the indicated location. After it's in place, peel the tape to reveal a set of steps.

6

Climb the steps to find the Course's first Comet Piece, then collect it to end your first visit.

Sticker Comet Piece: Unlocking the Path to World 3-9

This Course contains two pieces of the Sticker Comet, one of which opens an alternative route to a previously visited Course. Collect the Comet Piece along the right edge of the undergrowth to reveal the shortcut between World 3-11 and World 3-9.

Recommended Visit #2

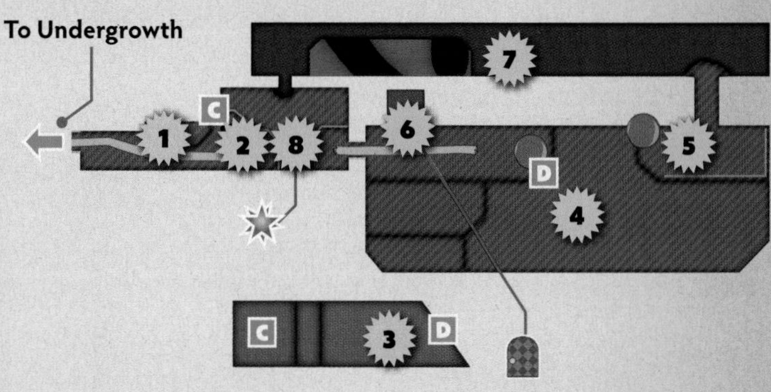

WORLD 3-11

After you collect the first Comet Piece, there's still plenty to do. Revisit the Course and follow the path through the undergrowth into the foothills. Approach the small platform at Point 1 to find a Toad being bullied by two Poison Bloopers.

It's a bit difficult to see, but there's a hole in the center of the toxic puddle at Point 2. Hop into the hole to drop to an underground passage—just make sure you avoid touching the poison surrounding it!

Toad Rescue: Holey Thicket

The third available Toad rescue takes place in the foothills of World 3-11. Pay the Poison Bloopers 50 coins to stop bullying the Toad, or simply defeat them in battle. The Poison Bloopers are fairly resilient, so consider using the Battle Spinner to earn at least one extra turn. Use two Hopslippers or some basic multi-target stickers to defeat them with ease.

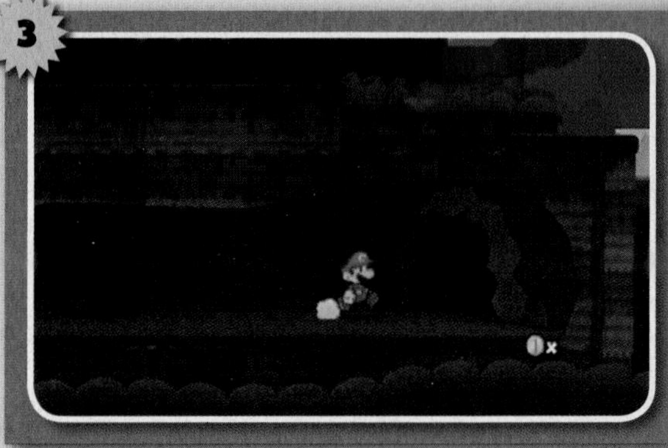

When you land, follow the path to the right and exit the passage.

When you emerge from the passage, search the nearby area for stickers. Before you head deeper into the Course, however, climb the steps to the left and explore the area along the back wall.

5

The Secret Door is at Point 5. Apply a Secret Door sticker to the marked location, then head inside to collect the Balloon.

THING: BALLOON

The Balloon is beyond the Secret Door. To find it, apply a Secret Door sticker to the marked location, then head inside.

6

The poison splattered at Point 6 marks an opening in the back wall. Approach the opening, then head inside to find a tunnel.

7

As you follow the tunnel to the left, take care to avoid the toxic puddles and poison pools along your path. A couple of Poison Bloopers patrol the area, too, so try to initiate combat while you're on dry ground.

8

After you emerge from the tunnel, collect the second Comet Piece to end your visit.

STICKER COMET PIECE: UNLOCKING WORLD 3-12

This Course contains two pieces of the Sticker Comet. To unlock World 3-12, collect the Comet Piece located in the foothills.

WORLD 3-12: WHITECAP BEACH

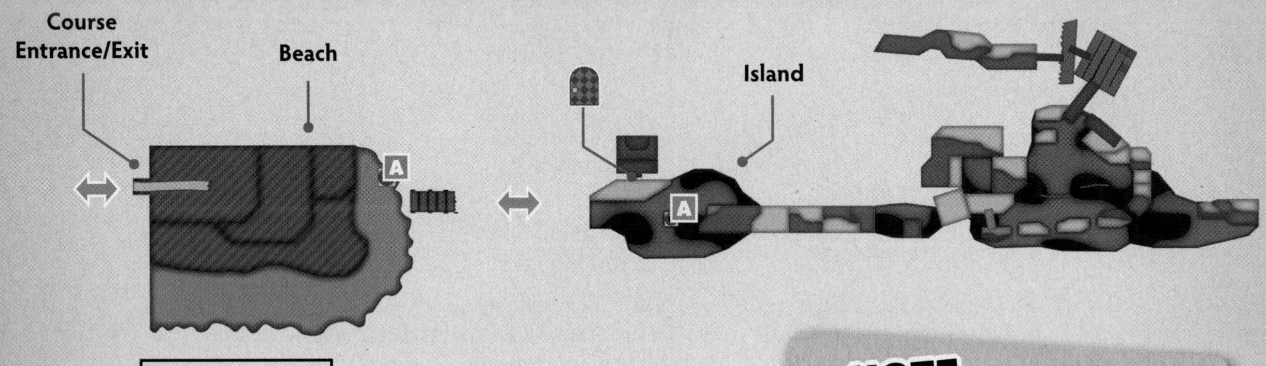

NOTE

The Warp Pipes indicated on this Course's maps appear only after you defeat the Gooper Blooper.

OVERVIEW

PREREQUISITES

To unlock this Course, you must collect the corresponding Comet Piece from the foothills in World 3-11. Make sure your Album contains a Secret Door sticker before you make your second visit. To reach the island off the coast, you must reassemble Wiggler in World 3-3.

NOTE

The Wiggler Segment that appears in this Course does so only after you find it in World 3-11.

ESSENTIAL THING STICKERS

NAME	THING LOCATION	NOTES
Sponge	World 3-9	Recommended for the boss battle.
Faucet	World 1-3	Recommended for the boss battle.

OBJECTIVES

This Course contains several objectives, some of which require an additional visit:

- **Collect the Pocket Watch.**
- **Defeat the Wiggler Segment.**
- **Find Luigi.**
- **Ride Wiggler to the island.**
- **Collect the Newspaper from the Secret Door.**
- **Traverse the poisoned island.**
- **Defeat the Gooper Blooper.**
- **Collect the Royal Sticker.**

IMPORTANT ITEMS AND LOCATIONS

DESCRIPTION	NOTES
Secret Door	The marked location is at the start of the island.
HP-Up Heart	None
Toad Rescue	None
Luigi Location	Luigi is on a rock formation near the pier.
Wiggler Diary Entry	None
Things	The Pocket Watch is on the beach. The Newspaper is through the Secret Door.

RECOMMENDED TACTICS

This Course contains some pretty intense battles, so make sure your Album is well stocked!

When you catch up with the fourth Wiggler Segment, it decides to attack. Two Poison Bloopers join the fight, so it's best to bring a few multi-target stickers. Stickers like Burnhammers and Shells help ensure the Poison Bloopers don't have an opportunity to attack, but there's always a chance the agile Wiggler Segment will dodge your initial attack—take advantage of the Battle Spinner!

The Cheep Cheeps throughout the island tend to leap into your path. Try to dodge them, then initiate each battle with a stomp or a Hammer strike. A basic selection of Battle Stickers should allow you to quickly dispatch these pesky enemies.

The Gooper Blooper is a fierce opponent, and its poison attacks can cause serious damage over the course of the battle. Use the Sponge to counter poison attacks, and use the Faucet to wash away any poison that makes it past your defenses. Bring high-damage stickers like Shiny Slaphammers and Shiny Eekhammers, and make sure you keep plenty of Mushrooms on hand.

RECOMMENDED VISIT #1

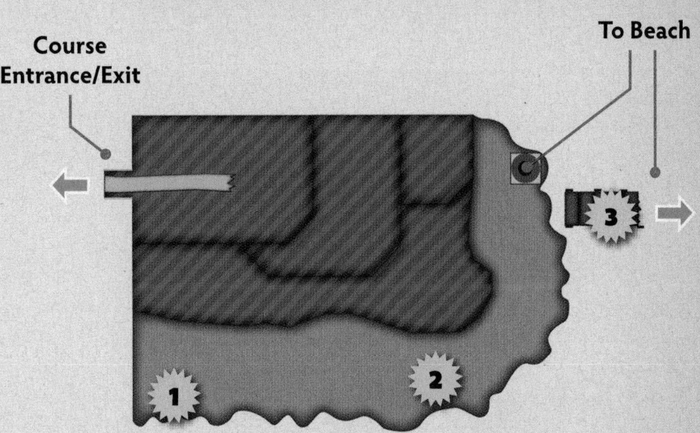

The Pocket Watch is buried in the sand at Point 1. When you enter the Course, move toward the foreground to find the top of the Pocket Watch near the coastline.

THING: POCKET WATCH

To collect the Pocket Watch, examine the metal loop protruding from the sand near the left edge of the beach.

When you approach Point 2, the Wiggler Segment jumps up and joins forces with the Poison Bloopers that carried it out of World 3-11! Take advantage of the Battle Spinner, and use multi-target stickers such as Shiny Fire Flowers and Shiny Ice Flowers to end the battle quickly.

After you defeat the Wiggler Segment, it moves to the pier. Wait for the Wiggler Segment to exit the Course, then examine the rock formations in the background to find Luigi. Use the Paperize ability to pull Luigi off of the rock formation, then follow the Wiggler Segment out of the Course.

Luigi Location: Whitecap Beach

Luigi is on one of the rock formations that can be seen from the pier.

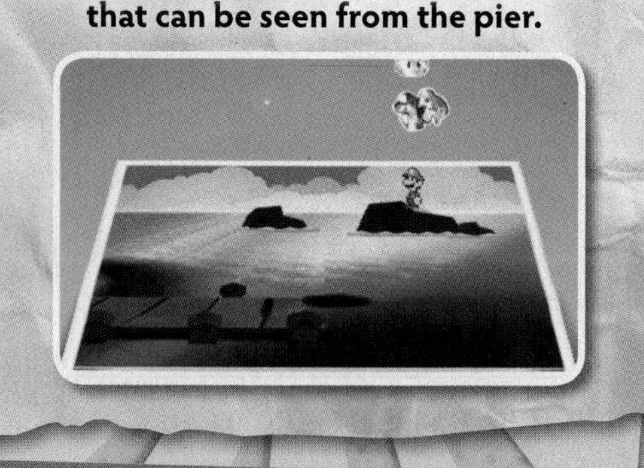

NOTE

After the Wiggler Segment leaves the Course, it flees to Surfshine Harbor. Retrieve the Wiggler Segment, use it to inspire any remaining diary entries, then deliver it to Wiggler in World 3-3.

Recommended Visit #2

Reaching the Island

Before you revisit World 3-12, make sure you reassemble Wiggler. Deliver all four Wiggler Segments to World 3-3, then use the Paperize ability to put Wiggler back together. When you do, Wiggler storms out of the tree house.

When you return to World 3-12, Wiggler is waiting on the pier. Speak to Wiggler when you're ready to travel to the island.

Thing: Newspaper

The Newspaper is through the Secret Door. When you reach the island, apply a Secret Door sticker to the marked location, then head inside.

TIP

There's an HP Block just before the boss battle, but there are a lot of potential fights along the way. If you'd rather not hop through the poison, you can return to collect the Newspaper after you purge the poison from the area.

1

When you're ready to face the Gooper Blooper, ride Wiggler out to the island. Wiggler drops you off near the Secret Door. Apply a Secret Door sticker to the marked location, then hop through the poison and enter the door to find the Newspaper.

2

As you follow the path across the island, watch out for Cheep Cheeps leaping from the water. Avoid them, or wait for them to land before you attack. Use the barrels scattered around the area to cross the poison between the platforms.

WORLD 3-12

As you search the area for stickers, don't forget to check the ? Block at Point 3. Use the barrel to move across the poison, or hop through the porthole in the wreckage.

As you approach Point 4, two large tentacles slam down in your path. Don't bother trying to attack them—just try to avoid getting hit.

Hop onto the barrel at Point 5, then adjust your position to keep from falling off as it moves across the surface of the poison.

There's a Hidden Block above the blue flower on the next ledge. Make sure you collect its contents before you continue through the area.

When you're finished searching for stickers, head into the wreckage at Point 6.

Use the Save Block and the HP Block, then follow the path to the next area.

When you approach Point 7, the Gooper Blooper bursts out from the wreckage.

GOOPER BLOOPER

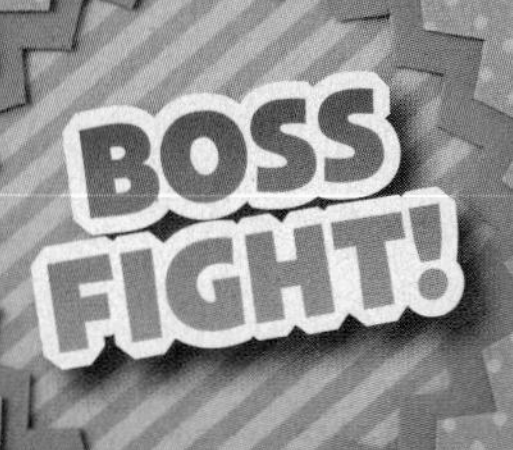

The Gooper Blooper turns dark purple just before it sprays poison. When you see it change color, use the Sponge sticker to counter the incoming attack. The Sponge not only absorbs the poison, it sprays it back at the Gooper Blooper. In addition to damaging your enemy, this compromises the Gooper Blooper's aim and damage resistance for the next several turns.

The Gooper Blooper has a lot of HP, so don't hesitate to use high-damage, single-target stickers. Shiny Slaphammers and Shiny Eekhammers are very effective, but if you have a selection of flashy stickers, consider using a few.

If you're hit by the Gooper Blooper's poison spray, use the Faucet sticker to purge yourself of the poison's effects. Use Mushroom stickers as needed, and continue to deal damage until you defeat this formidable foe.

8

After you defeat the Gooper Blooper, collect the Royal Sticker to complete your second visit.

The Cleansed Forest

When you defeat the Gooper Blooper, all of the Courses in World Three are cleansed! This grants safe access to areas that used to be poisoned, and you'll also find some new items in previously visited Courses:

- **Collect the HP-Up Heart from the end of World 3-1.**
- **Collect the Watch Battery from the drained pool at the beginning of World 3-8.**
- **Decline the quiz show in World 3-10 and collect the HP-Up Heart in the storage room.**

WORLD FOUR

WORLD FOUR COURSES

NUMBER	NAME
World 4-1	Snow Rise
World 4-2	Ice Flow
World 4-3	The Enigmansion
World 4-4	Shaved-Ice Cave
World 4-5	Whiteout Valley
World 4-6	Bowser's Snow Fort

World Four is covered in snow, and many of the enemies you'll encounter are immune to cold-based attacks. You'll also face a number of shiny enemy variants, so use the World 4-4 Sticker Shop to stock up on high-quality stickers.

Battle Ice Bros, Snow Spikes, Boos, and more as you make your way to Bowser's Snow Fort. Defeat the Bowser Ice Statue and the mysterious Mizzter Blizzard to add another Royal Sticker to your collection!

WORLD 4-1: Snow Rise

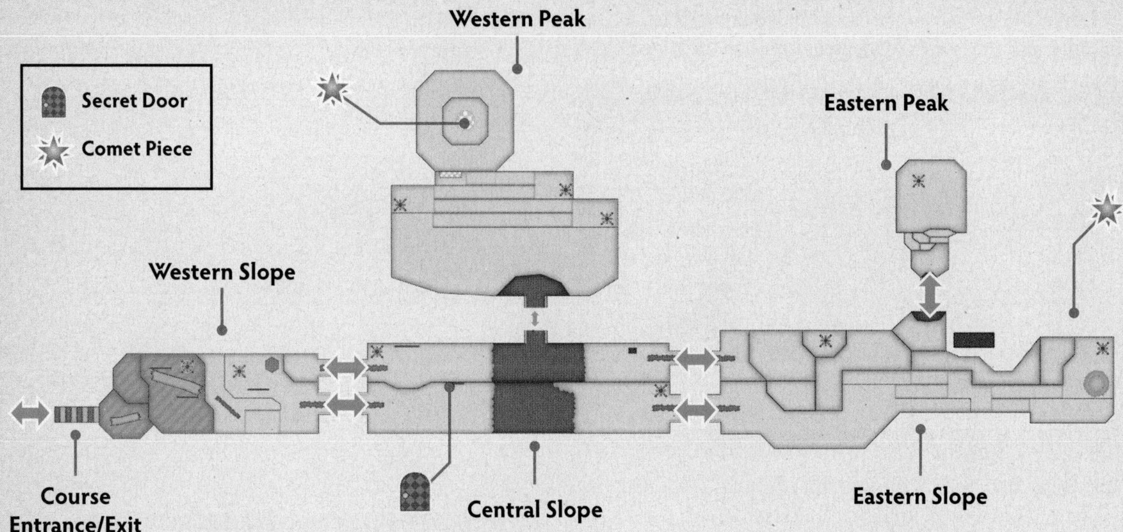

Overview

Prerequisites

This Course becomes available as soon as you defeat the Big Cheep Cheep in Surfshine Harbor. Before you enter the Course, make sure your Album contains a Secret Door sticker, a Fire Flower, and the Radiator Thing Sticker.

ESSENTIAL THING STICKERS

NAME	THING LOCATION	NOTES
Radiator	World 3-10	Needed to melt the central slope.

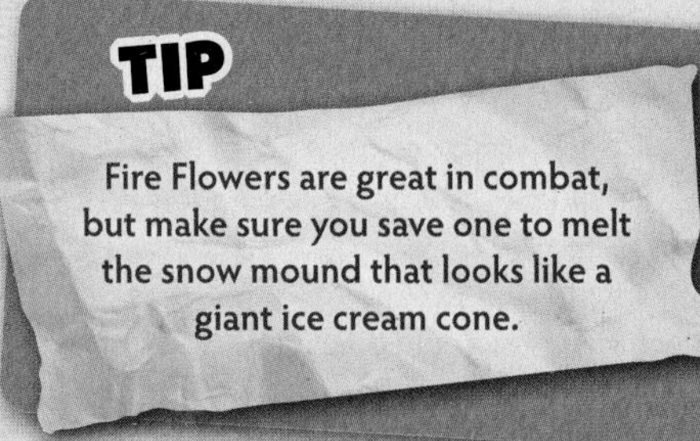

Fire Flowers are great in combat, but make sure you save one to melt the snow mound that looks like a giant ice cream cone.

Objectives

This Course contains several objectives, at least one of which requires an additional visit:

- **Use a Fire Flower to melt the giant ice cream cone.**
- **Use the Radiator to melt the central slope.**
- **Collect the Cell Phone from the Secret Door.**
- **Collect the Goat.**
- **Collect the Pipe in a Cave scrap.**
- **Collect the Comet Piece to unlock World 4-2.**
- **Apply the Pipe in a Cave scrap to the proper location.**
- **Collect the Comet Piece to unlock World 4-5.**

IMPORTANT ITEMS AND LOCATIONS

DESCRIPTION	NOTES
Secret Door	The marked location is hidden under the central slope.
HP-Up Heart	None
Toad Rescue	None
Luigi Location	None
Wiggler Diary Entry	None
Things	The Cell Phone is through the Secret Door. The Goat appears on the eastern peak.

Recommended Tactics

This Course introduces some significantly tougher enemies that pose new problems both in and out of battle. Make sure you stock up on higher-quality stickers, and stay alert as you move through each area.

The Shiny Goombas and Shiny Paragoombas are much more durable than their basic counterparts, and they tend to attack in large groups. Powerful, multi-target stickers such as Shiny Shells work well, but a properly used Spike Helmet is very effective against large groups of Shiny Goombas.

Snow Spikes tend to attack from higher ground, so be cautious when climbing the Course's various inclines. Use your Hammer to destroy incoming Snowballs, and watch out for additional enemies that might be riding the projectiles heading toward you. Once you initiate combat, use shiny stickers to help ensure you do sufficient damage with each attack.

Western Slope

From Central Slope

1

Course Entrance/Exit

To Central Slope

1

The western slope contains a few enemies and stickers, and it also contains a hidden scrap! Move to the formation that looks like a giant ice cream cone. Activate the Paperize ability and apply a Fire Flower to the indicated spot.

The ice melts, revealing the Pipe in a Cave scrap. To collect the scrap, however, you must approach the platform from the right. When you're ready, follow the path to the central slope.

central slope—part 1

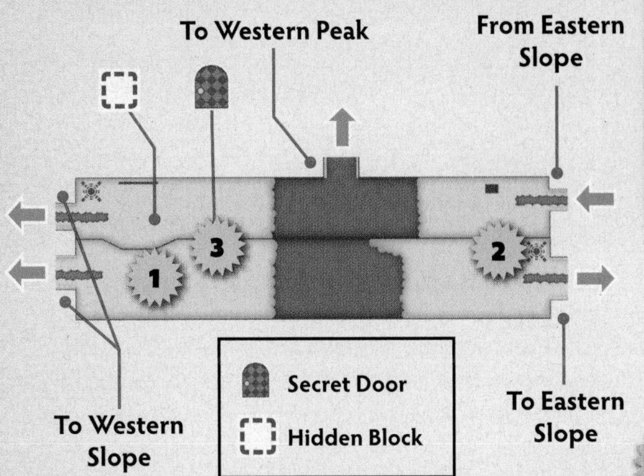

1

The first time you visit the central slope, the area is covered in fresh snow. As you move through the area, dodge the Cooligans sliding through your path.

2

When you reach the right edge of the fresh snow, activate the Paperize ability.

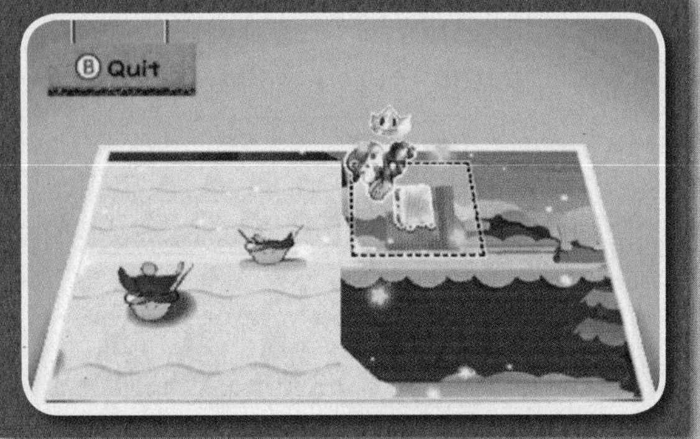

Apply the Radiator sticker to the marked spot on the ledge above you. Once the Radiator's in place, it melts the fresh snow. This not only reveals some hidden areas, it prevents the Cooligans from moving through the area.

3

After the snow melts, move back to the left and apply a Secret Door sticker to the marked location at Point 3. Head inside to find the Cell Phone. When you're finished, continue along the path to find the eastern slope.

thing: cell phone

The Cell Phone is through the Secret Door. Use the Radiator sticker to melt the fresh snow, then apply a Secret Door sticker to the marked location. When the door is in place, head inside and collect the Cell Phone.

WORLD 4-1

Eastern Slope—Part 1

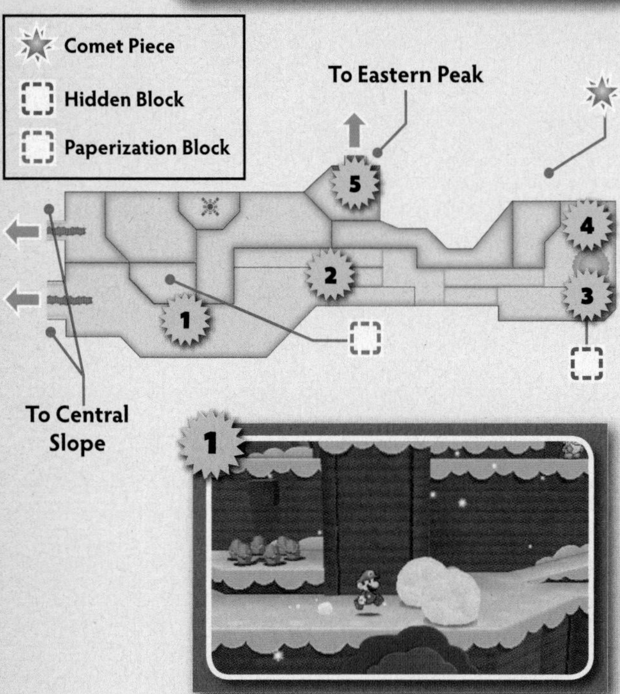

Look for the Paperization Block above the ledge at Point 1, then use your Hammer to clear the Snowballs out of your path.

As you approach Point 2, watch out for incoming Snowballs! You'll find Snow Spikes along most inclines, so use your Hammer to protect yourself. When you reach the first Snow Spike, defeat it in battle, then follow the path to the right.

caution

When you're hit by a Snowball, it not only does damage, it carries you back down the hill! It only takes one Hammer strike to destroy a Snowball, but proper timing is essential.

As you follow the path, stay near the foreground to arrive at Point 3. After you collect the Pipe in a Cave scrap, return to this area and apply it to the wall. For now, however, locate the Hidden Block above the blue flower, then follow the path to the ledge above you.

The snow mound at Point 4 covers a hole in the ground. After you apply the Pipe in a Cave scrap to the indicated spot back at Point 3, you can drop through the snow mound and warp over to the Comet Piece floating in the background. For now, follow the path to the left and continue to the top of the slope.

When you reach the top of the slope, follow the path through the back wall to find the eastern peak.

Eastern Peak

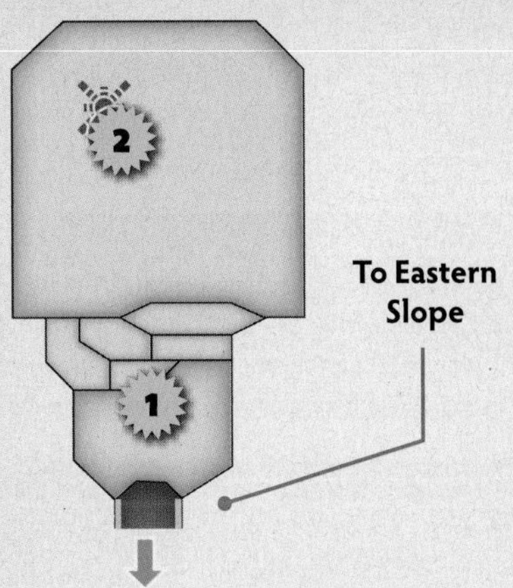

Thing: Goat

When you reach the top of the eastern peak, the Goat is barely visible in the background. Strike the nearby tree with your Hammer until the Goat moves into reach.

The eastern peak is a very small area. Hop up along the steps to reach the top.

A single tree stands at the top of the eastern peak. Strike the tree with your Hammer until you trigger a short cinematic. The Goat appears in the area when the cinematic ends. Collect the Goat, then follow the path back down to the eastern slope.

Eastern Slope—Part 2

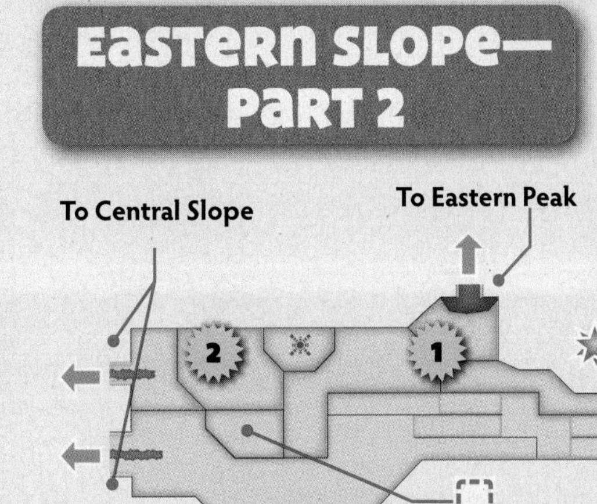

After you return to the eastern slope, drop down from the ledge to the left.

When you land, move to the right to enter a small cave. As you collect the stickers from the back wall, watch out for the Shiny Goomba lurking in the area. When you're ready, follow the path to the left.

Make sure you use the HP Block and Save Block at Point 2, then continue along the path and return to the central slope.

Central Slope—Part 2

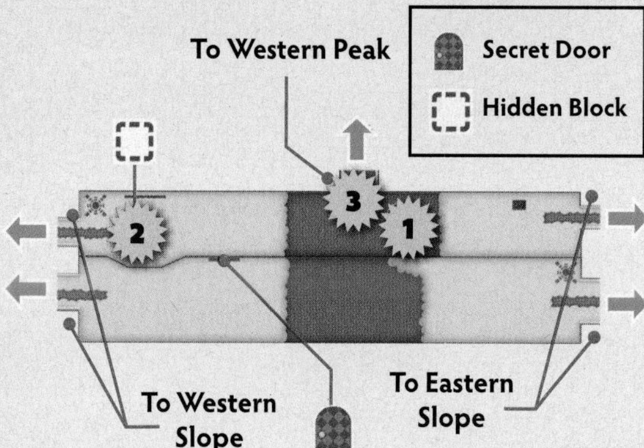

Follow the central slope's upper ledge past the small opening in the back wall. This passage leads to the western slope. Before you head inside, however, take a moment to collect the Pipe in a Cave scrap. Follow the path to the left and continue through the area.

As you approach the left edge of the central slope, look for the Hidden Block above the blue flower at Point 2. Collect the nearby stickers, then continue to the left to collect the Pipe in a Cave scrap from the western slope.

After you collect the Pipe in a Cave scrap, turn back and return to the central slope.

Return to the passage in the middle of the central slope and follow it to the western peak.

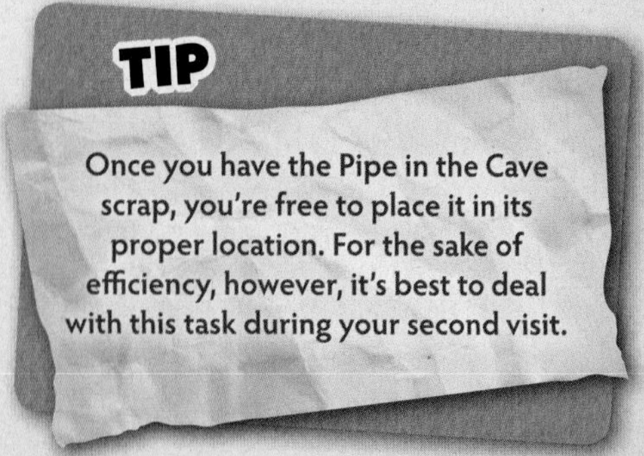

TIP

Once you have the Pipe in the Cave scrap, you're free to place it in its proper location. For the sake of efficiency, however, it's best to deal with this task during your second visit.

HOW TO USE THIS GUIDE
HOW TO PLAY
STICKERS
ENEMIES
WALKTHROUGH
DECALBURG
SURFSHINE HARBOR
WORLD 1
WORLD 2
WORLD 3
WORLD 4
WORLD 5
WORLD 6
CHECKLISTS

Western Peak

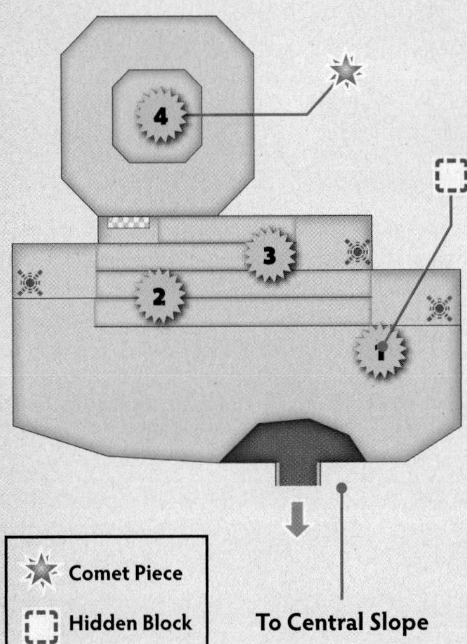

The western peak is fairly large, and it's packed with enemies. Use the HP Block at Point 1 to top off Mario's HP before you head up the first incline.

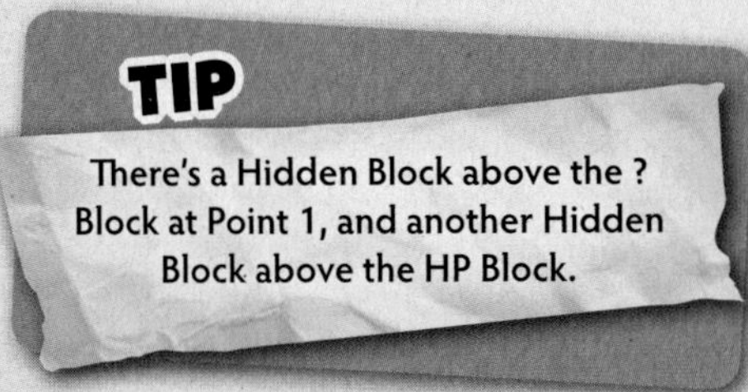

TIP

There's a Hidden Block above the ? Block at Point 1, and another Hidden Block above the HP Block.

The Snow Spike at the top of the first incline makes your initial ascent particularly difficult. Use the small alcoves along the back wall to dodge the Snowballs that roll toward you. When you reach the top of the incline, clear out the enemies on the first plateau.

Continue to ascend the peak one incline at a time. If you're unable to dodge incoming Snowballs, hit them with your Hammer and defeat the Shiny Goombas that ride them.

When you reach the top of the western peak, collect the Comet Piece to end your first visit.

STICKER COMET PIECE: UNLOCKING WORLD 4-2

This Course contains two pieces of the Sticker Comet. To unlock World 4-2, collect the Comet Piece at the top of the western peak.

RECOMMENDED VISIT #2

After you end your first visit, you must revisit the Course to collect the remaining Comet Piece. Return to the eastern slope's right edge and apply the Pipe in a Cave scrap to the indicated spot.

After the warp pipe is in place, climb up to the snow mound on the ledge above you. Stand at the center of the mound, then move toward the background until you drop down to the warp pipe. When you're ready, use the warp pipe to travel to the background.

When you emerge in the background, hop down from the pipe and collect the Comet Piece to the left.

STICKER COMET PIECE: UNLOCKING WORLD 4-5

This Course contains two pieces of the Sticker Comet. To unlock World 4-5, apply the Pipe in a Cave scrap to the indicated spot in the eastern slope, enter the warp pipe, and collect the Comet Piece from the background.

Mini-Boss: Bowser Jr.

Once you've collected the first three Royal Stickers and visited World 4-1, World 5-1, or World 6-1, Bowser Jr. prepares an ambush at the center of the World-Map. This battle is fairly simple if your Album is stocked with plenty of Jump-based stickers and a few Mushrooms, but stickers such as Throwing Stars, Boomerangs, and Hurlhammers are also very handy. Make sure you're prepared! Bowser Jr. is an airborne enemy, so take care when you plan each attack!

Bowser Jr. is usually vulnerable to Jump-based attacks, but the Bob-ombs he occasionally uses will counter such attacks. When he's armed, use stickers such as Hurlhammers, Throwing Stars, and Boomerangs to knock the Bob-ombs out of his hand. If you don't have an appropriate sticker, use a Jump sticker to detonate the Bob-ombs, then heal yourself with a Mushroom.

When Bowser Jr. is unarmed, use a few of your more powerful Jump-based stickers to deal heavy damage. Defend yourself from his attacks, and use Mushrooms to heal yourself as needed. Combine these tactics with the Battle Spinner to defeat Bowser Jr. with ease!

WORLD 4-2: Ice Flow

IMPORTANT ITEMS AND LOCATIONS

DESCRIPTION	NOTES
Secret Door	The marked location is in the first ice cave.
HP-Up Heart	The HP-Up Heart is along the second frozen river.
Toad Rescue	None
Luigi Location	None
Wiggler Diary Entry	None
Things	The Curling Stone randomly appears on the first frozen river. The Hair Dryer is through the Secret Door. A randomly selected Thing appears on the second frozen river.

Recommended Tactics

This Course contains a variety of enemies, and they tend to attack in large groups. You'll find plenty of useful stickers along the way, but consider building a good selection of shiny stickers and flashy stickers before you enter the Course.

An Ice Bro's attack not only deals significant damage, it temporarily incapacitates you. When you approach an Ice Bro, try to dodge its attacks. Once the battle begins, block its attacks to prevent yourself from freezing. Try to initiate each battle with a Hammer strike, and avoid using any stickers that deal freezing damage.

Overview

Prerequisites

To unlock this Course, you must collect the corresponding Comet Piece from the western peak in World 4-1. Make sure your Album contains a Secret Door sticker before you enter the Course.

Objectives

This Course contains several objectives, all of which can be completed on a single visit:

- **Collect the Curling Stone.**
- **Collect the Hair Dryer from the Secret Door.**
- **Collect the randomly selected Thing.**
- **Collect the Comet Piece to unlock World 4-3**

Most of this Course's battles involve large groups of enemies, so make sure you carry plenty of multi-target stickers. Since some of this Course's enemies are immune to freezing damage, it's best to use stickers like Shiny Shells, Shiny Fire Flowers, and Burnhammers when you want to end a fight quickly. As always, battles are much easier when you take advantage of the Battle Spinner.

Hop onto the first frozen river and follow it toward the background. The path is fairly simple, but the Cooligans sliding along the ice can be a serious nuisance! Dodge the enemies and collect the coins as they slide toward you. If you collect enough, you'll earn a Big 1UP sticker!

FIRST FROZEN RIVER

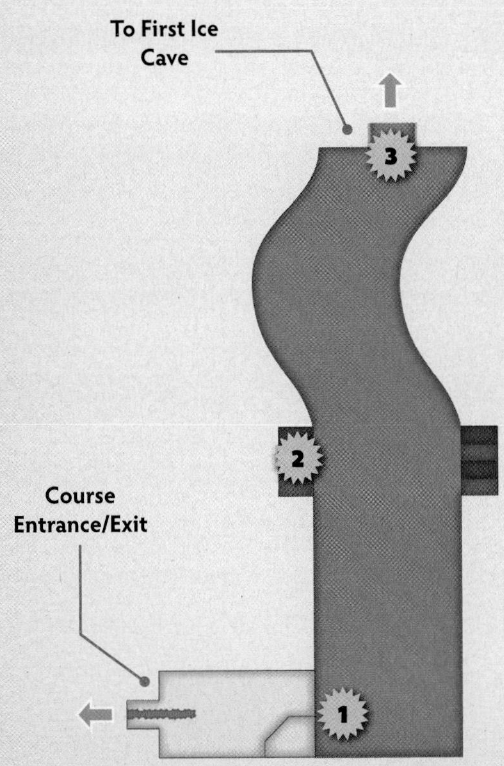

When you reach the ? Block at Point 2, hop off of the ice and wait for a Thing to slide down the first frozen river.

When the Curling Stone appears, hop onto the ice and grab it. If you've lost any HP, collect the Heart in the nook to the right before you leave the area.

THING: CURLING STONE

The Curling Stone randomly appears on the first frozen river. To make sure you find it, wait for a Thing to appear on the first frozen river. If the Curling Stone appears, move into its path and collect it when it reaches you.

FIRST ICE CAVE

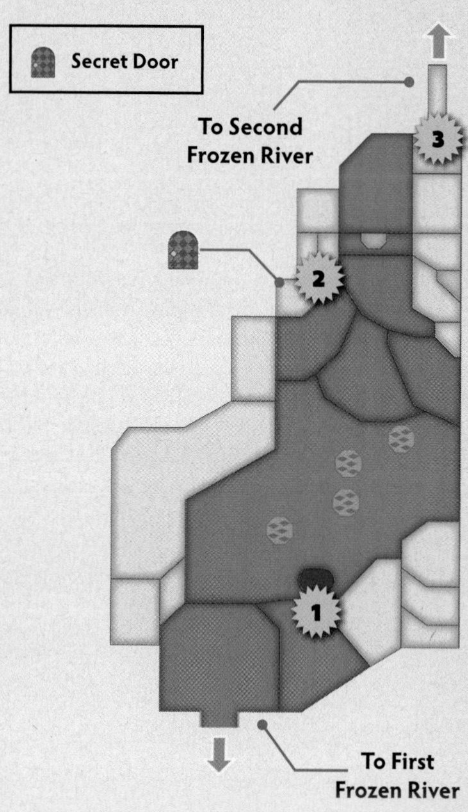

When you reach the end of the path, head through the opening to enter the first ice cave.

When you enter the cave, a Shiny Slaphammer can be seen through a large hole in the wall. To collect this sticker you must drop down from a hidden opening on the ledge above it.

Climb up the steps and deal with the Ice Bro patrolling the area. There are several spike-filled holes scattered around the cave, but the hole just above the Shiny Slaphammer is covered with ice. Break through the ice, then drop down and collect the sticker. Move to the left and exit the enclosure, then climb back up the steps and continue through the first ice cave.

The Secret Door is on a high platform on the left side of the cave. To reach it, climb to the top of the waterfall, then move to the left wall and walk toward the foreground until you drop off the ledge.

After you land, apply a Secret Door sticker to the marked location, then head inside to find the Hair Dryer.

Thing: Hair Dryer

Climb the waterfall in the first ice cave, then move to the left wall and drop from the ledge to find the Secret Door. Apply a Secret Door sticker to the marked location, then head inside to find the Hair Dryer.

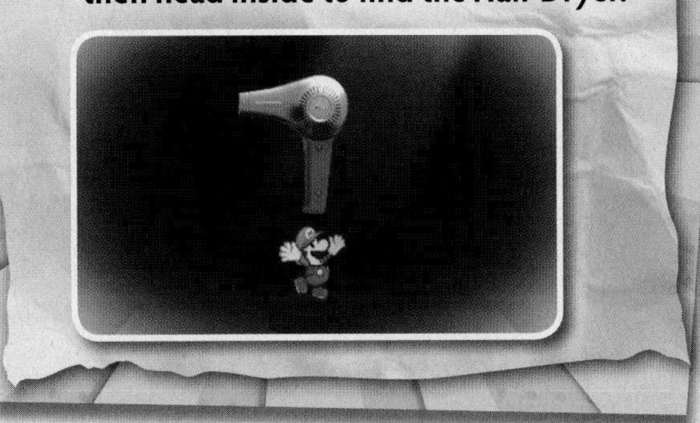

When you're finished exploring the first ice cave, climb back up the waterfall and follow the path out to the second frozen river.

Second Frozen River

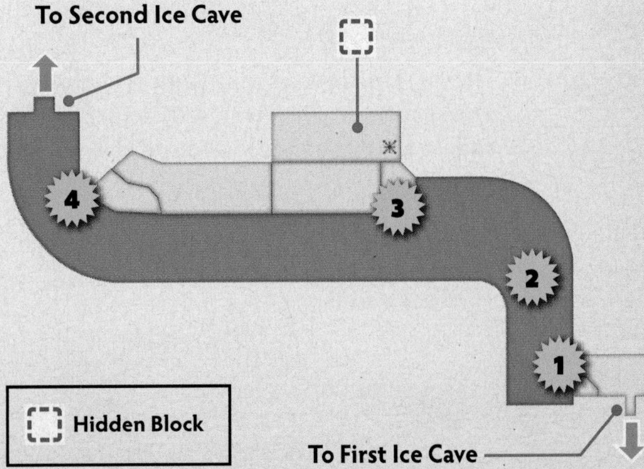

WORLD 4-2

The second frozen river is similar to the first, but it's a bit more hazardous. The ice path takes you through some sharper turns, which makes it much more difficult to spot incoming Cooligans. Additionally, the Cooligans in each group frequently change positions, so stay alert!

As you negotiate the second frozen river, collect the coins that appear. If you collect enough, you'll receive a Big Shiny 1UP sticker! Additionally, a randomly selected Thing eventually appears in the area. This will be a Thing that you've previously collected, but one that is not currently in your Album (as a Thing or a sticker).

There's an HP-Up Heart on the platform at Point 3. When you're in range, hop up and collect it, then search the nearby platforms to find an HP Block and a Hidden Block floating above a blue flower.

HP-Up Heart: Ice Flow

The HP-Up Heart is on a platform along the second frozen river. Make sure you collect it as you move through the area.

When you're ready, hop back down to the ice and continue through the area. As you move past the platforms, the incoming Cooligans tend to slide on their bellies. Rather than slip between them, simply jump over (or on) the sliding Cooligans and follow the path to the second ice cave.

Second Ice Cave

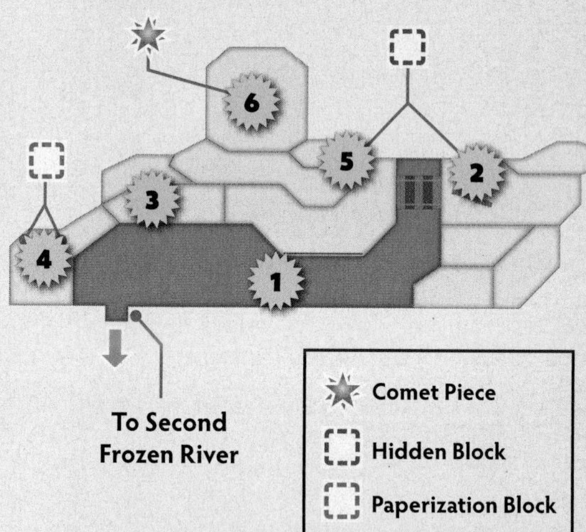

Stay alert as you explore the cave! It can be difficult to spot patrolling Ice Bros before they attack.

There are some stickers high on the wall at Point 2. To reach them, you must find the many Hidden Blocks in the area. Jump up to reveal the Hidden Blocks directly below them, then continue through the area to find some higher ground.

The path splits at Point 3. Before you climb up to the Comet Piece, make sure you explore the platforms to the left.

If your Album contains any unneeded stickers, use them to reveal the Paperization Blocks above the stumps at Point 4.

Before you collect the Comet Piece, use your Hammer to reveal the blue flower at Point 5.

Use your Hammer to reveal the Hidden Blocks to the right, then jump across the waterfall and collect the stickers on the wall back at Point 2.

When you're finished searching the area, climb back up to the top of the ice cave and collect the Comet Piece to complete your visit.

Sticker Comet Piece: Unlocking World 4-3

This Course contains only one piece of the Sticker Comet. To unlock World 4-3, simply collect the Comet Piece at the end of World 4-2.

WORLD 4-3: THE ENIGMANSION

GROUND FLOOR

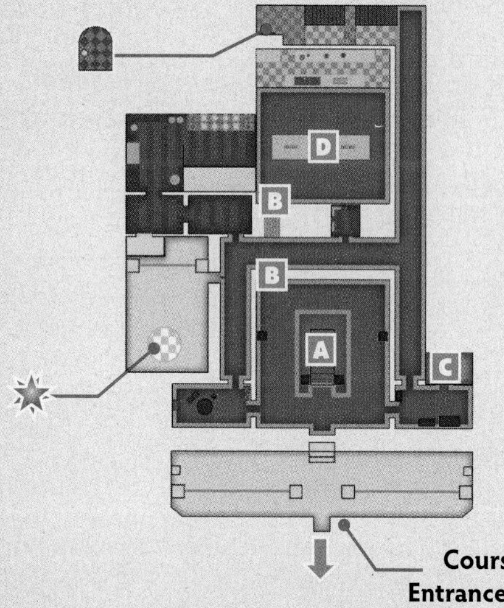

SECOND FLOOR

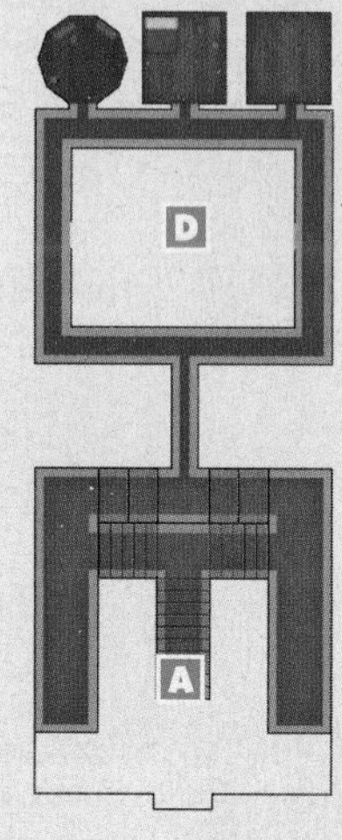

CELLAR

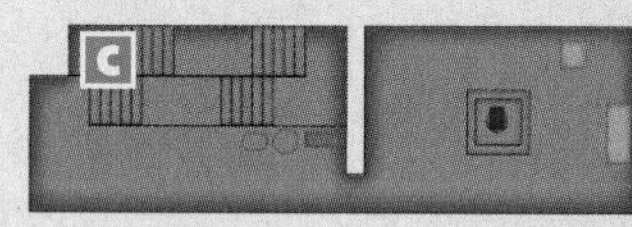

NOTE

Many of the areas shown on the map can only be reached as the scraps scattered throughout the Course are moved to the proper locations. The Comet Piece appears only after you defeat the Big Boo in the cellar.

OVERVIEW

PREREQUISITES

To unlock this Course, you must collect the Comet Piece at the end of World 4-3. Before you enter this Course, make sure your Album contains a Secret Door sticker and a water-based Thing Sticker.

ESSENTIAL THING STICKERS

NAME	THING LOCATION	NOTES
Soda	World 2-1	Used to reveal the Big Boo when it vanishes.

OBJECTIVES

This Course contains several objectives, one of which requires an additional visit:

- Collect the Book of Sealing.
- Find and defeat all of the hidden Boos.
- Collect the Oven.
- Collect the Refrigerator.
- Move the Mansion Door scrap from the library to the lobby walkway.
- Collect the Stapler.
- Open the Decalburg shortcut through the Secret Door.
- Move the Mansion Bookcase scrap from the ground-floor office to the central hallway.
- Swap the Mansion Wall scraps in the antechamber.
- Collect the Watering Can.
- Move the Mansion Safe scrap from the living room to the ground-floor office.
- Move the Steward's Portrait scrap from the lobby walkway to the bedroom.
- Move the Big Bookcase scrap from the second-floor office to the library.
- Collect the Cake.
- Place the Book of Sealing in the cellar.
- Defeat the Big Boo.
- Collect the Forebear's Portrait scrap.
- Collect the Comet Piece to unlock World 4-4.
- Collect the HP-Up Heart.

HOW TO USE THIS GUIDE
HOW TO PLAY
STICKERS
ENEMIES
WALKTHROUGH
DECALBURG
SURFSHINE HARBOR
WORLD 1
WORLD 2
WORLD 3
WORLD 4
WORLD 5
WORLD 6
CHECKLISTS

TIP

Various water-based Thing stickers can be used to reveal the Big Boo, but if you intend to purchase an item from the Thing Shop, the Soda is your least expensive option!

IMPORTANT ITEMS AND LOCATIONS

DESCRIPTION	NOTES
Secret Door	The marked location is at the top of the rear staircase.
HP-Up Heart	After you complete World 4-5, the HP-Up Heart appears in the living room.
Toad Rescue	None
Luigi Location	None
Wiggler Diary Entry	None
Things	The Oven and Refrigerator are in the kitchen. The Stapler appears in the right hall. The Watering Can is in the greenhouse. The Cake is on the dining room table.

NOTE

The Forebear's Portrait scrap found in this Course is needed to progress through World 4-5.

Recommended Tactics

This Course contains Scaredy Rats, Boos, and a Big Boo. A good selection of stickers should help you meet all challenges.

Scaredy Rats aren't particularly tough, but they often attack in groups. Use multi-target stickers to quickly end these battles—when a Scaredy Rat attacks, it has a chance to steal one of your stickers!

The mansion is absolutely packed with Boos, and the steward wants you to defeat them all. Boos are fairly durable, so it's best to use high-quality stickers. Shiny stickers are usually sufficient if you take advantage of the Battle Spinner—just make sure you carry both single-target and multi-target stickers.

The Boo Stack hiding in the Course is made up of 82 separate enemies, and their combined might is formidable. Luckily, this Course contains some Flashy Infinijump stickers. Consider using one of these rare stickers to end the battle in a single turn.

The Big Boo is a tough opponent, but a Flashy Infinijump sticker will end the fight quickly. Shiny Hopslippers are also quite effective if you'd rather save your rare stickers. The Big Boo disappears in the middle of the battle, and you'll need to use a Soda (or a similar water-based Thing Sticker) before you can resume your attacks. Make sure you're prepared!

WORLD 4-3

Recommended Route—Part 1

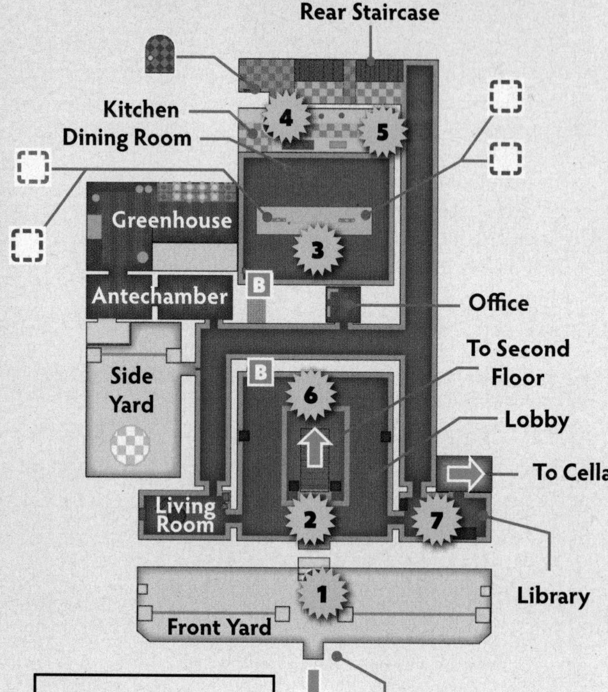

1 When you first visit the Course, the mansion's steward is in the front yard. Speak to the Toad on the steps to gain the Book of Sealing, then head inside.

2 The lobby contains several doors, a staircase, an HP Block, and a Save Block. The steward wants you to recapture the Boos hiding throughout the mansion, which means you have a lot of battles ahead of you. Return to the lobby and replenish Mario's HP as needed.

When you're ready, head through the door on the back wall to find the dining room and kitchen.

3 When you enter the dining room, the Boos swirl around the area and retreat to their hiding places. The Cake is sitting out of reach on the dining room table. To collect it, you must drop down from the second floor. For now, investigate the small kitchen along the back wall.

4 Move to the kitchen's left side to collect the Oven, then follow the counters to the right.

HOW TO USE THIS GUIDE
HOW TO PLAY
STICKERS
ENEMIES
WALKTHROUGH
DECALBURG
SURFSHINE HARBOR
WORLD 1
WORLD 2
WORLD 3
WORLD 4
WORLD 5
WORLD 6
CHECKLISTS

THING: Oven

The Oven is on the left side of the kitchen. Inspect the Oven to pull it away from the wall and collect it.

When you reach the end of the counters, open the Refrigerator to find the first Boo. Defeat this enemy to capture it in the Book of Sealing, then collect the Refrigerator.

THING: Refrigerator

The Refrigerator is on the kitchen's right side. Before you collect the Refrigerator, you must open it and defeat the Boo hiding inside.

When you're ready, head back into the lobby. Explore the area behind the stairs until you find the Boo hiding in the area. Capture the Boo in the Book of Sealing, then head through the door on the lobby's right wall to find the library.

When you first enter the library, three pieces of furniture are floating around the room. Hop onto the chest near the left wall. When the table floats into range, hop on and ride up to the small platform in the corner of the room.

Hop onto the platform, then jump and hit the candle above you. When the room is dark, you can see the Boos that have been manipulating the furniture. Attack one of the Boos to face all three in a single battle. Defeat the Boos to add them to the Book of Sealing.

After the battle, climb onto the bookcases along the right wall and collect the Mansion Door scrap. When you're ready, head through the door in the back wall to enter the hallway along the mansion's right edge.

NOTE

When you explore the second floor, you must replace the Steward's Portrait scrap with the Mansion Door scrap to access the rooms beyond the lobby. After you recover the Big Bookcase scrap from the second-floor office, use it to complete the library's back wall.

Recommended Route—Part 2

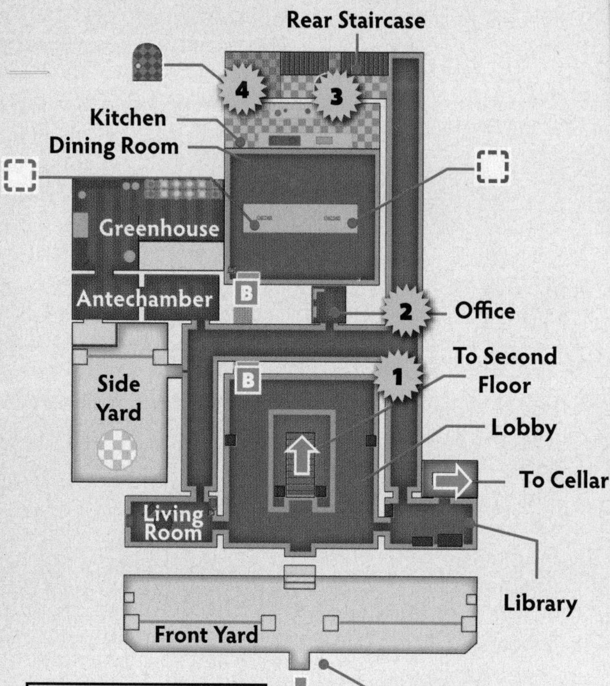

As you follow the hallway along the mansion's right edge, the Stapler bursts through one of the windows. Collect the Stapler and follow the hallway toward the background.

Thing: Stapler

The Stapler appears in the mansion's right hallway as you move through the area. Collect the Stapler after it collapses.

When you reach the intersection at Point 2, continue moving toward the background to find the mansion's rear staircase.

TIP

After you explore the rear staircase, return to this intersection and search the rooms along the central hallway.

Before you climb the rear staircase, search the area under the steps to find a Boo being bullied by two Scaredy Rats. When you approach them, they team up and attack you. Defeat all three enemies to capture another Boo in the Book of Sealing.

4

After you capture the Boo, climb the steps and apply a Secret Door sticker to the marked location at the top of the rear staircase.

This Secret Door actually creates a shortcut to Decalburg! Pass through the door, then use your Hammer to knock down the loose wall to emerge near the Decalburg Thing Shop. Take care of any business you might have in town, then head back through the shortcut to return to the mansion's rear staircase. Leave the area and head to the central hallway.

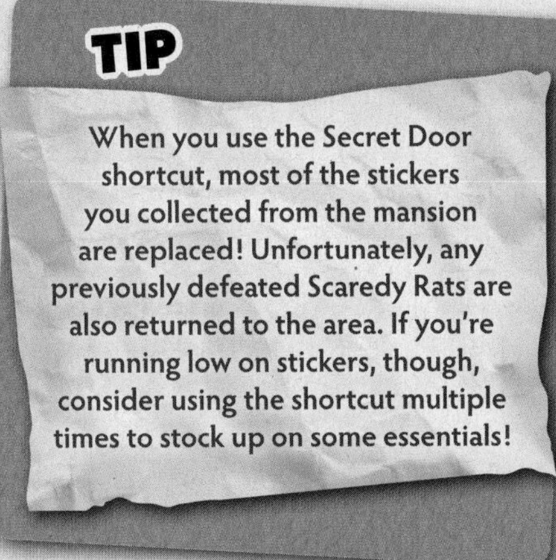

TIP

When you use the Secret Door shortcut, most of the stickers you collected from the mansion are replaced! Unfortunately, any previously defeated Scaredy Rats are also returned to the area. If you're running low on stickers, though, consider using the shortcut multiple times to stock up on some essentials!

Recommended Route—Part 3

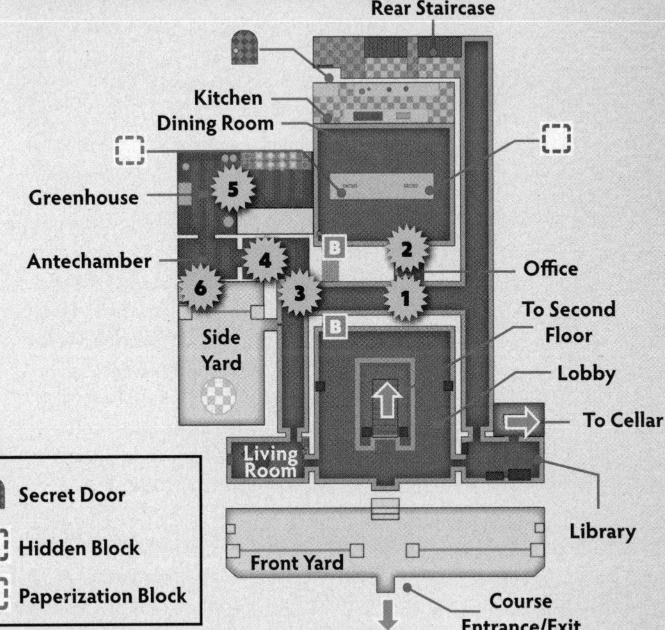

1

Soon after you enter the central hallway, some Scaredy Rats charge in to attack you. After you defeat these enemies, approach the hallway's first door. There's a scrap missing from the central hallway—luckily, it's close by. Head through the door and search the ground-floor office.

2

The bookcase in the office is upside down! Activate the Paperize ability and peel the Mansion Bookcase scrap off of the wall.

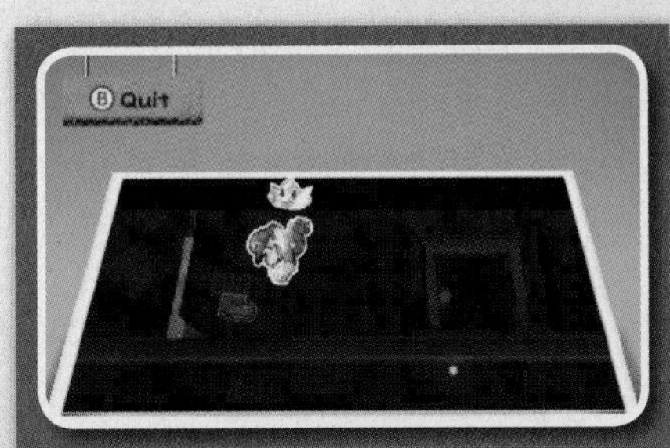

Exit the office and apply the scrap to the spot in the central hallway. Once it's in place, you can reach the Flashy Infinijump sticker! This sticker is very powerful, so make sure you save it for a powerful enemy.

NOTE

After you collect the Mansion Safe scrap from the living room, apply it to the hole you created when you peeled the Mansion Bookcase scrap from the office wall.

3

Follow the central hallway until it meets the mansion's left hallway. Open the door at the intersection and enter the antechamber.

4

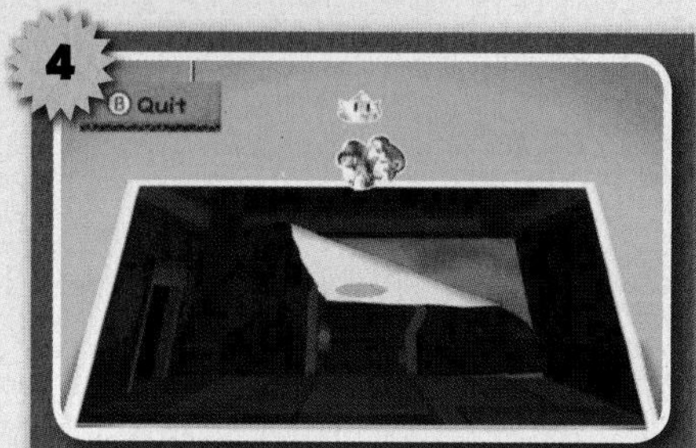

The door in the right half of the antechamber leads to a small enclosure outside of the greenhouse. Before you can enter the greenhouse, you must move the door! Activate the Paperize ability and peel the first Mansion Wall scrap off of the background.

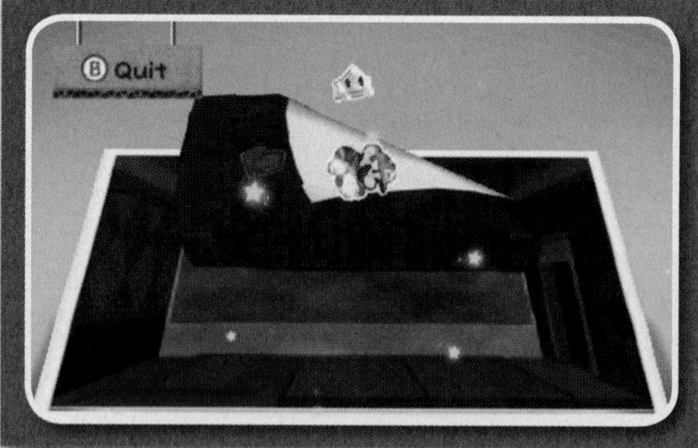

Move to the left half of the antechamber and peel the second Mansion Wall scrap off of the background.

After you've collected both of the Mansion Wall scraps, you must swap their original positions. Place the first Mansion Wall scrap in the left half of the antechamber, and place the second Mansion Wall scrap in the right half of the antechamber. When you're ready, head through the repositioned door to enter the greenhouse.

TIP

Don't forget to collect the Flashy Infinijump sticker from the second Mansion Wall scrap. The small table in the right half of the antechamber allows you to reach this rare sticker!

5

The Watering Can is on the shelves along the back wall. Hit the shelves with your Hammer until the Watering Can falls to the ground. After you collect it, attack the Boo to the right. Defeat the Boo to capture it in the Book of Sealing.

When you exit the greenhouse, move to the left wall and follow it to the foreground.

The path leads to a small enclosure in the mansion's side yard. Defeat the Scaredy Rats and search the ? Block, then head back inside. Follow the path back through the antechamber and return to the hallway.

Recommended Route—Part 4

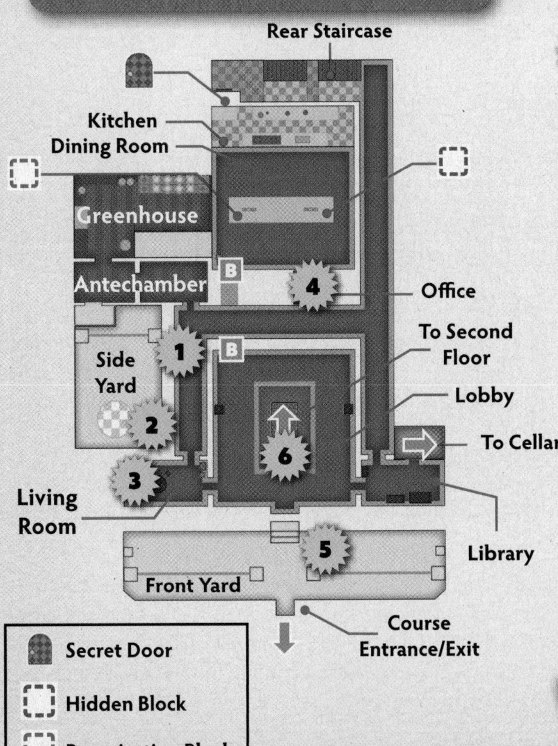

Follow the hallway down the mansion's left side. When you reach the first window, use your Hammer to knock it out of the wall. Jump through the opening and explore the rest of the side yard.

When you reach the end of the side yard, attack the Boo floating outside the living room window. Defeat the Boo to capture it in the Book of Sealing, then head back to the window and return to the hallway.

Follow the hallway toward the front of the mansion and enter the living room. Move over to the left wall and climb onto the fireplace. Strike the picture on the wall to reveal the Mansion Safe scrap, then drop down and collect it.

After you collect the Mansion Safe scrap, return to the ground-floor office and place it on the back wall.

Open the safe to discover another Boo. Defeat the Boo to add it to the Book of Sealing. When you're done, head back to the lobby and exit to the front yard.

TIP

The Boo in the safe may look strange, but it behaves just like any other Boo. Use your preferred tactics to defeat it!

When you return to the front yard, the steward is warming himself by a bonfire. Use your Hammer to put out the bonfire, then attack the Boo lurking behind the steward. Defeat the Boo to add it to the Book of Sealing, then head back inside.

Use the HP Block to top off Mario's HP, collect any stickers that may have reappeared when you used the Secret Door shortcut, and head up the stairs to the second floor.

Recommended Route—Part 5

Office

Bedroom

Empty Room

Dining Room/ Kitchen Walkway

To Ground Floor

Lobby Walkway

To Ground Floor

When you first visit the second floor, only the lobby is accessible. Use the Paperize ability to peel the Steward's Portrait scrap off of the back wall, then place the Mansion Door scrap you collected from the library in its place.

After you apply the Mansion Door scrap, head through the door to find the walkway above the kitchen and dining room.

As you follow the walkway toward the back wall, look for the gap in the railing. When you're ready to return to the ground floor, drop down from the walkway to land on the dining room table. Before you do, however, make sure you search the rooms along the back wall.

TIP

Use your Hammer to flip the doormats along the back wall. There's a sticker hiding under one of them!

3

Enter the door on the left edge of the back wall to find the second-floor office. The area is fairly small, but it contains a big surprise! Open the cabinet to reveal 82 Boos. When the battle begins, the Boos join forces to form a Boo Stack.

Use one of the Flashy Infinijumps you collected on the ground floor to defeat the entire Boo Stack in a single turn. Press Ⓐ each time you land on the Boo Stack to maintain your attack until the battle ends. If you miss an attack, use some Hopslippers to finish the job.

After the battle, collect the Big Bookcase scrap from the cabinet door.

There's still one Boo hiding in the office. Hop onto the desk and strike the clock with your Hammer. When the Boo appears, defeat it to capture it in the Book of Sealing.

4

After you leave the second-floor office, enter the door to the right to find the bedroom. Activate the Paperize ability and apply the Steward's Portrait scrap to the back wall.

Use your Hammer to topple the trash bin near the right wall and wait for battle to begin. Defeat the Boo to add it to the Book of Sealing, then move to the foreground.

As you approach the room's exit, a Boo appears in the portrait on the back wall. Investigate the portrait to begin the battle, then defeat the Boo to capture it in the Book of Sealing.

5

After you leave the bedroom, enter the door to the right to find an empty room with three pictures on the back wall. Examine the pictures to draw five Boos out of hiding, then defeat them to capture them in the Book of Sealing. If you've captured the Boos from all currently accessible areas, the Book of Sealing should now be full! Leave the empty room and return to the walkway above the kitchen and dining room.

WORLD 4-3

6

When you're ready, hop through one of the gaps in the walkway's railing and drop to the dining room table.

Collect the Cake at the center of the table. Before you drop to the ground, look for the Paperization Block and the Hidden Block floating above the nearby flowers.

THING: Cake

The Cake is on the dining room table. To reach it, you must climb up to the second floor and drop from the kitchen/dining room walkway.

Recommended Route—Part 6

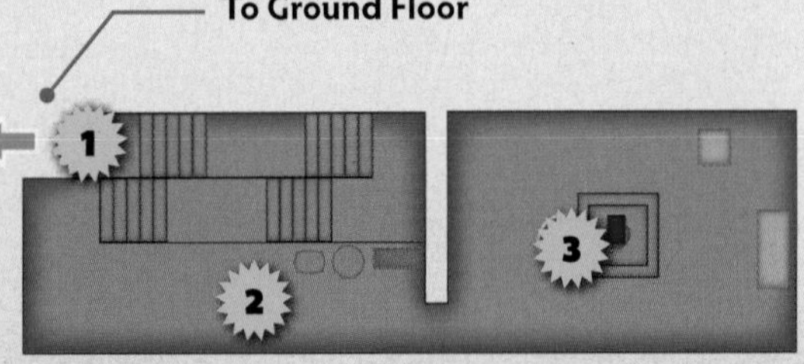

1

When you're ready to enter the cellar, return to the library. Apply the Big Bookcase scrap you collected from the second-floor office to the hole on the back wall. After the secret passage slides open, head inside and peel the Bowser tape on the ground to free the cellar stairs.

2

Follow the stairs down to the cellar floor, then head past the shelves to the right.

3

The second room contains a small bookstand. If you've captured all 100 Boos, place the Book of Sealing on the stand. The room lights up and Kamek appears. If the Book of Sealing isn't full, search the mansion for any Boos you haven't yet captured.

Caution

After you defeat the Big Boo, the mansion undergoes some significant changes. Make sure you've collected all desired stickers before you place the Book of Sealing on the stand!

Boo Locations

The mansion contains a total of 100 Boos spread out across 13 hiding spots:

- In the kitchen, inside the Refrigerator
- In the lobby, behind the stairs
- In the library, after you turn off the lights
- In the rear staircase, below the stairs
- In the greenhouse
- In the side yard
- In the ground-floor office, inside the safe
- In the front yard, after you extinguish the bonfire
- In the second-floor office, inside the cabinet
- In the second-floor office, inside the clock
- In the bedroom, inside the trash bin
- In the bedroom, hiding in the portrait
- In an empty room, hiding in the portraits

After a brief conversation, Kamek leaves you to deal with a Big Boo. Defeat this oversized enemy to put the mansion back in order.

Mini-Boss: Big Boo

When the battle starts, use powerful Jump-based stickers to deal heavy damage to the Big Boo. The Flashy Infinijump is particularly effective, but a few Shiny Hopslippers will yield similar results.

The Big Boo's attacks deal significant damage. Defend yourself just before it sweeps you up in its tongue. If the battle lasts long enough for the Big Boo to land multiple attacks, consider replenishing Mario's HP with a Mushroom sticker.

As the Big Boo weakens, the candles on the wall ignite. While the room is lit, the Big Boo is invisible. Before you can land additional attacks, you must force the Big Boo to reappear. Use the Soda (or a similar water-based Thing Sticker) to douse the candles on the wall. When the Big Boo reappears, continue your attacks until you defeat it.

WORLD 4-3

Recommended Route—Part 7

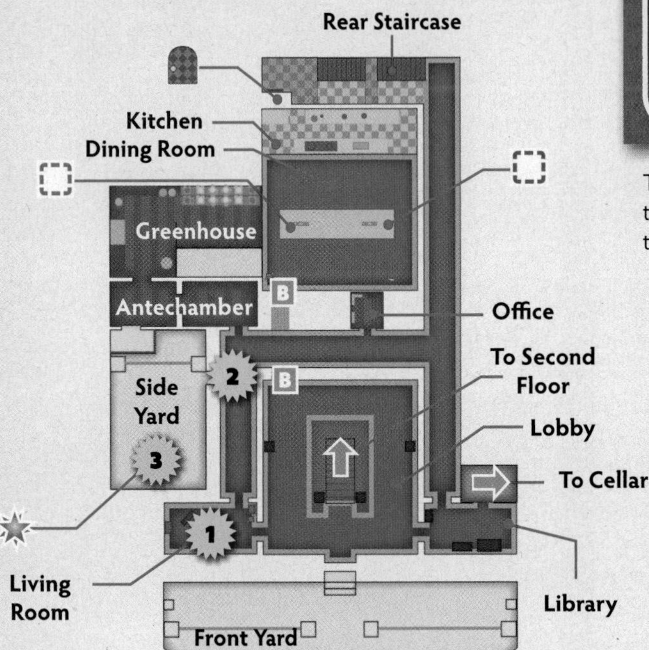

After you defeat the Big Boo, head back to the living room to have a chat with the steward. Sit down in the vacant chair and listen to the steward, then examine the photograph on the back wall.

The after a short conversation, the steward tells you to take the photograph. Collect the Forebear's Portrait, then head though the door on the back wall.

NOTE

When you reach World 4-5, use the Forebear's Portrait to access the chairlift.

Follow the hallway along the mansion's left edge and jump through the open window to return to the side yard.

3

When you're ready, collect the Comet Piece just outside the living room window to complete your visit.

Sticker Comet Piece: Unlocking World 4-4

This Course contains a single piece of the Sticker Comet. To unlock World 4-4, collect the Comet Piece that appears in the side yard after you defeat the Big Boo.

Recommended Visit #2

After you complete World 4-5, return to the mansion to find the forebear in the living room. Sit in the vacant chair and wait for the steward to arrive. After offering you a cup of tea, the steward rewards you with an HP-Up Heart.

HP-Up Heart: The Enigmansion

After you complete World 4-5, return to the living room and sit down with the forebear. After the steward enters the room, he gives you an HP-Up Heart.

WORLD 4-4: SHAVED-ICE CAVE

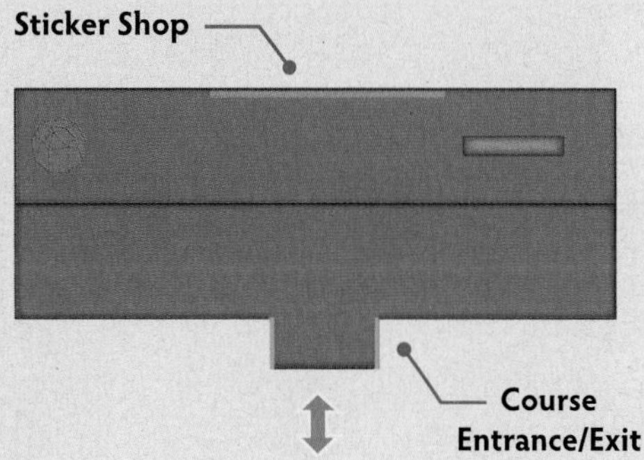

OVERVIEW

PREREQUISITES

To unlock this Course, you must collect the Comet Piece from World 4-3.

OBJECTIVES

This Course's only objective is to complete a single visit. Since this Course contains one of the game's Sticker Shops, however, you may find yourself making regular visits!

IMPORTANT ITEMS AND LOCATIONS

DESCRIPTION	NOTES
Secret Door	None
HP-Up Heart	None
Toad Rescue	None
Luigi Location	None
Wiggler Diary Entry	None
Things	None

RECOMMENDED TACTICS

This Course contains no enemies!

THE STICKER SHOP

This small, friendly area houses one of the game's Sticker Shops. Enter the Course, then speak to the frozen Toad to browse the available stickers. When you're ready, exit the Course to complete the only available objective!

TIP

The World 4-4 Sticker Shop is a great place to stock up on powerful stickers. Stop by whenever you need to supplement your sticker selection.

WORLD 4-5: WHITEOUT VALLEY

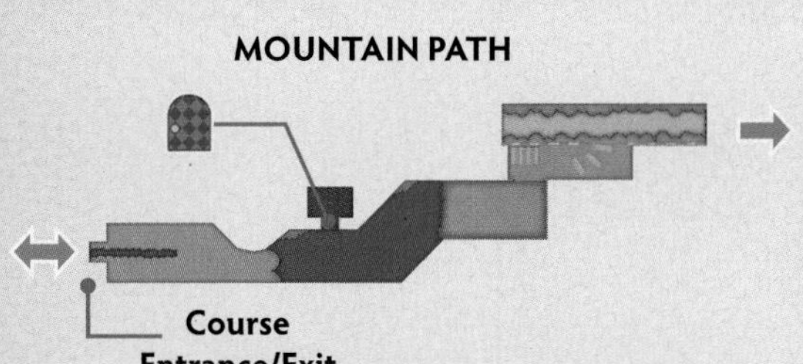

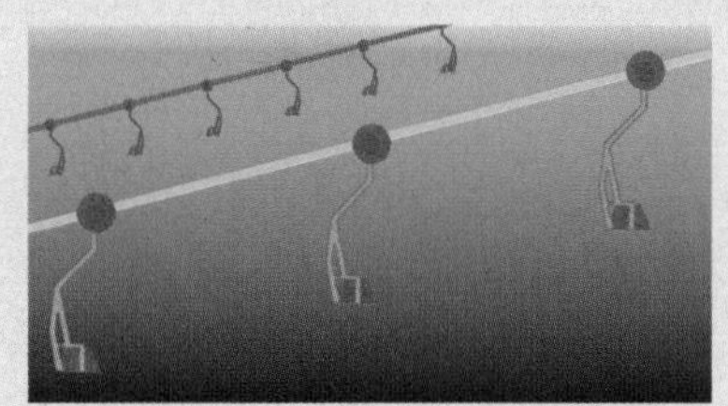

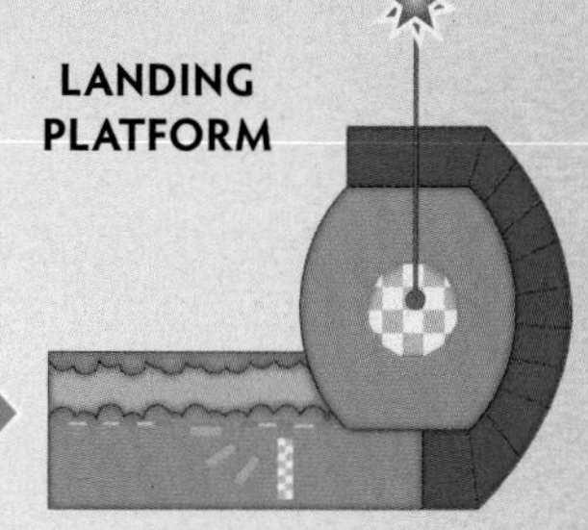

OVERVIEW

PREREQUISITES

To unlock this Course, you must collect the corresponding Comet Piece from the background of World 4-1. To access the chairlift, you must also collect the Forebear's Portrait from World 4-3. Before you enter the Course, make sure your Album contains a Secret Door sticker.

OBJECTIVES

All of this Course's objectives can be completed during a single visit:

- **Collect the Flashlight from the Secret Door.**
- **Place the Forebear's Portrait scrap at the end of the mountain path.**
- **Ride the chairlift.**
- **Collect the Comet Piece to unlock World 4-6.**

IMPORTANT ITEMS AND LOCATIONS

DESCRIPTION	NOTES
Secret Door	The marked location is on the mountain path, below the icicles.
HP-Up Heart	None
Toad Rescue	None
Luigi Location	Luigi appears near the end of the chairlift.
Wiggler Diary Entry	None
Things	The Flashlight is through the Secret Door.

RECOMMENDED TACTICS

This Course is packed with enemies, but the majority of battles can be avoided. Still, it's best to make sure you bring a nice selection of Battle Stickers.

Most of the Ice Bros in this Course keep their distance, but you'll find an Ice Bro patrolling the mountain path. When you attack, a second Ice Bro joins the battle. Carry some Burnhammers or similar multi-target stickers.

The chairlift is infested with Fuzzies! You should be able to knock most of them off of the cable before they attack, but chances are good at least a few will reach you. These enemies aren't particularly tough, however. Bring a large supply of basic stickers to deal with any Fuzzies that manage to attack you.

This Course also contains some Shiny Goombas and Shiny Paragoombas. As with the Fuzzies, you can avoid most of these enemies, but make sure you bring plenty of multi-target stickers to deal with unexpected encounters.

MOUNTAIN PATH

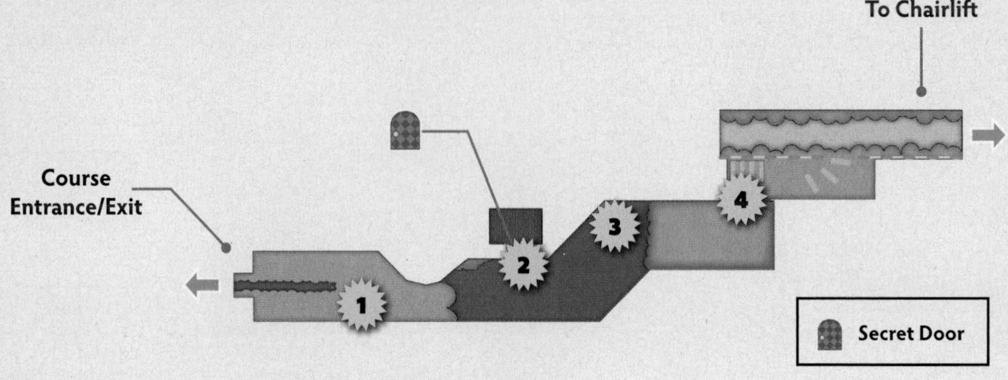

Stay alert as you collect the stickers at the start of the Course! The Ice Bro just up the path usually starts attacking before you spot him.

After you defeat the Ice Bro, head under the icicles and apply the Secret Door sticker to the marked location on the back wall. When the door is in place, head inside to find the Flashlight.

THING: FLASHLIGHT

The Flashlight is through the Secret Door. Apply a Secret Door sticker to the marked location on the mountain path, then head inside and collect the Flashlight.

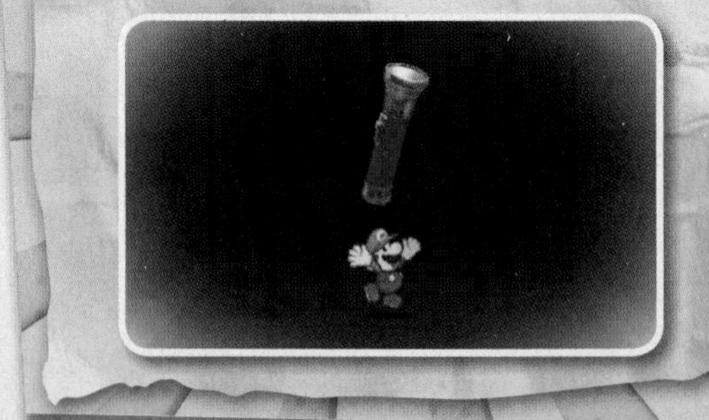

Point 3 offers an HP Block and a Save Block. There are a lot of potential battles ahead of you. Before you hop onto the chairlift, make sure you're in fighting shape.

CHAIRLIFT

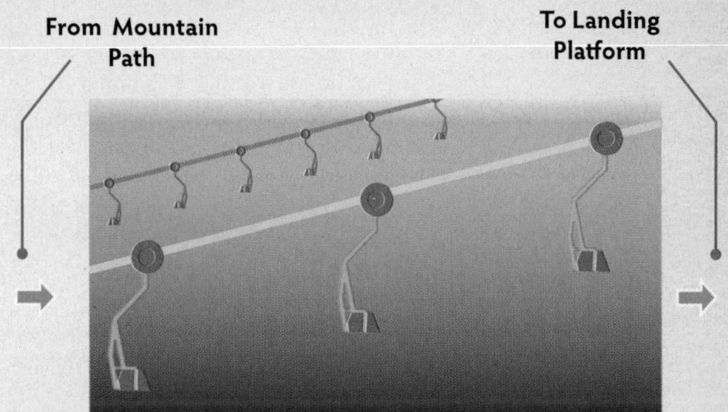

When you reach the end of the path, place the Forebear's Portrait scrap from World 4-3 on the wall. After a moment, the path to the chairlift appears.

Approach the booth and speak to the forebear to activate the chairlift. When you're ready, hop onto one of the chairlift's seats to leave the area.

The chairlift carries you along a set path, so you don't need to worry about navigating the area. You can take steps to defend yourself from incoming enemies, however. When Ice Bros and Paragoombas attack, slide the Circle Pad to the left and right to swing your seat in the corresponding direction. When a Fuzzy attempts to board your seat, press Ⓐ to shake it loose with a small hop.

As you approach the end of the chairlift, enemies stop appearing. Watch the seats in the background to find Luigi riding in the opposite direction.

TIP

If you time your maneuvers properly, you shouldn't have any trouble avoiding most of the enemies on the chairlift. Enemies do become more aggressive as the ride continues, however. Say alert!

When you reach the cave, Fuzzies attack in large groups. Be patient, and hop just as the last member of the group reaches the hinge above your seat.

The Shiny Paragoombas attack by leaping from nearby seats. As each enemy attacks, swing out of its path.

Luigi Location: Whiteout Valley

As you approach the end of the chairlift, Luigi appears on one of the seats in the background. Activate the Paperize ability and pull Luigi out of his seat.

LANDING PLATFORM

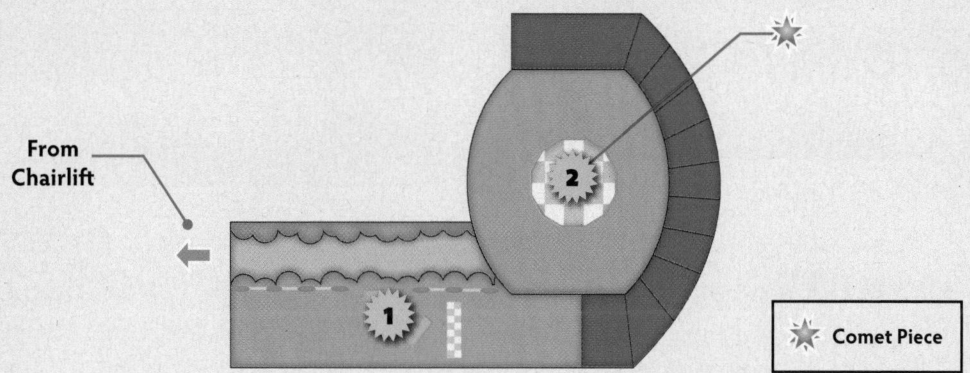

When you reach the landing platform, hop off of the chairlift and follow the path to the right.

When you're ready, collect the Comet Piece at the top of the stairs to complete your visit.

STICKER COMET PIECE: UNLOCKING WORLD 4-6

This Course contains only a single piece of the Sticker Comet. To unlock World 4-6, collect the Comet Piece from the landing platform.

WORLD 4-6: BOWSER'S SNOW FORT

RIDE QUEUE

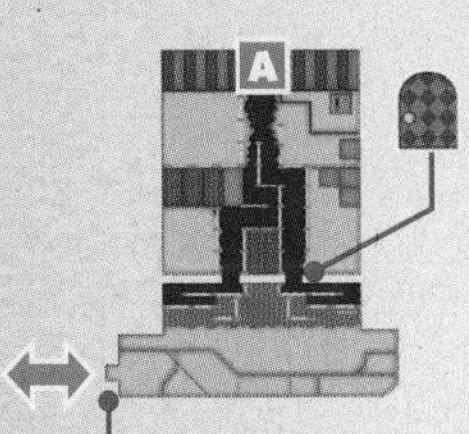

Course Entrance/Exit

FIRST MINE-CART RAIL

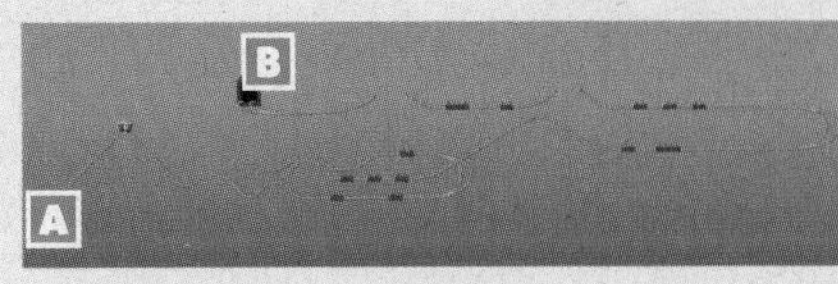

SECOND MINE-CART RAIL

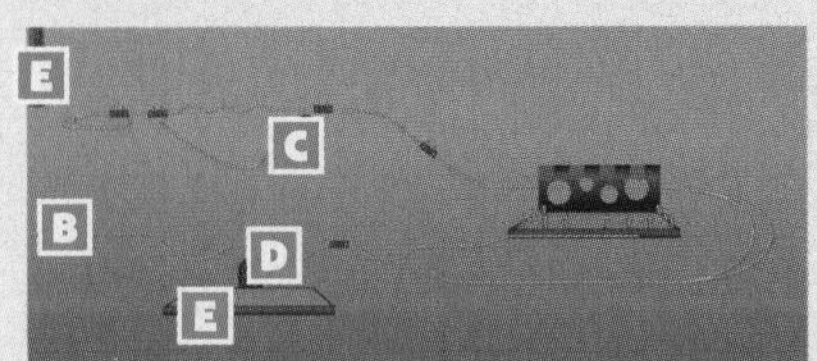

BOSS PLATFORM

NOTE

After you reach the boss platform, you can hop over the railing to return to the line queue.

Overview

Prerequisites

To unlock this Course, you must collect the Comet Piece from World 4-5. This Course actually contains a Secret Door sticker, but you're free to bring one of your own. To defeat the Bowser Snow Statue and Mizzter Blizzard at the end of the Course, it's important to bring plenty of heat-based Thing Stickers and Battle Stickers.

ESSENTIAL THING STICKERS

NAME	THING LOCATION	NOTES
Hair Dryer	World 4-2	Recommended for boss battle.
Oven	World 4-3	Recommended for boss battle.

NOTE

The Hair Dryer and Oven are conveniently located in nearby Courses, but any powerful heat-based stickers can be used. With a good supply of Flashy Fire Flowers, you can easily defeat the Bowser Snow Statue and Mizzter Blizzard without using any Thing Stickers.

Objectives

This Course contains several objectives, most of which can be completed in a single visit:

- **Rescue the bullied Toad.**
- **Collect the Sewing Scissors near the Secret Door.**
- **Collect and apply the first Mine-Cart Rail scrap.**
- **Reposition the second Mine-Cart Rail scrap.**
- **Collect the Megaflash Chillhammer sticker.**
- **Collect and apply the Mine-Cart Exit scrap.**
- **Defeat the Bowser Snow Statue and Mizzter Blizzard.**
- **Collect the Royal Sticker.**
- **Collect the Megaflash Line Jump.**

IMPORTANT ITEMS AND LOCATIONS

DESCRIPTION	NOTES
Secret Door	The marked location is to the right of the ride queue.
HP-Up Heart	None
Toad Rescue	The bullied Toad is to the left of the ride queue.
Luigi Location	None
Wiggler Diary Entry	None
Things	The Sewing Scissors are on the right side of the ride queue, near the Secret Door

Recommended Tactics

This Course contains a variety of enemies, and some of them are immune to cold-based attacks. Keep plenty of heat-based stickers on hand, but make sure you save enough to complete the boss battle at the end of the Course.

The Shy Guys bullying the Toad are extremely durable. The battle is sure to last several turns, but the Battle Spinner can be a big help. Combine Shiny POW Blocks with high-damage stickers to reduce incoming attacks as you chip away at their HP.

Toward the end of the Course, you'll face some Ice Bros and Shiny Bob-ombs. Stock up on Burnhammers to help ensure that you have no trouble with more diverse groups of enemies.

The Bowser Snow Statue and Mizzter Blizzard are both vulnerable to heat-based stickers. Thing Stickers like the Hair Dryer and Oven are very helpful, but Flashy Fire Flowers are just as effective.

Ride Queue

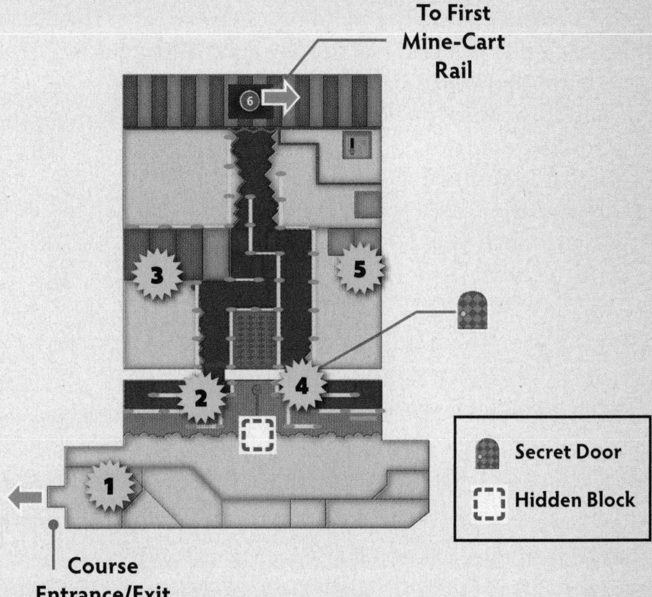

1 When you enter the Course, follow the steps up to the ride queue.

2 Approach the Shy Guys lined up along the ramp to the left. Hop over the railing and try to slip past the enemies. Watch out! The Shy Guys don't appreciate you cutting in front of them. A battle begins each time you make contact with an enemy.

3 There are two Shy Guys tormenting a Toad on the left side of the building. Once you're inside, hop over the railing and confront the bullies. End the conflict to complete another Toad rescue and collect a Secret Door sticker.

Toad Rescue: Bowser's Snow Fort

The wandering Toad is in trouble again! Follow the ride queue into the building, then hop over the railing to the left. Pay the Shy Guys 100 coins to leave the Toad alone, or simply defeat them in battle. After you rescue the Toad, he rewards you with a Secret Door sticker.

Thing: Sewing Scissors

The Sewing Scissors are on the crates along the building's right wall. To collect them, head through the Secret Door or fight your way to the head of the ride queue. When you reach the front of the line, hop over the railing and move to the crates near the right wall.

4

After you rescue the bullied Toad, hop back over the railing and slip out of the building. Climb the ramp to the right and apply a Secret Door sticker to the marked location. When you're ready, use the Secret Door to bypass the Shy Guys in the ride queue.

5

After you pass through the Secret Door, climb up to the front of the queue. Before you hop into a mine-cart, however, jump over the railing to the right and double back to find the Sewing Scissors near the building's right wall.

6

When you're ready, move to the front of the ride queue and hop into the first available mine-cart.

First Mine-Cart Rail

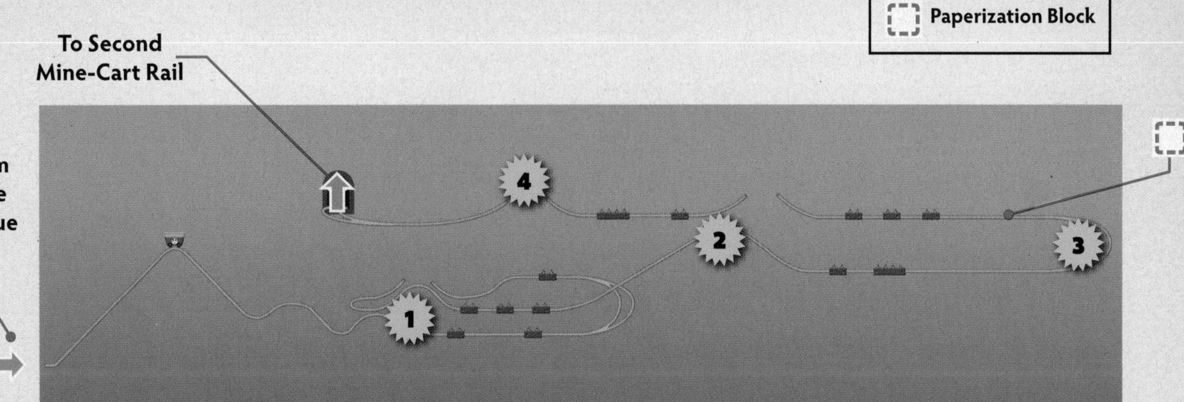

As you ride the mine-cart, press Ⓐ to hop over hazards like spikes and gaps in the rail.

As you make a second loop around the area, a Shy Guy appears on the rail above you. The first Mine-Cart Rail scrap is hanging from the Shy Guy's mine-cart; before you can leave the area, you must find a way to collect the scrap.

As you move through the next turn, activate the Paperize ability and use a sticker from your Album to reveal the Paperization Block in the Shy Guy's path.

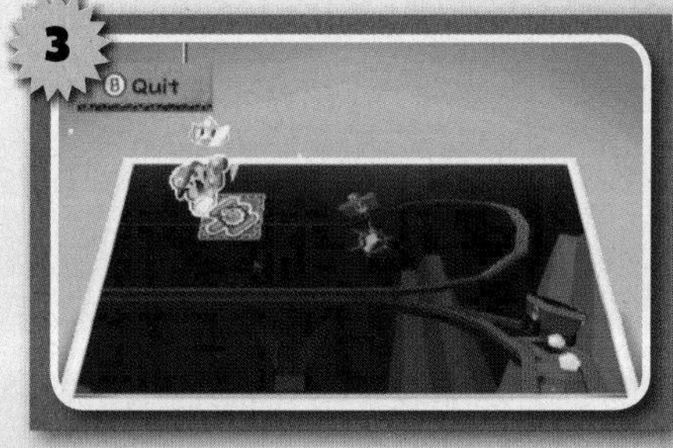

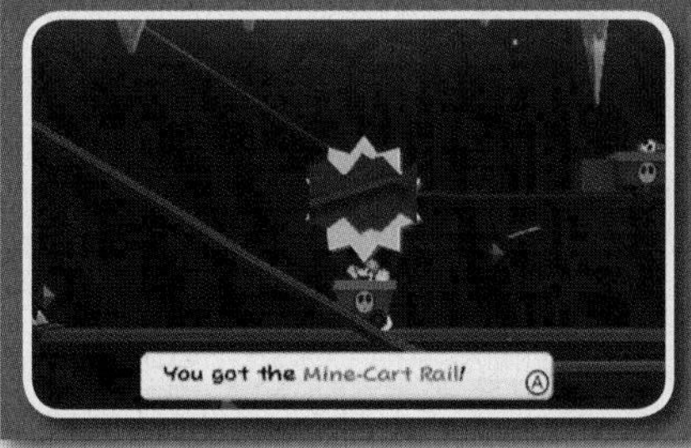

When the Shy Guy crashes into the Paperization Block, the dangling scrap breaks loose and lands in your path.

Place the first Mine-Cart Rail scrap in the gap at Point 4. The scrap extends the rail, but it doesn't complete it. Hop over the remaining gap and continue to the next area.

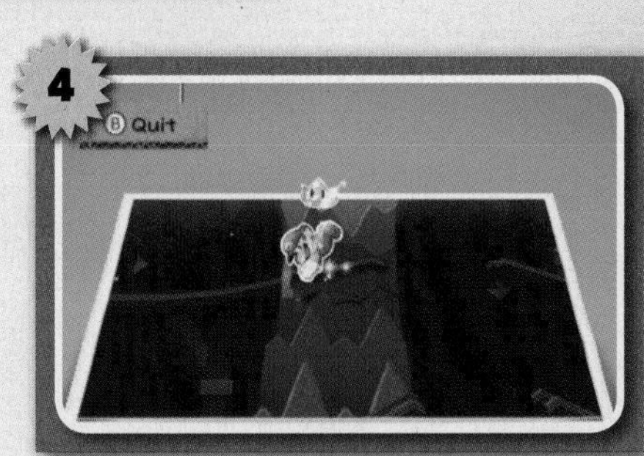

Second Mine-Cart Rail

To Boss Platform

From First Mine-Cart Rail

To Ride Queue

In addition to spikes and gaps, you must hop over the Bob-ombs that appear along the second mine-cart rail.

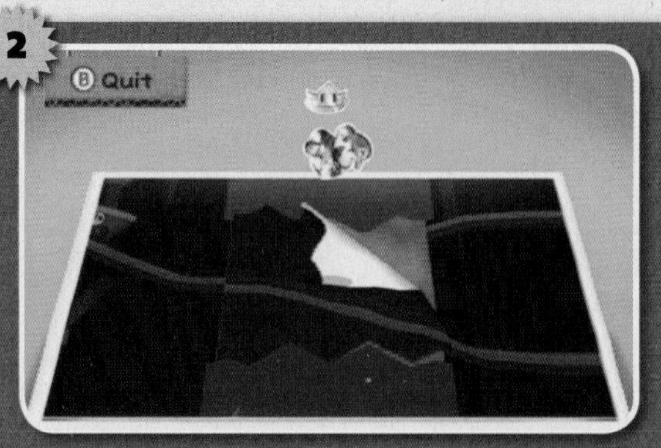

As you approach Point 2, activate the Paperize ability and peel the second Mine-Cart Rail scrap out of your path. Reapply the scrap in the same spot to change the rail's decline to an incline!

After you reposition the second Mine-Cart Rail scrap, the cart stops at a the large, enemy-infested platform.

The ? Block just left of the HP Block contains a Megaflash Chillhammer! Make sure you collect this rare sticker before you leave the area.

Examine the left side of the platform to find the Mine-Cart Exit scrap on the back wall, then use the HP Block and Save Block to the right.. When you're ready, hop back into the mine-cart and continue along the rail.

As you approach Point 4, look for the hole in the back wall. Apply the Mine-Cart Exit scrap to the hole, then ride the mine-cart out of the area.

NOTE

If you fail to apply the Mine-Cart Exit scrap to the indicated spot (or if you fail to jump the nearby gap), you fall to a small platform below the rail. From this location, you can either enter the warp pipe to return to the rail or head through the door to return to the ride queue.

BOSS PLATFORM

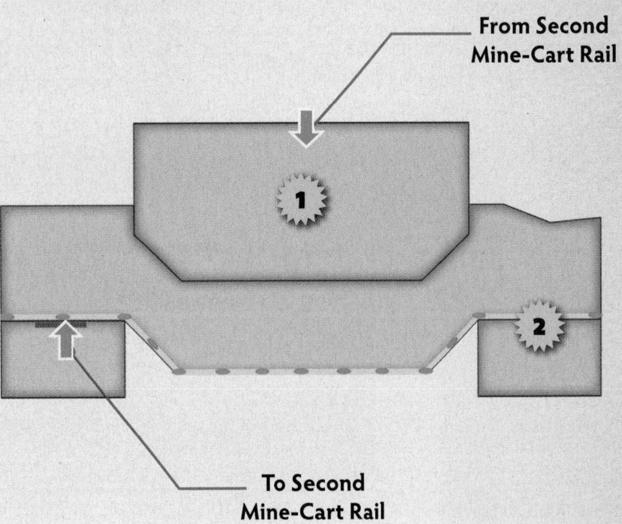

When the mine-cart crashes on the boss platform, the Bowser Snow Statue attacks. Defeat the Bowser Snow Statue and the deceptive Mizzter Blizzard to reveal another Royal Sticker.

BOSS FIGHT! BOWSER SNOW STATUE AND MIZZTER BLIZZARD

The Bowser Snow Statue is fairly durable, but it's vulnerable to heat-based attacks. Use the Battle Spinner to earn extra attacks on each turn, and combine Flashy Fire Flowers and any heat-based Thing Stickers you have in your Album.

As you damage the Bowser Snow Statue, it undergoes a physical change. First the snow falls off of its surface, then the ice shatters to reveal a smaller version of the Bowser Snow Statue. Repeat the process to reveal an even smaller Bowser Snow Statue.

The first two statues are large enough to stomp you, but the third statue dumps snow on you. Defend yourself from each attack, and continue dealing damage until you reveal Mizzter Blizzard.

Mizzter Blizzard isn't quite as impressive as the Bowser Snow Statue, but he can absorb a bit of damage. Don't let up! Defend yourself from his attacks, and use Flashy Fire Flowers and Burnhammers to defeat him.

When you defeat Mizzter Blizzard, he drops a Royal Sticker. Before you collect it, look for the ? Block floating beyond the boss platform's front-right corner. This ? Block contains a Megaflash Line Jump sticker! If you try to collect it, however, Kersti insists that you collect the Royal Sticker. Do as she asks to complete your first visit.

Recommended Visit #2

Revisit the Course and ride a mine-cart up to the boss platform. Move to the front-right corner of the platform and jump over the railing. Collect the Megaflash Line Jump sticker from the ? Block, then drop down to the ride queue. When you're ready, exit the Course to complete your visit.

WORLD 5-1

WORLD FIVE

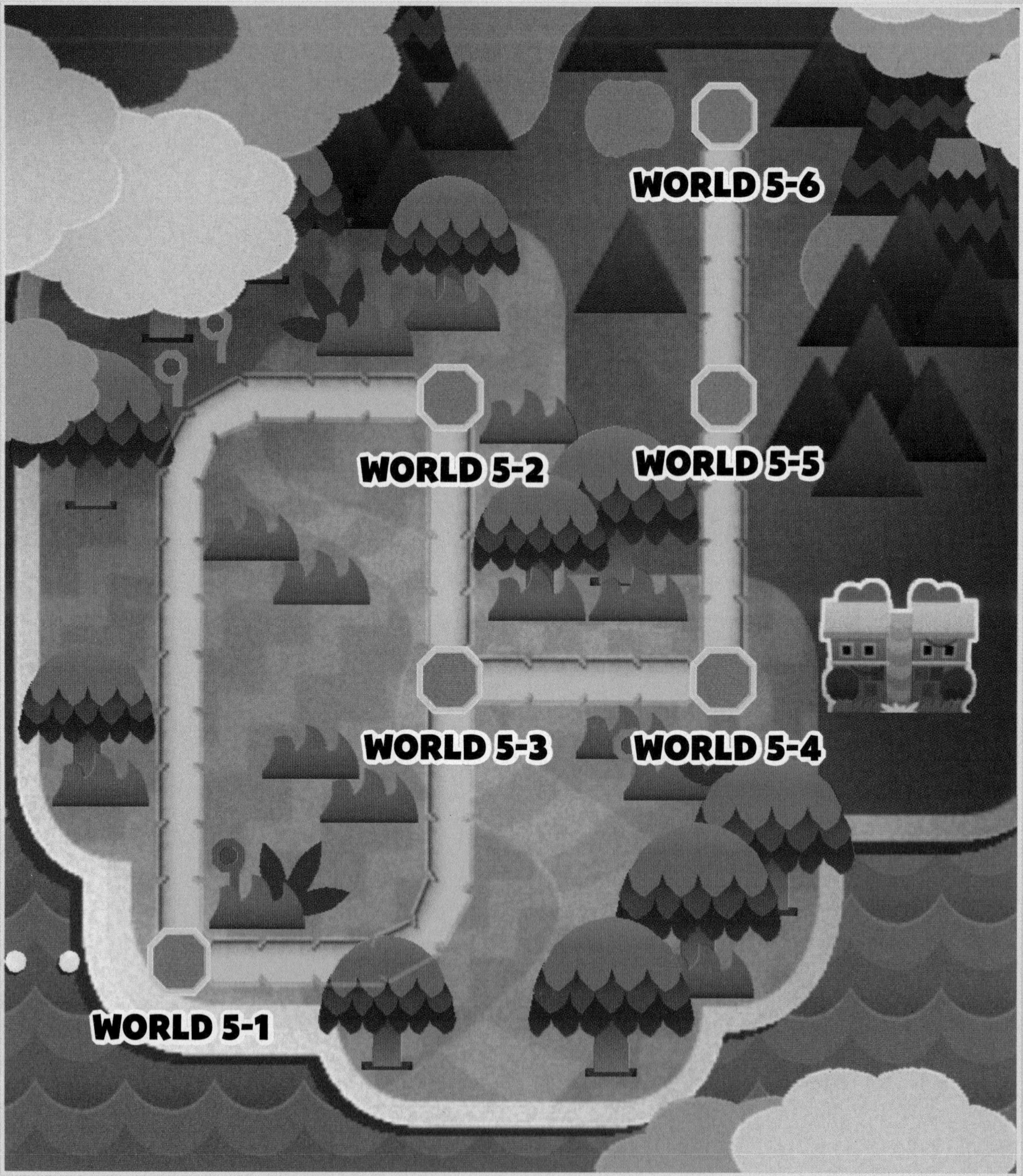

WORLD 5-6

WORLD 5-2

WORLD 5-5

WORLD 5-3

WORLD 5-4

WORLD 5-1

WORLD FIVE COURSES	
NUMBER	NAME
World 5-1	Shy Guy Jungle
World 5-2	Jungle Rapids
World 5-3	Long Fall Falls
World 5-4	Chomp Ruins
World 5-5	Rugged Road
World 5-6	Rumble Volcano

World Five contains dense jungles, wild rivers, and plenty of lava. These areas are filled with some very tough enemies, so plan on spending your hard-earned coins in the game's many Sticker Shops. Battle your way to Petey Piranha and claim the last Royal Sticker needed to unlock the gate in World 6-1.

WORLD 5-1: SHY GUY JUNGLE

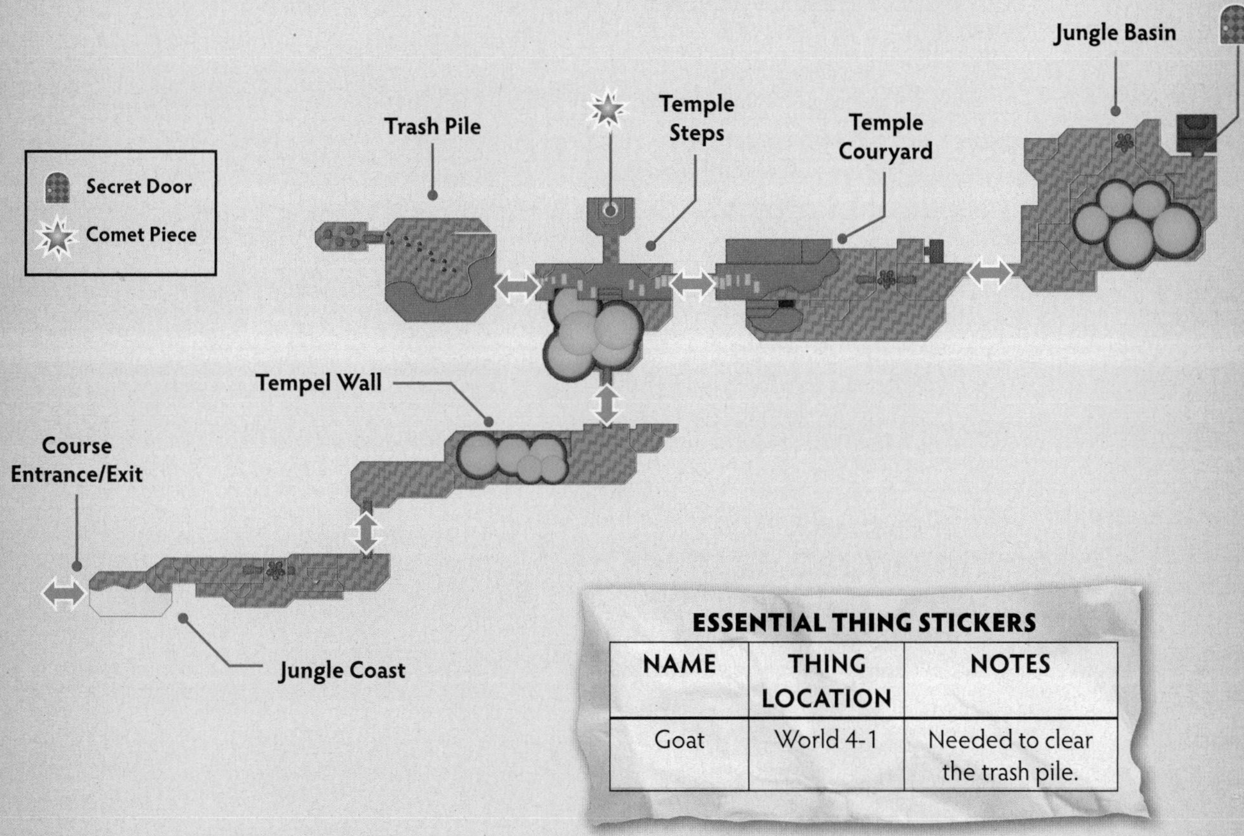

ESSENTIAL THING STICKERS		
NAME	THING LOCATION	NOTES
Goat	World 4-1	Needed to clear the trash pile.

OVERVIEW

PREREQUISITES

This Course becomes available as soon as you defeat the Big Cheep Cheep in Surfshine Harbor. Before you enter the Course, make sure your Album contains a Secret Door sticker and a Goat sticker.

NOTE

If you prefer, you can substitute the Vacuum or the Upright Vacuum for the Goat.

Objectives

This Course contains several objectives, all of which can be completed during a single visit:

- Collect the Toy Bat.
- Use the Goat to clear the trash pile.
- Collect the Megaflash Hurlhammer.
- Collect the HP-Up Heart.
- Collect the Powder Puff.
- Collect the Tailor Shears.
- Collect and assemble all three Bridge Part scraps.
- Collect the Comet Piece to unlock World 5-2.

IMPORTANT ITEMS AND LOCATIONS

DESCRIPTION	NOTES
Secret Door	The marked location is near the jungle basin's right wall.
HP-Up Heart	The HP-Up Heart is in a hidden area near the temple courtyard.
Toad Rescue	None
Luigi Location	None
Wiggler Diary Entry	None
Things	The Toy Bat is behind the temple wall. The Powder Puff is hidden in the jungle basin. The Tailor Shears are through the Secret Door.

Recommended Tactics

This Course contains some Hammer Bros, Boomerang Bros, and Piranha Plants, but most encounters will involve the Spear Guys scattered throughout each area.

Before you attack a Spear Guy, check the position of his weapon. When one of these enemies points his spear toward you, he can counter most Hammer-based attacks. When the spear is pointing upward, the Spear Guy can counter most Jump-based attacks. Take care to select the right sticker for the job, and keep plenty of powerful multi-target stickers on hand.

Jungle Coast

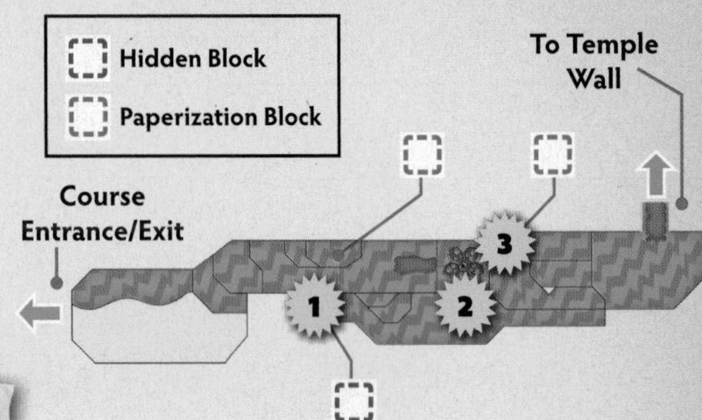

To reveal the Hidden Block at Point 1, jump onto the ? Block floating near the ledge and jump straight up.

The giant red flower at Point 2 is carnivorous, so don't step on its petals without taking the proper precautions. Drop down from the main path and search the area for stickers. When you're ready to move on, strike the carnivorous flower with your Hammer to temporarily stun it. Hurry back up to the main path and move across the flower before it recovers.

After you reveal the Paperization Block at Point 3, use it as a platform to reach the ? Block just above it. When you're finished searching the area, follow the path to the temple wall.

There's a hidden passage between the vine-covered trees at Point 2. Move into the background, then duck behind the tree to the right to find the hidden area behind the temple wall. Continue to the far end of the area to find the Toy Bat.

Temple Wall

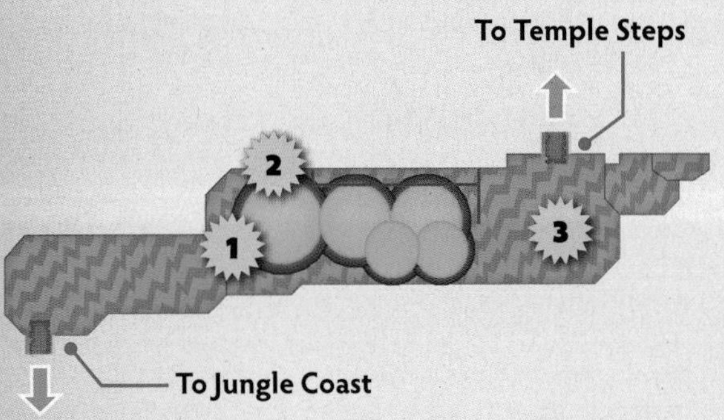

Thing: Toy Bat

The Toy Bat is hidden behind the temple wall. To find it, move between the vine-covered trees near the wall's left edge. Follow the path to the right and collect the Toy Bat from the hidden area.

The foliage around the temple wall is particularly high, making it difficult to spot lurking enemies. As you move through the area, watch for any shadows and spear tips that might betray an enemy's location.

When you approach Point 3, a Spear Guy hops into a collapsible bush and begins throwing spears. As you close in on the enemy, use the spear's shadows to help you dodge each attack. Hit the collapsible bush with your Hammer to destroy the hiding spot and confront your attacker. When you're ready, follow the path to the temple steps.

WORLD 5-1

Temple Steps

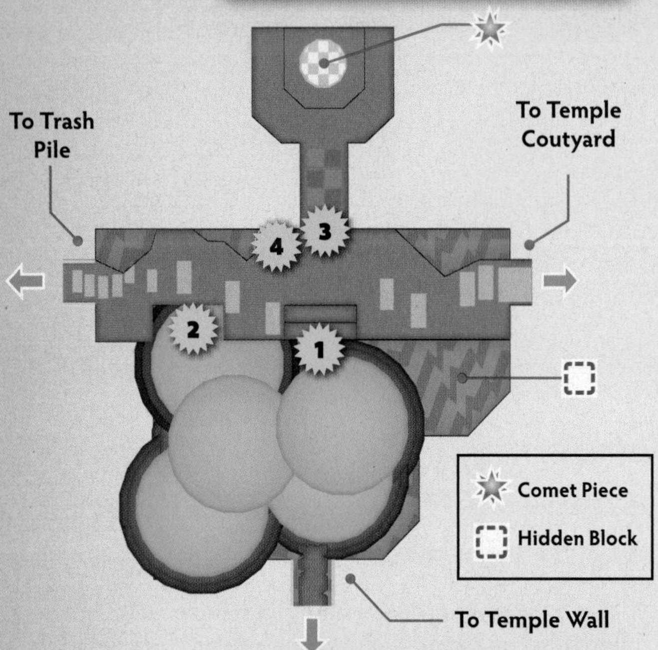

Each of the three Spear Guys at the top of the temple steps holds a Bridge Part scrap. When you approach them, they scatter in three different directions. To reach this Course's Comet Piece, you must recover the scraps and assemble the bridge on the temple steps.

One of the Spear Guys jumps down the steps and hides in the foliage. When he does, more Spear Guys appear in the area. While most of the enemies are aggressive, the Spear Guy carrying the scrap runs away from you. Defend yourself from any attackers, then chase the scrap-bearing Spear Guy into the nook at Point 2.

After you trap the Spear Guy, defeat him to collect the first Bridge Part scrap.

The Comet Piece is at the top of the temple steps, but you must recover the two remaining Bridge Part scraps before you can collect it. Once you have all three scraps, return to this area and use them to assemble the missing bridge.

Use the HP Block and the Save Block at Point 4, then follow the path to the left to find the trash pile.

HOW TO USE THIS GUIDE
HOW TO PLAY
STICKERS
ENEMIES
WALKTHROUGH
DECALBURG
SURFSHINE HARBOR
WORLD 1
WORLD 2
WORLD 3
WORLD 4
WORLD 5
WORLD 6
CHECKLISTS

Trash Pile

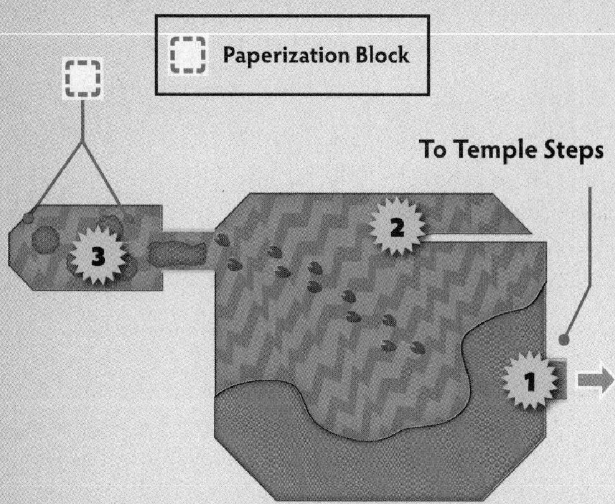

After you clear the area, defeat the exposed Spear Guy to collect the second Bridge Part scrap.

Before you leave the area, look for the Paperization Blocks at Point 3. When you're ready, return to the temple steps and follow the path to the temple courtyard.

The second scrap-bearing Spear Guy is hiding in the area, but the trash pile blocks your path.

Use the Goat sticker to clear the area and reveal the Spear Guy.

WORLD 5-1

TEMPLE COURTYARD

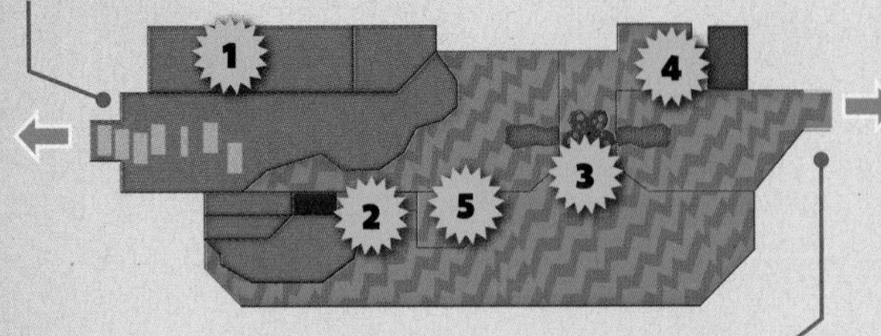

After you search the area, pass under the carnivorous flower at Point 3 to find a hidden path.

After you defeat the Hammer Bros at Point 1, search the ? Blocks to find a Megaflash Hurlhammer!

Follow the path to find a small cave in the back of the area, then head inside to collect an HP-Up Heart.

Use your Hammer to smash the collapsible bush at Point 2, then peel the Bowser tape to reveal some small steps.

HP-UP HEART: SHY GUY JUNGLE

To find this Course's HP-Up Heart, slip past the carnivorous flower near the temple courtyard and head into the hidden cave.

When you're ready, strike the carnivorous flower with your Hammer and race back to the main path. You don't have much time before the flower recovers, so use the steps left behind by the Bowser tape to shave a couple of seconds off of the trip.

The last scrap-bearing Spear Guy is hiding in the jungle basin. Clear the more hostile enemies from the foliage, then turn your attention to the scrap bearer.

Move quickly to make it safely across the flower and follow the path to the jungle basin.

Like the Spear Guy below the temple steps, this enemy flees from you. Chase the Spear Guy up the ramp at Point 2, and follow the ledge toward the background.

Jungle Basin

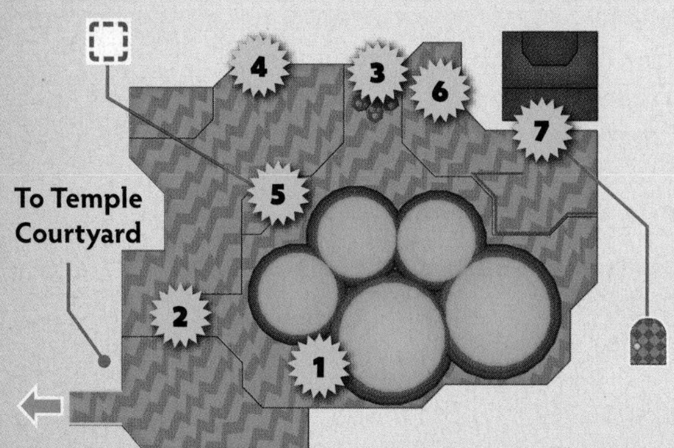

Secret Door

Hidden Block

Chase the Spear Guy all the way to the carnivorous flower. When the Spear Guy attempts to cross the gap, the flower eats him and spits the scrap to the far ledge.

Before you deal with the carnivorous flower, hop over the grass in the background and move left to find the Powder Puff in a hidden area.

After you cross the carnivorous flower, collect the final Bridge Part scrap from the ledge.

Drop from the ledge and move to the blue flower at Point 5. Use your Hammer to reveal the Hidden Block on the ground, then run over and stun the carnivorous flower. Dash back to the Hidden Block and climb up to the ledge, then cross over the carnivorous flower before it recovers.

Follow the ledge along the basin's right wall until you reach Point 7. Apply a Secret Door sticker to the marked location, then head inside to find the Tailor Shears.

THING: POWDER PUFF

To find the Powder Puff, climb up to the jungle basin's rear-left corner. Hop over the grass in the background and follow the path to the left to find a small area hidden in the background.

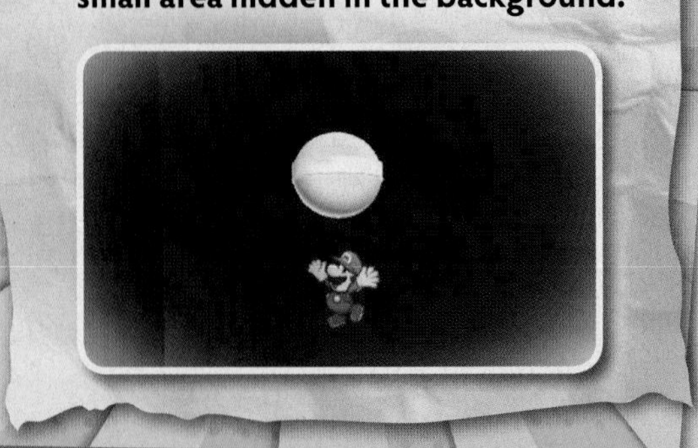

HOW TO USE THIS GUIDE
HOW TO PLAY
STICKERS
ENEMIES
WALKTHROUGH
DECALBURG
SURFSHINE HARBOR
WORLD 1
WORLD 2
WORLD 3
WORLD 4
WORLD 5
WORLD 6
CHECKLISTS

THING: TAILOR SHEARS

The Tailor Shears are located through the Secret Door. Apply a Secret Door sticker to the marked location on the right side of the jungle basin, then head inside to find the Tailor Shears.

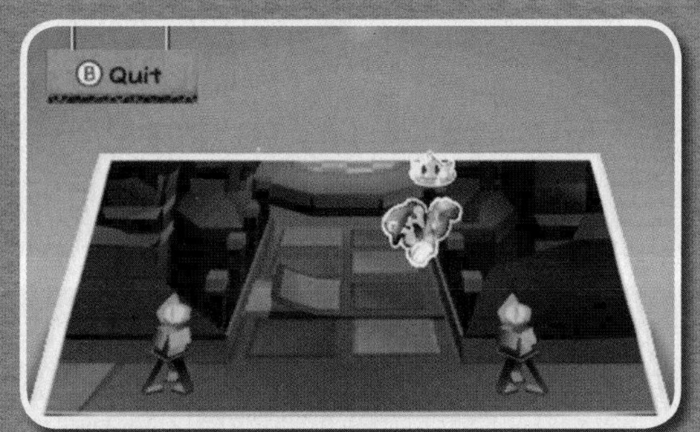

When you're ready, follow the path out of the jungle basin and through the temple courtyard. Return to the top of the temple steps and assemble the three Bridge Part scraps.

Cross the completed bridge and collect the Comet Piece to end your visit.

STICKER COMET PIECE: UNLOCKING WORLD 5-2

This Course contains a single piece of the Sticker Comet. To unlock World 5-2, collect the Comet Piece at the top of the temple steps.

WORLD 5-2: JUNGLE RAPIDS

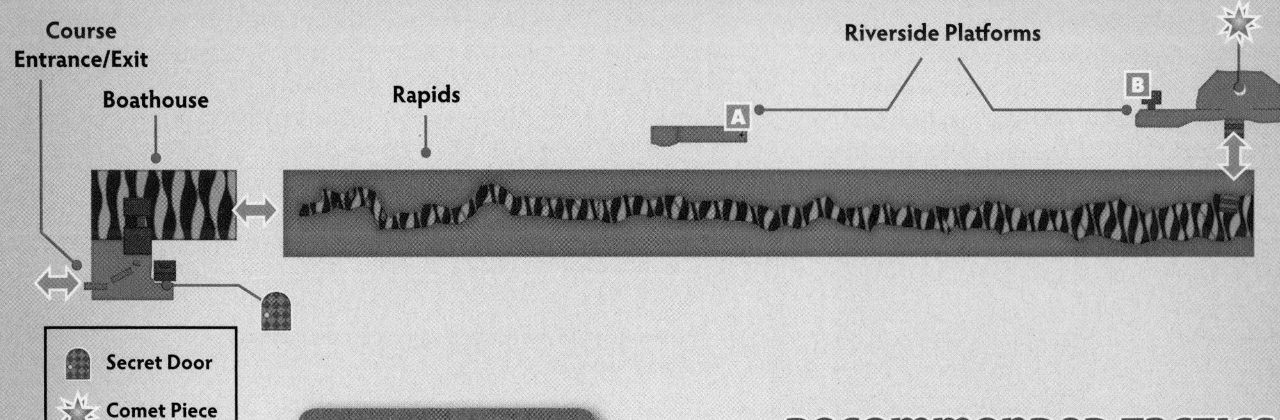

OVERVIEW

PREREQUISITES

To unlock this Course, you must collect the Comet Piece from the temple steps in World 5-1. Before you enter this Course, make sure your Album contains a Secret Door sticker.

OBJECTIVES

This Course contains several objectives, all of which can be completed during a single visit:

- **Collect the Mini Vacuum from the Secret Door.**
- **Navigate the raft down the rapids.**
- **Collect the Rubber Ducky.**
- **Rescue the bullied Toad.**
- **Collect the Comet Piece to unlock World 5-2.**

IMPORTANT ITEMS AND LOCATIONS

DESCRIPTION	NOTES
Secret Door	The marked location is near the boathouse.
HP-Up Heart	None
Toad Rescue	The bullied Toad is on one of the riverside platforms.
Luigi Location	None
Wiggler Diary Entry	None
Things	The Mini Vacuum is through the Secret Door. The Rubber Ducky appears in the water toward the end of the rapids.

RECOMMENDED TACTICS

This Course contains very few battles, but there are a few Spear Guys on the riverside platforms.

The Spear Guys near the Comet Piece are happy to ignore you, but they will defend themselves if you attack them. If you choose to fight the Spear Guys bullying the Toad, you must defeat a fairly large group. Use a Shiny Shell sticker to clear them out with a single attack.

BOATHOUSE

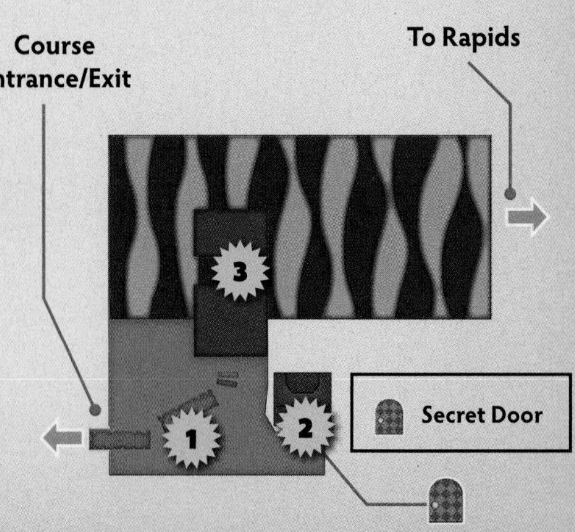

To reach the end of this Course, you must navigate a raft over a series of waterfalls. Before you enter the boathouse, take a moment to investigate the area outside.

Move to the small nook on the right edge of the area, then apply a Secret Door sticker to the marked location. Head inside to find the Mini Vacuum.

Thing: Mini Vacuum

The Mini Vacuum is through the Secret Door. Look for the marked location to the right of the boathouse, apply a Secret Door sticker, then head inside to collect the Mini Vacuum.

When you're ready, enter the boathouse and use your Hammer to smash the Block holding the raft in place. Ride over the first fall and continue down the rapids.

Rapids

To steer the raft, slide and hold the Circle Pad to the left or right as needed. This allows you to collect the coins floating above the water, but more importantly, it allows you to avoid the hazards throughout the rapids. Each time the raft hits an obstacle, one of its logs breaks loose. Take care to keep the raft intact.

As you navigate the rapids, Spear Guys drop new hazards into the water. Run clear of incoming spears and steer the raft around the barrels that fall into your path.

As you approach the next waterfall, a giant barrel drops into the water. Steer the raft to the left to ensure you slip past it without crashing.

When you reach Point 4, look for the bullied Toad in the background. Remember to help him when you reach the end of the rapids.

Toward the end of the rapids, Fish Bones attack your raft. Use your Hammer to knock them loose before they can cause serious damage.

As you defend your raft from the Fish Bones, watch for the Rubber Ducky that appears in the water. Steer the raft into the Rubber Ducky's path to catch it on its way through the area. Defend yourself from the remaining Fish Bones until you reach the riverside platforms.

RIVERSIDE PLATFORM

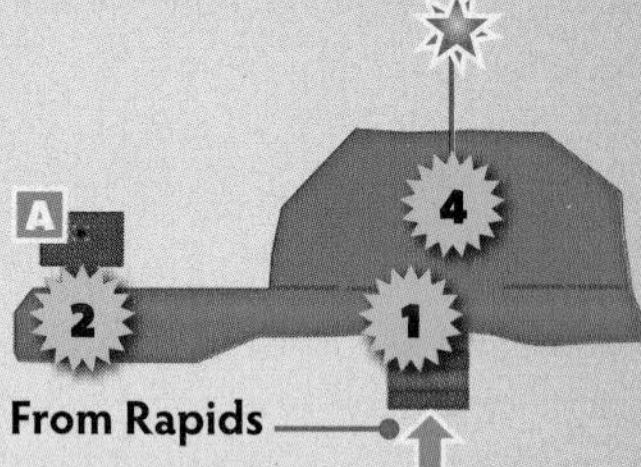

After you navigate the rapids, you land on one of the riverside platforms. Before you collect the Comet Piece, find the path to the bullied Toad.

Step off the dock and follow the bank to the left. Enter the cave at the end of the path, then use the warp pipe inside.

THING: RUBBER DUCKY

The Rubber Ducky appears toward the end of the rapids. Move into the Rubber Ducky's path to catch it on your raft.

3

After you emerge from the warp pipe, follow the path to the left to find two Spear Guys tormenting the wandering Toad. Bribe or defeat the Spear Guys to complete the game's fifth and final Toad rescue!

4

When you're ready, head back through the warp pipe. Slip between the dancing Spear Guys and collect the Comet Piece to complete your visit.

Toad Rescue: Jungle Rapids

Enter the cave to the left of the Comet Piece and use the warp pipe to reach the bullied Toad. Pay the Spear Guys 500 coins to leave the Toad alone, or simply defeat them in battle. Once the Toad is safe, he decides to retire from his life of adventure.

Sticker Comet Piece: Unlocking World 5-3

This Course contains one piece of the Sticker Comet. To unlock World 5-3, collect the Comet Piece from the riverside platforms.

TIP

After you complete all five Toad rescues, return to Decalburg's residential area. Enter the house on the right and read the green postcard near the right wall to reveal an HP-Up Heart.

WORLD 5-3: LONG FALL FALLS

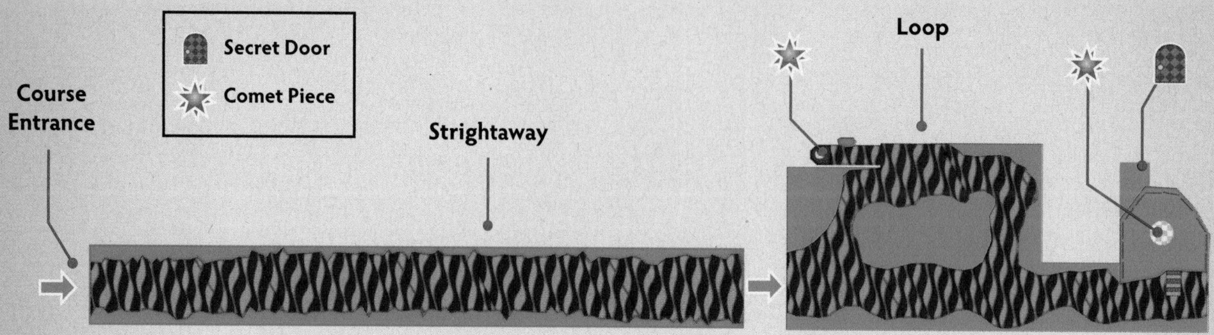

OVERVIEW

PREREQUISITES

To unlock this Course, you must collect the Comet Piece from the end of World 5-2. Before you enter this Course, make sure your Album contains a Secret Door sticker.

OBJECTIVES

This Course contains several objectives, some of which require an additional visit:

- **Evade the Big Cheep Chomp on the straightaway.**
- **Reposition the Jungle Flood Gate scrap.**
- **Collect the Megaflash Infinijump sticker.**
- **Collect the Comet Piece to unlock World 5-4.**
- **Collect the Big Shiny Infinijump Sticker.**
- **Collect the Luxurious Bed from the Secret Door.**
- **Collect the Comet Piece to unlock the path to World 5-1.**

IMPORTANT ITEMS AND LOCATIONS

DESCRIPTION	NOTES
Secret Door	The marked location is near the Comet Piece at the end of the river.
HP-Up Heart	None
Toad Rescue	None
Luigi Location	None
Wiggler Diary Entry	None
Things	The Luxurious Bed is through the Secret Door.

RECOMMENDED TACTICS

The Big Cheep Chomp is the only enemy in this Course, and there's no way to attack it. Your only option is to stay away from this beast!

STRAIGHTAWAY

You begin the Course on a raft heading toward a large waterfall. Once again, you must use the Circle Pad to steer the raft out of danger.

As you float down the straightaway, a Big Cheep Chomp appears behind you. Once it does, this persistent creature repeatedly attacks you. Any part of the raft caught in the enemy's path will break loose. If the Big Cheep Chomp lands a direct hit, however, it can swallow you whole.

As you continue along the straightaway, the Big Cheep Chomp's attacks become more and more difficult to predict. Because the raft isn't built for sudden maneuvers, it's generally helpful to keep moving. Drift gently from side to side until you can identify the Big Cheep Chomp's path. As the enemy approaches, you must then decide whether to pick up the pace or reverse direction.

The Big Cheep Chomp has a variety of attacks, but this doesn't affect your basic strategy. When you can't see the enemy itself, look for the shadow that indicates its position. Continue to evade the Big Cheep Chomp until your raft drops down to the loop at the base of the waterfall.

LOOP

After you drop off of the waterfall, steer the raft to the river's left edge. When you spot the turnoff, steer the ramp out of the main path and into the loop.

Follow the loop to the structure at the edge of the area, then activate the Paperize ability. Peel the Jungle Flood Gate scrap from the wall, then reapply it to the same spot.

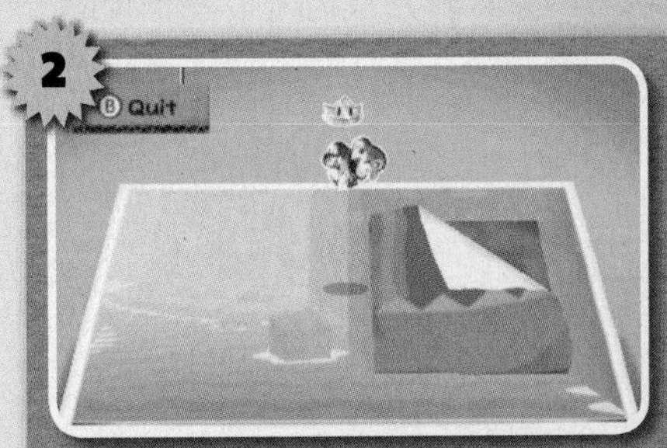

WORLD 5-3

After you align the scrap, steer the raft into the structure.

TIP

If you fail to align the scrap or steer the raft in time, just make a second pass around the loop.

The raft carries you to the Course's first Comet Piece. Before you collect it, however, look for the hidden area through the pillars to the right.

Search the ? Block in the hidden area to find the Megaflash Infinijump sticker.

When you're ready, leave the hidden area and collect the Comet Piece to end your first visit.

Sticker Comet Piece: Unlocking World 5-4

This Course contains two pieces of the Sticker Comet. To unlock World 5-4, collect the Comet Piece from the structure on the river's loop.

Recommended Visit #2

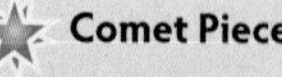

Secret Door

Comet Piece

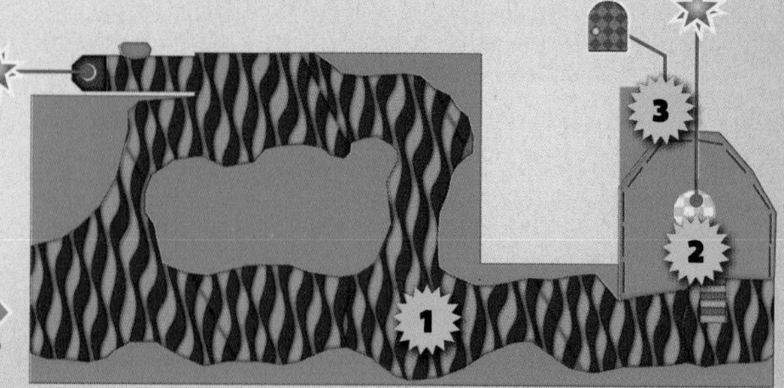

From Straightaway

1

After you collect the first Comet Piece, you must revisit the Course to complete the remaining objectives. Evade the Big Cheep Chomp until you reach the waterfall, then ride the raft past the loop and continue to the end of the river.

2

The second Comet Piece is floating near the dock, but take a moment to explore the area before you collect it.

CAUTION

After you collect the Course's first Comet Piece, the Big Cheep Chomp becomes much more aggressive! It's much more difficult to dodge its attacks when you revisit this level.

3

Hop over the fence to the left and place a Secret Door sticker on the marked location. Search the ? Block hidden behind the grass, then head through the Secret Door to find the Luxurious Bed.

THING: LUXURIOUS BED

The Luxurious Bed is behind the Secret Door. Apply a Secret Door sticker to the marked location near the second Comet Piece, then head inside to collect the Luxury Bed.

When you're ready, collect the sticker Comet Piece at the end of the river to complete your visit.

STICKER COMET PIECE: UNLOCKING THE PATH TO WORLD 5-1

This Course contains two pieces of the Sticker Comet. Collect the Comet Piece at the end of the river to unlock the path between World 5-3 and World 5-1.

WORLD 5-4: CHOMP RUINS

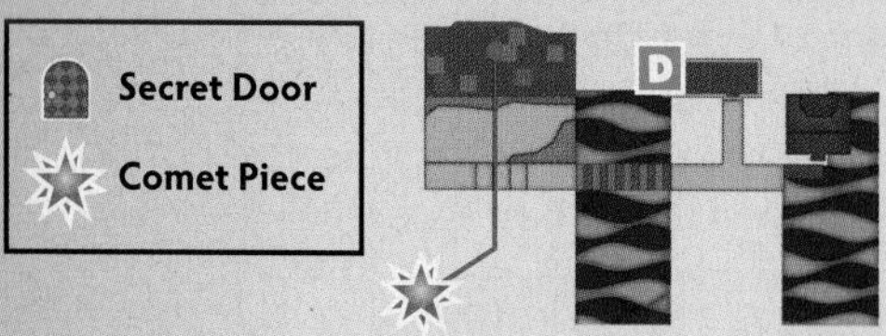

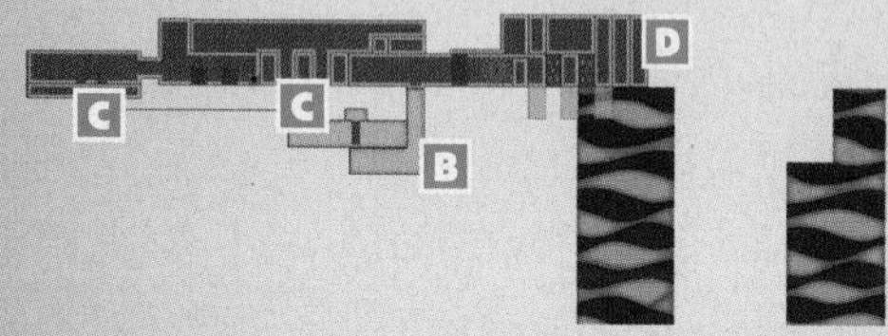

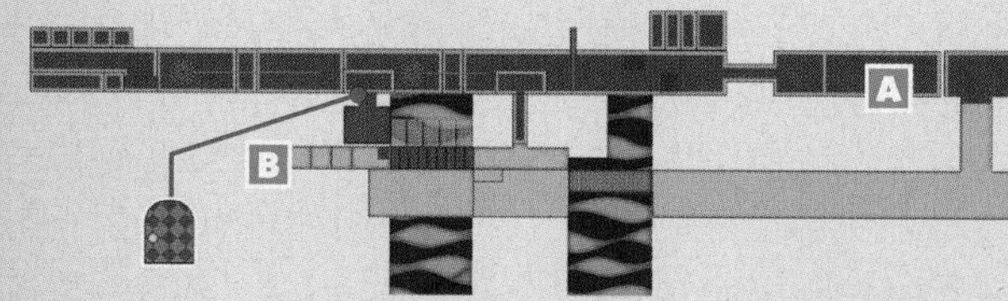

Overview

Prerequisites

To unlock this Course, you must collect the corresponding Comet Piece from the structure along the river's loop in World 5-3. Before you enter the Course, make sure your Album contains a Secret Door sticker.

Objectives

This Course contains several objectives, all of which can be completed during a single visit:

- **Collect the Megaflash Eekhammer sticker.**
- **Reposition the Ruin Slope scrap.**
- **Collect the Big Shiny Clone Jump sticker.**
- **Collect the Air Conditioner from the Secret Door. Collect the Megaflash Baahammer sticker.**
- **Collect the Megaflash Hurlhammer sticker.**
- **Collect the Megaflash Hopslipper sticker.**
- **Reposition the Bomp scrap.**
- **Collect and apply the Ruin Floor scrap.**
- **Collect the D-Cell Battery.**
- **Collect the Teapot.**
- **Free the Big Chain Chomp.**
- **Collect the Comet Piece to unlock World 5-5.**

TIP

The camera flips each time you move between the ruins' interior and exterior. Keep this in mind when referring to the Course's maps!

IMPORTANT ITEMS AND LOCATIONS

DESCRIPTION	NOTES
Secret Door	The marked location is on a second-floor platform.
HP-Up Heart	None
Toad Rescue	None
Luigi Location	None
Wiggler Diary Entry	None
Things	The Air Conditioner is through the Secret Door. The D-Cell Battery is on the third-floor balcony. The Teapot is near the fourth-floor walkway, behind a waterfall.

RECOMMENDED TACTICS

This Course contains a variety of enemies, most of which you've faced before. Bring a large assortment of high-quality stickers to overcome each challenge you face.

Familiar enemies like Hammer Bros, Spike Tops, Spear Guys, and Piranha Plants combine to make formidable teams. Keep plenty of powerful Jump-based stickers and Hammer-based stickers, and plenty of multi-target stickers as well. Burnhammers, Chillhammers, and Shells can end most of this Course's battles with ease.

Rather than defeat the Big Chain Chomp, free this slumbering enemy from its bonds before you begin the battle. Use basic stickers to progress the battle until the Big Chain Chomp wakes up.

GROUND FLOOR

The Bomps hiding at Point 1 react to your presence. If you choose to follow the main path, move slowly to draw these creatures out from the wall before they can knock you off of the path.

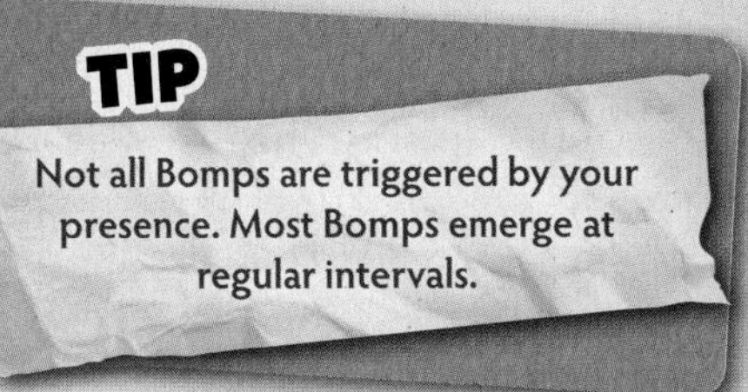

TIP

Not all Bomps are triggered by your presence. Most Bomps emerge at regular intervals.

Instead of crossing the bridge at Point 2, use the raft chained to the grass. Hop on the raft, then use your Hammer to pound the stake into the ground.

When the raft stops, search the nearby ? Block to find the Megaflash Eekhammer. When you're ready, climb the steps and enter the ruins.

Once inside, activate the Paperize ability and peel the Ruin Slope scrap from the center of the room.

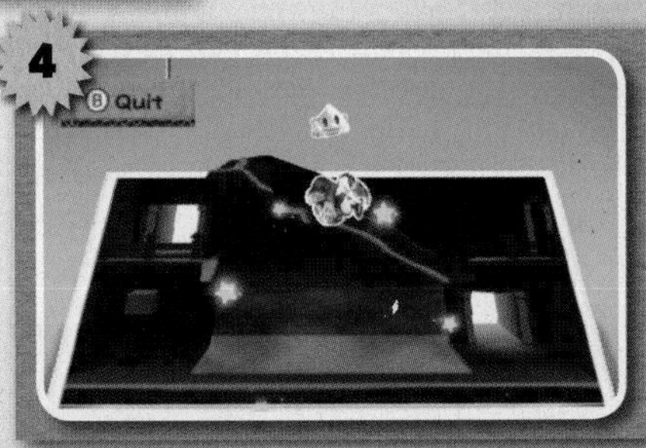

Reapply the scrap to create a ramp to the rest of the second floor.

> **TIP**
>
> There's an HP Block just outside the room's upper door. If you need to refill Mario's HP, after you adjust the scrap use the steps outside the room to reach the HP Block.

SECOND FLOOR

To Ground Floor

To Third Floor

Comet Piece

Hidden Block

Drop down through one of the trapdoors at Point 1, then clear out the enemies near your landing spot. Move to the back wall and follow it to the right to find a hidden room in the darkened area. Search the ? Block to collect a Big Shiny Clone Jump sticker, then make your way back up to the main path.

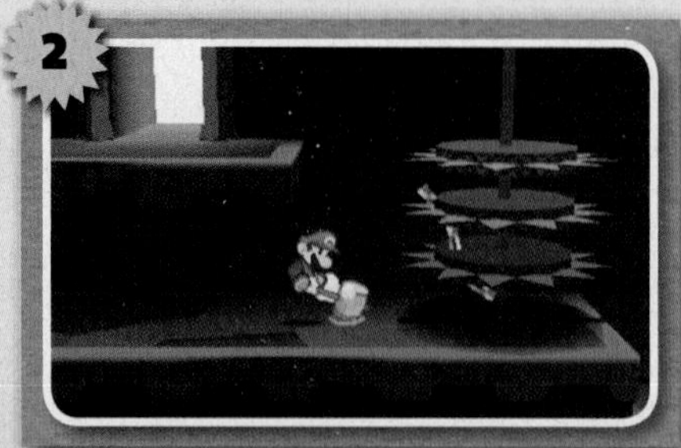

The saw blades at Point 2 are chained to the ground. Strike the stake with your Hammer to free them.

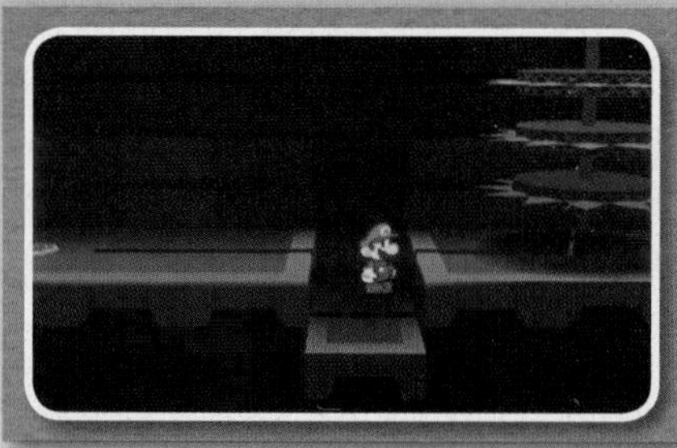

Follow the saw blades and drop into the small pit to the right. Wait for the blades to pass over you, then hop out of the pit and continue through the area.

When you reach the end of the hall, move to the foreground to find some small steps. After you search the ? Block at the bottom of the steps, climb back up to the hallway.

Stand below the Shiny POW Block sticker at Point 4 and jump to reveal the Hidden Blocks above you. Climb onto the Hidden Blocks, peel the sticker, and wait for the saw blades to approach. When you're ready, jump on the saw blades and ride to the next platform.

When you reach the next platform, hop off of the saw blades and apply a Secret Door sticker to the marked location. Head inside to find the Air Conditioner.

THING: AIR CONDITIONER

The Air Conditioner is through the Secret Door. Ride to the platform between the saw blades and apply a Secret Door sticker to the marked location. Head inside and strike the back wall with your Hammer until the Air Conditioner falls to the ground.

Hop onto the next set of saw blades and ride to the platform at Point 6. When you're ready, follow the path to the walkway outside.

Peel the Bowser tape at Point 7 to create a bridge over the water. Search the nearby ? Blocks and, if needed, use the HP Block to the right.

When you're ready, climb back up to the walkway and follow the path to the left. As you make your way across the bridge at Point 8, avoid the Bomps that emerge from the waterfall. Continue up the steps to reach the third floor.

TIP

A shadow appears just before each Bomp emerges—move out of the way before it pushes you off the bridge!

THIRD FLOOR

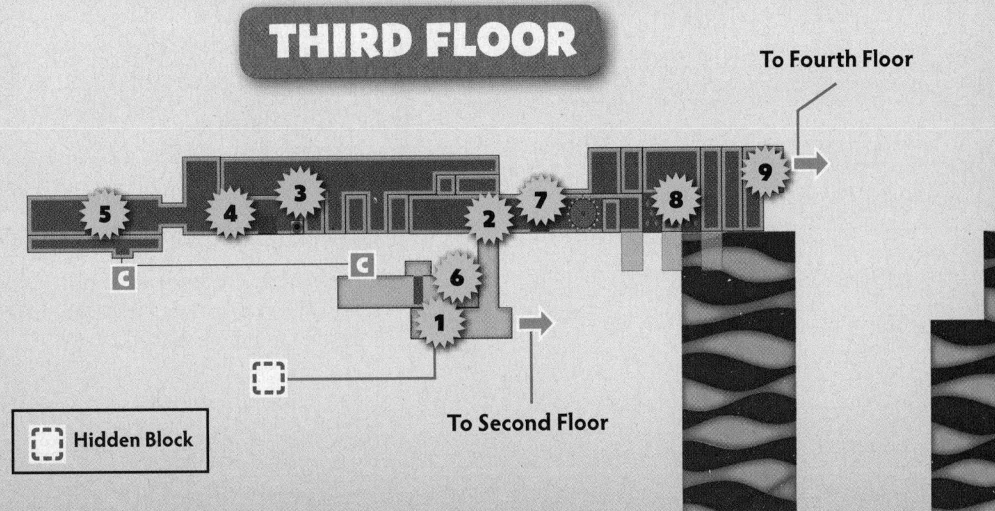

WORLD 5-4

Before you enter the third-floor hallway, reveal the Hidden Blocks above the blue flower.

When you enter the third-floor hallway, There's a Flashy Infinijump sticker on the back wall. You can't reach the sticker at this time, but remember to collect it before you complete your visit. Before you can follow the path to the left, you must recover the Ruin Floor scrap.

Drop down from the main path and peel the Bowser tape to reveal a set of stairs. A Spear Guy patrols the area, so watch out for incoming attacks.

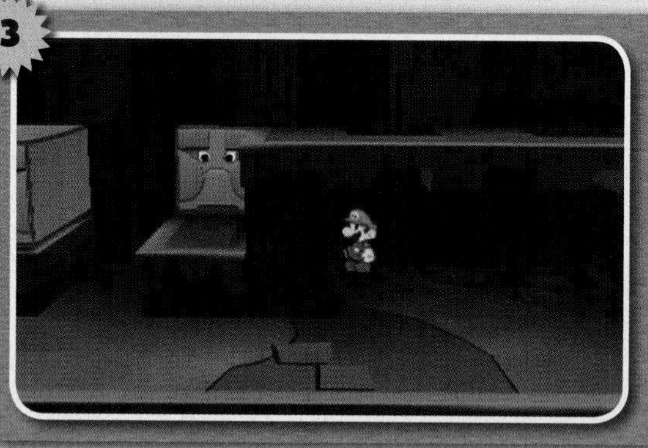

Move past the Bomps along the back wall and clear the area of enemies. Duck under the main path and enter the warp pipe hidden just past the last Bomp.

When you emerge from the warp pipe, search the nearby ? Blocks to find a Megaflash Baahammer, a Megaflash Hurlhammer, and a Megaflash Hopslipper! After you collect all three stickers, use the warp pipe to leave the hidden area.

When you're ready, climb back up to the main path and hop along the Bomps as they emerge from the wall. Keep moving to the right to find a small room.

The small room contains two Bomps, but one of them is stuck in the wall. Activate the Paperize ability and peel the Bomp scrap from the wall.

Reapply the Bomp scrap, climb up to the door at the top of the room, and head outside.

After you emerge on the balcony, move to the right to collect the Ruin Floor scrap.

One of the panels on the back wall is loose. Strike the panel with your Hammer to reveal the D-Cell Battery. After you collect it, drop down to the Hidden Blocks below you and grab the Big Shiny Baahammer. Hop down the steps and reenter the third-floor hallway.

THING: D-CELL BATTERY

When you reach the third-floor balcony, strike the loose panel with your Hammer to reveal the D-Cell Battery.

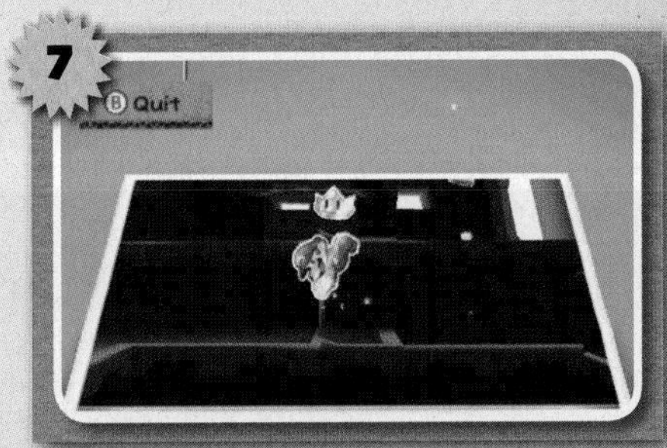

Use the Ruin Floor scrap to patch the hole at Point 7.

Use your Hammer to smash through the newly patched floor and then follow the path to the left.

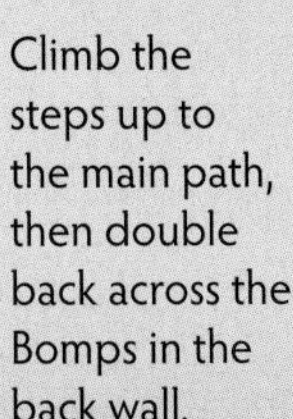

Climb the steps up to the main path, then double back across the Bomps in the back wall.

WORLD 5-4

Hop onto the saw blades and ride over to grab the Flashy Infinijump sticker to the right.

When you're ready, move back to the left and exit through the door at the top of the steps to reach the fourth floor.

THING: TEAPOT

Use your Hammer to reveal the Hidden Blocks on the right edge of the fourth-floor walkway. Follow the Hidden Blocks to the secret area behind the waterfall and collect the Teapot.

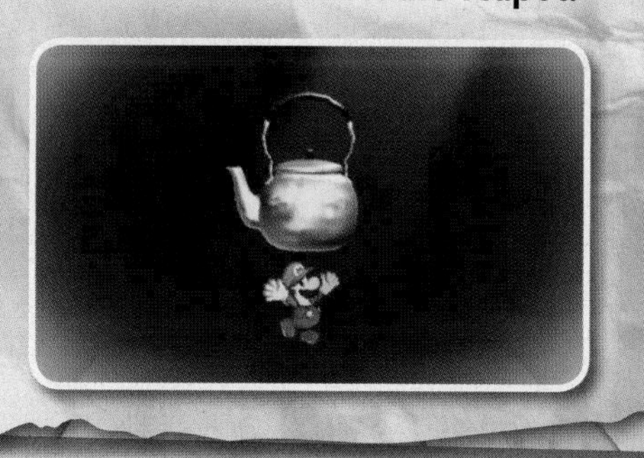

FOURTH FLOOR

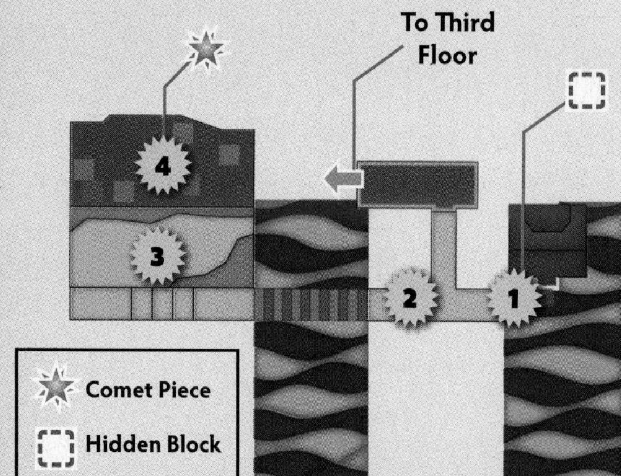

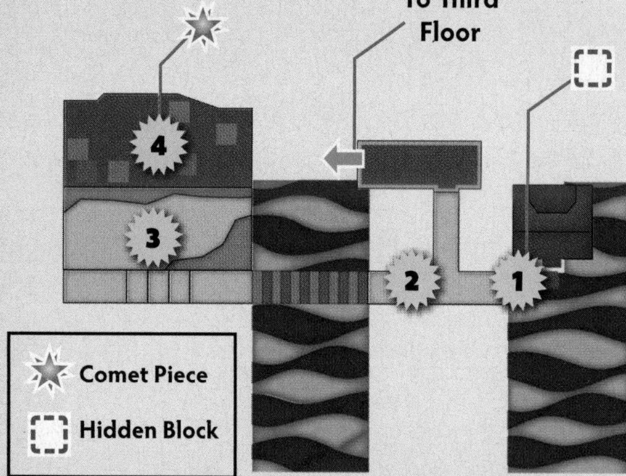

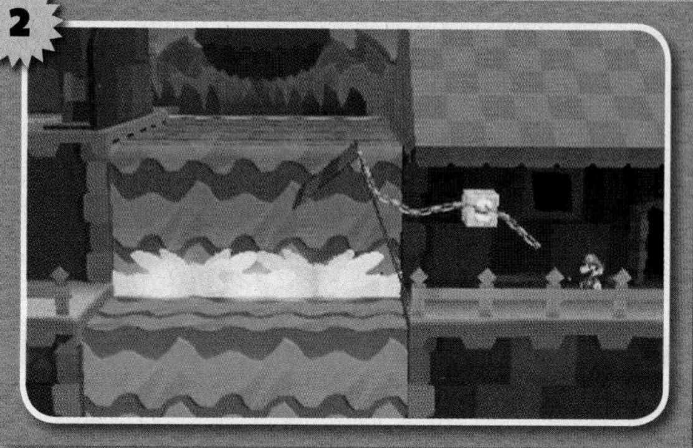

There's a stake at Point 2. Strike it with your Hammer to reveal the bridge to the left.

After you step onto the fourth-floor walkway, use your Hammer to reveal the Hidden Blocks to the right. Follow the Hidden Blocks to the center of the waterfall, then move toward the background to find the Teapot in a hidden area.

Climb the steps to find the Big Chain Chomp at Point 3. Free the sleeping enemy to reveal the Course's Comet Piece.

MINI-BOSS: BIG CHAIN CHOMP

Before you begin the battle, slip behind the Big Chain Chomp and strike the stake with your Hammer.

Once the Big Chain Chomp is free, attack it to begin the battle. The creature stays asleep for the first few turns, so you must progress the battle until it wakes up. Use a surplus sticker to end each turn as quickly and efficiently as possible.

When the Big Chain Chomp wakes, it attacks. You can't defend yourself from this lunge! Just absorb the damage and wait for the enemy to leave the area.

4

As the Big Chain Chomp thrashes around you, it topples a nearby wall. After the creature leaves the area, move toward the background and collect the Comet Piece to end your visit.

STICKER COMET PIECE: UNLOCKING WORLD 5-5

This Course contains only a single piece of the Sticker Comet. To unlock World 5-5, collect the Comet Piece near the Big Chain Chomp.

WORLD 5-5: RUGGED ROAD

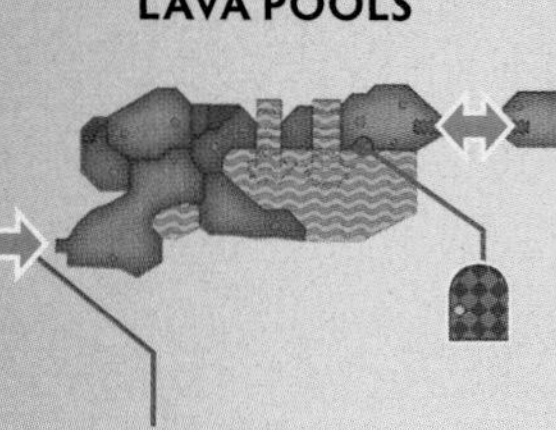

OVERVIEW

PREREQUISITES

To unlock this Course, you must collect the Comet Piece from World 5-4. Before you enter this Course, make sure your Album contains a Secret Door sticker and a cold-based Thing Sticker.

ESSENTIAL THING STICKERS

NAME	THING LOCATION	NOTES
Shaved Ice	World 2-4	Needed to freeze the lava pools.

NOTE

If you prefer, you can use the Refrigerator sticker or the Air Conditioner sticker instead of the Shaved Ice.

OBJECTIVES

This Course contains several objectives, all of which can be completed during a single visit:

- Freeze the lava pool with a cold-based Thing Sticker.
- Collect the Turkey.
- Collect the Basin from the Secret Door.
- Collect the Megaflash Burnhammer sticker.
- Swap the Mountain Hole scrap and the Mountain Boulder scrap.
- Drop the first big boulder into place.
- Collect the Car Sponge.
- Collect the Megaflash Slaphammer sticker.
- Find Luigi.
- Collect and apply the Cracked Boulder scrap.
- Drop the second big boulder into place.
- Collect the Megaflash Iron Jump sticker.
- Reposition the Big Boulder scrap.

IMPORTANT ITEMS AND LOCATIONS

DESCRIPTION	NOTES
Secret Door	The marked location is in the large lava pool.
HP-Up Heart	None
Toad Rescue	None
Luigi Location	Luigi is in the hot springs near the second lava flow.
Wiggler Diary Entry	None
Things	The Turkey is in the small lava pool. The Basin is through the Secret Door. The Car Sponge is hidden near the first lava flow.

Recommended Tactics

This Course contains some fairly tough enemies. Bring a wide variety of powerful stickers to deal with Fire Bros, Ice Bros, Fire Piranhas, Shiny Paratroopas, and Bony Beetles.

Megaflash stickers are certainly effective, but your Album can only accommodate so many. Adding to the challenge, many of the Course's enemies are immune to at least one type of attack. Shiny Paratroopas can avoid many of your strongest multi-target stickers. Bony Beetles have retractable spikes that counter most Jump-based attacks. Several enemies are immune to fire-based damage.

Before you use any fire-based stickers, Jump-based stickers, or Hammer-based stickers, make sure you evaluate each enemy in the group. Use the Battle Spinner to select multiple, high-quality stickers on a single turn. It's best to bring a large assortment of stickers, but a combination of Shiny Shells and Shiny Hopslippers will prove effective against most groups.

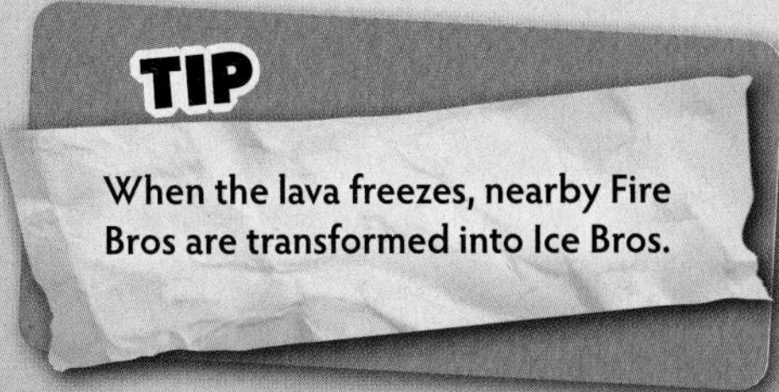

TIP

When the lava freezes, nearby Fire Bros are transformed into Ice Bros.

Lava Pools

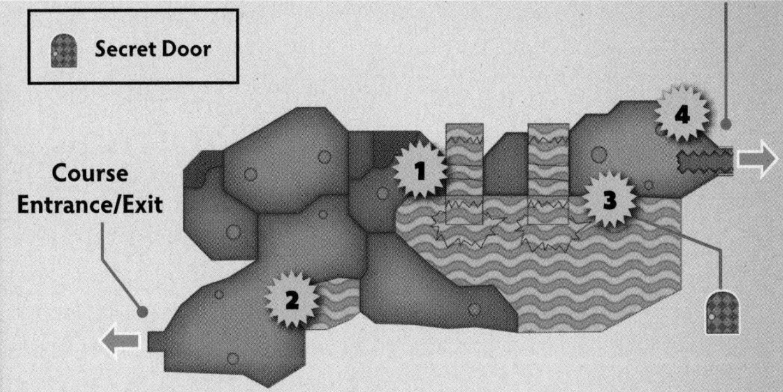

When you first visit this Course, the lava pools are blocking your path. Activate the Paperize ability and apply the Shaved Ice sticker (or any cold-based Thing Sticker) to the background.

After the lava pools freeze, you can safely explore the area.

2

The small pool serves as an entrance to a hidden area. Drop into the pool and search the ? Block, then move to the left to find the Turkey in a hidden area.

THING: BASIN

The Basin is located through the Secret Door. Apply a Secret Door sticker to the marked location in the large pool. Pass through the door and collect the Basin.

THING: TURKEY

After you freeze the lava pools, drop into the small pool and search the wall to the left to find the Turkey in a hidden area.

4

There's a hidden area near Point 4. To find it, slip behind the rock in the background.

3

Apply a Secret Door sticker to the marked location near the large pool's right edge. Head inside and collect the Basin.

Search the ? Block in the hidden area to find a Megaflash Burnhammer. After you collect it, return to the main path and continue to the first lava flow.

FIRST LAVA FLOW—PART 1

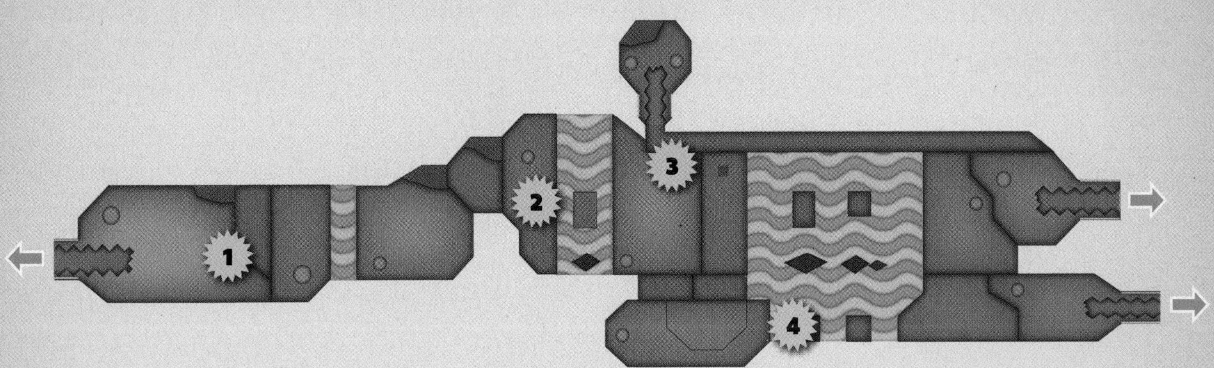

The Fire Piranhas at Point 1 attack while you approach. Dodge the incoming fireballs and clear these troublesome enemies from your path.

When you reach Point 3, activate the Paperize ability and peel the Mountain Hole scrap out of the background.

As you move through the area, chunks of molten rocks fall toward you. Watch for the shadow that indicates each point of impact. Keep moving to avoid taking damage.

After you collect the scrap, move to the foreground and climb down to the lower path. Hop across the lava and follow the path to the first big boulder.

FIRST BIG BOULDER—PART 1

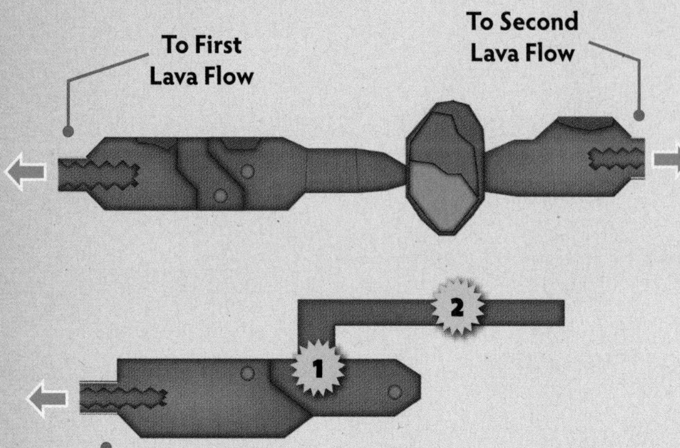

Apply the Mountain Hole scrap to the open spot to create a new path, then follow it through the mountain.

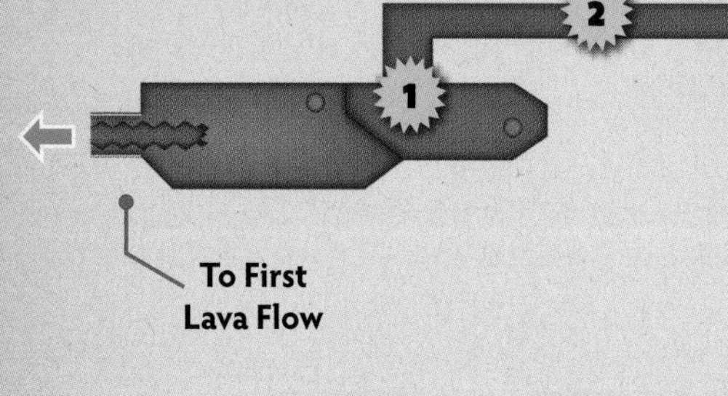

When you reach Point 1, activate the Paperize ability and peel the Mountain Boulder scrap from the wall.

When you reach the cracked rock formation at the end of the path, strike it with your Hammer. When the formation splits, the first big boulder drops down to create a bridge above you. Turn around and follow the path back to the first lava flow.

FIRST LAVA FLOW—PART 2

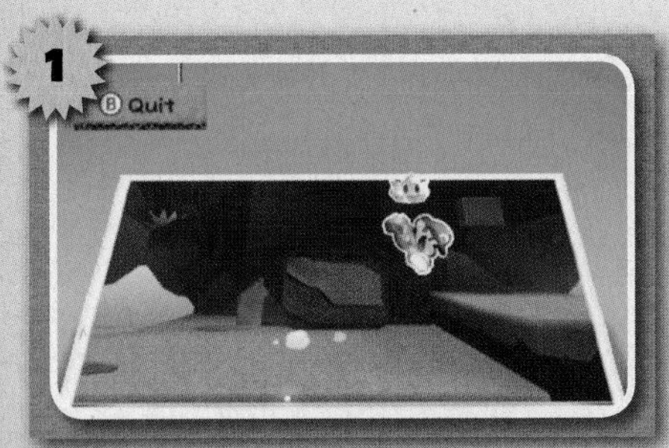

Climb back up to the main path and apply the Mountain Boulder scrap to the space left by the Mountain Hole scrap.

After the scrap is in place, hop onto the boulder and up to the ledge.

Follow the ledge to the left to find a hidden area containing the Car Sponge.

THING: Car Sponge

The Car Sponge is hidden behind the first lava flow. After you place the Mountain Boulder scrap in the appropriate spot, climb up to the ledge on the back wall and follow it to the left.

After you collect the Car Sponge, leave the hidden area and follow the ledge across the lava flow. Hop down from the ledge and search the area. When you're ready, follow the main path back toward the first big boulder.

FIRST BIG BOULDER—PART 2

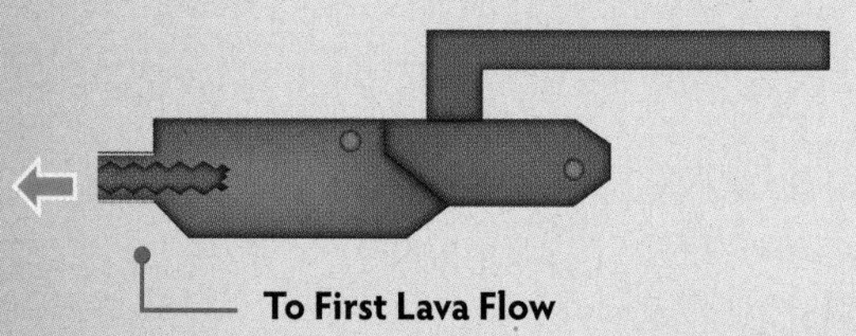

Follow the path across the first big boulder and continue through the area.

Be particularly mindful of the falling rocks when you use the HP Block and the Save Block at Point 2—draw a molten rock away from the Blocks, then run in and use them before the next one arrives. When you're ready, follow the path to the second lava flow.

SECOND LAVA FLOW

1

Some of the terrain around the second lava flow is destructible. Stand on the X at Point 1 and wait for a molten rock to approach. When the shadow appears, move away and wait for the rock to tear a hole in the ground.

Drop down through the hole to find a hidden area. Search the ? Block to collect a Megaflash Slaphammer sticker.

2

When you leave the hidden area, you emerge at Point 2. Search the area for stickers, then climb back up to the main path.

There's another hidden area below Point 3. Draw another molten rock to the X below the Fire Bro's ledge. After the impact, drop down to find the hot springs.

3

4

After you land, investigate the hot springs to find Luigi sitting in the small pool to the left.

LUIGI LOCATION: RUGGED ROAD

Luigi is sitting in the hot springs below the second lava flow. Approach the smaller pool on the left edge of the background, activate the Paperize ability, and pull Luigi out of the hot springs.

5

On your way out of the hot springs, make sure you collect the Cracked Boulder scrap at Point 5.

After you leave the hot springs, climb back up to the main path and search the area for any remaining stickers. When you're ready, hop along the platforms that appear in the lava flow.

Once you're safely across the lava, climb the steps up to the ledge and search the background for hidden enemies and stickers. When you're ready, return to the main path and continue to the second big boulder.

Second Big Boulder

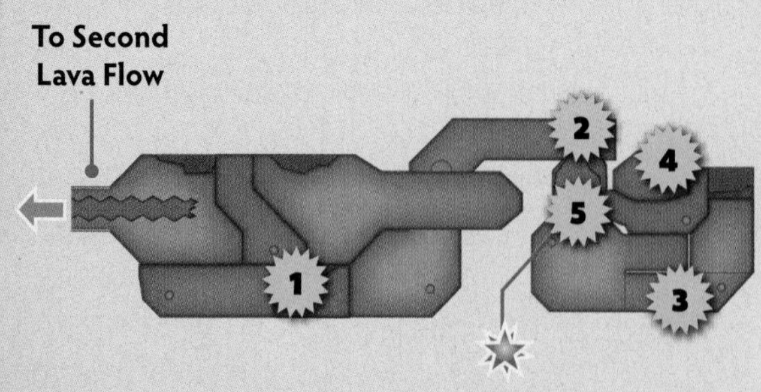

As you approach the second big boulder, take the steps down to the bottom of the area and follow the path to the right.

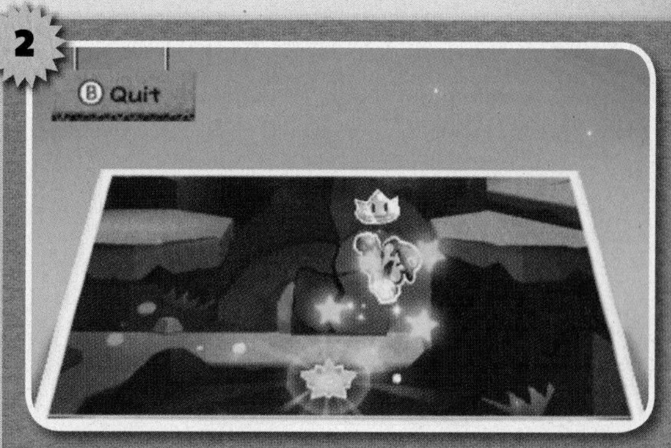

Apply the Cracked Boulder scrap to the hole at Point 2. Hit the crack with your Hammer to topple the big boulder above you. When it lands, it crushes the nearby comet piece.

Before you collect the comet piece, climb the ramp to the right.

4

Draw a molten rock to the X at the top of the ramp. After the impact, drop through the opening to find another hidden area.

Search the ? Block to collect a Megaflash Iron Jump sticker, then exit the hidden area to emerge at the bottom of the ramp.

5

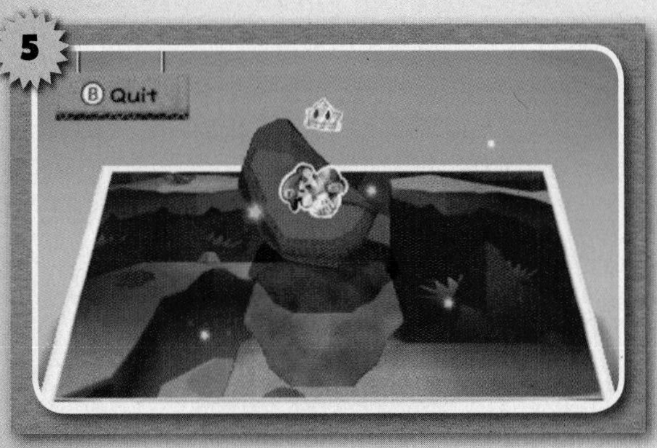

Approach the toppled boulder and activate the Paperize ability. Peel the Big Boulder scrap from the ground, then reapply it to reveal the Comet Piece.

When you're ready, collect the Comet Piece to complete your visit.

Sticker Comet Piece: Unlocking World 5-6

This Course contains one piece of the Sticker Comet. To unlock World 5-6, collect the Comet Piece pinned beneath the second big boulder.

WORLD 5-6: RUMBLE VOLCANO

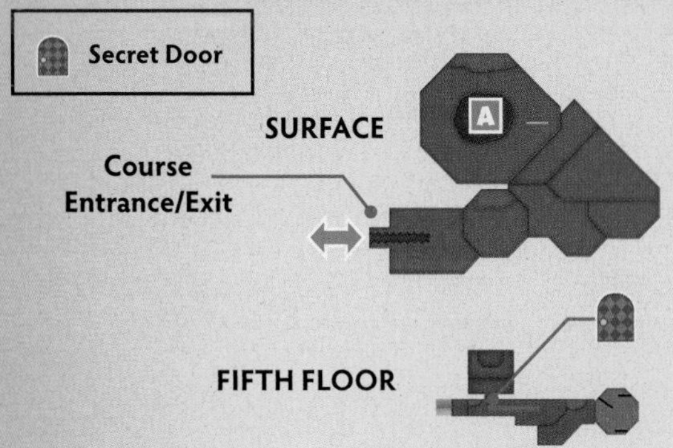

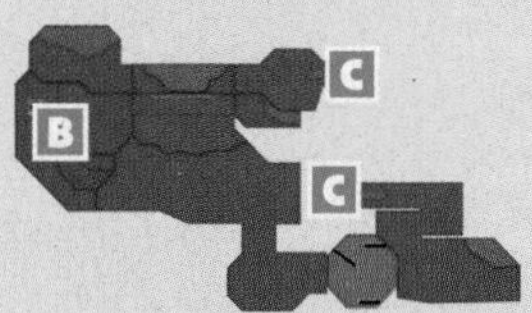

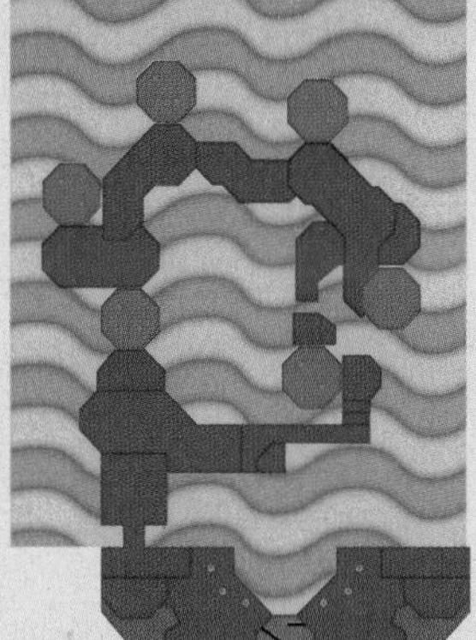

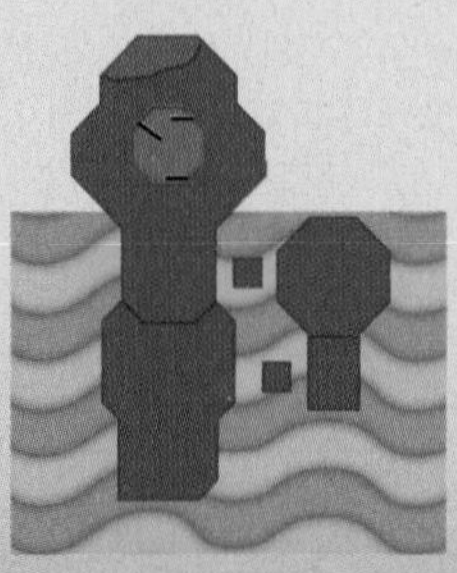

NOTE

The central lift allows you to move between the volcano's floors, but you must free all three Big Chain Chomps before it becomes fully functional.

overview

Prerequisites

To unlock this Course, you must collect the Comet Piece from the end of World 5-5. Before you enter the Course, make sure your Album contains a Secret Door sticker, some Mushroom stickers, and plenty of coins for the Course's Sticker Shop. The Squirt Gun sticker is useful during the boss battle, so consider bringing one.

ESSENTIAL THING STICKERS

NAME	THING LOCATION	NOTES
Squirt Gun	World 1-6	Useful during the boss battle.

caution

This Course contains no HP Blocks or Save Blocks, and after you drop into the volcano, you must defeat Petey Piranha before you can return to the surface. You can purchase everything you'll need at the Sticker Shop, but make sure you begin the Course with enough stickers to get there safely.

HOW TO USE THIS GUIDE
HOW TO PLAY
STICKERS
ENEMIES
WALKTHROUGH
DECALBURG
SURFSHINE HARBOR
WORLD 1
WORLD 2
WORLD 3
WORLD 4
WORLD 5
WORLD 6
CHECKLISTS

OBJECTIVES

This Course contains several objectives, one of which requires an additional visit:

- **Reach the volcano's central lift.**
- **Lead the first Big Chain Chomp to the central lift.**
- **Draw the second Big Chain Chomp to the central lift.**
- **Collect the Big Shiny 1UP sticker.**
- **Collect the Megaflash Clone Jump sticker.**
- **Draw the third Big Chain Chomp to the central lift.**
- **Collect the HP-Up Heart.**
- **Defeat Petey Piranha.**
- **Rescue Kersti.**
- **Collect the Royal Sticker.**
- **Collect the Guitar from the Secret Door.**

IMPORTANT ITEMS AND LOCATIONS

DESCRIPTION	NOTES
Secret Door	The marked location is on the fifth floor.
HP-Up Heart	The HP-Up Heart is on the second floor.
Toad Rescue	None
Luigi Location	None
Wiggler Diary Entry	None
Things	The Guitar is through the Secret Door.

RECOMMENDED TACTICS

Soon after you enter the Course, Petey Piranha kidnaps Kersti. This means the Battle Spinner is unavailable until you recover your companion. Fill your Album with the most powerful multi-target stickers available, but make sure you bring a supply of Mushroom stickers as well.

This Course contains Fire Piranhas, Fire Bros, Spear Guys, and a variety of beetle-based creatures. Megaflash stickers are certainly useful, but it's difficult to carry a sufficient supply. Use Shiny Shells to clear out groups of weaker enemies, and save your more powerful stickers for tougher enemies. When a single sticker isn't enough to end the battle, use POW Blocks or Baahammers to incapacitate the group, then take them out one at a time.

One of the Course's three Big Chain Chomps attacks before you can free it. Use a Baahammer to put it to sleep, then run from the battle. There are Baahammer stickers scattered throughout the Course, so make sure you grab one before you approach this enemy.

Petey Piranha is a formidable foe, but the proper strategy should put him right out of commission. Use the Course's Sticker Shop to stock up on Shiny POW Blocks and Big Shiny Hopslippers. When Petey Piranha makes himself dizzy, use these stickers to deal heavy damage!

SURFACE

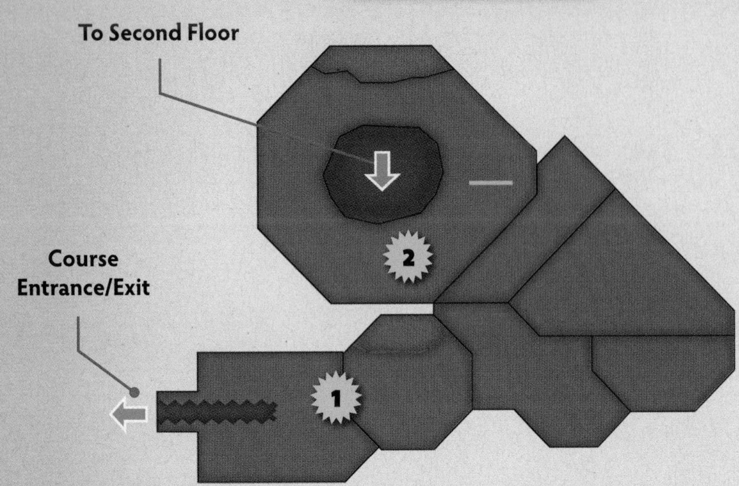

NOTE

When you first visit this Course, this area contains a hole that leads to the volcano's second floor. If you revisit the Course after you defeat Petey Piranha, a warp pipe that connects the surface to the second floor appears in the area.

As you climb the steps on the volcano's surface, consider avoiding the enemies along the path. You have plenty of battles ahead of you, and it's best to ration your stickers until you gain access to this Course's Sticker Shop.

When you're ready, enter the volcano through the hole at Point 2.

NOTE

When you first visit this Course, you must visit the floors in a predetermined order. You start on the second floor, descend to the first floor, soar up to the fifth floor, and work your way back down. If you revisit the Course after you defeat Petey Piranha, use the central lift to carry you from floor to floor.

SECOND FLOOR—PART 1

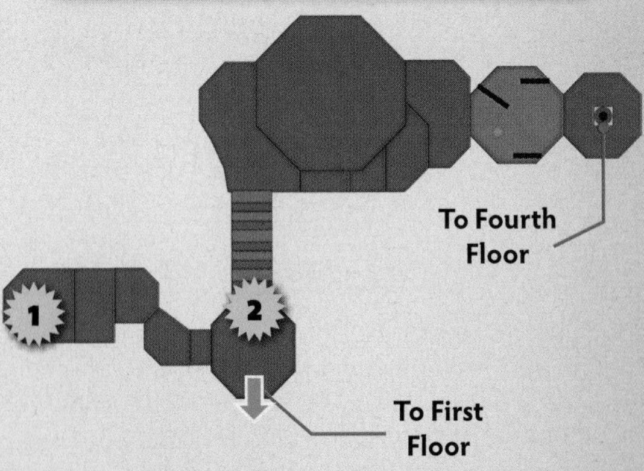

NOTE

The volcano's second floor contains Petey Piranha's platform and a warp pipe that leads to the Sticker Shop on the fourth floor. After you defeat Petey Piranha, a warp pipe leading to the surface appears at Point 1.

When you drop down from the surface, you land on the volcano's second floor. This floor contains Petey Piranha's platform, as well as a warp pipe that leads to the Sticker Shop on the fourth floor. Follow the path to the right to find Petey Piranha.

When Petey Piranha appears, he swallows Kersti and retreats to his platform. Unfortunately, the hole in the bridge prevents you from following him. Peel the Bowser tape at Point 2 to drop to the volcano's first floor.

First Floor

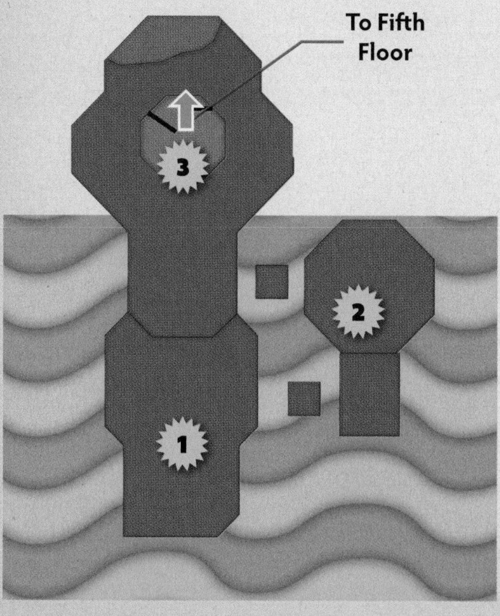

> **NOTE**
>
> The volcano's first floor serves as the central lift's starting point.

After you drop to the first floor, move to the right. As you do, watch out for incoming attacks from the Fire Piranhas on the ledge.

Hop along the platforms on the right side of the area to reach the volcano's central lift.

When you're ready, step on the lift to ride all the way up to the fifth floor.

WORLD 5-6

FIFTH FLOOR

NOTE

The fifth floor contains the Secret Door location, the first Big Chain Chomp, and several items hanging from chains.

When the lift stops on the fifth floor, there are several stickers and enemies hanging from the chains above you. These chains are anchored to the stakes on the third floor. Search the nearby ? Block and continue to the left.

The Secret Door is on the wall at Point 2. Unfortunately, you can't use the Paperize ability until you rescue Kersti. After you defeat Petey Piranha, revisit this area and apply a Secret Door sticker to this location.

Approach the lava at the edge of the area to coax the first Big Chain Chomp out of hiding. Run back out to the lift. When the Big Chain Chomp follows you, it embeds itself in the lift. When you're ready, hop onto the lift to drop to the fourth floor.

FOURTH FLOOR

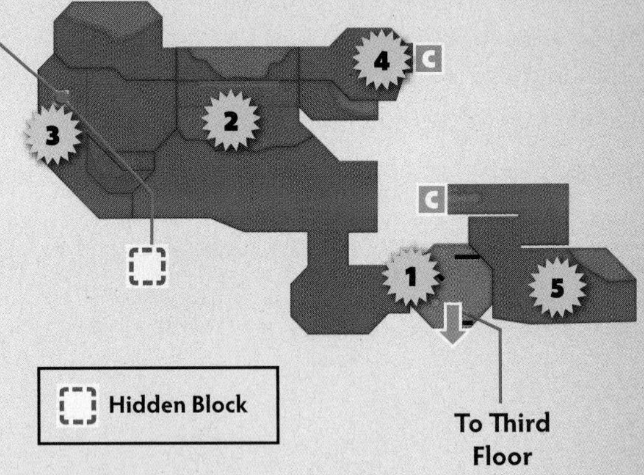

NOTE

The fourth floor contains the World 5-6 Sticker Shop and the second Big Chain Chomp.

1

When you reach the fourth floor, the second Big Chain Chomp is on the ledge to the right. To reach it, you must loop around the entire area. Follow the path to the left to find the Course's Sticker Shop.

2

Stop by the Sticker Shop and make sure your Album is ready for battle. Stock up on Big Shiny Hopslippers, Shiny POW Blocks, Shiny Mushrooms, and any other stickers you might need.

3

The warp pipe near the Sticker Shop leads to the second floor, but the lava geyser supporting the lift blocks the path to Petey Piranha. Look for the Hidden Block near the warp pipe, then follow the path up the steps.

4

Search the area for stickers and defend yourself from any attackers, then follow the path to the right.

5

Make sure your Album contains some type of Baahammer, then approach the Big Chain Chomp at Point 5.

When the battle starts, attack it with a Baahammer. Once the enemy is asleep, run from the battle.

Move behind the sleeping Big Chain Chomp and hit the stake with your Hammer. Restart the encounter and use basic stickers to progress the battle until the Big Chain Chomp wakes up. You can't block its lunge, so just absorb the damage and allow it to leave the area. When the battle ends, drop down from the ledge and ride the lift to the third floor.

TIP

If Mario's HP is running low, use a Mushroom sticker while you wait for the Big Chain Chomp to wake up.

THIRD FLOOR

NOTE

The third floor contains eight stakes that anchor the chains on the fifth floor. This area also includes a large chamber that extends down to the lava.

When you arrive on the third floor, there are four stakes on each side of you. If you hit one of these stakes with your Hammer, the enemy or sticker attached to the anchored chain falls down from the fifth floor. Before you deal with the stakes, however, follow the path to the left and explore the connected chamber.

When you first enter the chamber, look for the Bowser tape on the ledge in the background.

To reach the Bowser tape, you must negotiate the platforms throughout the chamber. Many of the platforms serve as small lifts. Each time the path seems to end, hop onto a lift and ride to a new platform.

The path is fairly simple, but there are plenty of enemies along the way. There are some very useful stickers along the way, too, so make sure you check each of the ? Blocks you find.

When you're finished exploring the platforms, use the lift at Point 4 to ride up to the ledge.

Climb up to the Bowser tape and peel it off of the chain. Move toward the foreground, hop down from the ledge, and return to the stakes near the central lift.

Use your Hammer to hit the stake on the far left. When you do, a sticker drops down from the fifth floor. There's a Spear Guy hanging from the next chain, so consider skipping it. Hit the third stake to receive a Big Shiny 1Up sticker!

Move across the central lift and hit the stake on the far right to collect a Megaflash Clone Jump sticker! Skip the stake next to it, then hit the two stakes to the left. The last stake drops the third Big Chomp Chain onto the lift. After you collect the stickers, hop onto the lift and ride back down to the second floor.

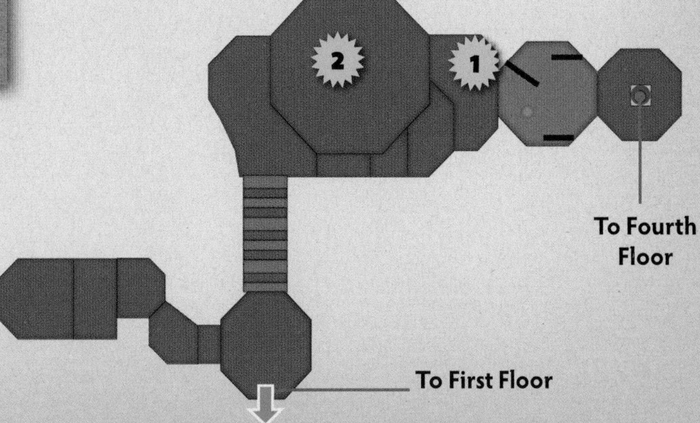

1 When you return to the second floor, the lift lands between a warp pipe and Petey Piranha's platform. If you're not prepared for battle, use the warp pipe and purchase Shiny POW Blocks and Jump-based stickers from the Sticker Shop. If you're ready, collect the HP-Up Heart to the left and continue up the nearby steps.

HP-UP HEART: RUMBLE VOLCANO

The HP-Up Heart is on the volcano's second floor, just left of the central lift. Grab it on your way to face Petey Piranha.

2 Climb to the platform at Point 2 to find Petey Piranha. To rescue Kersti and claim another Royal Sticker, you must defeat this fiend!

After you defeat Petey Piranha, collect the Royal Sticker to end your first visit.

NOTE

After you collect the five available Royal Stickers, you can unlock the gate in World 6-1.

RECOMMENDED VISIT #2

After you defeat Petey Piranha, revisit the volcano's fifth floor and apply the Secret Door sticker to the marked location. Head inside to find the Guitar.

THING: GUITAR

After you regain the Paperize ability, apply a Secret Door sticker to the marked location on the volcano's fifth floor. Pass through the door and collect the Guitar.

BOSS FIGHT!

PETEY PIRANHA

Until you recover Kersti, you're limited to a single sticker during each of your turns. Use basic stickers to progress the battle until Petey Piranha performs a spin attack. Once he's dizzy, use a POW Block, an Eekhammer, or a Slaphammer to knock him off his feet.

While Petey Piranha is down, use Big Shiny Hopslippers to do serious damage to him. Repeat the process until Kersti Pops out of his mouth.

Each time you use a Jump-based sticker, there's a chance that a Dry Bones will appear. After you rescue Kersti, use the Battle Spinner to perform multiple attacks during each turn.

If not, simply use the Battle Spinner to deal high-damage attacks with Shiny Hopslippers and Big Shiny Hopslippers. Keep attacking until you defeat Petey Piranha!

WORLD SIX COURSES	
NUMBER	NAME
World 6-1	Gate Cliff
World 6-2	Bowser Jr.'s Flotilla
World 6-3	Bowser's Sky Castle

WORLD 6-1: GATE CLIFF

OVERVIEW

PREREQUISITES

This Course becomes available as soon as you defeat the Big Cheep Cheep in Surfshine Harbor. To complete the available objectives, however, you must first collect the Royal Stickers from World One, World Two, World Three, World Four, and World Five.

OBJECTIVES

This Course contains only two objectives, both of which can be completed during a single visit:

- **Use the Royal Stickers to reveal the gate.**
- **Reposition the Hidden Bowser Castle scrap.**

IMPORTANT ITEMS AND LOCATIONS

DESCRIPTION	NOTES
Secret Door	None
HP-Up Heart	None
Toad Rescue	None
Luigi Location	None
Wiggler Diary Entry	None
Things	None

Recommended Tactics

This Course contains no enemies, so there's no need to worry about combat.

Unlocking the Gate

When you arrive in the area, a large cliff blocks your path. Exit the boat's cabin and listen to Kersti.

After you use all five Royal Stickers, activate the Paperize ability and peel the Hidden Bowser Castle scrap from the cliff. Reapply the scrap to the same spot.

Select each of the Royal Stickers from your Album's cover to illuminate a corresponding location on the cliff.

After you replace the scrap, Bowser's Sky Castle soars into the air. Reenter the cabin and activate the captain's wheel to complete your visit.

WORLD 6-2: BOWSER JR.'S FLOTILLA

Secret Door
Comet Piece

UPPER DECKS

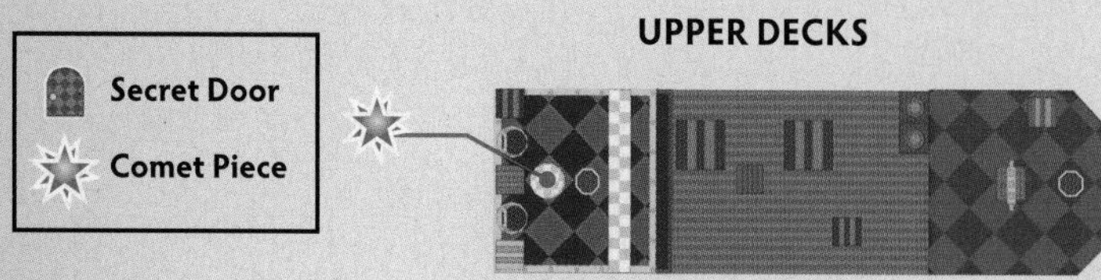

MAIN DECK

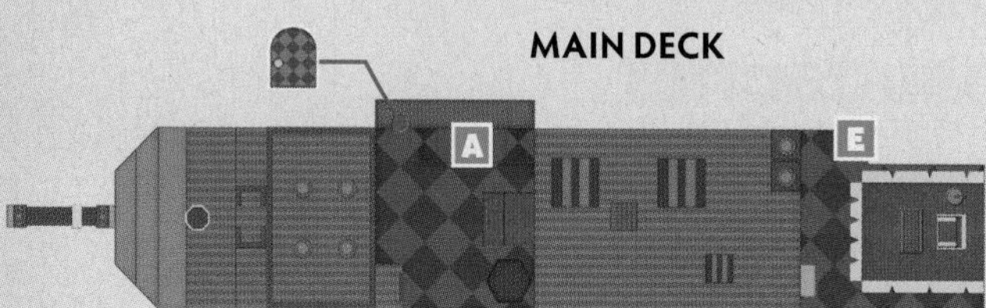

GUN DECK

HOLD

OBJECTIVES

This Course contains several objectives, all of which can be completed during a single visit:

- **Collect the Megaflash Jump sticker from the Secret Door.**
- **Drop the stowed cannon into place.**
- **Reposition the Banzai Bill Cannon scrap.**
- **Defeat Bowser Jr.**
- **Collect the Comet Piece to unlock World 6-3.**

IMPORTANT ITEMS AND LOCATIONS

DESCRIPTION	NOTES
Secret Door	The marked location is just inside the ship's cabin.
HP-Up Heart	None
Toad Rescue	None
Luigi Location	None
Wiggler Diary Entry	None
Things	None

RECOMMENDED TACTICS

This Course contains some fairly difficult encounters, so don't pull any punches! You'll face Rocky Wrenches, Broozers, a variety of Bros, and more. Stock your Album with the best available stickers.

Rocky Wrenches appear in groups of three, so bring plenty of powerful multi-target stickers. If you attack one to initiate battle, the crafty critter will hide in its hole. Just walk up and make contact when you're ready to pick a fight.

OVERVIEW

PREREQUISITES

To unlock this Course, you must reposition the Hidden Bowser Castle scrap in World 6-1. To reach this Course, you must visit Wiggler in World 3-3. Before you speak to Wiggler, make sure your Album contains a Secret Door sticker and a large supply of Mushrooms and Jump-based stickers.

Broozers are very tough enemies. The frequently become enraged, which allows them to deflect most attacks. POW Blocks, Snowballs, Boomerangs, and Bombs are always effective, however. You should pick up some Bomb stickers and Boomerang stickers on your way through the Course, so make sure you save them for Broozer encounters.

Bros are always tough, and this Course contains several of them. When you're facing a particularly formidable group of Bros, use the Battle Spinner to combine a Shiny POW Block with more powerful multi-target attacks.

With his car's new canopy, Bowser Jr. is tougher than ever! This battle can be won using only Tail stickers, but doing so requires precision timing. If you haven't mastered the required Attack Commands, consider bringing a supply of Super Boots and high-damage Jump-based stickers.

Main Deck—Part 1

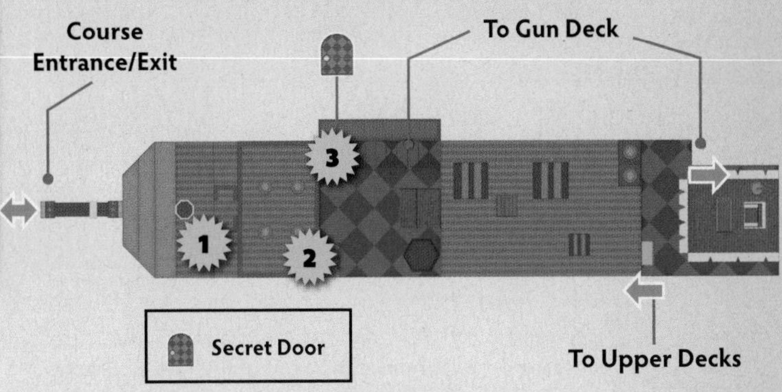

NOTE

When you're ready to enter World 6-2, return to World 3-3 and look for Wiggler in his tree house. The newly transformed Flutter carries you straight to Bowser Jr.'s Flotilla!

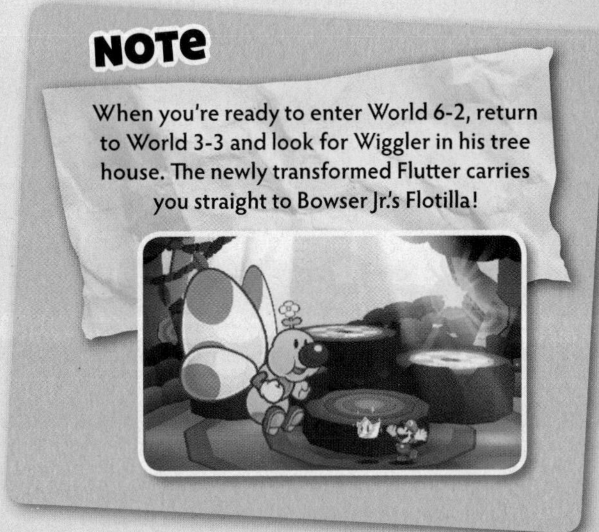

1

When Flutter drops you off on the ship, move to the right to find a Save Block.

WORLD 6-2

As soon as you drop down to the main deck, the nearby Rocky Wrenches pop out of their holes. Dodge the incoming attacks and clear the enemies hiding in the area.

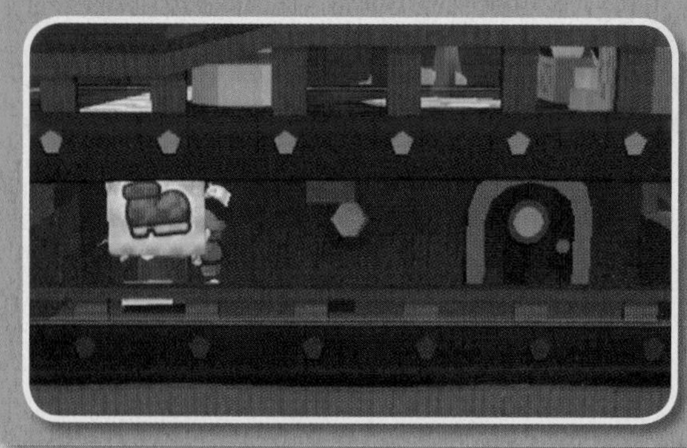

Head through the Secret Door to find two ? Blocks, one of which contains a Megaflash Jump sticker.

When you're ready, head through the door at Point 2.

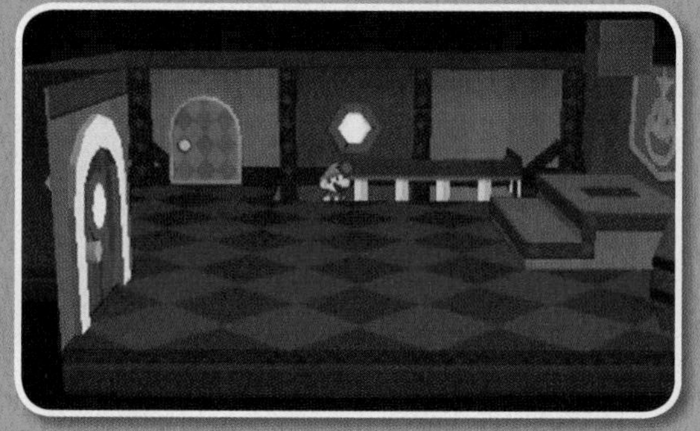

When you're ready, head back inside. Use the steps just to the right of the Secret Door to enter the ship's gun deck.

As you enter the room, watch out for incoming attacks from the nearby Ice Bro. Defend yourself, then apply a Secret Door sticker to the marked location on the back wall.

Gun Deck

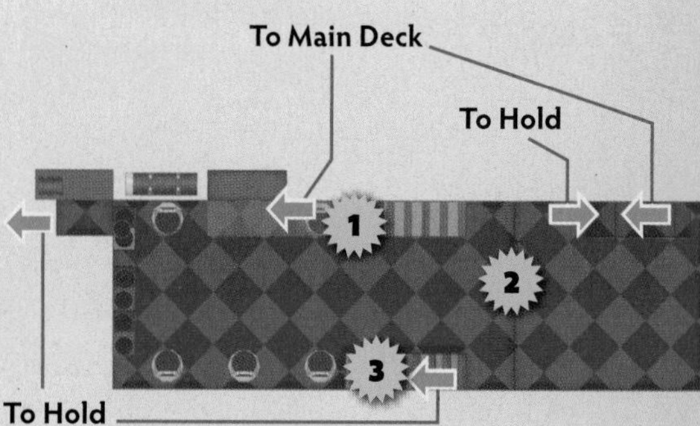

The gun deck is filled with enemies, so be ready to defend yourself. Take care of the Shiny Koopa Troopa on the ledge, then drop down and allow the Bob-ombs to attack you. Win each battle for a chance to collect some very useful Bomb stickers.

The opening in the back wall leads to a walkway, but that path isn't ready to use at this time. Move to the foreground and follow the stairs down to the ship's hold.

TIP

Make sure you let the Bob-ombs make the first move! If you've been collecting the available HP-Up Hearts, your Hammer strikes should be powerful enough to finish each Bob-omb without initiating a battle.

HOLD

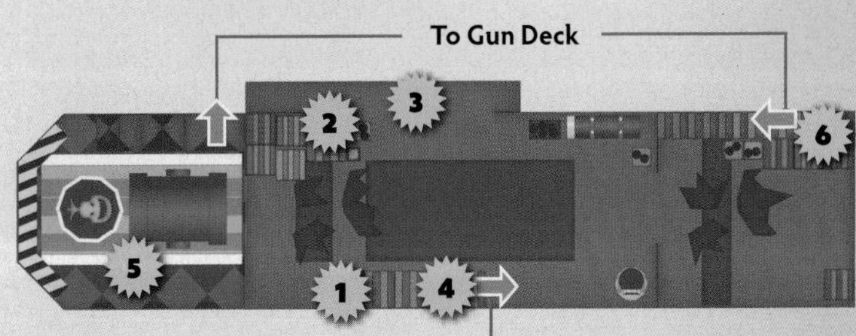

The Hammer Bros on the ledge attack whenever you're in range. You can't reach them at this time, so keep moving.

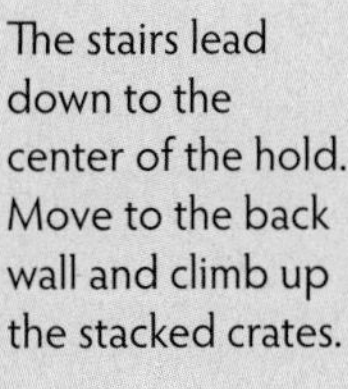

The stairs lead down to the center of the hold. Move to the back wall and climb up the stacked crates.

When you reach the top of the crates, peel the Bowser tape from the wall to drop the stowed cannon into place.

3

Step through the opening in the back wall to find a small walkway. As you search the area for stickers, use your Hammer to knock away the incoming Bullet Bills.

The cannon that you dropped into place can now be used as a platform. Defend yourself from the incoming Bullet Bills as you head for the opening to the right. Enter the ship and follow the steps back down to the hold.

4

When you're ready, climb back up the stairs.

5

When you reach the bottom of the stairs, activate the Paperize ability and peel the Banzai Bill Cannon scrap off of the floor.

Cut across the gun deck and head through the opening in the back wall.

Reapply the scrap to the same spot to aim the cannon into the ship. When the next Banzai Bill emerges, it smashes a path through the hold.

Follow the path left by the Banzai Bill. Climb the crates at the end of the hold and follow the stairs up to the gun deck.

Clear out the Hammer Bros on the gun deck, then follow the next set of stairs up to the main deck.

Main Deck—Part 2

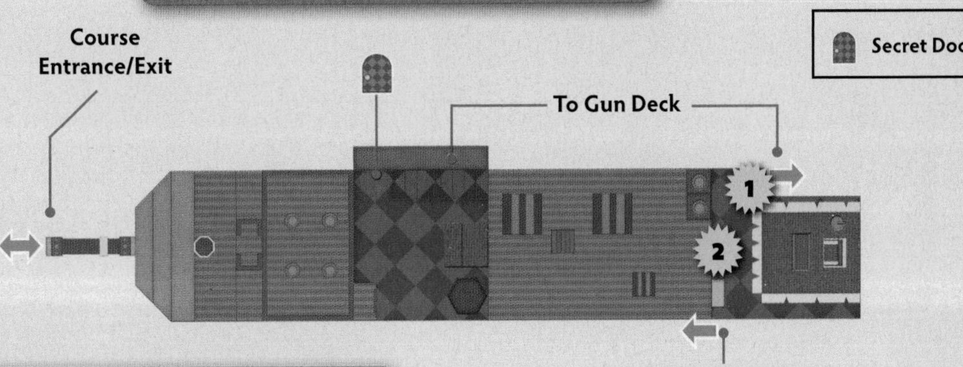

1

The small cabin at the top of the stairs contains a Fire Bro and a Boomerang Bro. These enemies have powerful allies, so make sure you're prepared for battle. Run in and clear the enemies out of the area.

After you clear the cabin, head through the door on the left wall to emerge between the ship's upper decks.

TIP

When you attack the Boomerang Bro, he's joined by two Broozers. When the Broozers become enraged, remember to use the Bomb stickers you collected from the Bob-ombs.

UPPER DECKS

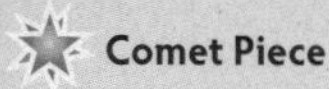

The upper decks are separated by a large portion of the main deck. After you leave the cabin, clear the Rocky Wrenches from the nearby steps and climb up to the deck on your right.

Use the HP Block at Point 2 to refill Mario's HP, then move toward the background and hop onto the ship's railing.

Follow the railing to the left and wait for the nearest crate to slide toward you. Hop onto the crate, then move along the crates to the left until you reach the next deck.

When you reach the next deck, Bowser Jr. appears. Before you can reach the Comet Piece, you must defeat him for a third and final time.

Mini-Boss: Bowser Jr.

If you've mastered the use of Tail stickers, use them to counter Bowser Jr.'s attacks. By doing this, you can defeat him without using the Battle Spinner or more valuable Battle Stickers. If you're worried about your timing, however, you can combine Super Boots and high-damage Jump-based stickers to attack and defend with ease.

If you opt to use Jump-based stickers, do so after applying a Super Boot to make the most of each attack. Use high-quality Hopslippers, Infinijumps, and Clone Jumps to deal significant damage on each attack.

At the end of each turn, use the Super Boot to dodge Bowser Jr.'s attacks. No matter which tactic you choose, proper timing should allow you to stay healthy for the duration of the battle. Bowser Jr. is fairly powerful, though, so keep an eye on Mario's HP if any of his attacks land. Use Mushrooms as needed, and use your selected tactics until you defeat Bowser Jr.

5

After you defeat Bowser Jr., collect the Comet Piece to complete your visit.

Sticker Comet Piece: Unlocking World 6-3

This Course contains one piece of the Sticker Comet. To unlock World 6-3, you must collect the Comet Piece from the upper decks.

WORLD 6-3: BOWSER'S SKY CASTLE

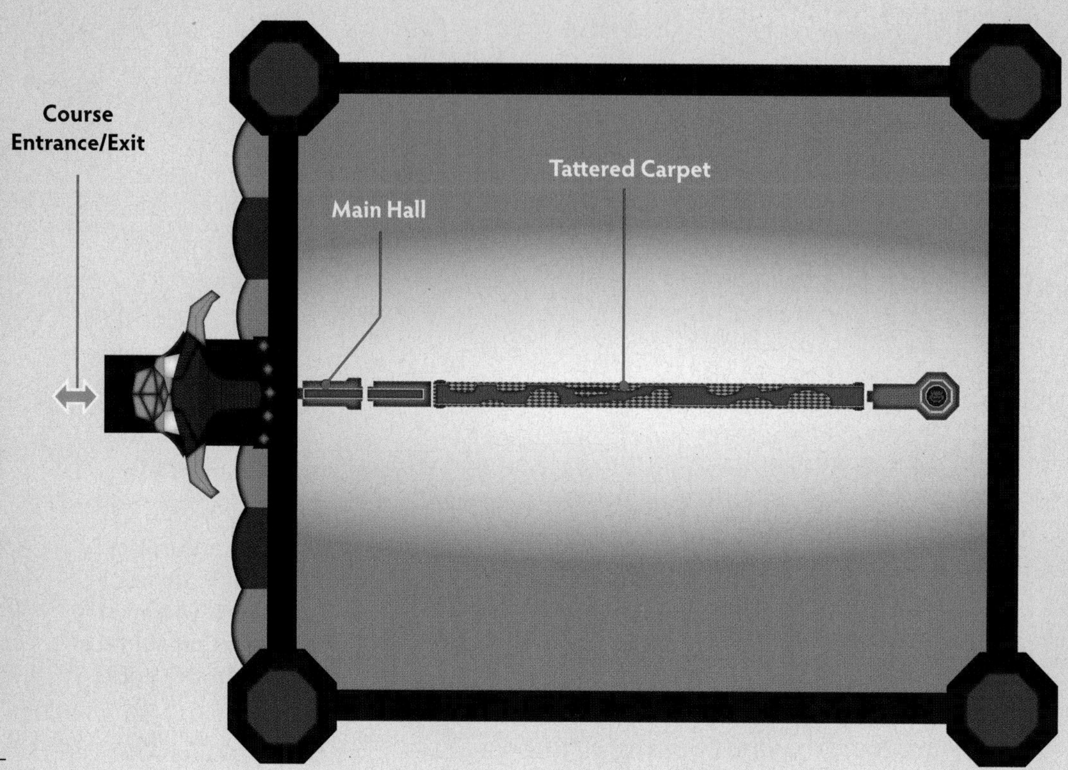

OVERVIEW

PREREQUISITES

To unlock this Course, you must collect the Comet Piece from the upper decks of World 6-2. This Course consists of a long series of battles, so make sure your Album contains all the stickers you'll need. Bring plenty of Super Boots (or Frog Suits), Jump-based stickers, and Mushrooms, then fill the rest of your Album with as many Battle Stickers and Thing Stickers as you can carry. Virtually every sticker can be used at some point in the Course. Bring a variety of multi-target stickers, single-target stickers, POW Blocks, and defensive stickers—anything that might help you meet an unexpected challenge. Purchase high-quality stickers, and revisit completed Courses to collect Megaflash stickers, Infinijumps, and other rare items the Sticker Shops don't carry.

> **TIP**
>
> The game ends when you complete World 6-3. Before you enter the Course, make sure you take care of any unfinished business. Collect any Things, Comet Pieces, and HP-Up Hearts you missed along the way. Complete the Sticker Museum, find all of Luigi's hiding spots, and reveal every Secret Door in the game—complete all of the conditions listed on the Super Flags in Decalburg.

ESSENTIAL THING STICKERS

NAME	THING LOCATION	NOTES
Tape	World 3-8	Used during the first Bowser battle.
Hair Shears	World 2-4	Used during the second Bowser battle.
Shaved Ice	World 2-4	Used during the third Bowser battle.
Paper Fan	World 2-2	Used during the third Bowser battle.
Baseball Bat	World 2-3	Used during the fourth Bowser battle.

IMPORTANT ITEMS AND LOCATIONS

DESCRIPTION	NOTES
Secret Door	None
HP-Up Heart	None
Toad Rescue	None
Luigi Location	None
Wiggler Diary Entry	None
Things	None

TIP

Any related stickers can be used in place of the recommended Thing Stickers. For instance, you could bring the Thumbtack, Scissors, Refrigerator, Bellows, and Toy Bat stickers in place of the recommended selection. Larger stickers do more damage, but they also take up more valuable Album space!

Objectives

This Course contains several objectives, all of which must be completed to complete the game:

- **Defeat Kamek.**
- **Complete the first Bowser battle.**
- **Complete the second Bowser battle.**
- **Complete the third Bowser battle.**
- **Complete the fourth Bowser battle.**
- **Defeat Bowser.**
- **Free Peach.**

Recommended Tactics

This Course contains some of the game's most difficult encounters. While the proper tactics should allow you to claim victory, it can be a long and dangerous process. Some of your stickers will be destroyed along the way. You can take some precautions, but be ready to improvise if you lose a particularly important sticker.

The battle with Kamek is much simpler if you score a jackpot on the Battle Spinner. Once again, Kamek transforms all of your stickers into Sandals for the duration of the battle. Use any three stickers to defeat the Kamek clones in a single turn.

The recommended Thing Stickers are very useful in dealing with Bowser's many allies, but you'll also need a good selection of powerful Battle Stickers. Bring plenty of Super Boots and Jump-based stickers, but make sure to bring some multi-target stickers as well. You'll also need at least one Eekhammer to topple a particularly tough Whomp.

WORLD 6-3

The final encounter is much easier with the right combination of stickers. Combine Super Boots with Infinijumps and other powerful Jump-based stickers to deal reliable damage on each turn. Bowser destroys some of your stickers as the battle progresses, so make sure you bring a suitable supply.

> **TIP**
>
> Don't underestimate the importance of Super Boot stickers! They increase the damage done by your Jump-based attacks, protect you from Bowser's spikes, and allow you to dodge most incoming attacks. Make sure you stock up!

Main Hall

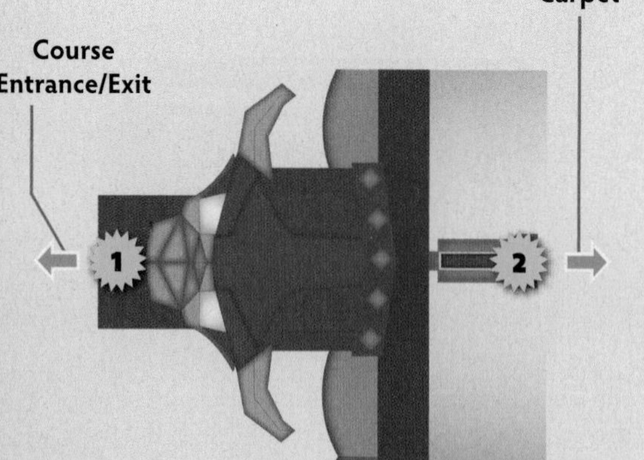

When you arrive at the castle, climb the steps to the entrance and head inside.

Follow the main hall to the next door. Kamek attempts to block your path.

Defeat Kamek for a third and final time, then follow the path to the tattered carpet.

HOW TO USE THIS GUIDE
HOW TO PLAY
STICKERS
ENEMIES
WALKTHROUGH
DECALBURG
SURFSHINE HARBOR
WORLD 1
WORLD 2
WORLD 3
WORLD 4
WORLD 5
WORLD 6
CHECKLISTS

MINI-BOSS: KAMEK

When the battle starts, Kamek transforms all of your stickers into Sandals. Try to remember each sticker's true form, and avoid using your more valuable stickers until the battle ends and the effect wears off. Kamek also summons two clones. If you manage to score a jackpot on the Battle Spinner, select three Sandals from your Album and use each one to defeat a Kamek. To deal sufficient damage, remember to press Ⓐ each time the Sandal sparkles.

If you fail to end the battle during your first turn, the battle becomes significantly harder. Not only does Kamek replace any lost clones, but at least one of your enemies is likely to move out of your attack range. If this happens, try not to waste stickers attempting to hit airborne enemies.

Kamek's attacks can deal damage, put you to sleep, or destroy some of your stickers. Make sure your current Album page contains stickers you can afford to lose.

Use the Battle Spinner and attack your enemies whenever you can. Defeat Kamek and his clones to end the battle.

TATTERED CARPET

To Main Hall

To Bowser's Chamber

1 2 3

When you hop onto the tattered carpet, it begins to roll up. Move quickly and avoid the holes in the carpet to avoid falling onto the spikes below you.

As you approach the end of the carpet, several bars appear in your path. Hop over each obstacle to maintain your speed.

After you make it past the last bar, move to the end of the tattered carpet and wait for it to carry you to Bowser's chamber.

BOWSER'S CHAMBER

From Tattered Carpet

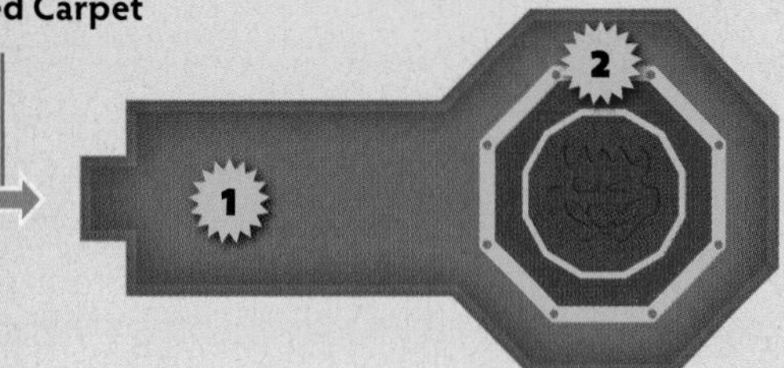

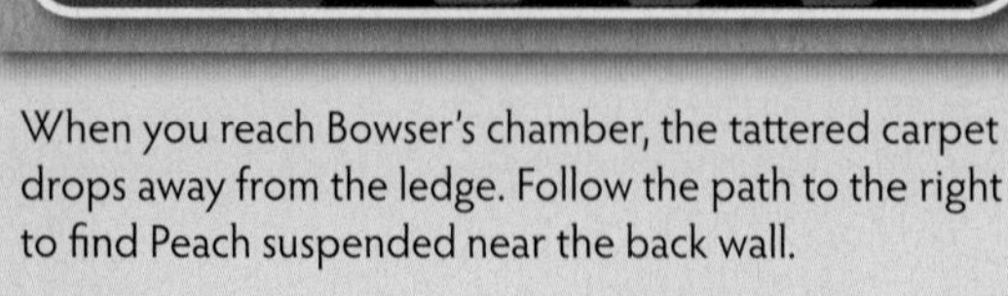

When you reach Bowser's chamber, the tattered carpet drops away from the ledge. Follow the path to the right to find Peach suspended near the back wall.

As you approach Peach, Bowser blocks your path and sends Peach down a hidden hallway. To find Peach, you must survive a series of battles against Bowser and his minions.

FIRST BOWSER BATTLE

During the first Bowser battle, enemies emerge from the three panels on the wall.

To prevent new enemies from emerging throughout the battle, use a Tape Thing Sticker to seal the panels on the wall. This also temporarily incapacitates the enemies. Use some multi-target attacks to clear out Bowser's minions before they recover.

Bowser's spikes protect him from most Jump-based attacks, but the Super Boot allows you to overcome his defenses. Use the Battle Spinner to combine Super Boot stickers with Jump-based stickers. Defend yourself from his attacks, and use Mushroom stickers to heal yourself as needed.

TIP

Make sure you save plenty of Super Boot stickers and Jump-based stickers for the final encounter. If your supply is running low, use Hammer-based stickers, POW Blocks, and any other Battle Stickers that deal damage.

When Bowser absorbs around 100 points of damage, he withdraws from the battle. After this happens, you automatically follow him to the next encounter.

Second Bowser Battle

When the next battle begins, Bowser heals himself and hides behind a Whomp. The Whomp is a very tough enemy, but it does have an exploitable weakness. Use the Battle Spinner to earn at least one extra attack, then select an Eekhammer and the Hair Shears Thing Sticker. Land at least two hits with the Eekhammer to topple the Whomp. The Hair Shears will finish the downed enemy.

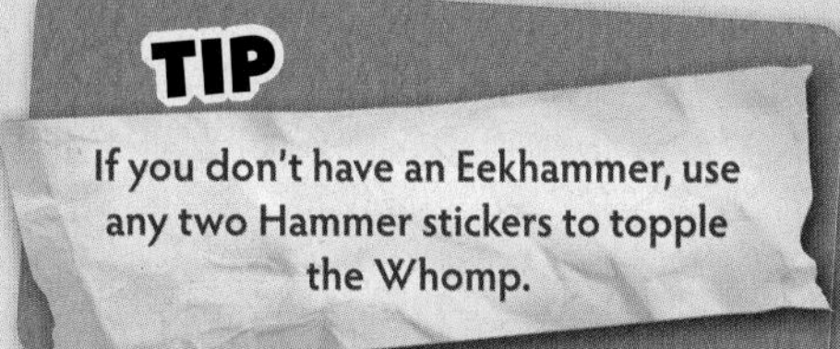

TIP

If you don't have an Eekhammer, use any two Hammer stickers to topple the Whomp.

Once Bowser's on his own again, employ the same tactics as earlier. Use the Battle Spinner to earn at least one extra attack during each turn, and combine Super Boot stickers with Jump-based stickers.

When Bowser absorbs around 200 points of damage, he withdraws from the battle and heads to his next group of minions.

WORLD 6-3

THIRD BOWSER BATTLE

When the next battle begins, Bowser heals and surrounds himself with Lava Bubbles.

Use the Battle Spinner to earn at least one extra turn, then select the Shaved Ice sticker and the Paper Fan sticker. The Shaved Ice sticker freezes all of the enemies, then the Paper Fan sweeps them up in a whirlwind.

The damage caused by the two Thing Stickers is enough to end the battle! When Bowser recovers, he withdraws to his remaining minion.

FOURTH BOWSER BATTLE

During the next battle, you must face Bowser and a Chain Chomp while Peach watches from the background. Use the Baseball Bat sticker to end the battle on your first turn.

If you don't have a bat-type Thing Sticker, use a Tail sticker to counter the Chain Chomp's first attack. Either method will knock the Chain Chomp into Bowser. The impact sends both enemies tumbling off the platform.

Peach is dangling out of reach, so you can't rescue her at this time. Meet Kersti at the edge of the platform to begin the final battle.

HOW TO USE THIS GUIDE
HOW TO PLAY
STICKERS
ENEMIES

WALKTHROUGH
DECALBURG
SURFSHINE HARBOR
WORLD 1
WORLD 2
WORLD 3
WORLD 4
WORLD 5
WORLD 6
CHECKLISTS

BOSS FIGHT!

Bowser

When Bowser emerges, he's bigger and stronger than ever. When the encounter starts, use Jump-based stickers to damage Bowser's hands. Each impact does only one point of damage, so sticker quality isn't a factor at this time. Use Hopslippers and basic Jumps to chip away at Bowser's HP. There's no need to use Super Boots. If your Album contains any Infinijumps, save them for the battle's next phase.

Bowser's attacks do fairly heavy damage, so make sure you defend yourself. Keep an eye on Mario's HP, and use Mushrooms or 1UP stickers to keep your health up.

As the battle progresses, Kersti appears in your Album. Use the Kersti sticker to move into the battle's second phase. Once you do, the Battle Spinner automatically grants you five attacks on each turn, and your Battle Stickers are much more effective.

After you use the Kersti sticker, select a Super Boot and the four most powerful Jump-based stickers left in your Album. High-quality Infinijumps, Clone Jumps, and Hopslippers do massive damage while a Super Boot is active, so don't hold back! If you're running low on these stickers, combine a Frog Suit with high-quality Burnhammers, Chillhammers, and any other powerful multi-target stickers in your Album.

Don't use Jump-based attacks on Bowser's head without first selecting a Super Boot. If you do, his spikes will counter everything aside from the Iron Jump. When Bowser breathes fire, the flames destroy a few of your stickers. If you run out of Super Boots, finish him off with Hammers, Shells, POW Blocks, and any other non-Jump stickers left in your Album. Keep attacking and defending until you defeat Bowser.

When you defeat Bowser, the sixth and final Royal Sticker floats down to you.

After you collect the Royal Sticker, peel the Bowser tape holding Peach off the ground. After you free Peach, you've completed the game! Watch the final cinematic to see how the story ends.

The Sticker Museum is a great place to keep track of the Battle Stickers and Things you've managed to collect, but it can be a little more difficult to keep track of other special items, locations, and events. Use these checklists to review the tasks you've completed, and to help determine which tasks you might have missed as you played through the game.

SECRET DOORS

LOCATION	NOTES
❑ World 1-1	The marked location is on one of the hills beyond the waterfall.
❑ World 1-2	The marked location is in the foothills toward the end of the Course.
❑ World 1-3	The marked location is in the drain below the Bowser fountain.
❑ World 1-4	The marked location is in the hidden garden at the end of the Course.
❑ World 1-5	The marked location is in the underground passage.
❑ World 1-6	The marked location is near the middle of the eastern wall.
❑ World 2-1	The marked location is at the top of the pyramid.
❑ World 2-2	The marked location is on the ground floor, on the north edge of the sphinx.
❑ World 2-3	The marked location is through Door 4 (or Door 5).
❑ World 2-4	The marked location is on the outer ring, near the path to the oasis.
❑ World 2-5	The marked location is just inside the Course's entrance.
❑ World 3-1	The marked location is on a large tree among the flooded platforms.
❑ World 3-2	The marked location is near the steps in the eastern cluster.
❑ World 3-3	The marked location is in the living room, at the top of the ramp.
❑ World 3-4	The marked location is near the lakeside steps.
❑ World 3-5	The marked location is near the Boomerang Bro in the southern cavern.
❑ World 3-6	The marked location is below the Sticker Shop.
❑ World 3-7	The marked location is behind the Hammer, on the ledge in the burrow's first chamber.

Secret Doors

LOCATION	NOTES
❑ World 3-8	The marked location is just inside the Course entrance.
❑ World 3-9	The marked location is beside the second pool, below the poison gas.
❑ World 3-10	The marked location is in the storage room.
❑ World 3-11	The marked location is near the center of the foothills.
❑ World 3-12	The marked location is at the start of the island.
❑ World 4-1	The marked location is hidden under the central slope.
❑ World 4-2	The marked location is in the first ice cave.
❑ World 4-3	The marked location is at the top of the rear staircase.
❑ World 4-5	The marked location is on the mountain path, below the icicles.
❑ World 4-6	The marked location is to the right of the ride queue.
❑ World 5-1	The marked location is near the jungle basin's right wall.
❑ World 5-2	The marked location is near the boathouse.
❑ World 5-3	The marked location is near the Comet Piece at the end of the river.
❑ World 5-4	The marked location is on a second-floor platform.
❑ World 5-5	The marked location is in the large lava pool.
❑ World 5-6	The marked location is on the fifth floor.
❑ World 6-2	The marked location is just inside the ship's cabin.

HP-Up Hearts

LOCATION	NOTES
❑ Decalburg	After you complete all five Toad rescues, return to Decalburg's residential area. Enter the house on the right and read the postcards inside.
❑ Surfshine Harbor	Reposition the Warehouse Door scrap, then follow the path to the upper floor.
❑ World 1-2	Replace the ruined flowers in the windy garden.
❑ World 1-4	Defeat the Big Buzzy Beetle to earn an HP-Up Heart.
❑ World 2-1	The HP-Up Heart is on a platform near the pyramid.
❑ World 2-2	The HP-Up Heart is on the sphinx's north side, on the right rear foot.
❑ World 2-3	The HP-Up Heart is in a sarcophagus through Door 3.
❑ World 3-1	After the forest is cleansed, the HP-Up Heart appears at the end of the Course.
❑ World 3-3	The HP-Up Heart is through the Secret Door.
❑ World 3-8	The HP-Up Heart is hidden on the forest floor, behind one of the large trees.
❑ World 3-9	The HP-Up Heart is hidden under the steps at the left edge of the second pool.
❑ World 3-10	After you cleanse the forest, the HP-Up Heart appears in the storage room.
❑ World 4-2	The HP-Up Heart is along the second frozen river.
❑ World 4-3	After you complete World 4-5, return to the living room and speak to the steward.
❑ World 5-1	The HP-Up Heart is in a hidden area near the temple courtyard.
❑ World 5-6	The HP-Up Heart is on the second floor.

Toad Rescues

LOCATION	NOTES
❑ World 1-2	Two Goombas are bullying a Toad on the hilltop.
❑ World 2-1	The bullied Toad is on a platform among the sand dunes.
❑ World 3-11	The bullied Toad is on the left edge of the foothills.
❑ World 4-6	The bullied Toad is to the left of the ride queue.
❑ World 5-2	The bullied Toad is on one of the riverside platforms.

Luigi Locations

LOCATION	NOTES
❑ World 1-6	As you approach the central tower, look for Luigi in the background.
❑ World 2-5	Luigi is on the tower's fourth floor, along the outer walkway.
❑ World 3-12	Luigi is on a rock formation near the pier.
❑ World 4-5	Luigi appears near the end of the chairlift.
❑ World 5-5	Luigi is in the hot springs near the second lava flow.

Wiggler Diary Entries

LOCATION	NOTES
❑ Surfshine Harbor	This entry is automatically earned when you collect the Wiggler Segment from Surfshine Harbor.
❑ World 3-2	Lead a Wiggler Segment to the dandelion in the northern cluster, then walk through the flower.
❑ World 3-6	Bring a Wiggler Segment to the overlook near the Course entrance.
❑ World 3-8	Lead the Wiggler Segment to the poisoned hot springs.
❑ World 3-10	Complete the quiz show a second time while the Wiggler Segment watches.

PRIMA OFFICIAL GAME GUIDE

WRITTEN BY: NICK VON ESMARCH

Product Manager: Jesse Anderson

Design & Layout: Tigereye Design Studio

Copyedit: Deana Shields

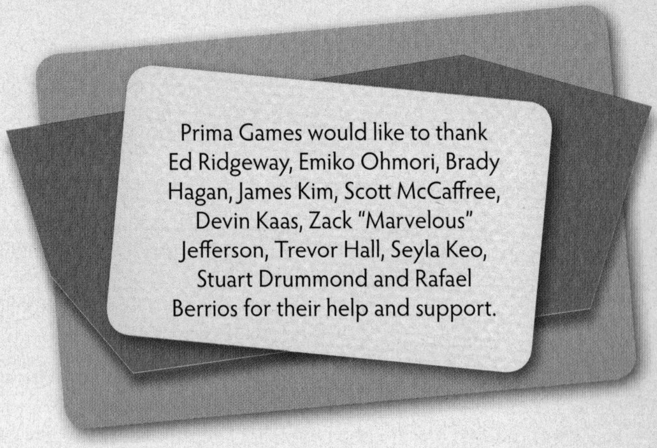

Prima Games would like to thank Ed Ridgeway, Emiko Ohmori, Brady Hagan, James Kim, Scott McCaffree, Devin Kaas, Zack "Marvelous" Jefferson, Trevor Hall, Seyla Keo, Stuart Drummond and Rafael Berrios for their help and support.

Prima Games

An Imprint of Random House, Inc.

3000 Lava Ridge Court, Suite 100
Roseville, CA 95661

www.primagames.com

Full Size ISBN: 978-0-307-89673-5
Mini Size ISBN: 978-0-307-89675-9

Printed in the United States of America

12 13 14 15 LL 10 9 8 7 6 5 4 3 2 1